IIAS Series: Governance and Public Management

International Institute of Administrative Sciences (IIAS)

IIAS
International Institute
of Administrative Sciences

The International Institute of Administrative Sciences is an international association with scientific purpose based in Brussels. As a non-governmental international organisation its activities are centred on the study of public administration and on providing a forum in which comparative studies – including both practical experiences and theoretical analyses of experts in public administration from all cultures – are presented and discussed. The Institute is interested in all questions related to contemporary public administration at national and international levels.

Website: http://www.iias-iisa.org

Governance and Public Management Series
Series edited by:
Gérard Timsit, Emeritus Professor, University of Paris 1 Panthéon Sorbonne;
Wim van de Donk, Tilburg University, The Netherlands

Series Editorial Committee:

Gérard Timsit, IIAS Publications Director
Rolet Loretan, IIAS Director General
Wim van de Donk, Member and Series Editor
Michiel De Vries, Member
Christopher Pollitt, Member, IRAS Editor in Chief
Fabienne Maron, IIAS Scientific Administrator and Publications Coordinator

The *Governance and Public Management* series, published in conjunction with the International Institute of Administrative Sciences (IIAS), brings the best research in public administration and management to a global audience. Encouraging a diversity of approaches and perspectives, the series reflects the Institute's commitment to a neutral and objective voice, grounded in the exigency of fact. How is governance conducted *now*? How could it be done better? What defines the law of administration and the management of public affairs, and can their implementation be enhanced? Such questions lie behind the Institute's core value of *accountability*: those who exercise authority must account for its use – to those on whose behalf they act.

Governance and Public Management series

Titles in the series include:
Eberhard Bohne
THE WORLD TRADE ORGANIZATION
Institutional Development and Reform

Michiel S. De Vries
THE IMPORTANCE OF NEGLECT IN POLICY-MAKING

Michiel S. De Vries, P.S. Reddy, M. Shamsul Haque (*editors*)
IMPROVING LOCAL GOVERNMENT
Outcomes of Comparative Research

Wouter Van Dooren and Steven Van de Walle (*editors*)
PERFORMANCE INFORMATION IN THE PUBLIC SECTOR

Per Lægreid and Koen Verhoest (*editors*)
GOVERNANCE OF PUBLIC SECTOR ORGANIZATIONS
Proliferation, Autonomy and Performance

Also by Koen Verhoest:

Geert Bouckaert, B. Guy Peters and Koen Verhoest
THE COORDINATION OF PUBLIC SECTOR ORGANIZATIONS
978–0–230–24015–5

Koen Verhoest, Paul G. Roness, Bram Verschuere, Kristin Rubecksen and
Muiris MacCarthaigh
AUTONOMY AND CONTROL OF STATE AGENCIES
978–0–230–57765–7

Governance and Public Management Series
Series Standing Order ISBN 978–0230–50655–8 (hardback)
978–0230–50656–5 (paperback)

You can receive future titles in this series as they are published by placing a standing order. Please contact your bookseller or, in case of difficulty, write to us at the
address below with your name and address, the title of the series and the ISBN
quoted above.

Customer Services Department, Macmillan Distribution Ltd, Houndmills,
Basingstoke, Hampshire RG21 6XS, England

Governance of Public Sector Organizations

Proliferation, Autonomy and Performance

Edited by

Per Lægreid
Professor, Department of Administration and Organization Theory,
University of Bergen, Norway

and

Koen Verhoest
Associate Professor and Research Manager, Public Management Institute,
Catholic University of Leuven, Belgium

First published 2010 by
PALGRAVE MACMILLAN

Palgrave Macmillan in the UK is an imprint of Macmillan Publishers Limited,
registered in England, company number 785998, of Houndmills, Basingstoke,
Hampshire RG21 6XS.

Palgrave Macmillan in the US is a division of St Martin's Press LLC,
175 Fifth Avenue, New York, NY 10010.

Palgrave Macmillan is the global academic imprint of the above companies
and has companies and representatives throughout the world.

Palgrave® and Macmillan® are registered trademarks in the United States,
the United Kingdom, Europe and other countries

Neither the COST Office nor any person acting on its behalf is responsible
for the use which might be made of the information contained in this
publication. The COST Office is not responsible for the external websites
referred to in this publication.

EUROPEAN
SCIENCE
FOUNDATION ESF provides the COST Office through an EC contract

COST is supported by the EU RTD Framework programme

ISBN 978–0–230–23820–6   hardback

This book is printed on paper suitable for recycling and made from fully
managed and sustained forest sources. Logging, pulping and manufacturing
processes are expected to conform to the environmental regulations of the
country of origin.

A catalogue record for this book is available from the British Library.

Library of Congress Cataloging-in-Publication Data

Governance of public sector organizations : proliferation, autonomy
    and performance / edited by Per Lægreid, Koen Verhoest.
        p. cm. — (Governance and public management)
    Includes bibliographical references.
    ISBN 978–0–230–23820–6 (hardback)
    1. Administrative agencies—Cross-cultural studies.   2. Comparative
government.   I. Lægreid, Per.   II. Verhoest, Koen.
JF1601.G685 2010
351—dc22

2010023831

10   9   8   7   6   5   4   3   2   1
19   18   17   16   15   14   13   12   11   10

Printed and bound in Great Britain by
CPI Antony Rowe, Chippenham and Eastbourne

Contents

List of Tables and Figures

Tables

Figures

Notes on Contributors

Tobias Bach, Research Fellow, University of Hannover, Germany
Dario Barbieri, Research Fellow and Assistant Professor, SDA Bocconi School of Management, Italy
John P. Burns, Professor, University of Hong Kong, China
Tom Christensen, Professor, University of Oslo, Norway
Paolo Fedele, Assistant Professor, Udine University, Italy
Davide Galli, Assistant Professor, SDA Bocconi School of Management, Italy
Marieke van Genugten, Assistant Professor, University of Twente, the Netherlands
György Hajnal, Senior Researcher/Head of department, ECOSTAT Government Research Institute, Department of Public Administration Research, Hungary
John Halligan, Professor, University of Canberra, Australia.
Claude Laurin, Professor, HEC Montreal, Canada
Per Lægreid, Professor, University of Bergen, Norway
Martino Maggetti, Senior Researcher/Lecturer, University of Zurich and University of Lausanne, Switzerland
Joery Matthys, Researcher, Catholic University Leuven, Belgium
Falke Meyers, Expert, Flemish Agency for Personnel and Organization, Belgium
Edoardo Ongaro, Professor, SDA Bocconi School of Management, Italy
Martin Painter, Professor, City University of Hong Kong, China
Marie-Ève Quenneville, Lecturer, HEC Montreal, Canada
Vidar Wangen Rolland, Adviser, Norwegian Social Science Data Services, Norway
Jan Rommel, Researcher, Catholic University Leuven, Belgium
Paul G. Roness, Professor, University of Bergen, Norway
Andrew Sulle, Research Fellow, Catholic University Leuven, Belgium
Nicole Thibodeau, Assistant Professor, Willamette University, USA
Koen Verhoest, Associate Professor and Research Manager, Public Management Institute, Catholic University Leuven, Belgium
Bram Verschuere, Assistant Professor, University College Gent, Belgium
Way-Hang Yee, Senior Research Associate, City University of Hong Kong, China
John-Erik Ågotnes, Adviser, Directorate of Fisheries, Norway

Preface

This book contains studies focusing on the governance of public sector organizations in the era of New Public Management (NPM) and the recent post-NPM reforms such as 'Whole-of-Government' initiatives. Its empirical focus is on government agencies in Australia, Belgium, Canada, Germany, Hong Kong, Hungary, Italy, the Netherlands, Norway, Switzerland and United Kingdom. We apply a multi-theoretical approach embracing structural instrumental features, tasks, political design, cultural–institutional trajectories and external pressure to understand the process and effects of agencification and administrative reforms.

A main aim of our study is to examine specialization and proliferation, autonomy and control, coordination and complexity and implication and results of public sector organizations in a period of comprehensive administrative reforms. A central argument is that there is a layering or sedimentation process going on producing composite and hybrid organizational forms. Rather than replacing old reforms new reform initiatives tend to be added to old reforms and mix with them in rather complex ways. Another is that different organizational forms matter and affect the way the public organizations operates and work in practice.

There are a number of individuals and organizations to whom we own our thanks. First, we would like to thank contribution of the members of the Comparative Public Organization Data Base for Research and Analyses (COBRA) network, which is an academic research collaboration in the field of public management. The COBRA network gathers and analyses similar survey data on agencies in a large number of participating countries, allowing comparison of agency types and features operating in different political–administrative systems.

In a similar way we would like to thank our colleagues of the COST Action on 'Comparative Research into Current Trends in Public Sector Organization'. Within this network, high-quality European public administration research teams from 22 countries are joining their forces in a common research strategy on public sector organization. A central research focus in this work is the changing autonomy, control and coordination of government agencies, as well as explanation and consequences of this trend.

Many of the chapters in this book have also been presented at the European Group of Public Administration's (EGPA) Study Group on

Governance of Public Sector Organizations and we thank the participants at that group for their comments and advice.

Among this excellent group of scholars we especially would like to thank Geert Bouckaert at Catholic University of Leuven who has been the entrepreneur and driving force of these research networks. We also would like to thank Wim van de Donk, Kenneth Keraghan, Werner Jann, Sandra van Thiel and Kutsal Yesilkagit for their help. Thanks are also due to Alexandra Webster and her colleagues at Palgrave Macmillan, to Marleen Soers and the rest of the secretariat at the Public Management Institute in Leuven. We would also thank the Catholic University of Leuven for granting a fellowship for Per Lægreid which made this book project possible and to our home institutions for granting us time and support to do this study.

This publication is supported by COST. Therefore, we gratefully acknowledge the European Science Foundation and COST for allowing the COST Action ISO601 to fund the involved network activities, which has further enabled this comparative research.

Per Lægreid and Koen Verhoest

COST

COST – the acronym for European Cooperation in Science and Technology – is the oldest and widest European intergovernmental network for cooperation in research. Established by the Ministerial Conference in November 1971, COST is presently used by the scientific communities of 35 European countries to cooperate in common research projects supported by national funds. The funds provided by COST – less than one per cent of the total value of the projects – support the COST cooperation networks (COST Actions) through which, with €30 million per year, more than 30,000 European scientists are involved in research having a total value which exceeds €2 billion per year. This is the financial worth of the European added value which COST achieves. A 'bottom up approach' (the initiative of launching a COST Action comes from the European scientists themselves), 'à la carte participation' (only countries interested in the Action participate), 'equality of access' (participation is open also to the scientific communities of countries not belonging to the European Union) and 'flexible structure' (easy implementation and light management of the research initiatives) are the main characteristics of COST.

As precursor of advanced multidisciplinary research COST has a very important role for the realisation of the European Research Area (ERA) anticipating and complementing the activities of the Framework Programmes, constituting a 'bridge' towards the scientific communities of emerging countries, increasing the mobility of researchers across Europe and fostering the establishment of 'Networks of Excellence' in many key scientific domains such as: Biomedicine and Molecular Biosciences; Food and Agriculture; Forests, their Products and Services; Materials, Physical and Nanosciences; Chemistry and Molecular Sciences and Technologies; Earth System Science and Environmental Management; Information and Communication Technologies; Transport and Urban Development; Individuals, Societies, Cultures and Health. It covers basic and more applied research and also addresses issues of pre-normative nature or of societal importance.

Web: http://www.cost.eu.

1
Introduction: Reforming Public Sector Organizations

Per Lægreid and Koen Verhoest

1.1 Introduction

New Public Management (NPM) assumes that task specialization results in efficiency gains (Hood 1991). Following this logic governments have structurally disaggregated major monolithic public sector organizations into smaller parts, with some degree of autonomy. Since the 1980s, this has been visible in the increase in decentralization and devolution, as well as in a clear expansion of the types and numbers of autonomous agencies. Two other changes in the political–administrative system occurred at the same time. First, the split between politics and administration was re-emphasized; secondly, the different phases in the policy cycle, i.e. policy design, policy implementation and policy evaluation, were organizationally split (Bouckaert *et al.* 2010).

This development has brought about the emergence of a broad range of specialized and autonomous organizations with single-purpose tasks that are active in one of the now disconnected phases of the policy cycle. It was argued that these changes would result in better performance because it would 'make managers manage', or allow 'managers to manage'. Managers now have their own budget, which they can spend with some degree of freedom, including on personnel. Government control of such bodies is mainly based on *ex post* evaluation of performance as agreed upon in a contract instead of on an *ex ante* input control system. In response to this performance-based control and increased managerial autonomy, agencies are assumed to be improving their performance by adopting management tools from the private sector. However, empirical proof of the beneficial effects of agencification is quite limited and rather inconclusive (Verhoest *et al.* 2004a; Pollitt 2004a).

Specialization resulted in two mechanisms for organizational proliferation. The number of autonomous organizations within the public sector increased, while the reduction in standardization and uniformity in management practices made organizations more heterogeneous and diverse. Agencies with different legal forms were created, producing diversity within the agency landscape in terms of formal autonomy and control arrangements (OECD 2002a). But even agencies with the same legal form seem in many countries to have different levels of autonomy and different degrees of control (Verhoest *et al.* 2004a; Pollitt *et al.* 2004). As a result of its not being compensated for by additional coordination mechanisms, this proliferation of public organizations was perceived to have resulted in a fragmentation of government (OECD 2002a; Verhoest *et al.* 2007b; Bouckaert *et al.* 2010).

This development leads us to our first set of research questions:

RQ 1: How much evidence is there of a straightforward process of increased specialization and organizational proliferation in central government? How can this specialization and proliferation be explained? To what extent has this proliferation resulted in coordination and control problems?

RQ 2: What patterns of autonomy and control of agencies are visible in different countries? How do changes in formal organization affect the *de facto* autonomy and forms of control within the administrative system? What other factors can affect the perceived autonomy and control of public sector bodies?

RQ 3: To what extent do increased autonomy, result control, and the use of private management techniques in agencies lead to better performance, as expected by NPM?

The narrow task definition of agencies, their focus on organizational performance targets, their drive for autonomy, and the decoupling of implementation from policy design creates centrifugal forces, with central and parent departments perceiving a loss of coordination capacity. For instance, Peters (Peters and Savoie 1996: 295–6; Peters forthcoming) states that such NPM changes have increased the capacity of individual programmes and organizations to resist coordination efforts.

Recently, governments in many NPM frontrunner countries put a renewed emphasis on coordination of policy and management (6 2005; Bogdanor 2005; Gregory 2006; Halligan 2006; Richards and Smith 2006; Christensen and Lægreid 2007). But also in more NPM-resistant countries, like France or Belgium, governments invest in better coordination and collaboration (Bouckaert *et al.* 2010). 'Whole of government' initiatives like 'Joined-up Government' (UK), 'Horizontalism' (Canada), 'connecting government' (Australia), and 'Reviewing the Centre' (New Zealand) focus on horizontal collaboration and integrated service delivery between public organizations and governmental levels. Moreover, renewed attention is being devoted to strengthening the capacity of central government, increasing political control 'bringing the state back in'. Mergers of departments and the reintegration and standardization of agencies are interpreted as elements in this new trend (Christensen and Lægreid 2007a).

An increasing number of scholars are arguing that these post-NPM trends, focusing on whole-of-government, are a reaction to the organizational proliferation and resulting fragmentation induced by NPM-inspired reforms (Pollitt 2003b; Pollitt and Bouckaert 2004; Boston and Eichbaum 2007; Gregory 2006; Halligan 2006; Christensen and Lægreid 2007a; Bouckaert *et al.* 2010). However, it remains unclear what these 'whole-of-government' initiatives imply in terms of the autonomy, control and coordination of central agencies and other public sector organizations. Have NPM reforms really diminished central control and enhanced autonomy, and do the new reforms really address the failures and shortcomings of the old reforms? To answer these questions it is important to examine to what degree the new need for coordination and stronger control is enhancing post-NPM movements with 'whole-of-government' features and rebalancing the autonomy-control trade-off. This leads us to our fourth research question:

> RQ 4: What do the 'whole-of-government' reforms imply? How do they foster horizontal coordination and increased central control over a proliferated governmental apparatus? Have these post-NPM reforms replaced the NPM reforms or are they supplementing them, producing increased complexity in public sector organizations?

1.2 Central concepts

The different contributions in this book focus on some core concepts that are useful for describing and understanding the above-mentioned changes. These concepts include organizational forms, the autonomy and control of these organizational forms, specialization, coordination, and performance.

Organizational form – agencies. Agencies have been described variously as non-departmental public bodies, hybrids, quangos, fringe bodies, non-majority institutions, quasi-autonomous public organizations, and distributed public governance (Greve *et al.* 1999; Flinders 2004b). What an agency is and what it does varies considerably across national and organizational cultures, legal systems, and political systems (Smullen 2004; Christensen and Lægreid 2006). In this book we will mainly use Pollitt and associates' (Pollitt *et al.* 2004; Pollitt and Talbot 2004) rather narrow definition of an agency as a structurally disaggregated body, formally separated from the ministry, which carries out public tasks at a national level on a permanent basis, is staffed by public servants, is financed mainly by the state budget, and is subject to public legal procedures. Agencies have some autonomy from their respective ministry in policy decision-making and over personnel, finance, and managerial matters, but they are not totally independent, because political executives normally have ultimate political responsibility for their activities.

Autonomy. The focus is on the autonomy of a single agency *vis-à-vis* the responsible minister and department and the control of them by the minister/department. The academic discussion of concepts and the relationships between them is rich and evolving (e.g. Christensen 2001). We define autonomy as the level of decision-making competency (discretion) of an organization (Verhoest *et al.* 2004a). Control focuses on the constraints which ministers/departments can impose to influence the actual use of this decision-making competency, in order to influence the decisions made. Making an agency more autonomous involves shifting decision-making competency from external actors to the agency itself by delegation, devolution, or decentralization. We distinguish between managerial autonomy (the choice and use of financial, human, and other resources) and policy autonomy (objectives, target groups, policy instruments, quality and quantity of outputs, processes and procedures, issuing of general regulations, or decisions in individual cases), each on a strategic or operational level. We will address perceived actual autonomy but also to some degree formal, legal autonomy.

Control in this research refers to the cycle of guidance, control, and evaluation (Kaufmann *et al.* 1986), encompassing the mechanisms and instruments used by the government to intentionally influence the decisions and the behaviour of the agency in order to achieve government objectives. In this study three dimensions of control will be distinguished: timing (*ex ant–e-ex post*), focus (inputs–outputs), and control techniques (see Kaufmann *et al.* 1986).

Ex ante control emphasizes the 'before-the-fact' formulation of detailed rules, regulations, standard operating procedures, and approval requirements that give directions to actors so that the desired objective (from the viewpoint of the ministers/departments) will be achieved. The intention is 'to minimize risks and to increase certainty of perform-ance processes before they begin' (Wirth 1986).

Ex post control emphasizes whether the intended organizational goals have been achieved by the agency and whether there is a need for cor-rective future action. Elements of *ex post* control are objective setting, monitoring, evaluation, audit, and sanctions. Both *ex ante* and *ex post* control may have their principal focus on the choice and use of inputs, or the delivery of the outputs, although in practice they mostly appear in pairs (*ex ante* on inputs, *ex post* on outputs).

Control techniques may be hierarchical, market-like and/or network-based: for example (1) structural control, achieved by influencing the agencies' decisions through hierarchical and accountability lines through the agency head or the supervisory board; (2) financial control, achieved by changing the level of budget granted to the agency, the composition of its income, and the level of risk-turnover to influence agency deci-sions; (3) control achieved by making the agency compete with other organizations; (4) control achieved by creating cooperation networks of which the agency is part.

Specialization. In organization and management theory specialization (or work division, differentiation) (Gulick 1937) and coordination are seen as closely related, even complementary matters (Mintzberg 1979; Heffron 1989). In a public sector context, specialization may be defined as the creation of new public sector organizations, with limited objec-tives and specific tasks, out of traditional core-administrations which have many tasks and different, sometimes conflicting objectives (Hood and Dunsire 1981; Pollitt and Bouckaert 2000). It may emerge in two forms (cf. Heffron 1989): (1) horizontal specialization defined as 'the splitting of organizations at the same administrative and hierarchical level (...) and assigning tasks and authority to them'; (2) vertical special-ization defined as the 'differentiation of responsibility on hierarchical levels, describing how political and administrative tasks and authority are allocated between forms of affiliation' (Lægreid *et al.* 2003). The level of vertical specialization depends upon the extent to which tasks and policy cycle stages are transferred from the core administration to the more peripheral parts of the public sector.

Coordination in a public sector inter-organizational context is the purposeful alignment of tasks and efforts of units in order to achieve a defined goal. Its aim is to create greater coherence in policy and to reduce redundancy, lacunae, and contradictions within and between policies (Peters 1998). Inter-organizational coordination can be predominantly vertical or horizontal and can be achieved by using hierarchical mechanisms, market incentives, contracts, network-like bargaining mechanisms and multi-level governance approaches (Thompson *et al.* 1991; Peters 1998; Bouckaert *et al.* 2010)

Performance has served as a core concept in public service modernization initiatives in many countries. Performance management was a key element in the NPM movement and beyond. At the core of this concern with performance is the idea that we need to shift our attention from what goes into public administration towards what comes out of it. In this book we do not interpret performance in a narrow, efficiency-oriented way. We define performance more widely, including effectiveness, equity, user-satisfaction, and quality (for an even wider performance concept, see Heffron 1989). Thus performance is not some value-free, purely technical concept. It has many dimensions and in each dimension certain key public service values are embedded. In this book, both objective measures of performance and perceived performance are used.

1.3   Theoretical foundation

The theoretical basis for the study of public sector organizations is drawn from different schools. We avoid single-factor explanations and instead aim to gain a better understanding of change in public sector organizations and its effects by combining different theoretical approaches.

A main assumption in the book is that organizational forms have behavioural consequences for the organizations and policy areas involved. How state agencies are organized is not solely a technically neutral question. Organizing always involves selection, so different organizational forms mobilize different biases and facilitate or constrain access to different actors, issues, priorities, and resources (Schattschneider 1965). Organizational practice therefore cannot merely be regarded as a response to external forces and shocks, or as the result of conscious political decisions, procedures, cultures, traditions, and dynamics (Olsen 1992).

In practice, public organizations' mode of operation will be characterized by a complex interplay between political and administrative governance and design, negotiations and promotion of self-interest, cultural features, and adaptation to external pressure and influence (Christensen *et al.* 2007). We will assume that organizational circumstances associated with proliferation, coordination, autonomy and control are particularly decisive for organizational conduct.

This transformative approach sees public sector reforms and the ability of the political–administrative leadership to design and redesign the system as contingent on three sets of contexts (Christensen and Lægreid 2001a, 2007b). First of all, the actions of the leadership can be constrained by formal structures in political–administrative systems, like constitutions, main type of election and representational system, whether the civil service is homogeneous or heterogeneous, etc. (Christensen and Lægreid 2001a). Certain combinations of structural factors offer better preconditions for deciding on and implementing reform. Westminster systems, for example, with their 'elective dictatorships' allow the winning party in principle to implement radical reforms if it chooses to do so. In systems with multiple parties, where there are often minority coalition governments, or systems with many checks and balances, like in the USA, the situation is very different. According to this perspective, organizations are regarded as tools or instruments for achieving certain goals viewed as important in society. It regards public sector organizations and their designers as acting with instrumental rationality according to a logic of consequentiality. Hence the design of public sector organizations is influenced by structural factors in the wider political–administrative regime. But the structure of public sector organizations, in turn, determines how its members will actually behave. In that perspective, the structure, autonomy, and control of public sector organizations will determine both behaviour and performance. Instrumental rationality can thus involve both the effects of organizational structure and the process whereby that structure is determined and formed (Christensen *et al.* 2007b). This structural–instrumental perspective is the main approach in this book and inspires almost all the empirical chapters (except for Chapter 12).

One specific group of theories within the structural–instrumental approach that is used in several chapters is rational choice institutionalism. This book refers to ideas from economic organization theory, including principal agent theory, property rights theory (Chapter 11), and transaction cost theory (Chapter 9). The focus of the latter is on which governance structures – in our case, which organizational form – are most suitable to support transactions of a given kind from an efficiency point of view. The argument is that the governance structure should ideally match the characteristics of the transactions and should minimize transaction costs.

Principal agent theory deals with the design and control problem a principal has when delegating a task to a specialized and autonomous agent. It refers to the agency problem a government faces when dealing with autonomous public bodies. The theory advocates the use of result-based management tools and incentives, in order to counterbalance agencies' autonomy and to increase their performance (Chapter 11).

A closely related rational choice concept, which has been elaborated in political science literature, is the concept of *credible commitment* (Chapters 3, 4, and 10). The central argument of this explanation of agency design is that in order to be effective a policy needs to be credible to the enacting coalition and to external stakeholders (Majone 1997a). Policy credibility is the expectation that an announced policy will be carried out in a way that creates credible policy commitments *vis-à-vis* stakeholders, citizens, and consumers.

The second context is related to cultural processes. Public organizations evolve gradually by adapting to internal and external pressure. In a process of institutionalization they develop distinct cultural features represented by their informal norms and values (Selznick 1957). In contrast to the structural instrumental perspective, which applies a logic of consequentiality, this perspective introduces a logic of appropriateness (March and Olsen 1989). This means that decision-makers act in accordance with their experience of what has worked well in the past or with what feels fair, reasonable, and acceptable in the environment in which the person works. Actors will gain experience of an institutional culture by learning what is appropriate. Institutionalization processes are related to path-dependency, i.e. the norms and values that characterized the organization when it was established will influence and constrain its further development (Krasner 1988). When reforms are introduced, cultural sensitivity and compatibility are important. Reforms that are culturally compatible will be adapted and implemented easily, while reforms that are incompatible will be bounced back or adopted only partially in a pragmatic way (Brunsson and Olsen 1993). Moreover, the specific path of a single public sector organization will to some extent determine how it will deal with its autonomy and how it will react to control from its principals.

The third set of contextual factors relates to *environmental factors*. The *technical environment,* for instance – whether in the form of external factors like globalization or the financial crisis or internal economic, social, political, or technological pressures – may have an important influence on the direction taken by reforms and administrative policy. The technical environment refers to all aspects of the environment potentially relevant to goal-setting and goal-attainment, or more narrowly as the sources for inputs, markets for outputs, competitors, and regulators (Verhoest *et al.* 2010).

The other part of the environment, the institutional environment, may exert ideological pressure as international and national concept entrepreneurs try to further new ideologies, ideas, concepts, and myths about how to organize the public sector. Certain ideas come to be 'taken-for-granted' as they are taken on board and promoted by dominant professions, consulting firms, or international and national commercial actors. Isomorphism and loose coupling between talk and action are special features of this sociological institutional perspective (Meyer and Rowan 1977; Brunsson 1989; DiMaggio and Powell 1983). This perspective is used in Chapters 2, 7, and 11.

We also apply a task-specific perspective, which can be viewed as a sub-variant of a structural–instrumental perspective. Formal organizational structures and rules define how and by whom tasks are to be carried out within the organization. However, a task-specific perspective is also linked to an environmental perspective, emphasizing the relevance of agencies' technical environments. The specific kind of task an organization executes relates to features of the task-related environment, like stable or shifting, homogeneous or heterogeneous environments (Thompson 1967), or to goals and means–ends relations which are either clear or unclear (DeLeon 2003). The main argument here is that tasks matter for both the design of organizations and the way those organizations behave. Task-specific features, such as the measurability of tasks or the level of political salience, will influence organizational reforms and actions. Moreover, there will be variations between organizations working mainly with policy advice, service delivery or regulatory tasks (Wilson 1989; Pollitt 2004a). The importance of tasks in understanding organizational forms, their autonomy, and their control is analysed in Chapters 5–7. The relevance of task environment for organizational performance is also studied in Chapters 8 and 11.

Taken together, these sets of constraining factors may at one extreme tend to favour modern reforms, as studies of NPM have shown (Christensen and Lægreid 2001b; Pollitt and Bouckaert 2004). Countries facing economic crises or strong normative pressure from international organizations, and that have an accommodating culture and 'elective dictatorships' might adopt reforms of this kind most easily. Other countries might lag behind because of less external pressure, less accommodating cultures and more problematic structural preconditions. Between these extremes, there are many other variants conditioned by the complex way (outlined by the transformative approach) that these main sets of international, national, and environmental factors interact. Additionally, factors at the level of individual public sector organizations, like their structural, cultural, or task-related characteristics, will also influence how international NPM and post-NPM ideas are applied to these specific public sector organizations (Verhoest *et al.* 2010).

Depending on the contexts outlined, the civil service in a given country may develop in several different ways. One scenario is a more or less wholesale adoption of NPM in place of the old public administration followed by a kind of pendulum swing back towards some of the main norms and values of the old public administrations in the form of post-NPM reforms in the late 1990s (Christensen *et al.* 2007d). Another is the preservation of some aspects of the old public administration and deinstitutionalization of others. In other words, only certain aspects of NPM have been implemented, while post-NPM has become only partially institutionalized leading to a hybrid structure and culture that contains elements of the old public administration, NPM, and post-NPM. One way to describe this is as a process of layering or sedimentation (Streeck and Thelen 2005; Olsen 2009).

Since, as noted above, all the empirical chapters use one or several of the theoretical perspectives described, this book allows a multi-theoretical explanation of organizational design and behaviour within the public sector.

1.4   Data, method and selection of case countries

We will address the research questions by applying a comparative approach. The importance of differences between countries will be contrasted with differences between organizational forms, tasks, and policy areas. State agencies, mostly at the central level, form the main object of the study. They will be studied in a broader context that encompasses several actors and several governmental levels but also with respect to their own top governance structure, their internal management, their organizational culture, and their performance.

We have selected countries from different political–administrative cultures and state systems to cover frontrunners as well as latecomers to NPM reforms. By doing this we have tried to control for the more radical NPM reformers such as Australia and Canada (Chapter 11) and also to some degree Hong Kong (Chapter 6), and the more modest NPM reformers anchored in a continental Weberian bureaucratic system, such as Germany (Chapter 5), the Netherlands (Chapter 9), and Switzerland (Chapter 10), or a Napoleonic bureaucratic system, like Italy and Belgium (Chapters 4, 7, and 11). The Scandinavian counties with their large welfare states, here represented by Norway, are somewhere in between (Chapters 2 and 13). We have also included one of the new EU members from Central Europe (Hungary) to see how these countries' integration into the EU has affected the organization of their administrative apparatus (Chapter 3) This is important because most of the previous NPM-related studies have been preoccupied with the Western OECD countries.

The idea behind this selection of countries is to control for the different state traditions, (Nordic, Continental, Latin, East European, Anglo-Saxon and Asian) as well as for different starting points and stages of reforms (front-runners versus laggards) and to examine whether the same empirical phenomena and the same causal patterns hold in different administrative cultures. Conducting a strict comparison of countries is, however, difficult in this selected design since we do not compare countries within single articles, and the dependent variables are to some extent different from one chapter to another. That said, we believe that by including Anglo-American countries, Continental Europe (the old West and the new East), Scandinavia, and the Far East will enable us to find out to what degree there is a convergence in public sector organization towards NPM reforms and also post-NPM reforms across countries with different state traditions and administrative cultures or whether there is still a lot of variety and divergence. Moreover, by comparing similar processes across administrative cultures, we may study to what extent similar explanatory models and theories (e.g. credible commitment theory) hold in different cultural settings.

Each chapter uses a different methodological approach, some quantitative, others qualitative. The data basis in many of the chapters is a comprehensive comparative survey approach in different countries, but comparative case studies are also used. More specifically, some chapters build on data gathered by (longitudinal) mapping methodologies (Chapters 2, 3, and 4), surveys (Chapters 5, 6, 7, and 11), and statistical data mining (Chapter 8). Other chapters use qualitative approaches, comparative case studies (Chapters 9 and 10), document studies and interviews (Chapters 9 and 12), and media coverage (Chapter 10). The surveys were conceived within the Comparative Public Organization Data Base for Research and Analysis (COBRA) network (http://www.publicmanagement-cobra.org/). Surveys with similar questions and targeting similar respondents (CEOs of state agencies) are replicated in the different countries. The COBRA network gathers and analyses similar survey data on agency autonomy and control in a number of countries, allowing a comparison of agency types and features operating in different politico-administrative cultures. The COBRA survey is one of the methodologies used within a larger network, the COST Action ISO601 'Comparative Research into Current Trends in Public Sector Organization' (www.soc.kuleuven.be/io/cost). Within this network, high-quality European public management research teams from 22 countries have joined forces in a common research project on public sector organizations, focusing on the changing autonomy, control, and coordination of public agencies, as well as on the explanations and consequences of this trend.

1.5   Design of the book

The aim of this book is to contribute to an understanding of the changes going on in the formal structure of central governmental administration in contemporary democracies by focusing on organizational forms. There is a considerable need in society for knowledge in this field in a period when new forms of cooperation and governance are challenging traditional structures. In this book we will focus on four interconnected topics:

1.5.1   Proliferation and specialization

What is happening in the organization of central government? This is the empirical–descriptive challenge of describing and mapping the changing formal structures of the state agencies. Here we will focus on the proliferation of central government systems, the increasing number of central agencies, processes of vertical and horizontal specialization that result in increasing proliferation of the administrative apparatus, more complexity and eventually in an increased need for coordination. We address different consequences of the observed proliferation.

Part I of the book is linked to the first set of research questions (RQ1) and describes the processes of proliferation, fragmentation, and agencification in different countries in the NPM era in three chapters. Chapter 2, by Per Lægreid, Vidar W. Rolland, Paul G. Roness, and John-Erik Ågotnes, addresses the structural anatomy of the Norwegian state in the period 1985–2007. The chapter examines the form and extent of vertical and horizontal specialization and de-specialization in the Norwegian state from the mid-1980s onwards. The authors ask whether the Norwegian state administration has experienced increased specialization or pendulum shifts as a result of changes in government or following the adoption of international and national administrative doctrines. The empirical basis is changes in the formal structure of Norwegian civil service organizations outside the ministries, state-owned companies, and governmental foundations. Taking international doctrines, ideas, and reform movements as the point of departure, the chapter examines how these are filtered, modified, translated, and interpreted by domestic political–administrative culture and by instrumental choices made by political and administrative leaders.

Chapter 3 is by György Hajnal, who examines the agency landscape in Hungary. This chapter offers an overview of how agencification has travelled to Hungary and it also contributes to existing explanations of why agencies exist, for what purpose, and how they are used by politicians. The author focuses on the extent to which agency-type organizations have proliferated in the Hungarian central government structure in general and in the various policy areas in particular. He also addresses whether any change trends can be identified regarding such proliferation. One central question is whether Hungarian regulatory agencies support the credible commitment hypothesis as an explanation for the autonomy of regulatory agencies. Another is to what extent the formal–legal features of Hungarian agencies have changed since their creation and what patterns and explanatory factors can be identified in these changes. The empirical basis of the research is a data base covering all structural changes in central government organizations between 2002 and 2006.

Chapter 4 by Jan Rommel, Koen Verhoest, and Joery Matthys addresses the mapping of specialization, proliferation, and fragmentation of regulatory administration. They study the way regulatory bodies in Belgium and Flanders are organized as part of broader regulatory arrangements and ask to what extent regulators are specialized both vertically and horizontally. They also examine whether regulatory area or governmental level matters most – i.e. to what extent can differences in the level of specialization and fragmentation be explained by level of government (federal versus regional) or by different regulatory areas (economic versus social)?

1.5.2 Autonomy and control

Part II of the book focuses on autonomy and control of central agencies. We ask how changes in formal organization affect the *de facto* autonomy and forms of control within the administrative system. What other factors can affect perceived autonomy and control? What is the role of tasks, policy area, and other organizational features? This part deals with our second set of research questions. Different dimensions of autonomy, such as policy autonomy and managerial autonomy, will be explored.

The multi-dimensional character of autonomy is evident, because autonomy can be related to issues of management or policy, to legal position, and to financial dependence. There is growing awareness that real autonomy can be quite different from formal–legal autonomy (Verhoest *et al.* 2004a). However, measurement and knowledge of different kinds of autonomy is still relatively underdeveloped. It is unclear how tasks, political salience, policy field, polity features, and national political–administrative culture affect the autonomy of public sector organizations in different countries and sectors. It is important to discern different kinds of autonomy, how they can be operationalized and measured, and to describe and explain different patterns and trajectories of autonomy.

External control also seems to be multidimensional, with differences between formal and factual, *ex ante* and *ex post*, and input-oriented versus output-oriented, and structural, financial, and contact-based control. Control might change over time and depend on tasks, policy field and country-specific, path-dependent factors (Pollitt *et al.* 2004). Little systematic research exists on the exact influence of these factors. In this section we aim to conceptualize different forms of steering and control, to observe empirically different patterns and trajectories of steering and control and to explain them.

Part II of the book will address the problems of agency autonomy by focusing on different dimensions, such as policy autonomy and managerial autonomy and the efforts of controlling semi-autonomous agencies by use of *ex post* and *ex ante* control tools.

Chapter 5, by Tobias Bach, examines policy and management autonomy of federal agencies in Germany. The chapter describes the perceived managerial and policy autonomy of agencies and analyses variations in perceived autonomy by legal category as well as by features of the parent ministry. Its empirical basis is a comprehensive survey of all federal agencies. The chapter tests the assumption that legal categories will play a major role in determining agency autonomy and ministerial control, as one would expect from the rule-of-law tradition of Germany's administrative system. As a result of the strongly defended principle of departmental sovereignty, it will elaborate on how much autonomy the agencies under respective parent departments have. The chapter distinguishes between agency characteristics and features of the oversight ministries as key explanatory factors, and draws on different strands of organization theory to explain observed similarities and differences.

Whereas the previous chapter discusses policy autonomy of agencies in an archtypical European *Rechtsstaat*, Chapter 6 by Martin Painter, John P. Burns, and Wai-Hang Yee bring us to Hong Kong, where agencies function in a quasi-democratic political regime (at best). The contribution discusses perceived management and policy autonomy of different types of public sector organizations. It examines to what extent formal legal structure, the nature of tasks, and the policy domain explain patterns of autonomy. Regarding legal structure the vertical specialization in departments and non-departmental organizations is central. With respect to tasks the authors focus on political salience, regulatory tasks, and whether the 'targets' of organizations are private citizens or public bodies.

Chapter 7 by Dario Barbieri, Paulo Fedele, David Galli, and Edoardo Ongaro examines determinants of result-based control of central agencies in Italy, a country with a Latin, legalistic politico-administrative culture and a Napoleonic administrative legacy. Italian agencies are controlled in different ways by their parent minister and department. This contribution aims to describe and explain this control, using structural–instrumental, cultural–institutional, and environmental perspectives. The focus is on *ex post* based result-based control between agencies and their parent ministries, and factors such as agency age, size, tasks, and policy field are used to examine variations in the control pattern. The chapter investigates whether the systems of steering and control of central agencies in Italy have changed since the 1999 reform programme and how variations in control can be understood.

1.5.3 Performance and results

Part III of the book focuses on the consequences of different organizational forms for the performance of public sector organizations. As already mentioned, NPM expects agencification, result control, and 'modern' management tools to produce performance gains. However, can agencies deliver what they promise? What is the impact of different modes of government and what is the long-term performance of decentralized agencies?

The results of studies on organizational performance of public sector organizations are rather inconclusive. Generally there is a lack of reliable knowledge about the effects of different organizational forms on performance. Studying changes in the performance of public sector organizations in relation to changes in their organizational form (like agencification) appears to be very difficult, because of the lack of valid and long-term performance information. However, other ways of studying the issue of performance have been used with more success, such as the perception of different stakeholders (Burger and Treur 1996). Moreover, performance information has recently improved.

In this section we will address the third set of research questions (RQ3) by focusing on the implications of changes in organizational forms and in the level of autonomy and control of a public sector organization. The effects will be studied with respect to performance and internal management of agencies. We will measure and explain variation in the performance of central agencies along different dimensions. In the first two chapters performance is measured by more objective measures such as standardized performance reports and efficiency measures. The last two chapters use more subjective measures such as reputation and agencies' own assessment of their performance.

Chapter 8 by Marie-Eve Quenneville, Claude Laurin, and Nicole Thibodeau addresses the long-term performance of decentralized agencies in the Canadian province of Québec. This study examines the performance of agencies over time along multiple dimensions. In the specific case of Québec, reforms can be traced back to the mid-1990s when the government moved to decentralize operational authority in exchange for more accountability in some government organizations. The contribution studies the effect of the introduction of result-based management and managerial autonomy on the performance of 16 agencies. One central question is whether the reported performance of agencies improved following the introduction of the autonomy reform in 2001. To do this the authors analyse the output, efficiency, and financial and performance indicators of the agencies from 2002 to 2007. They formulate some possible explanations for agency differences in performance.

Chapter 9 by Marieke van Genugten compares the impact of modes of governance. Public services are provided through a variety of modes of governance. The aim is to study one type of public service under alternative institutional arrangements. This contribution studies the relative efficiency and performance of these modes using a comparative case study of household waste collection in eight Dutch municipalities with high urbanization. The author conducts a comparative institutional analysis of different forms of in-house and out-sourcing arrangements. The Transaction Cost Economics, originally developed by Williamson (1985), is applied to a variety of public governance structures – municipal service, public companies, and contracting out. A main question is whether alignments between governance structures and transactions really matter for efficiency. Another aim is to study the relative efficiency of different modes of governance in terms of transaction costs.

Chapter 10, by Martino Maggetti, asks whether agencies can deliver what they promise. Two main rationales drive the delegation of power from governments to formally independent regulatory agencies: an increase in policy credibility (through independence), and the enhancement of decision-making efficiency (through expertise). The two goals are expected to be incompatible, because they require two opposite structures of delegation, one promoting de facto independence, the other implying the need to retain control. In order to contribute to this discussion, the author examines the reputation of agencies in two contrasting cases (the British and Swiss Competition Commissions), according to credibility and efficiency criteria, by doing a content analysis of major national newspapers during the years 2006–2007. The chapter illustrates the expected variations in agencies' reputations, with reference to a set of organizational and institutional variables that systematically differ across the selected countries.

The last contribution in Part III, Chapter 11, by Koen Verhoest, Bram Verschuere, Falke Meyers, and Andrew Sulle addresses the performance of public sector organizations by focusing on the importance of management techniques and management quality. The authors challenge the view that the import of managerial tools from the private sector to public sector organizations will increase their efficiency, effectiveness, and quality. Using data from a survey of 124 public sector organizations in Flanders (Belgium), ranging from departments to private law agencies, they analyse to what extent management matters for the performance of public sector organizations. Based on neo-institutional economics and sociological neo-institutionalism, the possible influence of specific management tools on the self-assessed performance of public sector organizations is investigated. It is also controlled for specific contextual factors, like managerial quality, managerial flexibility and incentives, organizational culture, tasks, and organizational resources.

1.5.4   Whole-of-government: horizontal coordination and increased complexity

The last part of the book examines what has happened in the aftermath of New Public Management. Have the NPM reforms peaked? Is NPM dead and been replaced by post-NPM features or are we just seeing a revision and moderate change to the organizational models in the new millennium? The question is whether we can see 'beyond NPM trajectories', implying a tendency towards reassertion of the centre and an increased focus on horizontal coordination.

The proliferation of semi-autonomous organizational forms in the public sector is one of the reasons why many countries have now launched initiatives to enhance coordination and to manage 'cross-cutting' and 'whole-of-government' issues. In such initiatives, strengthening the link between individual public sector organizations and the larger objectives of government as well as with other public sector organizations seems crucial.

In this part we address these questions and reveal the main features of post-NPM reforms, such as an increased focus on integration and a strengthening of central policy-making capacity and control. One core question is the focus on horizontal coordination that is a central feature of the 'whole-of-government' reforms. Another question is whether post-NPM reforms, such as whole-of-government reforms, are replacing the NPM reforms or whether they are supplementing them, producing increased complexity in public sector organizations. In addition, the final set of research questions RQ4 is addressed.

Chapter 12, by John Halligan, examines proliferation, horizontal coordination, and whole-of-government initiatives in Anglo-Saxon countries. He addresses the issue of greater fragmentation, which is one of the challenges of increased proliferation of central government administration. In the post-NPM era there has been a global movement away from disaggregation and increasing efforts to bring a fragmented state together again through various whole-of-government initiatives and an enhanced focus on horizontal coordination. Using illustrations from Australia, the author discusses new modes of coordination and whole-of-government tools such as different types of integrating structures including multilevel governance approaches. The chapter examines the drivers of different types of horizontal coordination and their significance and impact in different sectors with reference to the experience of other countries.

Chapter 13 by Tom Christensen, and Per Lægreid focuses on increased complexity in public organizations and links this to the challenges and implications of combining NPM and post-NPM features. Both the NPM and the post-NPM reform waves have stressed different elements of increased autonomy or increased control. This has resulted in highly complex combinations and layering of autonomy and control in different public organizations. Focusing on the complex interplay of autonomy and control, they study two main research questions. First, what characterizes the new complexity and layering of NPM and post-NPM reforms in public organizations? A brief overview is given of the shift from NPM to post-NPM reforms. This is followed by empirical illustrations from four Norwegian reform processes in the sectors of hospitals, welfare administration, regulation, and immigration, in which balancing control and autonomy has added complexity. The second research question is how the development of this complexity might be analysed. What is the role of the political and administrative leadership in this development and to what extent do other factors come into play? Within a transformative theoretical perspective, negotiative, cultural, and environmental factors are discussed in terms of whether they limit or foster potential hierarchical control in designing complexity and balancing political control and autonomy. Finally, in Chapter 14 the authors link the main findings of the different parts in the book, and discuss theoretical, methodological, and practical implications.

Part I
Proliferation and Specialization

2
The Structural Anatomy of the Norwegian State: Increased Specialization or a Pendulum Shift?

*Per Lægreid, Vidar W. Rolland, Paul G. Roness
and John-Erik Ågotnes*

2.1 Introduction

In this chapter we will address structural change over time in the Norwegian state apparatus by focusing on specialization. Changing the principles and practice of specialization will influence coordination and steering in the public administration and will affect whether various aspects are viewed together or separately. What gets attention and what is ignored or neglected in the state apparatus changes when the specialization of the apparatus changes (Lægreid and Roness 1999).

The structural anatomy of the state can be described in terms of a vertical and a horizontal dimension (Egeberg 1989; Christensen and Egeberg 1997; Lægreid and Roness 1998; Roness 2007). The vertical dimension concerns centralization and decentralization (Pollitt 2005), in other words, how responsibility for political and administrative tasks is allocated among organizations at different levels of the hierarchy. The horizontal dimension focuses on how tasks and responsibility are allocated among different organizations at the same hierarchical level.

Agencies and other bodies at arm's length from the central political authorities have existed for a long time in the Norwegian state (Christensen and Roness 1999; Roness 2007). However, like in other countries, the introduction of new types of civil service organizations and the conversion of existing ones into structurally more devolved forms has been linked to the doctrines of New Public Management, which prescribe increased specialization along the vertical as well as along the horizontal dimension (Christensen *et al.* 2007d). Increased vertical and horizontal specialization tends to increase the proliferation of state organizations and thus enhance coordination problems.

We examine the form and extent of specialization and de-specialization in the Norwegian state from the mid-1980s onwards. The aim is to find out whether changes of government or the adoption of new doctrines has brought about increased specialization or pendulum shifts, and if so to what extent. In order to identify these tendencies, the period we are looking at is divided into sub-periods, mainly corresponding with the party constellations in government and the prevailing international and national administrative policy doctrines.

We will first specify the central concepts and present our theoretical approach, emphasizing a transformative perspective. Secondly, we will outline the database and the method used. Thirdly, we will describe the Norwegian reform context by focusing on the main components of the administrative policy that different governments have pursued. Fourthly, we will describe the formal structure of the Norwegian state by focusing on the main organizational forms. Fifthly, we will present our empirical data on changes in the formal structure over time. The chapter concludes with a discussion of the main findings on the form and extent of specialization and de-specialization and once again underlines the relevance of a transformative perspective.

2.2   Central concepts

Specialization is a core feature in organization theory going back to the founding fathers of bureaucratic theory (Weber 1997 [1922]) and scientific management (Taylor 1998 [1911]). The different forms of specialization (Gulick 1937; Simon 1946; Mintzberg 1979) and the relationship between specialization and coordination (Verhoest *et al.* 2007b) have been the subject of a major debate. In this chapter we will focus on specialization and de-specialization in the formal organizational structure, distinguishing between vertical and horizontal specialization and de-specialization across organizational boundaries.

Vertical specialization can take the form of structural devolution, meaning conversion of existing state organizations into units that are organizationally further away from the central political authorities. It also includes the transfer of tasks to existing units that have a structurally more devolved form, and an increase in the number of new organizations with a structurally more devolved form. Vertical de-specialization implies the movement of units and tasks in the opposite direction, in other words a decrease in the number of units with a structurally more devolved form. For the vertical dimension we will here focus on changes involving the transfer of whole units from one hierarchical level to another.

Horizontal specialization may mean that existing organizations are split into smaller sub-units or that new organizations are founded at the same hierarchical level, while horizontal de-specialization generally involves the merger, absorption or termination of existing organizations. For the horizontal dimension we will also focus on changes involving whole units, i.e. the splitting, secession, founding, merging, absorption, termination or complex reorganization of organizations. Thus, we will not examine the transfer of tasks from one organization to another at the same hierarchical level.

2.3   Theoretical approach

We will examine structural changes and ask to what degree the changes can be understood as resulting from international administrative doctrines, the national historical-institutional context or domestic reform programmes. We regard the form and extent of vertical and horizontal specialization as dependent variables and discuss reforms and changes in specialization from a neo-institutional and a transformative perspective (cf. Christensen and Lægreid 2001a, 2001b, 2007).

One variety of neo-institutional organization theory emphasizes that organizations exist in institutional environments that prescribe socially defined norms for their structural and procedural arrangements (Meyer and Rowan 1977; DiMaggio and Powell 1983). Organizations are exposed to and constrained by institutionalized standards that are widely accepted prescriptions for how organization should be structured (Røvik 1996). They can be seen as solutions looking for problems (March and Olsen 1976; Kingdon 1984) and thus as a response to outside actors offering a shopping basket of organizational tools to state organizations.

Different waves or tides of reform have also highlighted different aspects or doctrines at different times. Reform tools tend to follow a cyclical pattern, coming into and going out of fashion (Røvik 1996; Light 1997; Talbot 2005). They reflect shifting organizational trends observed among similar actors or organizations in the environment. The increased use of organizational tools may also be triggered by supply-side considerations. Public and private professionals, groups of experts and international organizations, and consultants have all been promoters and carriers of new administrative doctrines (Saint-Martin 2000; Sahlin-Andersson and Engwall 2002). According to this perspective administrative doctrines are frequently introduced and spread easily across organizations, policy areas and countries (Sahlin-Andersson and Engwall 2002). This neo-institutional perspective argues that the main reason for the popularity of such tools is persuasive rhetoric and 'taken-for-grantedness' (Nørreklit 2003). Generally the volatility in such doctrines is great, and they are often rather unstable and shifting. The perspective also predicts that the doctrines will lead to changes in the formal structure but not necessarily to change in the actual practice within the organizations.

According to this neo-institutional perspective we would expect that international doctrines about organizational forms to be adopted easily and quickly by Norwegian reform policy and be adapted in actual reorganizations. The argument is that the Norwegian government will follow isomorphic pressure in a direct way. More specifically we would expect NPM doctrines on vertical and horizontal specialization from 1985 onwards to have found their way into Norwegian reform programmes of that time and to have resulted in structural reforms following these doctrines. When in the late 1990s international doctrines began to move towards post-NPM doctrines emphasizing more vertical and horizontal de-specialization we would likewise expect this trend to have been easily and quickly incorporated into Norwegian reform policy and to have resulted in structural reforms enhancing centralization and mergers.

According to a transformative perspective, national reform concepts and programmes do not constitute a simple adjustment to current international administrative doctrines. Rather, the doctrines are filtered, interpreted and modified by two nationally based processes. One is a country's unique political–administrative history, culture, traditions and style of governance, which have evolved gradually over time; the other is instrumental actions taken by political and administrative executives to further collective goals through administrative design and active administrative policy (Olsen 1992; Olsen and Peters 1996).

Individual organizations are not only passive adopters of external standards and doctrines. Their leaders can choose among different doctrines and also transform the instruments and reshape them to fit their own organization (Friedland and Alford 1991; Sahlin-Andersson 1996). The doctrines are not merely a diffusion of standardized solutions. Normally the transfer of such organizational tools also involves local adaptation, modification and interpretation (Pollitt 2004b).

When they are applied to national political–administrative systems internationally generated reform concepts and processes may to some extent be translated and therefore have varied and ambiguous effects and implications. Political leaders may take a pragmatic approach and use only parts of externally generated reforms or else they may try to redefine ambiguous reform elements in a national context in order to match instrumental goals. They may also consciously manipulate the reforms, pretending to implement them, but actually having little intention of doing so. The reforms then acquire the status of myths and symbols designed to further the leaders' legitimacy through double-talk – i.e. separating talk, decisions and action, or saying one thing and doing another (Brunsson 1989).

Our argument is that there will not be a convergence towards a common administrative model across different countries but that we will face considerable divergence, and far more divergence in practice than we would expect from policy documents and programmes (Pollitt 2001). Thus, from a transformative perspective it is important to distinguish between reform efforts, actual changes and the effects and implications of reforms and changes (Lægreid and Roness 2003).

2.4 Data and method

The empirical basis for the chapter is the comprehensive and detailed Norwegian State Administration Database (NSA), which covers changes in the formal structure of the Norwegian ministries, civil service organizations outside the ministries, state-owned companies and governmental foundations from 1947 onwards. An organization is included in the database if it meets one of the following four criteria (cf. Rolland and Roness 2009):

(a) It is a ministry or subunit within a ministry, such as a division, section or office.
(b) It is legally part of the state and separate from but subordinated to a parent ministry or to parliament. Organizations of this kind are labelled civil service organizations outside the ministries.
(c) It is state-owned or partly (i.e. majority) state-owned. These organizations are labelled state-owned companies (SOCs).
(d) It is a self-owned organization founded by a ministry or a civil service organization. These are labelled governmental foundations.

For the organizations that are included in the NSA, all changes in organizational structure from the founding of an organization to its termination are recorded. A predefined categorization that classifies organizational change in three main categories is used: changes related to the founding of an organization, changes related to the maintenance of an organization, and changes related to the termination of an organization. For each main category of changes there are several sub-categories, including splitting, secession, merger, absorption and movement of organizations vertically and horizontally within the state apparatus, and into or out of it (cf. Rolland and Roness 2009).

As of 2007, the database covered about 3,400 [unique] organizations, about 2,100 of which are internal units within the ministries. These organizations have gone through about 10,500 organizational events, indicating a substantial degree of turbulence and structural change of various kinds in the state apparatus. This indicates that reorganization is a very popular administrative reform tool (cf. Peters 1988), that the structure of the state is subject to continuous change and that this has been going on for a long time (Lægreid *et al.* 2003). This data set reveals that the idea that public sector organizations are stable is incorrect.

2.5   Administrative arguments and doctrines

With regard to the structural anatomy of the state, NPM quite consistently prescribes increased specialization along the horizontal as well as along the vertical dimension (Christensen *et al.* 2007d; Roness 2007). Increased horizontal specialization implies single-purpose organizations and a differentiation (inside or between state organizations) between the government's roles and functions as owner, administrator, regulator, purchaser and provider (Boston *et al.* 1996). Increased vertical specialization implies structural devolution and more autonomy for agencies and other state organizations outside the (core) ministries, where authority and responsibility are delegated to lower hierarchical levels.

Over the past decade a number of post-NPM reform features have come to the fore that have supplemented and modified the NPM reforms, especially in the most radical NPM countries such as the United Kingdom, Australia, New Zealand and Canada. These reforms have tended to pay greater heed to the problems of horizontal coordination by focusing on 'joined-up government' (Pollitt 2003b) and 'whole-of-government' initiatives (Christensen and Lægreid 2007, 2008b). Regarding horizontal specialization there has been a tendency to merge organizations and to build various networks and partnerships between organizations. Regarding vertical specialization we have seen a trend towards a reassertion of the centre. So the main post-NPM features involve both horizontal and vertical de-specialization.

The reform programmes of various Norwegian governments from the mid-1980s until the late 1990s were pragmatic and cooperative rather than ideological and confrontational, and they aimed to enhance efficiency more than to roll back the state. Reform strategies tended to be sector-based rather than comprehensive. The reform style was maintenance and modernization rather than radical change aimed at marketization or minimizing the state (cf. Christensen and Lægreid 2008b; Pollitt and Bouckaert 2004). The reform arguments and doctrines emphasized a strong and modernized state that combined old Weberian features with some elements from the NPM movement. More management than market elements of NPM were taken on board, and visions of a decline of the public sector brought about by privatization scarcely featured in the Norwegian reform programmes (Christensen and Lægreid 1998a).

The Norwegian adoption of NPM through an active administrative policy under the auspices of the political executive has since the early 1990s mainly taken the form of increased structural devolution and the introduction of Management-by-objectives-and-results (MBOR) (Christensen and Lægreid 2001b). Norway has a long tradition of having central agencies (directorates), but the agency model has been rather unified with little horizontal specialization. There is also a tradition of strong political control of state-owned companies in Norway within a system of ministerial governance. The Hermansen commission (NOU 1989: 5) and subsequent governments emphasized the relationships between ministries and state-owned companies and governmental foundations. The commission discussed the coupling of tasks and organizational forms and suggested that various standardized forms of state-owned companies should be used more actively. Governmental foundations were not recommended, because of accountability and steering problems connected to this form of affiliation.

When NPM was introduced, Norway did not jump on the band-wagon but remained a reluctant reformer for the next 10–15 years (Olsen 1996). This modest strategy came under pressure in the 1990s and Norway then became a more eager NPM reformer. The result was more autonomy for central agencies and state-owned companies. Under the Labour government of 2000–2001 (Stoltenberg I), a partial privatization of Telenor (the national telecommunications company) and of Statoil (the large state-owned oil company) was initiated and implemented. Another big reform initiated under this government was the hospital reform. In 2002, responsibility for Norwegian hospitals was transferred from the counties to central government, thus introducing centralized state ownership. The reform also set up new management principles for the hospitals based on a decentralized enterprise model (Lægreid *et al.* 2005). This was a hybrid reform, which combined centralizing elements of post-NPM with decentralizing elements of NPM.

The most marked NPM-oriented reform period was during the Conservative-Centre government's term in office from 2001 to 2005. The slogan of the Bondevik II government (2001-2005) –'From words to action'– indicated a wish to weaken the symbolic elements of administrative reform and to enhance its substantive outcome (Christensen and Lægreid 2003a). The new and active minister of government administration assigned a prominent role to structural devolution, single-purpose organizations, competitive tendering, efficiency measures, consumer choice and the decentralization of service provision (Christensen and Lægreid 2003b). The government eagerly proceeded with a comprehensive programme for converting civil service organizations into state-owned companies. The most controversial reform attempt concerned regulatory agencies (Christensen, Lie and Lægreid 2008). The basic ideas were that regulatory agencies should have more autonomy and unambiguous roles, thus breaking with the Norwegian tradition of integrating different roles and functions. This was an argument for more vertical specialization and also for horizontal specialization of roles and single-purpose organizations, as prescribed by the OECD (1997, 2002), but the most radical elements in these initiatives were modified by the parliament, and the reform initiative eventually assumed a rather hybrid form.

Before the national election in 2005 the Labour Party formed an alliance with the Centre Party and the Socialist Left Party. This alliance ran pretty much on an anti-NPM ticket arguing that NPM reforms should be stopped or modified because of their negative consequences, such as reduced political control and increased fragmentation. The alliance won the election and formed a Red-Green government (Stoltenberg II). The programme of this government was pursued under the slogan 'a strong and efficient public sector' and this renewal strategy has featured some post-NPM measures such as a 'whole-of-government' initiative as well as a reassertion of the centre that has modified but not replaced NPM elements.

In our empirical description of the actual changes in the formal organization of the state apparatus from the mid-1980s onwards we will distinguish five periods. The first period (1985–1990) represents the last two years of the Conservative–Centre Willoch government, which presented the first NPM-inspired modernization programme in 1986, and the Labour Brundtland government which came to power in 1986 and launched its renewal programme the year after. These two programmes were pretty similar. For most of the second period (1991–1996) a Labour

Party minority government more or less continued the renewal pro-gramme begun in 1987. The third period (1997–2001) mainly covers the term of the Bondevik I government, which was a rather weak minority Centre government that pursued a moderate modernization programme under the slogan 'a simplified Norway'. During the fourth period (2002–2005) a Conservative–Centre government launched a more radi-cal NPM-inspired programme. The last period (2006–2007) covers the first two years of the Centre-Left government, which was elected on an anti-NPM ticket and is the first majority government since 1985.

2.6 The formal structure of the state apparatus

The recent and existing forms of state organizations in Norway are out-lined in Table 2.1. Those closest to the central political authorities are at the top of the table, while the degree of formal autonomy and structural devolution increases as one moves down the table.

One can distinguish between internal structural devolution, whereby civil service organizations are converted from one sub-category into another, giving them more autonomy from the political executive, and external structural devolution, whereby civil service organizations are converted into some sort of state-owned company or governmental foun-dation (Lægreid and Roness 1998). The main aim of structural devolution is to distance the provision and control of an activity or service from poli-ticians and to secure commercial benefits and professional autonomy. This is done by delegating some formal powers from the minister to a central agency or a state-owned company, where they can be exercised with a degree of autonomy from ministerial control, even though the responsible minister does not relinquish his or her authority entirely.

The major formal dividing line runs between civil service organizations and state-owned companies (SOC) (cf. Christensen and Lægreid 2003a; Roness 2007). There is also a significant difference between SOCs and governmental foundations. Civil service organizations outside the min-istries are, legally speaking, government entities subject to ministerial directions and directly subordinated to ministerial control. In contrast to state-owned companies, the state budget, the state collective wage agreement, the state pension scheme, the Freedom of Information Act, the Public Administration Act and the Civil Servants Act regulate central agencies and other civil service organizations. Government administra-tive enterprises are given enhanced budgetary leeway.

SOCs are primarily characterized by their independent legal status, by having their own control or scrutiny bodies, by holding responsibility

Table 2.1 Different forms of affiliation for units in the Norwegian state and the number of units in each category (1985 and 2007)

	Form of affiliation/type of unit	1985	2007	Example
	Ministries	*18*	*18*	Ministry of Finance
	Civil service outside the ministries	*293*	*173*	
F	Directorates, central agencies	74	59	Directorate of Fisheries
O	Other ordinary civil service organizations	193	69	Norwegian Institute of Public Health
R	Civil service organizations with extended authority	5	36	Research Council of Norway
M				
A	Government administrative enterprises	9	4	Norwegian Mapping Authority
L	Financial institutions, funds	12	5	National Insurance Scheme Fund
	State-Owned Companies (SOC)	*40*	*65*	
A	Hybrid companies established by special law	2	5	Innovation Norway
U	Government-owned companies by law of 1965	4	–	SIVA – Industrial Development Corporation of Norway
T				
O	Government-owned companies	–	4	Norwegian Power Company
N	Health Enterprises	–	5	Western Norway Regional Health Authority
O	Government limited companies (100% state owned)	21	32	Electronic Chart Centre
M				
Y	Limited companies with the state as majority owner	13	19	Statoil
	Governmental Foundations	*45*	*73*	
	Central foundations	28	46	Norwegian Institute for Urban and Regional Research
	Fringe foundations	17	27	Institute of Transport Economics
	Total outside the ministries	378	311	

Low → High

for their own economic resources, and by their closely observing the laws regulating private companies (Zuna 2001). When the ownership of the hospitals was transferred to central government in 2002 they changed their organizational form from public administration bodies at the county level to state health enterprises regulated by a special law. The government controls the SOCs through its ownership position, manifested in an annual general assembly and in some cases a continuous dialogue between the owner and the companies, but also through its role as regulator via laws and regulations. The companies' income comes from the market but also from the government. SOCs can handle their own budget independently of economic decisions made in the Storting (Parliament) and they can borrow money to finance their activities.

Governmental foundations are separate legal entities, founded either by a ministry (central foundations) or by a civil service organization outside the ministries (fringe foundations). Like state-owned companies, they are not covered by the civil service rules and regulations. In contrast to state-owned companies they are self-owned entities and thus have more formal autonomy from the ministry than SOCs. The government can control the foundations by general laws and regulations, by the formulation of statutes and by recruiting board members. These control devices are, however, weaker and less precise than for the other forms of affiliation.

2.7 Changes in the formal structure

In this section we will concentrate on the changes in formal structure that have actually taken place by focusing on the number of units and the extent of vertical and horizontal specialization and de-specialization in the state apparatus.

2.7.1 Size of the state

The number of ministries in Norway has remained quite stable throughout the 1985–2007 period, ranging from 16 to 18. However, in the empirical description below we will not examine the ministries but only units outside the ministries that report directly to a ministry.

Table 2.1 reveals that within the three main forms of affiliation – civil service organizations outside the ministries, state-owned companies and government foundations – there are 13 different sub-forms. In the civil service outside the ministries, organizations covering certain regions of the country that have similar tasks are grouped together and counted as one unit. In 1985 there were a total of 378 state organizations outside the ministries and in 2007 the number had dropped to 311. Civil service organizations outside the ministries had the biggest reduction, while there was an increase in state-owned companies and government foundations, indicating a vertical specialization process. Within the civil service we see a significant increase in civil service organizations with extended authority, indicating vertical specialization through an internal structural devolution process. The strong reduction in civil service organizations outside the ministries also implies that horizontal de-specialization has occurred at this level.

Table 2.2 reveals that there was a quite steady decline in the number of civil service organizations from the mid-1980s onwards, and particularly in the 1991–1996 period. The number of state-owned companies increased somewhat, particularly in the 2002–2005 period. For governmental central foundations there was quite a steady increase until the mid-1990s, followed by a stable number of units for a decade and some decline in the most recent years. However, even in the second half of the 2000s there are more central foundations than there were in the second half of the 1980s.

2.7.2   Organizational changes in the state

We will distinguish between three main categories of organizational change: founding of organizations, organizational maintenance, and termination of organizations.

Table 2.2 summarizes organizational changes that influence the number of units for our three main forms of affiliation. We distinguish between two types of founding and termination of organizations: Pure foundings are new organizations with no prior organizational history, while organizations founded on the basis of existing units are created from one or more existing organizations. This may take the form of splitting an existing organization into two or more new organizations, or of secession, where a new organization is created based on parts of an existing organization. Similarly, pure terminations are changes where no parts of the unit are continued in other units, while termination into existing units denotes changes where all or some parts of an organization continue in one or more existing units. This may take the form of a merger of two or more existing organizations or the absorption of an organization into another existing organization. More complex reorganizations involving foundings and terminations based on existing units may also occur. Moreover, pure immigration implies that an existing unit outside the main form of affiliation in question is converted into this form, while pure emigration implies that an existing

Table 2.2 Organizational changes influencing the number of units (1985–2007)

Affiliation	Period	No. at the start of the period =	Pure foundings +	Foundings based on existing units +	Pure immigration +	Pure emigration −	Terminations into existing units −	Pure terminations −	No. at the end of the period =
Civil service outside the ministries	1985–90	293	19	20	4	11	34	11	280
	1991–96	280	22	15	2	13	79	10	217
	1997–01	217	12	18	1	13	49	1	185
	2002–05	185	15	18	1	4	39	1	175
	2006–07	175	2	4	1	4	7	0	171
	1985–07		70	75	9	45	208	23	
State-owned companies	1985–90	40	5	2	2	4	3	2	40
	1991–96	40	5	6	5	1	5	4	46
	1997–01	46	2	4	4	6	0	1	49
	2002–05	49	4	22	13	11	11	2	64
	2006–07	64	1	2	3	3	2	0	65
	1985–07		17	36	27	25	21	9	
Governmental (central) foundations	1985–90	28	13	2	7	1	3	0	46
	1991–96	46	7	0	1	0	2	1	51
	1997–01	51	1	1	1	1	0	0	53
	2002–05	53	1	3	0	1	10	0	46
	2006–07	46	0	0	0	0	0	0	46
	1985–07		22	6	9	3	15	1	
Total	1985–90	361	37	24	13	17	40	14	364
	1991–96	364	34	22	10	13	86	14	317
	1997–01	317	16	33	12	25	50	2	301
	2002–05	301	20	32	7	13	59	3	285
	2006–07	285	2	6	3	5	9	0	282
	1985–07		109	117	45	73	244	33	

unit within the main form of affiliation in question is converted into another form.

Table 2.2 reveals quite a complex pattern of change across the main forms of affiliation and time periods. With regard to civil service organizations outside the ministries, foundings based on existing units are somewhat more common than pure foundings, except for the 1991–1996 period. The number of pure terminations is much lower than the number of pure foundings, particularly from 1997 onwards. On the other hand, the number of terminations into existing units is higher than the number of foundings based in existing units, particularly in the 1991–1996 period. During this period, many higher education organizations merged into the new group of more comprehensive university colleges, contributing to a high level of horizontal de-specialization. Throughout the whole period, the number of units being converted from civil service organizations outside the ministries is also higher than the number of units converted into this form of affiliation. As shown below, this normally implies vertical specialization.

With regard to state-owned companies, the number of changes was greatest in the 2002–2005 period. However, even in this period most new state-owned companies were based on existing companies or units having another form of affiliation, and several existing state-owned companies were terminated by being absorbed into existing companies. Of the 25 state-owned companies converted into other forms of affiliation from 1985 onwards, 24 were privatized (5 in the 1985–1990 period, 11 in the 1997–2001 period and 8 in the 2002–2005 period).

For central governmental foundations, until the mid-1990s the increase was brought about primarily by the founding of new units, but in the 1985–1990 period some existing units with other forms of affiliation were also converted into central foundations. On the other hand, the decrease from the early 2000s onwards was primarily due to terminations into existing foundations, i.e. through absorptions and mergers. These are also examples of horizontal de-specialization. An interesting observation is that pure termination of central governmental foundations is quite uncommon.

This picture reveals that there have been a lot of changes in formal organizational structure and that most of the changes have been terminations of organizations into existing units or foundings of new organizations based on existing ones, but there are also a significant number of pure foundings. Most of the organizations terminated do not die but continue within new organizational structures. Pure terminations happen rather seldom, but the statement that 'government organizations are immortal' (Kaufman 1976) is not entirely true either. Over the 23 years studied, 33 state organizations were terminated.

2.7.3 Vertical specialization and de-specialization

Taking civil service organizations outside the ministries as the point of departure, we will now examine the extent of vertical specialization and de-specialization by looking at the emigration of units out of or immigration of units into the civil service. For vertical specialization we distinguish between regionalization (transfer to counties and municipalities), corporatization (transfer to state-owned companies and governmental foundations), privatization (transfer to non-profit organizations and profit-oriented market organizations), and agencification (transfer from ministries). Likewise, for de-specialization we distinguish between de-regionalization, de-corporatization, de-privatization and de-agencification movement of units in the other direction.

Figure 2.1 covers the whole period, and shows that vertical specialization is much more widespread than vertical de-specialization. While 79 civil service organizations outside the ministries were involved in vertical specialization from 1985 onwards, only 15 moved in the opposite direction. Vertical specialization through corporatization is most common.

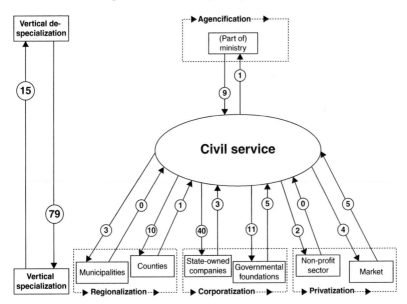

Figure 2.1   Vertical specialization and de-specialization: central node – civil service outside the ministries (number of units involved in changes, 1985–2007)

There were 40 conversions of civil service organizations into state-owned companies. There are also a number of instances of vertical specialization through regionalization (particularly transfer to counties), while the extent of privatization is very low. Thus, only six civil service organizations were privatized, and this was even counterbalanced by a similar number of organizations being de-privatized. Only one non-ministerial civil service organization was moved into a ministry during the 1985–2007 period. On the other hand, nine ministerial units moved in the opposite direction. From these figures we can conclude that external structural devolution involving organizations moving downwards and outwards from the civil service is much more common than the type of internal structural devolution where units are moved from ministries to central agencies.

Figure 2.2 shows, for each sub-period, the yearly average number of units involved in different forms of vertical specialization and

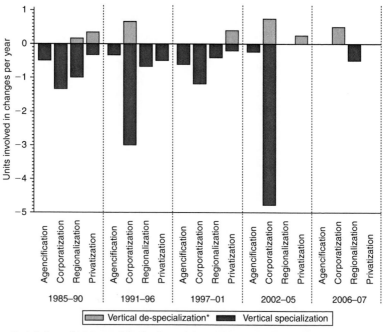

*Labels for vertical de-specialization (area above 0-line) are opposite of vertical specialization: De-agencification, de-corporatization, de-regionalization and de-privatization.

Figure 2.2 Vertical specialization and de-specialization divided into periods: central node – civil service organizations outside the ministries (units involved in changes per year, 1985–2007)

de-specialization, taking civil service organizations outside the ministries as the point of departure. In general, movements of units along the vertical dimension were much less common in the most recent period than it was before. Vertical specialization through corporatization was particularly widespread in the 2002–2005 period and in the 1991–1996 period, but did not occur in the 2006–2007 period. In the last period, however, there is one instance of vertical de-specialization through de-corporatization. In the 2002–2005 period there were no instances of regionalization or de-regionalization, but in each of the periods before and later on some units moved between counties or municipalities and the civil service. There were no privatizations of civil service organizations from 2002 onwards, and before that on average less than one civil service organization per year was privatized. Occurrences of de-privatization and agencification are quite evenly distributed across the periods before 2006.

2.7.4 Horizontal specialization and de-specialization

As noted above, horizontal specialization and de-specialization may take different forms. Figure 2.3 shows, for each sub-period, the yearly average number of units founded or terminated in the civil service (net changes, cf. Rolland and Roness 2009).

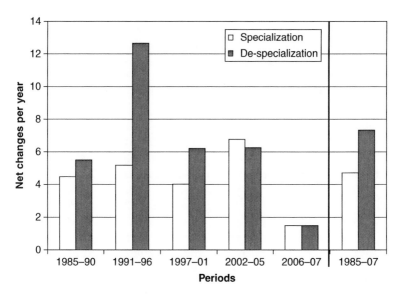

Figure 2.3 Horizontal specialization and de-specialization in civil service organizations outside the ministries divided into periods (net changes per year, 1985–2007)

Overall, the extent of horizontal de-specialization is greater than the extent of horizontal specialization, but not after 2002. Like for the vertical dimension, changes along the horizontal dimension were much less common in the most recent period than before. While occurrences of horizontal specialization are quite evenly distributed across the periods before 2002, there are some differences across time for horizontal de-specialization. The large extent of horizontal de-specialization in the 1991–1996 period was, as noted above, partly due to the merger of many higher education organizations into more comprehensive university colleges.

2.7.5   Extent of change

Summing up, the main findings in this analysis are, first, that there were a large number of structural changes in the state apparatus during the period in question. Secondly, over time we find a significant decrease in the number of civil service organizations outside the ministries and an increase in the number of state-owned companies. For central governmental foundations a steady increase in the number of units until the mid-1990s was followed by a slow decline.

Thirdly, along the vertical dimension, specialization was more widespread than de-specialization. Taking the non-ministerial civil service as the point of departure, vertical specialization though corporatization is the most common form, but there are also several instances of regionalization and agencification. There was not much privatization, not even in the period 2002–2005 when the government was most enthusiastic about NPM.

Fourthly, along the horizontal dimension, for all main forms of affiliation we find many instances of specialization, but for civil service organizations outside the ministries an even larger extent of de-specialization. For these organizations, hierarchical de-specialization was primarily due to mergers or absorptions of existing organizations.

Fifthly, there are some variations with regard to the form and extent of vertical and horizontal specialization and de-specialization across sub-periods. The extent of change was markedly lower in the most recent period than before, in line with the Stoltenberg II government's sceptical attitude to NPM. For civil service organizations outside the ministries, vertical specialization through corporatization was most prominent from 1991 to 1996 and especially in the 2002–2005 period, but did not occur at all in the 2006–2007 period. The difference between the Bondevik II government's enthusiasm for NPM and the scepticism of the Centre-Left government towards NPM is clearly expressed in the extent of corporatization. Here there was a clear pendulum shift away from corporatization. Along the horizontal dimension within the non-ministerial civil service there were more instances of de-specialization than specialization until 2001, but since then specialization has been more prevalent. Here, too, we see a clear difference between the Bondevik II government and the Stoltenberg II government, which scores very low on horizontal reorganizations.

Finally, there are also several sector- and organization-specific differences. For example, in the sphere of immigration a decision was taken in 2004 to bring the immigration authorities back under closer government control (Christensen *et al.* 2006a), and the hospital reform of 2002 also had strong centralizing elements. The recent reform of the welfare administration in Norway (the NAV reform) is informed by post-NPM doctrines on 'whole-of-government' (Christensen *et al.* 2007c).

2.8 Isomorphism and transformation revisited

The findings show clearly that there is little support for the expectations based on a neo-institutional perspective emphasizing isomorphism. There is not a simple, automatic and quick adoption of shifting international reform doctrines into the Norwegian administrative reform policy. The NPM doctrines on vertical and horizontal specialization from the mid-1980s onwards are not automatically reflected in the pattern of structural changes in the Norwegian state apparatus, and the same is the case for the post-NPM doctrines on increased vertical and horizontal de-specialization from the end of the 1990s.

Our findings are more in line with a transformative perspective in which international doctrines are modified by institutional and cultural values in the Norwegian political–administrative apparatus and by specific deliberative domestic action and choices. Some elements of international NPM doctrines, such as privatizations, are more or less rejected. Structural devolution is, however, strong and remains so into the post-NPM period. The post-NPM features are primarily represented by mergers and horizontal de-specialization, but some of these trends actually start before the post-NPM doctrines from the end of the 1990s.

In line with the national administrative doctrines in Norway from the early 1990s onwards, many of the reform efforts involving increased vertical specialization resulted in conversions of civil service organizations into state-owned companies. Likewise, in line with a recent reorientation towards post-NPM doctrines, no further conversions were made in 2006–2007, but only one state-owned company was reconverted into a civil service organization. With regard to horizontal specialization, in the Norwegian case the reforms of regulatory agencies based on streamlining and single-purpose organizations have, at least so far, not been implemented to the extent prescribed, and many central agencies still combine regulatory tasks with other types of tasks in their task portfolio (Christensen and Lægreid 2008a).

In the case of Norway the trend is not uniformly towards more horizontal and vertical specialization. There is no linear development in the direction of more fragmentation of the state apparatus in line with NPM doctrines. But neither is there a clear cyclical process representing a reaction and a return to the 'old' system. Rather than clear pendulum shifts we generally see dual processes of vertical specialization and horizontal de-specialization, especially in the 1990s.

The general picture is not one of increased fragmentation and proliferation, but rather a movement of organizations further away from the central political authorities combined with mergers. This can be seen as a co-evolution of reform ideas and administrative practice producing hybrids and complex organizational solutions (cf. Christensen *et al.* 2007d). There is a trend towards single-purpose organizations, but this trend is divided into two parallel processes. On the one hand, integrated organizations having both regulatory tasks and service provision tasks have been separated into different organizations through splitting. On the other hand, different organizations with similar tasks have merged. This concerns regulatory tasks, such as when five regulatory agencies merged into one regulatory food agency (2004); and service provision tasks, such as when 27 different types of higher education organizations merged into one group of similar organizations (1994).

What we see is a combination of robustness in organizational forms and a large degree of turbulence and change activity within and across these forms. This produces a more complex structural anatomy through a sedimentation process, involving a mixture of rather unstable vertical and horizontal specialization. These findings are in line with Pollitt's (2007) characterization of the Nordic states as Neo-Weberian states or strong modernized states that have been able to combine old Weberian bureaucratic features, NPM doctrines and post-NPM structural elements. A Neo-Weberian state of the Norwegian type implies that some of the main features of the Weberian bureaucracy such as specialization are still a main feature of the state apparatus. But the specific types of specialization and the mixture of vertical and horizontal specialization have changed and been affected by international administrative doctrines such as NPM and post-NPM reform trends.

The public administration in Norway has been subjected to considerable reform efforts, and significant changes have also occurred in the structural anatomy. From the end of the 1980s organizational changes in central government took on a new character, moving from change through construction to change through reconstruction (cf. Lægreid and Pedersen 1999; Lægreid *et al.* 2003). What we have seen since the mid-1980s is a fever of reorganization in the state apparatus.

Overall, the historical ties, traditions and established routines that characterize the Norwegian state have influenced the changes that have occurred in the last two decades. Reforms are to a large extent reactions to, or consequences of, earlier reforms. The historical legacy of a governmental model of ministerial rule has clearly affected changes in the formal organizational structure of central government in Norway. The existence of strong sector ministries and a government administration ministry with weak horizontal coordinative power means that reform processes are more often driven by sector-specific initiatives than by comprehensive and binding general reform programmes from the government.

One important lesson of the reforms in Norway is that the coupling of visions, reform measures and actual changes is not always very tight (Lægreid and Roness 1999, 2003). This can be illustrated by the fact that, in contrast to the policy signals from the Hermansen commission in 1989, the number of governmental central foundations continued to increase throughout the 1990s. Thus, it is important to distinguish between general administrative policy documents, specific reform measures and actual changes, and generally between reform and change (Brunsson and Olsen 1993; Christensen *et al.* 2007). Not all administrative changes are the result of reforms, and not all reforms result in manifest changes. Nevertheless, over time, links between overarching and sector-based reform efforts have been strengthened. An example of this is the increased focus on autonomization and corporatization, in the reform programmes as well as in the actual changes made in public sector organizations over the past decades.

2.9   Conclusion

Our conclusion is that there is no one factor explaining change in the structural anatomy of the Norwegian state apparatus. We need to combine explanatory factors related to external pressure from internationally dominant administrative doctrines and national features related to domestic political–administrative culture and instrumental choices made through an active administrative policy.

Administrative reforms in Norway have largely taken place with the support of the state employees' unions (Roness 2001) in line with the participatory model of modernization in the Nordic countries (Pollitt 2007). We are confronted with a Norwegian version of public sector reform in which NPM seems to supplement established procedures and working methods rather than replacing them. The state organization in Norway seems to have adjusted to the new administrative reforms in a pragmatic, incremental and cautious manner, but it has done so within its strong tradition of solving problems by founding new public sector units or reorganizing existing units.

Administrative reforms undergo a screening process whereby they are filtered and refined (Røvik 1996; Sahlin-Andersson 1996). Established structural arrangements do not disappear but are gradually modified by the reforms. The Norwegian civil service has opened the door to certain parts of NPM, but at the same time the individual central agencies have their own 'gate-keepers' who transform, interpret and give meaning to the new administrative policy so that it becomes a natural extension of previous reforms (Christensen and Lægreid 1998b).

Our interpretation is that the Norwegian state apparatus is resistant to radical change, while simultaneously being loyal to administrative policy reform measures. New administrative reform measures are not wholly rejected but are adapted to the established culture and to the existing procedures and working routines in the ministries. The international concept of administrative reform and guidelines for good organization proposed by NPM doctrines is 'edited', implying that the reforms are adapted and modified. The measures are adjusted and interpreted to fit the national culture and tradition, but political initiatives appropriate to the particular situation of the individual country are also important.

In line with the established political–administrative culture in Norway, the concrete reform measures can be interpreted as a political cooperation process of finding solutions that are administratively and politically reasonable, appropriate and possible in the light of opposing views and demands (Olsen 1989). Administrative policy reform style corresponds with the general Norwegian policy-making style of peaceful coexistence and 'revolution in slow motion' based on common interests and consensus (Olsen *et al.* 1982). Under such conditions, successful reform will be more a question of keeping the reform process alive long enough to aggregate many small measures into a more comprehensive adjustment of the state apparatus.

We have shown that there are significant internal variations in the Norwegian state apparatus. This suggests a need for increased pluralism regarding administrative policy measures, and that standardization based on a single organizational ideal has clear limitations. We have revealed a combination of vertical specialization and horizontal de-specialization. It is not a linear development towards increased proliferation and fragmentation, but rather a combination of structural devolution, but not privatization, and merger of some similar types of organization to increase horizontal coordination. Administrative policy is not only a question of effective implementation of holistic and overarching centrally determined reform programmes, but also of how individual organizations and sectors launch their own reform initiatives and influence overall administrative policy. This implies that it is important to study administrative policy from the bottom-up, i.e. to look at how management and organization have changed in practice in the various parts of central government (Jacobsson 1995).

The challenge is to determine how much leeway there is for action for an active administrative policy in a situation characterized by demands for adjustment to a dominant administrative policy fashioned abroad, and by demands for adaptation to an established administrative culture and to the historical legacy of a national style of governance.

3
The Agency Landscape in Hungary, 2002–2006

György Hajnal

3.1 Introduction

The dismantling of large, integrated central government bureaucracies and the increasing creation of, and reliance on, single-purpose, task-specific organizations structurally separated from their parent ministry has been an emphatic direction of recent administrative reforms. Some would even call it a central proposition (Moynihan 2006b).

To some extent, similar processes seem to appear throughout the transitional countries of Central and Eastern Europe (CEE). At the same time, there are also important differences in the way 'agencification' travelled in relation to the implementation of various CEE administrative reforms as well as in relation to public and academic discourse on those reforms.

The quantity and the detail of published evidence – let alone scholarship – related to agencification is, by orders of magnitude, more modest than in Western Europe. Even international research which attempts to offer a broader geographical coverage (OECD 2002a, Pollitt and Talbot 2004, Pollitt *et al.* 2004,) tends to exclude this region from their focus. Moreover, the range of CEE countries covered by existing scholarship that targets specifically the issue of agencification is quite modest (for some examples see Moynihan 2006b on Slovakia, Tavits and Annus 2006 on Estonia, and Hajnal and Kádár 2008 on Hungary), as is the coverage of the topic within these countries (Moynihan 2006b, 1037; Hajnal and Kádár 2008, 1 and 8–9).

On the basis of available evidence, it seems that while certain phenomena (resembling or actually called agencies), are present, albeit to a largely varying extent, they conceal quite special and idiosyncratic substance and underlying motives. For example, Moynihan (2006b) traced and identified the various policy actors and their quite specific motives fundamentally influencing the interpretation of international policy exemplars and the construction of an Slovakian meaning of 'agency'.

I wish to contribute to the academic discourse now unfolding around the issues cited above, additionally lessening the 'Anglophone and Anglo-Saxon biases [...] particularly virulent [...] in this sub-field' (Pollitt *et al.* 2004, 12). I shall attempt to do so in two ways.

First, this chapter intends to partly compensate for the above-mentioned scarcity of information by offering a relatively detailed qualitative and quantitative description of Hungary's agencification process.

Secondly, and more importantly, it attempts to improve existing explanations of why agencies exist and for what purposes and in what ways they are used by politicians.

Section 3.2 specifies the research question and locates it in its relevant theoretical context while section 3.3 describes the context of the problem; the research design. The methods and the data used for the purpose of the research are outlined in section 3.4. Section 3.5 summarizes the findings reached and section 3.6 formulates the summary conclusions of the article.

3.2 Research questions

3.2.1 Proliferation of agencies

The extent of scholarship dealing with issues related to agencification in Hungary is very limited. While much of the relevant literature deals with legal–structural regulations of agency type organizations (Mónus 1994; Balázs 2004; Kilényi 2006; Vadál 2006), the term itself has been rarely an element of either academic or political discourse. Moreover, even on these rare occasions, the phenomenon is usually approached from a normative–legal perspective, lacking any empirical element. For one and a half decades, the only empirically oriented work on Hungarian agencies has been that of Nyitrai (1994). The *de facto* developments regarding agency formation and proliferation have not become the subject of any empirical work. This justifies the first one of the two broad research ambitions in the introductory section related to the exploratory description of the Hungarian agency population. This ambition can be expressed in terms of the following two research questions:

RQ1: To what extent have agency-type organizations proliferated, firstly, in Hungarian central government structures in general and, secondly, in the various functional/policy domains in particular?

RQ2: Can there be any change in trends identified with these types of proliferation?

3.2.2 Agency dynamics

The second broad ambition of this study is more explanatory than exploratory in nature: Here, the question of why agencies are created, maintained, and restructured/abolished is examined from different theoretical angles and using different methodological approaches.

Explaining why politicians choose to restrain their own control over government apparatuses and why they tend to do so to an extent broadly varying in space, time and across policy sectors has attracted much scholarly attention throughout the past few decades. In an overview covering a distinctly broad theoretical horizon, Pollitt *et al.* (2004, 13–18) has clustered these efforts as belonging to one of three categories: The epistemological realm of economic, traditional social science, and interpretive and social constructivist approaches. Focusing more on the second one of the above clusters, Thatcher (2002a) emphasizes, on the one hand, the importance of functional pressures such as (i) the technical complexity of certain regulatory tasks, (ii) politicians' urge to 'delegate responsibility' for unpopular policies – for example, racial and gender equality or competition – and (iii) the so called 'commitment problem'.

This latter explanation, based on the problem of commitment, lies at the heart of my third research question. It refers to one key, but specific, subset of agencies: the regulatory agencies.[1] The central argument of this explanation of agency formation is that, in order to be effective, certain policies need to be credible to major external stakeholders since in a world of increasing international exposure the most traditional and 'reliable' policy instrument – coercion – may no longer be available (Majone 1997b). Certain policy sectors are more prone to this problem than others. For example, this is the case in newly opened markets requiring policy-makers to attract new investors – such as with utilities privatization and liberalization –, which is clearly not a goal to be accomplished by coercion (Gilardi 2002, 877; see also Maggetti, Chapter 10, this volume). As politicians have to survive in a political market characterized by short-term cycles, the political hazard of long-term international investment is greatly increased. The most straightforward way of creating credibility for a policy regime – and thereby creating effective policies – is to delegate autonomy to regulators which are institutionally entrenched and isolated from direct, short-term political influence. There are, of course, factors counteracting this 'commitment logic', too. For example, Yesilkagit (2004) notes that, as principals, politicians strive to lessen the agency gap – that is, to exert effective control over bureaucratic apparatuses. According to Yesilkagit, this is a factor acting towards less bureaucratic autonomy.

Although the theoretical argument underlying the commitment based explanation seems well-founded, existing empirical results are controversial: For example, while Gilardi (2002) as well as Rommel, Verhoest and Matthys, Chapter 4, (this volume, focused on seven western European countries and found empirical support to the hypothesis, Yesilkagit and Christensen's (2006) work resulted in its rejection on the basis of Danish, Dutch and Swedish data. Hungary, being one of the European transition countries with a particularly exposed internationally economy, is abundant in regulatory tasks centring around newly opened and internationally exposed markets, privatized public utilities/services sectors, and the economic imperative of attracting foreign direct investment. Thus, my next research question is:

RQ 3: Does data on Hungarian regulatory agencies support the credible commitment hypothesis as an explanation of regulatory agencies' autonomy?

There may be different ways in which the credible commitment hypothesis can be operationalized and tested. One relatively simple way is to compare the presence of autonomous regulatory agencies in the field of economic vs. non-economic regulation (Gilardi 2002; Yesilkagit and Christensen 2006; for the conceptualization of economic vs social regulation, see e.g. Thatcher 2002a and Gilardi 2005b). Although the credibility problem might also be present in the field of social regulation, it is primarily economic regulation where one may expect the most direct and powerful role played by organized interests and, thus, the presence of the commitment problem. Consequently, the commitment model can be said to predict a greater extent of organizational autonomy in the economic, as opposed to the non-economic, regulatory domain. In such a case, the hypothesis is supported while, in the opposite case, the hypothesis is refuted.

The commitment hypothesis implies the functional superiority of more autonomous agencies in certain (mainly economic) policy areas and a similar superiority of the less autonomous agencies in other (mostly social) ones.

However, as Pollitt *et al.* (2004, 18) maintains, in addition to broad functional forces (such as the need for credibility) one might expect that other, non-functional factors also play a key role in shaping the agency field (see also Thatcher 2002a, Maggetti, Chapter 10, this volume, and Lægreid *et al.*, Chapter 2, this volume). These may include pre-existing institutional arrangements, administrative culture, and mimetic factors driving decision-makers to create institutional structures similar to those found elsewhere (van Thiel 2004a).

The third research question involves a replication of previous studies testing the commitment hypothesis. The next and final research question puts this explanation to further scrutiny, on the basis of more elaborate analyses of organizations' structural change dynamics and, thus, contributes to the additional development of explanations concerning agency dynamics beyond the scope of the commitment model.

> RQ4: To what extent and how do – in addition to/instead of the need for credibility – non-functional factors of agency formation shape the dynamics of Hungarian agencies?

This question can be broken down into two sub-questions.

First, the predominance of the commitment logic (or other functional forces) would imply monotonous change trends, leading from more-to-less or from less-to-more autonomy, or the level of autonomy being kept at a constant level. Alternatively, if no such consistent change patterns are found then other explanatory factors might come in the foreground. Therefore

> RQ4a is as follows: To what extent is the Hungarian universe of agencies characterized by clear, monotonous change trends in terms of their basic formal-structural features?

The commitment model suggests that certain agencies are granted more formal–legal autonomy because, in order to enable politicians to pursue successful policies, they need to be more autonomous indeed. Interpreted through the fundamentally formal–structural prism of this study more *de facto* autonomy would imply less frequent structural changes. If, however, the opposite is found then one may conclude that the functional logic of the commitment hypothesis does not perform well. In that case, other explanatory factors of agency formation are needed

> RQ4b: Are formally more autonomous agencies indeed more entrenched with outside political intrusion into their basic structural features?

3.3   Agencies and agencification in the post-1990 period: an overview of basic legal–institutional features

Throughout the past five election cycles the governing majority was always based on a party coalition of two or more parties. It is only the last one year when a single-party minority government is in office. The Hungarian central government is divided into ministries. To date, there are 13 of them, including the Prime Minister's Office (hereinafter: PMO). The core of the government is the PMO; ministries are chiefly responsible for policy-making while most of the implementation tasks are carried out by agencies;

Before 2006, there had been no single uniform law regulating the structural features on organizations in the executive branch. Ministerial competences were regulated by various, and frequently changing, government decrees; besides that, the government had extensive powers to establish the government structure within the broad limits specified by law and the Constitution.

An overarching feature of the 1990s and the early 2000s was the apparent lack of grand themes within regards to administrative policy; central government administrative structures usually changed mostly following short-term party political considerations. Likewise, decisions regarding the creation/restructuring of an agency were made in pursuance of a broad range of (party) political, sectoral, organizational and personal interests.

In the absence of general policies or legal constraints, the nineties preserved (and even exacerbated) the proliferation of less than optimally controllable and transparent structures inherited from the Socialist era. Ministries and sectors often could build up their 'empires' without substantive external oversight while the agencies could look for ways to dislodge their dependency on the centre. Thus, while the legal–constitutional regulation and the traditions narrowed the government's opportunities in establishing and reshaping organizations at the level of ministries, the lower levels of the organizational hierarchy ended up in a rather opaque proliferation.

Both academics and practitioners were dissatisfied with this unregulated characteristic of the agency universe and persistently argued in favour of common legal standards as a token of effective central government structure. In contrast to other countries (see e.g. Bouckaert *et al.* 2007b; 6 2004), the problem of policy coordination in the context of agencification has, throughout Hungary's post-transition period, not appeared in the academic discourse. On the level of practice it is mostly only the Regional Colleges of State Administration, responsible for improving territorial level policy implementation, that are worth mentioning as an arrangement specifically targeted at alleviating the consequences of the proliferation of specialized bodies. This relative lack of both interest and knowledge on the policy-related consequences of the proliferation of agencies can be probably much more attributed to the severe lack of policy-related research in Hungary than to the lack of coordination problems themselves. Scarcely available results (e.g. Hajnal 2008) suggest that the lack of coordination amongst administrative and policy sectors are major factors in policy failures.

In the period between 1990 and 2006, there has been only one significant event regarding agencies: The 2040/1992 Government Resolution (1992) created a three-category classification for agency-type organizations. Nevertheless, it did not classify the individually existing bodies themselves accordingly.

This Resolution could not settle the problem of unregulated proliferation of agencies because it would not be applied to bodies created previously. Moreover, in the next 14 years, a series of government resolutions repeatedly tried to eliminate opaque and overlapping agency structures and to develop and clarify the legal–structural principles underlying them (Hajnal and Kádár 2008, 5).

As the 2002 Government Resolution allowed deviations from, and exceptions to, the features declared for agencies to be created later on, the agencies' statutes don't exactly reflect either the typology or the terminology of this legislation. Still, the three genres outlined in the Resolution are also applied in the literature dealing with this subject (Balázs 2004; Sárközy 2006; Vadál 2006).

This typology defines three agency types:

(a) organizations with nationwide competence (*OHSZ*);
(b) central bureaus (*központi hivatal*); and
(c) ministry bureaus (*minisztériumi hivatal*).

The list above reflects a clear and institutionalized organizational hierarchy, going from the most to the least autonomous type of organization in terms of formal, legal-institutional autonomy. However, all three types of organization are separate, legal entities operating with nationwide competence and performing some specialized public administration task(s). The third type, however, excludes the creation of law-type rules. From the perspective of the current study, the significance of this is that the formal–legal autonomy of individual agencies will be operationalized according to their membership in this three-cluster typology. The autonomy granted to agencies by formal–legal measures is only one of several possible aspects of autonomy in the broader sense. Other dimensions of agency autonomy such as perceived (policy and operational) autonomy or *de facto* entrenchment from political influence may conflict with formal–legal autonomy. As the study will show, they often do.

Some additional features of the three agency types are outlined in Table 3.1.

Table 3.1 Typology of agencies based on their legal–structural features

Structural features	OHSZ	Central bureau	Ministry bureau
Founder/form of founding document (statute)	Parliament/law	Government/ government Decree	Minister/ ministerial Decree
Superior organ	Cabinet	Ministry	Ministry
Appointment/ dismissal of the leader	– By the Cabinet/ Prime Minister – Appointed for a term of 4–6 years	– By the Minister – Appointed for an indefinite period	– By the Minister – Appointed for an indefinite period
Remuneration of staff (according to Law on Civil Service)	Same as for ministry staff	Less than for ministry staff	Less than for ministry staff
Participation in the governmental decision-making bodies	– May participate in meetings of Permanent State Secretaries – May participate in Cabinet meetings	– May participate in meetings of Permanent State Secretaries	– May not participate in governmental decision-making bodies
Budgetary status (position in the Law on Budget)	Separate section in the Law on Budget	Subsection within the Ministry's section in the Law on Budget	Not included explicitly in the Budget

The temporal scope of this study is the period from 2002 to 2006. The starting year of this period largely reflects the set-up of the centre-rightist Orbán administration. The parliamentary elections held in that year led to a change in the governing coalition. Since the 2002 elections, the centre-left, Socialist-Liberal party coalition has been in power throughout the parliamentary cycle, although in 2004 Prime Minister Medgyessy was replaced by Prime Minister Gyurcsány. The same Socialist-Liberal party coalition won the next elections in 2006, too. Thus, the last year of the period studied here (2006) is signified by the incoming second Gyurcsány cabinet.

In 2006, in an attempt to create some order to more than a decade of mushrooming central government organizations and organizational units, the Parliament adopted a law regulating the basic structural features of agencies. The new law created a uniform regulation of central government organizations, including agencies. However, since the empirical investigation that follows focuses on the period between 2002 and 2006 these changes are not (or are only marginally) reflected in our data.

3.4   The design of the research

3.4.1   Data

The study uses two data sets:

(a) an organizational containing central government public administration organizations for the 2002–2006 period, and
(b) a structural change database containing basic data on structural changes database having occurred to the organizations included in the previous set (organizational) during the same time period (2002–2006).

These two databases are briefly described below.

3.4.1.1   Organizational data
Data collection began with the official database of the Hungarian civil service registry KÖZIGTAD, which covers all central, territorial and local government public administration organizations operated by the Prime Minister's Office. Among others, this database contains (a) a list of administrative organizations and (b) their staff size on 1 September of each year. In addition to these initial variables, the research team

supplemented the data set with additional ones. Thereby, each central government organization was categorized according to three features:[2]

(c) Ministerial affiliation (that is, the ministry to which the agency reports).
(d) Legal status of the organization (OHSZ, central bureau, or ministry bureau).
(e) The agency's regulatory function (that is, whether the agency's primary function includes regulation, and, if so, whether it involves economic or other types of regulation).

These latter three agency features were mostly identified with the help of electronic databases containing legislation related to these organizations.

In the data set, each organization existing in each of the five consecutive years under study (2002–2006) constitutes one observation (record). Altogether, there are 283 records (implying an average count of 57 organizations in each year).

3.4.1.2 Structural change data

The concept of structural change, as applied in this study, can be defined as follows: Structural change happens if one or more of an organization's key formal–structural features changes between two consecutive years. Thus, such a change happens if (i) the legal status or (ii) the ministry affiliation of the organization changes, or (iii) any organizational subunits are transferred between the organization at hand and any other organization. If any of these features change between two observations in two consecutive years then the organization at hand is said to be 'structurally altered'. In that case, a change event is associated with the relevant organization(s). In the absence of these conditions, however, no change is associated with the organization at hand.

The data set contains a total of 66 changes between 2002 and 2006. Each change is described by the following variables:[3]

– input (i.e., affected, pre-existing) organization(s), if any;
– output (i.e., affected, resulting) organization(s), if any;
– the year in which the change took place;
– a brief narrative description of the change.

The primary sources for change data were legal regulations defining the basic structural features of the agency in question. These pieces of legislation are amended two or three times a year on average, including both some minor as well as major changes. In some cases, other sources of information such as the internet, media research, and telephone interviews with agencies' managers were pursued.

3.4.2   Methods of analysis

Analyses related to RQs (1), (2) and (3) followed the way of simple quantitative, statistical procedures (cross tabulations, correlations analysis).

As to the fourth research question, the analysis of organizational change data followed different routes. I was looking for emergent change components, grasping certain important aspects of the changes whereby one change can be described by one or more such components. The qualitative analysis proceeded in a case-by-case, iterative manner, much resembling the so called 'open coding' used in grounded theory research (Strauss and Corbin 1998, 101 ff.; Ezzy 2002, 86–95; Ryan and Bernard 2002, sometimes also called 'qualitative coding'; see Kelle 1997) until a fine-grained typology emerged. The typology applied to change data file served as the input of further, simple statistical procedures. In addition to the above, producing certain kinds of information required the performance of relatively complex database queries rather than 'normal' statistical procedure

3.5   Findings

3.5.1   Prevalence of agencies and agency types

This subsection gives an overview of the findings related to the proliferation of agencies having either regulatory or non-regulatory tasks (RQs 1 and 2). In 2002, the incoming Socialist-Liberal government started its parliamentary cycle with 49 agencies. In subsequent years, this figure rose rapidly to 61 in 2005; consistent with the markedly activist attitude of the new (Medgyessy) cabinet in office from 2002 to 2004. In the final year of the parliamentary cycle (2006), this trend, however, took a reversal and the overall number of agencies dropped to 57. Most of the 2002–2005 increase occurred to the most autonomous type of agencies, OHSZs. The new Socialist-Liberal cabinet starting its parliamentary cycle in Spring 2006 rapidly decreased this number, whereby the number of OHSZs dropped, within one year, from 24 to 19.

At the other end of the autonomy spectrum, ministry bureaus continued to exhibit a modest but constant increase in number throughout the entire period. It is the ministry bureaus which exhibit the largest degree of stability overall.

Similar trends appear if staff sizes are used as the prime indicator of organizational weight, albeit with two differences. First, central bureaus

Table 3.2 Number of agencies and staff according to legal status (2002–2006)

	No. of agencies				Staff employed in agencies			
	OHSZ	Central bureau	Ministry bureau	Total	OHSZ	Central bureau	Ministry bureau	Total
2002	14	25	10	49	5 259	5 401	2 639	13 299
2003	17	28	11	56	6 301	5 604	2 528	14 433
2004	20	27	13	60	6 555	6 438	2 604	15 597
2005	24	24	13	61	7 377	6 346	2 621	16 344
2006	19	23	15	57	6 612	6 488	2 746	15 846

followed a partly different trend by producing a 15 per cent growth rate during the first three periods while avoiding staff decline in the last year. Secondly, total staff of ministry bureaus remained rather stable throughout the entire period, suggesting that quantitative changes occurring among the least autonomous agencies were more of a formal than of a substantive character.

3.5.2 Testing the credible commitment hypothesis

To reiterate, the credible commitment hypothesis – lying in the focus of Research Question (3) – focuses on a specific subset of agencies: Those having a primarily regulatory function. The hypothesis predicts more autonomous agencies to be present in the field of economic regulation rather than in social/public interest regulation. The explanatory variable is, thus, the domain or target group of the regulation, whereas the dependent variable – the extent of agency autonomy – is operationalized as the legal status of the agency – OHSZs being the most autonomous entities and ministry bureaus the least, with central bureaus somewhere between the two.

Throughout the analysed period, the number of (either economic or non-economic) regulatory agencies fluctuated in range between 25 and 30, lacking in any clear monotonous trend. Thus, a total of 139 observations of regulatory agencies in the 2002–2006 period served as the empirical basis of the analysis.

As Table 3.3 shows, the proportion of the most autonomous type of agencies (OHSZ) is definitely greater among economic than among other types of regulators. Likewise, the proportion of the least autonomous types of organizations (ministry bureaus) is significantly higher among non-economic than it is amongst economic regulators. The strength of this relationship is mediocre when measured by the nonparametric correlation coefficients but remains statistically strongly significant; the value of Kendall's tau-b was –0.184 (p = 0.014). To sum up, the data

Table 3.3   Prevalence of various agency types in the economic vs non-economic regulatory domains (average number of organizations in the 2002–2006 period)

	OHSZ	Central bureau	Ministry bureau	Total
Non-economic	1 (11%)	4.6 (52%)	3.2 (36%)	8.8 (100%)
Economic	6.2 (33%)	7.8 (41%)	5 (26%)	19 (100%)
Total	7.2 (26%)	12.4 (45%)	8.2 (29%)	27.8 (100%)

supports the credible commitment hypothesis: The prevalence of the most autonomous agencies (OHSZ) is larger, while the prevalence of the least autonomous agencies (ministry bureau) is smaller in the population of economic regulators than amongst other types of regulators.

3.5.3   Structural dynamics of Hungarian agencies

3.5.3.1   *Changes in organizations' lives*

The qualitative analysis of structural change data, aimed at the development of a set of fine-grained concepts effectively describing the change phenomena, resulted in thirteen so called codes, each representing a well-defined element of structural change. As the emergent categories were not necessarily mutually exclusive, a certain number of changes received two, or even three, codes. In the end, the total number of code occurrences assigned to the 66 changes is 78. Subsequently, the previously identified codes were grouped into three groups, signified by so called 'higher-order' codes used in the subsequent analyses.

The codes identified by the qualitative analysis, denoted by a code name and briefly explained by a brief code description, are listed in Table 3.4.

To sum up, the input to analyses aimed at answering RQ 4a was the organizational change database supplemented with an additional set of variables indicating the presence of three conceptually distinct features of change events: 'pro-NPM' changes are ones in line with the key structural propositions of NPM, such as creating more specialized (single-purpose) and more autonomous organizations; 'anti-NPM' changes point the opposite direction; while changes of a mere 'organizational–legal reshuffling' type lack such a clear conceptual direction.

In order to explain and justify the above grouping of the codes, some comments on individual codes, as follows, are necessary:

– The first two change components mentioned in Table 3.4 – turning ministry units into agencies and increasing the formal–legal autonomy

Table 3.4   Codes and code descriptions depicting different types of organizational changes

---

1. 'Pro-NPM' type changes:
Agencification (N = 14): Part of a ministry is moved into an agency (either existing or newly created).
Relative autonomization of organization (N = 5): Organization or its part moves 'upwards' in the agency hierarchy (i.e., becomes more autonomous).
Secession (N = 1): Re-shuffling of organizational boundaries, as a result of which the number of agencies and other NDPB's increases.

2. 'Anti-NPM' type changes:
Insourcing to Ministry (N = 7): Agency or its part is moved into a ministry.
Merger (N = 7): Re-shuffling of organizational boundaries, as a result of which the number of agencies and other non-departmental public bodies (NDPB's) decreases.
Relative de-autonomization of organization (N = 3): Organization or its part moves 'downwards' in the agency hierarchy (i.e., becomes less autonomous).

3. Organizational-legal reshuffling:
Horizontal shift (N = 10): Organization is put under the supervision of another (already existing) ministry.
Internal functional change (N = 4): Change in the size or tasks of the organization (not affecting basic functions), without any significant change other than change of the organization's name.
Realm of civil service contracted (N = 1): As a consequence of legislative changes, the scope of the CS regulation is narrowed so that the organization at hand is exempt (but continues to exist).
Realm of civil service expanded (N = 8): As a consequence of legislative changes, the scope of the CS regulation is broadened so that the organization at hand is included (and continues to exist there).
Supervising ministry reorganized (N = 14): The ministerial entity supervising the organization is transformed into a new one.
Transfer of organizational unit (N = 3): A component part of an agency is transferred to either another agency or to another type of NDPB. (Vertical transfer means agencification or insourcing.)

---

of existing agencies – realizes what many think is 'the most frequently adopted and far-reaching policy proposal' of NPM (Moynihan 2006b, 1029). If this is the case then movements in the opposing direction can be clustered as anti-NPM type changes.

- Disaggregating existing organizations into more units (that is, various forms of secession) can typically be expected to create more specialized and single-purpose organizations. Since the latter principle is a typical prescription of NPM-type reforms it is considered a 'pro-NPM' measure. For example, Hood considers the 'shift to *disaggregation* of units in the public sector' a major doctrinal component of NPM

(1991, 5; emphasis in the original). It follows from the above that the structural changes of the opposite direction – mergers – can be considered a step towards leading to larger, more integrated, multi-task organizations. They are, thus, assumed to be a step towards the direction opposing NPM principles.

– Contracting or expanding the legal domain of civil service regulation has an ambivalent relationship with NPM type structural propositions. Including an agency into the civil service domain would, ideally, mean both lesser managerial autonomy and greater policy/political autonomy by protecting the agency (especially the agency heads) from external political intrusion. Moreover, on the basis of mostly anecdotal evidence, it seems that such typically minor decisions are usually driven by completely different motives, such as being able to ensure pay raises and other benefits for employees. Therefore, contracting and expanding the realm of civil service are considered as changes lacking in NPM related conceptual roots.

Figure 3.1 displays information on the overall composition and the temporal dynamics of organizational changes on the basis of second-order codes.

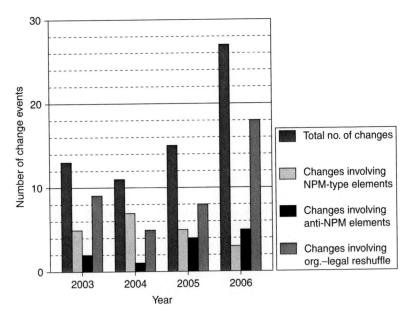

Figure 3.1   Frequencies of different types of change events broken down by year

The first observation regards the sheer amount of change happening to agencies. As opposed to the picture conveyed by the simple count of agencies shown earlier – whereby the yearly change ranged between one and six – the real intensity of structural change is much greater: The number of structural changes ranges between 11 and 27 in each of the four consecutive years, with the highest figure reached in the election year of 2006. In other words, 20 to almost 50 per cent of the agencies underwent at least one significant structural change in each year under study which, even in the lack of comparative data, seems a strikingly high figure. In regards to the direction/pattern of changes, the most peculiar feature of the data might be the convincing, absolute majority (40 out of 66) of changes involving an element of mere organizational-legal reshuffling of existing organizations.

It is probably a central observation emerging out of these data that, as hypothesized earlier, the changes seem to lack overall – or even temporal – consistency in terms of their orientation. Pro-NPM type elements are present in approximately 30 per cent of change events, while changes of the opposite nature (i.e. anti-NPM type changes) also have a significant presence, as their relative frequency amounts to about 18 per cent.

3.5.3.2 *Determinants of organizational stability*

The basic idea of the analysis that follows is that some agencies might have remained unaffected by structural changes and that the frequency distribution of such stable organizations across agency subgroups is a telling sign of both policy-makers' willingness to initiate structural changes and the constraints they face in doing so.

Table 3.5 presents the proportions of such stable organizations in the three groups of agencies defined by their legal status. Two remarks are necessary at this point. Firstly, the purpose of the present analysis is to

Table 3.5 Counts and percentage proportions of structurally stable agencies (2002–2006)

Agency type	Stable organizations (n)	All organizations in 2004	Stable organizations (%)
OHSZ (most autonomous)	8	20	40%
Central bureau	15	27	56%
Ministry bureau (least autonomous)	9	13	69%
Total	32	60	53%

reveal some politicians' motives in deciding on agency structure and agency restructuring. There is, however, one specific type of change – 'ministry restructuring' – that impliesa structural change to all agencies belonging to that ministry. However, a structural change occurring as a consequence of such a decision cannot be assumed to be motivated by factors specifically related to the affected agency or agencies. Consequently, if an agency is restructured only by a 'ministry restructuring' type of change then it is, for the purpose of the current analysis, not considered as one affected by any targeted restructuring decision.

Secondly, simple counts of stable organizations are, by themselves, meaningless. Therefore, relative frequencies were calculated using organization counts for the mid-point reference year (2004).

As the data in Table 3.5 shows, organizational stability seems to be directly related to agency autonomy: The least autonomous type of agencies (ministry bureaus) exhibited the largest extent of structural stability; the proportion of stable organizations (among these, least autonomous agencies) is approximately twice as much the same measure calculated for central bureaus and, specifically, the most autonomous cluster of OHSZs (Kendall's tau-b measure of rank order correlation is 0.22, $p < 0.0005$).

At first sight, this finding seems to contradict, firstly, the – somewhat intuitive – expectation that the more formal–legal autonomy an agency has, the stronger its entrenchment from outside political forces. More importantly, it also contradicts the conclusion reached concerning Research Question (3), i.e. that agencification occurs, at least in part, as a result of an overall functional pressure created by the commitment problem. However, if the hypothesis involving the commitment-based, functional explanation is disconfirmed then the Hungarian agency dynamics will need some – albeit tentative – alternative explanation(s).

Below I suggest two such alternative explanations. They are visualized in Figure 3.2.

The first explanation – depicted in the upper part of Figure 3.2 – is related to the political significance, or value, of the organization. This political value includes such things as: the opportunity to place senior party cadres or clientele into powerful, prestigious and well-paid positions (note that OHSZ leaders were, at the time, defined by law as having much greater prestige and higher salaries than leaders of less autonomous bodies). Yet, more generally, it also includes the ability to exert influence on much larger and more qualified apparatuses, budgets, and more significant policy arenas.

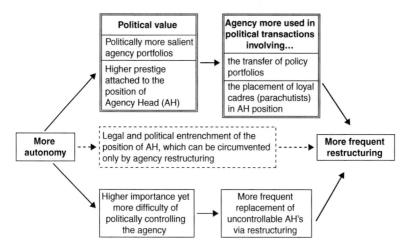

Figure 3.2 Alternative explanations of the dynamics of Hungarian agencies

Such political values placed on an organization are not only based on its present capacity to accommodate such needs but also on its future potential to do so – such as in the case of a political shift in the governing coalition or party. In other words, (some) agencies may play the important role of an organizational *Hintergrund* for party cadres and clientele.

The greater political value an agency has raises its 'currency' on the political market. In other words, more autonomous bodies are likely to play the role of exchange goods in political transactions more frequently than less autonomous ones.

However, utilizing an agency in a political transaction is likely to require, due to its political entrenchment (see middle part of Figure 3.2) more autonomous agencies, some kind of a structural change for the following reasons.

First, although the legal situation in this regard remained rather fuzzy throughout the period in question, one may say that 'simply' firing an OHSZ leader was, from a legal aspect, usually difficult if not impossible. Though, it becomes quite easy once justified by some reorganization effort. On the other hand, firing ministry bureau management posed no legal difficulties and, therefore, necessitated no structural change.

Secondly, irrespective of legal difficulties, firing the head of a highly visible OHSZ on purely political grounds is seen by Hungarian political public opinion as difficult to defend. There are very few, if any, examples of any government willing to pay the political price for such a decision. Instead, there is an expectation that the decision has to be presented as a logical consequence of a rational, policy-based (as opposed to political) decision, only one 'by-product' of which is a change in the agency management.

Thirdly, this need for 'window-dressing' agency-related decisions as ones based on seemingly policy-related grounds is characteristic not only for personnel decisions involving agency heads but for all administrative policy decisions. Thus, for example, if a significant element of the task portfolio is to be transferred to a new institutional location, this step is likely to occur in the framework of a series of large and 'noisy' restructuring measures.

The second possible explanation (not precluding the first one and depicted in the lower part of Figure 3.2) for the perverse pattern of structural volatility is related to the centrifugal forces present in the Hungarian central government machinery. There is growing literature on the limited ability of transition country governments to exert strategic control over their policies and apparatuses (Cooley 2000; Sotiropoulos 2002; Kovryga and Nickel 2004; Hajnal 2006,). As shown in section 3.2, the chaotic and opaque proliferation of various types of central government organizations have been detected by various authors, specifically in regards to Hungarian agencies, too. On the basis of anecdotal evidence concerning agency restructuring, it seems that in a number of cases agencies – and, most of all, charismatic agency heads, sometimes supported by some sort of (opposition) political support – tend to get out of political control. Moreover, an effective – and, in the short term, probably the only effective – means of regaining control over such organizations is to 'disable' it and its management by means of a 'professionally well-founded' reorganization. This cycle movement is present among OHSZs while ministry bureaus are easy to regulate using official, hierarchical means of control.

Despite the relative abundance of anecdotal evidence, it is difficult to cite specific documented cases to illustrate the mechanisms hypothesized above. This difficulty stems from such sources as the lack of empirical research in the field and that of courageous investigative journalism. One of the rare exceptions where the political value based explanation has appeared in the public discourse is the case of István Kolber. As he was a supporter of the governing Socialist Party's newly inaugurated Prime Minister Ferenc Gyurcsány, Gyurcsány wished to 'show his gratitude' towards Kolber by nominating him as a candidate for Minister of the Interior. However, as the incumbent Minister enjoyed the support of the Socialist Party's other, weighty factions, a new position had to be created for Kolber. Finally, as a Minister without portfolio he obtained via a diverse host structural changes – the National Bureau for Housing and Construction (*OLÉH*) and the National Bureau for Regional Development (*MTRFH*).

The above mentioned set of changes exemplifies, although in a way not covered by the news media, the second, political control-based mechanism, too. Prior to to the arrival on the scene of Prime Minister Gyurcsány Sándor Nagy, a prominent leader of a faction within the governing Socialist Party, had been in charge of supervising, among others, the legal predecessor the National Bureau of Regional Development (*MTRFH*). His political position has, however, gradually diminished as a result of changing power structures within the Socialist Party. The transfer of the regional development policy to Kolber may be viewed also in this context: Nagy's policy portfolio – a key part of which was regional development – continued to be slowly but surely weakened, until he eventually left the Prime Minister's Office in 2006.

The two hypothesized routes in which decisions aimed at changing agencies' structural features are used, are also congruent with – and are able to explain – the peculiar finding established earlier that structural change events, either individually or jointly, do not seem to involve any marked policy direction, or paradigm. Rather, it is the mere reshuffling of legal and structural features that takes up much of 'reform' activity.

3.6 Conclusion

The conclusions can be summarized as follows. As to RQs (1) and (2) regarding proliferation of agencies, it seems that in the Hungarian context the problem field of agencification is better to be conceptualized and explored not as a unidirectional and consistent pattern of administrative policy but as one often involving sharp reversals noticeable even within the short time frame of this research. In an absolute majority of structural decisions, change motifs of markedly opposing signs are present in each year under study. In addition, an absolute majority of changes are of a purely legal-structural nature, lacking in any recognizable pattern of administrative policy.

As to RQ (3) which aims to test the credibility hypothesis, it seems that Hungarian data supports the credible commitment hypothesis of the creation of agencies with a predominantly regulatory function. In other words, it is reasonable to assume that one of the motives driving politicians to grant (increased) autonomy to certain agencies is their strive to provide – at least apparent – institutional guarantees for key external stakeholders against future intrusions into regulatory matters driven by short-term political motives.

In the findings reached in relation to the patterns and directions of structural changes (RQ 4a), one may conclude, first, that structural changes are happening to agencies constantly and at a quick pace. Secondly, these changes seem to lack any clear direction or doctrinal orientation. Rather, various, often opposing elements appear not only within any given year but on several occasions within a single change event too (see also Lægreid *et al.*, Chapter 3, this volume). As to Research Question (4b), analysis revealed a peculiar and perverse relationship between agencies' *de facto* stability and their institutionally entrenched formal–legal autonomy. Namely, the more autonomous – and thus institutionally well-protected – an agency is, the greater the chance (and frequency) of political intrusion on that autonomy by making significant structural changes to the agency.

Findings reached in relation to RQs (4a) and (4b) suggest that more thorough analyses shed doubt over the functional, commitment based explanation thus far confirmed in relation to RQ (3). Elaborating upon and testing alternative explanations of Hungarian agency dynamics is not possible on the basis of available data. However, it is both possible and justifiable to elaborate some plausible hypotheses potentially orienting future research in this problem field. I propose two such hypotheses.

One of the hypotheses centres around the concept of agencies' political value. Greater autonomy implies a greater political value, involving such things as access to key policy areas, decisions, large and important apparatuses, and (managerial) prestige. As a consequence of constraints rooted in legal regulations and political feasibility, using these endowments in political transactions usually necessitates some kind of structural retrenchments. Thus, the argument goes, greater autonomy implies greater political value leading to higher 'currency' in political transactions, necessitating, at the end, more frequent reorganizations.

The other proposition regards reorganization as a primary means of ensuring political control over agencies that have 'broken-free'. Despite the existing means of control granted to politicians by legislation, it is often difficult to exert effective administrative policy and political control over (segments of) central government apparatuses as a consequence of complex legal, political and power relations. Consequently, a cyclical pattern of (formal or informal) autonomization coupled with loosening political control and reorganization leading to de-autonomization and tightened control, emerges (Christensen and Lægreid, this volume).

These explanations put the commitment-based explanation into a new, somewhat different light as they suggest that, in the Hungarian context, formal–legal autonomy is more of a symbolic rather than of a factual nature (Verhoest *et al.* 2004). To put it another way, agency autonomy is not only a conceptually complex organizational feature but also one that is difficult to be assessed by external stakeholders. Autonomy should, therefore, be conceived of in the context of the commitment-based explanation of agency formation, not as a 'hard' feature of agencies but more as a symbolic value conveyed to the public and, most of all, to weighty organized interest groups by the formal, legal–structural features of the organization. Somewhat perversely however, it is exactly these features that make these highly autonomous agencies – in a subtle way which is not visible to most external stakeholders – prone to frequent political intrusion in the form of restructuring decisions.

The symbolic – as opposed to instrumentally rational, problem-solving – character of certain government policies or measures is a relatively fresh and unconquered topic of public policy research (Newig 2003). For example, Hetling, McDermott and Mapps (2008) argue that government policies, such as the U.S. welfare reform of 1996, may significantly increase electoral satisfaction with the given government policy irrespective of the real effect of the policy change. Voss (1989, ch. 2) and other authors (e.g. Lübbe-Wolff 2000), however, suggest that the symbolic operation of policy measures may not only be a possibly unintended side-effect but a conscious choice of policy-makers, whereby laws are adopted not because they are expected to exert certain societal effects but because they serve as a medium for political messages sent to the electorate. Whether and, if so, to what extent this is the case with the legislative framework of Hungarian agencies is the promising subject of future research.

Notes

1. Throughout the study I use the concept of regulation in the sense of 'public administrative policing of (private) behaviour according to rules and laws prescribed in the public interest' (Mitnick 1980, 9).
2. For a somewhat similar solution see Rolland and Aagotnes (2003).
3. For more details on the data used see Hajnal and Kádár (2008).

4
Specialization and Fragmentation in Regulatory Regimes

Jan Rommel, Koen Verhoest and Joery Matthys

4.1 Introduction

In recent years, the regulation literature has reported a marked increase in the complexity of regulation. New regulatory organizations have emerged as a result of the hiving off of tasks from existing organizations (Jordana and Levi-Faur 2004). First, specialized regulators have been created in multiple sectors (Christensen and Lægreid 2006). Secondly, authority has been dispersed from central states towards multiple levels of government. National states delegated authority to subnational (e.g. regions) and supranational levels. These new organizations have not entirely replaced the old ones, which led to an accumulation of institutions.

Regulation is defined as the public administrative policing of a private activity with respect to a rule prescribed in the public interest (Mitnick 1980). It covers a range of activities, such as the definition and enforcement of public service obligations, competition rules, technical standards, and access prices. Regulatory bodies are involved in several tasks: translation of general policies in more concrete norms and standards (e.g. standards of interconnection); application of these norms in individual cases via licences and permits (e.g. building permission, licence for supply or approval of technologies); monitoring compliance (e.g. information gathering) and enforcement (e.g. application of sanctions and rewards) (Hood *et al.* 2001). Thus, regulation is conceptualized as a bundle of tasks, where the output of a preceding task forms the input for the following task. Although a regulatory regime normally includes all tasks, the literature has argued that these are often spread across several organizations. Many sectors are regulated by complex multi-actor and multi-level 'institutional constellations' (Jordana and Sancho 2004) or 'regimes' (Doern *et al.* 1999; Hood *et al.* 2001; Doern and Johnson 2006).

The central characteristic of these regimes is that competencies are fragmented across multiple, highly-specialized organizations (Black 2001). Actors are becoming increasingly interdependent, as regulations are the product of the interplay between multiple organizations. The practice of 'better regulation' considers fragmentation as harmful, because it increases administrative costs for regulatees. Recent reforms in many European countries (e.g. UK, Ireland, The Netherlands, Belgium) have sought to reduce the extent of fragmentation, for instance by merging small regulators. However, there is little empirical evidence on the extent to which these regimes are actually specialized. Previous empirical studies focused on describing the regulatory architecture in specific sectors, such as telecommunications (Hall *et al.* 2000), financial markets (Black 2003), or energy (Doern *et al.* 1999).

The objective of this chapter is to provide a systemic, cross-sector analysis of the structure of regimes in Flanders. The first research question is descriptive: *To what extent are regulators specialized, both vertically and horizontally?* The second research question is explanatory: *How can differences in the level of specialization be explained?* We use a database that contains information on a range of regulatory bodies in different sectors on the Belgian federal level and the Flemish regional level. The database maps which actors are involved in regulating a certain sector and which tasks and competencies they have. This allows us to assess the role each actor plays in the regulatory cycle. Moreover, it allows us to test to what extent the degree of specialization within the regulatory arrangement is determined by the regulatory area or the governmental level at which these bodies are active.

The chapter is structured as follows. In the next section, central concepts such as specialization and fragmentation are defined. We then discuss the potential effects of fragmentation and indicate how these have been targeted by recent 'better regulation' reforms. The following section introduces two theoretical frameworks (credible commitment and multi-level governance) and derives hypotheses to explain potential differences in specialization. Subsequently, the methodology and the main findings are presented. We end with a discussion and summary of the findings.

4.2   Specialization and fragmentation

Proliferation, which is the increase of public sector organizations, is associated with specialization. The core of specialization is the creation of new organizations with limited objectives and specific tasks, out of traditional core-administrations that had many tasks and different, some-times conflicting, objectives (Pollitt and Bouckaert 2000). Specialization seems to emerge in two forms. V*ertical specialization* is 'differentiation of responsibility on hierarchical levels, describing how political and administrative tasks and authority are allocated between forms of affiliation' (see also Chapter 13 in this volume). The extent to which a public sector system has a high level of vertical specialization depends upon the extent to which tasks and policy cycle stages are transferred from the core administration to the more peripheral parts of the public sector. This transfer is labelled as decentralization, devolution, delegation, agencification (Greve *et al.* 1999), outsourcing and even privatization.

A second form of specialization is when functionally homogeneous organizations responsible for a whole policy field are divided into different organizational units that are responsible for subparts of the domain. This trend is induced by the growing complexity and multi-facetedness of policy areas. This process is what Lægreid *et al.* call *horizontal specialization,* or 'splitting of organizations at the same administrative and hierarchical level ... and assigning tasks and authority to them' (Lægreid *et al.* 2003, 1). An example is the separation of the ministry of environment from the ministry of health since environmental policy grew in importance. Moreover, within a policy (sub)domain, the different stages of the policy cycle (policy design, development and preparation, policy implementation, policy evaluation and audit) are separated and assigned as specific tasks to different organizations. As a result, organizations specialize in a small number of tasks. They have smaller fields of competencies, to the extent of being single purpose bodies or task homogeneous bodies (Verhoest and Bouckaert 2004). Splitting up closely connected policy stages within an administration will lead to *fragmentation*, meaning that tasks are spread over a variety of organizations.

4.3   Specialization and regulatory reform

Fragmentation can have both positive and negative effects. One advantage of fragmenting tasks is that the time-consistency of policy may be increased. Fragmentation limits the mandate of each organization and prevents a single regulator from becoming too powerful. A second advantage is the existence of a back-up in case one regulator fails (Hood *et al.* 2001). A third advantage is that a fragmented and highly specialized regulatory arrangement may be able to more easily collect relevant information from the regulatees than a centralized one (Laffont and Martimort 1999). However, fragmentation is associated with *'siloization'*, meaning that organizations become confined within their own boundaries and are unaware of the mandates of other organizations (Gregory 2006). This may lead to a duplication of tasks, which increases administrative costs for companies when they must provide the same information to multiple organizations. Duplication of tasks will also create confusion and uncertainty if regulators contradict each other (Hansen and Pedersen 2006; Helm 1994). A second disadvantage is that companies can play regulators off against each other and exploit blind spots in rule enforcement ('functional underlap') (Hood *et al.* 2001; Geradin and McCahery 2004).

Regulatory reforms and the practice of 'better regulation' have mainly focused on the negative consequences of fragmentation. Unclear task divisions and 'siloization' are considered to be the main drivers of administrative burdens. In the UK, the *Hampton Review* formulated recommendations to improve the quality of regulation. The review identified fragmentation as a central problem:

> A highly fragmented [regulatory] system means that business is more likely to be on the receiving end of conflicting advice. For government, it means duplication of effort and cost. Regulated businesses are subject to overlapping inspections from different bodies, and asked to provide similar information to different government agencies, none of which has an overview of the effects of regulation on that business. Where joining up does occur, numerous stakeholders and complex data interactions make synergies hard to establish. Confusion in the system makes it more difficult for businesses to comply with regulation and fragmentation (...) could mean that riskier businesses are not inspected'. (Hampton 2005, 58).

According to the review, this fragmentation was caused by a proliferation of regulatory authorities, with regulatory inspection and enforcement being divided between 63 national regulators, 203 trading standards offices, and 408 environmental health offices in 468 local authorities (Hampton 2005, 6).

In Ireland, the High Level Group on Regulation published a 'White Paper on Regulating Better', in which it argued that the Irish regulatory landscape was highly fragmented. There were 213 different regulators, each with their own procedures and structures, resulting in red tape and a duplication of tasks. The report called for an audit of the current regulatory framework, which would map out the various rule-making and enforcement bodies and reporting arrangements (Department of the Taoiseach

2004, 15). Such an audit would help to reveal which organizations have overlapping competencies or are involved in the same procedures. Hence, having knowledge about how many regulators were operating and the areas they regulated was considered particularly important to minimize the potential for fragmentation and duplication (Humphreys and Mair 2006; Better Regulation Group 2007). In the Netherlands, the *'Commissie Stevens'* (2007) came to similar conclusions and argued for a streamlining of competencies across levels of government.

In Flanders, a study of the largest employer's organization indicated that the principal complaint of entrepreneurs is that they have to invest resources in providing information that had already been given to other government organizations (VOKA, 2006). They also complained that procedures for obtaining certain licenses were too long and complicated because different organizations imposed diverging information require-ments. The study suggested that government organizations are confined within their own boundaries, as they do not exchange information with organizations in other policy fields (see also Van Humbeeck 2006). In addition, multiple governmental levels were involved in the same procedures. As a result, 66 per cent of Belgian CEO's believe that there are many inconsistencies between regulations. Less than half of the respondents know which department or organization is responsible for a certain license or who they could contact to ask further information (Janssen *et al.* 2005; Unizo, 2007).

In these countries, regulatory reforms have sought to reduce fragmen-tation by joining-up regulators. Some bodies may be merged together, whereas others are encouraged to exchange information and co-ordinate their actions with each other, for instance by means of bundling inspec-tions. It is hoped that such co-ordination will also stimulate regulators to pay more attention to whole-of-government issues that have links with other policy fields besides their own (Christensen and Lægreid 2006).

4.4   Differences in specialization

4.4.1   Regulatory area

Regulatory fields can be grouped into different areas. Economic regula-tion focuses on the direct government intervention in corporations and market decisions in order to stimulate competition (e.g. pricing, market entry/exit). Social regulation is aimed at the protection of social values such as health, the environment and social cohesion. Finally, general legal regulation refers to the protection of individual rights, such as human rights, security, and immigration (Christensen and Yesilkagit 2006).

A popular theoretical argument for differences in specialization is the thesis of credible commitment. An important condition for economic growth is that rational investors can anticipate future moves of policymakers (North and Weingast 1989; Henisz 2000; Gilardi 2002). This can only be achieved when they are certain that politicians are committed to displaying the same behaviour in the future (Shepsle 1991). Thus, if governments want to attract new investors, they have to credibly signal their commitment to a certain policy, i.e. to bind themselves to a fixed and pre-announced course of action. However, politicians have a short time horizon, since elections may pressure them to suddenly change their preferences. This makes it difficult for politicians to be consistent over time (Gilardi 2002). The credibility problem can be solved when 'political sovereigns are willing to delegate important powers to independent experts' (Majone 1997b, 139–40). Such experts do not suffer from the short time horizon that constrains politicians (Gilardi 2002).

It has been argued that credibility matters more in sectors that are internationally interdependent or that have been subject to market opening (e.g. utilities, transport) (Thatcher 2002a; Elgie and McMenamin 2005). More generally, Gilardi (2002, 2004) has argued that credibility problems arise in *all* fields of economic regulation. He asserts that credibility is less necessary for other areas of regulation (e.g. social regulation and general legal regulation), because consumers, instead of investors, are the main target of these policies.

4.4.1.1 *Area and vertical specialization*

Credibility has previously been tested as a predictor of the creation of independent agencies. Since economic regulators need to credibly commit themselves, they are assumed to be more insulated from politicians (i.e. more independent) than other regulators (Gilardi 2002; Elgie and McMenamin 2005; Roness *et al.* 2007). However, Yesilkagit and Christensen (forthcoming) do not find any significant effect on the independence of agencies. Similarly, Roness *et al.* (2007) find no evidence that agencies in an economic policy area have more policy autonomy or financial management autonomy than other agencies. Lægreid *et al.* (2008) found that regulatory agencies are controlled much more than expected. One explanation for this poor empirical support may be that focusing on delegation to agencies alone is too narrow. Elgie and McMenamin (2005: 548) call 'to include a wider set of non-majoritarian institutions than has usually been the case'. Christensen and Yesilkagit (2006) point to a high number of collegiate boards to which authority has been delegated. These boards have a legal mandate that grants them some degree of autonomy and decision-making power.

Assuming that credibility is more important for economic regulators (Gilardi 2002, 2004), we should find that they are organized in different organizational forms than other regulators in regard to the level of *vertical specialization*. More precisely, if we define a range of organizational forms at different distances from government (ranging from government departments, to different forms of agencies, to collegiate boards to private sector regulators) we expect economic regulators to have an organizational form that is further away from government, and hence, is more located towards the end of this range. Therefore, we formulate the following hypothesis:

> H1: Economic regulation will be allocated to organizational forms that are at a further distance from government than social and general legal regulation.

4.4.1.2   *Area and task specialization*

General tasks. In order to signal credibility, the 'regulatory state' involves the separation of operational tasks from regulatory activities in some policy areas. In addition, policy tasks are separated from operational tasks, where the former are allocated to ministerial departments and the latter are allocated to independent agencies (Scott 2004, 148; Lægreid *et al.* 2008). Especially for economic regulation, governments need to separate regulation from service delivery in order to signal their credible commitment that they will not regulate in favour of the incumbent. Hence, if we define a number of general tasks (e.g. policy formulation, regulation, subsidies, service delivery), then we expect to find a separation of tasks, particularly in economic regulation:

> H2: Economic regulators will perform fewer general tasks, other than regulation, than social and general legal regulators.

Regulatory tasks. An additional solution to increase the credibility of commitments is to disperse regulatory authority over multiple actors. Institutional fragmentation makes regulators more interdependent, so that the capacity of a single actor to revise an entire arrangement is limited. When authority is more fragmented, the commitments made by governments are more credible, since the fragmentation makes future policy changes more difficult. Thus, fragmentation de facto increases the time-consistency of policy (Levy and Spiller 1996; Henisz 2000; Gilardi 2002).

If regulation is operationalized as a bundle of specific regulatory tasks, fragmentation implies that these are unbundled and allocated to different bodies. A regulatory regime should normally have all components, although the functions can be spread across several bodies within a sector. For instance, it is possible that a body is active in rule-making but has no competencies in monitoring or enforcement. If credibility is more important in economic regulation, then we should find more fragmentation in terms of regulatory task specialization than in other areas. We can derive the following hypothesis:

> H3: Economic regulators will perform less regulatory tasks than social and general legal regulators.

4.4.2 Level of government

A second theoretical argument for an increase in the number of regulatory bodies refers to the number of levels of government involved in regulation. National states have increasingly delegated tasks to other levels of government, both upward and downward. For example, national governments have delegated entire bundles of competencies upward to the supranational level. They also have decentralized tasks downward to the subnational level, for instance, to spur competition between regions or to increase the legitimacy of actions (Peters and Pierre 2005).

There are two ways to delegate tasks to other levels of government. The first option is to transfer competencies partially to another level, so that multiple levels *share* the authority over a specific field (Hooghe and Marks 2001; Bache and Flinders 2004). Doern and Johnson (2006, 3) define multi-level regulatory governance as a deliberative form of governance that involves 'interacting, reinforcing, and colliding rule-making and governance' at the various governmental levels (Doern and Johnson 2006: 3). Relations are characterized by mutual interdependence on each others' resources (Hooghe 1996), and sovereignty is predominantly shared with other levels (Börzel and Risse 2000).

The second option is to allocate entire bundles of competencies to one level. This level is then exclusively responsible for the regulation of a sector, which causes governmental levels to remain separated. For instance, dual federalist systems (e.g. Belgium) emphasize the institutional autonomy of the different levels, with their goal being the clear vertical separation of powers. Competencies are allocated to either the federal or regional level. Once a competence is allocated to a level, both the legislative and executive powers rest within this level (Börzel and Risse 2000).

The extent to which authority over a sector is shared by multiple levels may have an effect on the organizational characteristics of the regulators. Sociological neo-institutionalism has been concerned with processes of reproduction and homogenization (Thelen 1999). It focuses on how the institutional environment exerts influence on the formal structure of organizations. Organizations facing the same environment will show a tendency to resemble each other, because of isomorphism (Powell and DiMaggio 1991). Coercive isomorphism is characterized by the effect of political influence and the issue of legitimacy, which refers to the imposition of certain structures or processes by the legal and technical environment. Mimetic isomorphism is observed in situations of uncertainty (e.g. ambiguous goals, poor understanding of organizational technologies), where organizations imitate 'popular' organizations. Finally, normative isomorphism is closely related to processes of professionalization, whereby professional networks diffuse certain approaches and views. When multiple levels are active in the same policy field, they are confronted with pressures from the same institutional environment. If the environment imposes a certain extent of specialization, all organizations in the field will show a similar extent of specialization. In addition, when levels are interwoven, they may form relational networks with each other and engage in mutual learning processes about how to organize regulatory tasks.

Conversely, when governmental levels are separated, they may diverge and develop different objectives of regulation (Doern *et al.* 1999; Doern and Johnson 2006). Each level will develop its own 'style of regulation', resulting in a different extent of specialization. Since Belgium is considered to be a dual federal system (Kovziridze 2001; Deschouwer 2006; Swenden and Jans 2006), we expect that these levels will be separated. Hence, we expect both the Belgian federal and Flemish regional government to develop their own style of regulation and hence, we expect to find significant differences between these governmental levels:

H4 Bodies on the federal and regional level of government in Belgium will differ with respect to the organizational forms to which regulatory tasks are allocated.

H5 Bodies on the federal and regional levels of government in Belgium will differ with respect to the number of general tasks they perform.

H6 Bodies on the federal and regional levels of government in Belgium will differ with respect to the number of regulatory tasks they perform.

4.5 Method

4.5.1 Data collection

The data are drawn from a mapping database, which contains a list of regulatory bodies. The database was constructed using two different government yearbooks: the *Gids der Ministeries* is published by the federal government; the *Instellingenzakboekje 2008* is published by a private publisher. They both list all organizations that have a legal mandate and that are involved in performing public tasks in Belgium. They provide basic information on the legal mandate, the level of administration, legal status, and the internal structure of the organization. Both handbooks have a wide scope and include administrations and agencies, as well as boards or commissions and private professional organizations. Subsequently, the legal statutes of each regulatory body were used to acquire a comprehensive task description. Hence, the database should contain the entire population of Belgian regulatory bodies. In addition, using legal documents ensures the reliability of the data collection.

The data was collected in two phases. We first made a list of all institutions on the federal and the Flemish regional level that perform public tasks and have a legal recognition. The tasks of these organizations were coded into five categories: (1) policy preparation; (2) regulation; (3) other kinds of exercising authority; (4) general public services; (5) business services. For each organization, multiple tasks could be selected, based on the task description. We did not distinguish between major and minor tasks, so that an organization is defined as a regulatory body as soon as one of its tasks is coded as regulation. In the second phase of the data collection, we selected only the regulatory bodies from this large list and copied them into a new database.

Some cases were omitted from the analysis. First, we only included organizations with a central authority. When some tasks are performed by several provincial boards with identical tasks and structure, these boards are coded as one body, similar to Lægreid *et al.* (2003). Second, we only included bodies belonging to the executive branch of government, excluding legislatures and courts. The final database contained 278 organizations.

4.5.2 Dependent variables

An organization's *legal status* represents the extent of vertical specialization. We define this as an ordinal variable with four categories, where higher categories indicate more insulation from politicians than lower categories:

(1) Ministerial departments: are under the full hierarchical control of the minister.
(2) Agencies: perform their tasks with some formal independence from the minister. Several formal–legal types of agencies are included but these have been recoded to one category for most analyses.
(3) Commissions or boards: defined as collegiate bodies that are composed of interest groups and governmental organizations, to which regulatory tasks have been delegated by law. They usually have no formal structure, apart from an administrative secretariat (Christensen 2005; Christensen and Yesilkagit 2006);
(4) Private professional organizations: are legally recognized and have been delegated self-regulatory competencies by law (e.g. accountants, lawyers, doctors).

Each organization could have multiple general tasks, based on the task description. The *number of general tasks* represents the extent of general task specialization: a lower score indicates that the body will be more specialized in regulation. A cybernetic definition of regulation usually distinguishes three tasks: rule-making, monitoring, enforcement (Hood *et al.* 2001; Black 2002). This study separates rule-making into two tasks: the transition of general laws into concrete norms and the application of these norms on individual cases (Lowi 1999). Analytically, rule-making and application represent a different level of abstraction. Whereas rule-making is a general task aimed at achieving collective goals and not bound to individual cases, application is a very specific task and related to individual cases. In addition, empirically, an initial screening in the first phase of the data collection indicated that bodies may be involved in either rule-making or licensing, but not both. This suggests that rule-making and application are two separate tasks. Therefore, an organization was defined as regulatory when it has at least one of the four following *regulatory tasks*:

(1) *Transition of general laws to more concrete rules, norms, and standards*: Includes the setting of standards and norms. Standards indicate the acceptable levels and distributions of a specific risk (e.g. safety standards, goals in distributive justice, pollution, chemicals);
(2) *Application of rules and standards in individual cases (licensing)*: Includes decisions on giving permits or licenses in individual cases, based on

pre-existing norms (e.g. building permission, driver's license, permission to start a business,...);

(3) *Monitoring*: Includes all actions that are aimed at gathering information on the compliance of actors to rules. Information-gathering is defined as producing knowledge about current or changing states of a system (see Hood *et al.* 2001). In this paper, information-gathering can occur both through desk work and on-site inspections and audits;

(4) *Enforcement*: Includes organizations that are involved in modifying the behaviour of an actor by applying sanctions and rewards, forbidding to do an activity, or demanding a reversal/change of a decision. Courts belonging to the judiciary branch (e.g. criminal courts) are excluded.

An organization's *number of regulatory tasks* represents the extent of regulatory task specialization. A low score indicates that an organization is specialized in only a few regulatory tasks. A high score indicates that the body is active in (almost) the entire regulatory cycle. Assuming that any regulatory regime entails all four tasks, this variable is a proxy for the extent of fragmentation of the regime. A low mean score indicates a high extent of fragmentation in the regime, since the tasks are spread across multiple organizations. Alternatively, a high mean score indicates a low extent of fragmentation, because tasks are concentrated in a few organizations.

4.5.3 Independent variables

The *regulatory area* was taken from Christensen (2005) and Christensen and Yesilkagit (2006). This categorical variable groups all fields of regulation into three categories:

(1) Economic regulation (financial markets, competition, product standards, business conditions, utility regulation);

(2) Social regulation (labor market and employment law, environmental protection, consumer protection, worker's health and safety, social affairs, land planning);

(3) General legal regulation (penal law and policing, private law, public law, immigration and traffic law).

Finally, the *level of government* to which the body belongs is a dummy variable (federal or regional). Regulatory boards/commissions were allocated to the level that provides the administrative secretariat. Private bodies were coded as a missing value.

4.6   Empirical results

4.6.1   Descriptives

To answer the first research question, descriptives are shown in Table 4.1. Consistent with Christensen (2005) and Christensen and Yesilkagit (2006), we find that regulatory administration is rather complex and that boards are a particularly prominent form. Agencies are the second largest form, followed by ministerial departments and private professional organizations. For a small majority, regulation is the only general task and only 14 per cent perform three general tasks. General public services (72 organizations) and policy formulation (64 organizations) were the most frequent additional tasks. The former usually entails providing information to citizens, private companies, or other administrations. Regarding the spread of regulatory tasks, most organizations have two regulatory tasks and 60 per cent perform two tasks or less. Hence, the extent of both the general task specialization and the regulatory

Table 4.1   Features of regulatory administration in Belgium and Flanders

Variables	Categories	N	%
Legal status	Department	31	11.7
	Agency	59	22.3
	Board	154	58.1
	Private body	21	7.9
	Total	265	
No. of general tasks	1	145	52.2
	2	93	33.7
	3	38	13.8
	Total	276	
No. of regulatory tasks	1	76	27.8
	2	84	30.8
	3	49	17.9
	4	64	23.4
	Total	273	
Regulatory area	Economic	160	57.6
	Social	70	25.2
	General	47	16.9
	Total	277	
Level of government	Federal	170	69.7
	Regional	74	30.3
	Total	244	

task specialization seems rather high. However, further analysis reveals that, for regulatory task specialization, this number is explained by the high number of regulatory boards that are very specialized. Ministerial departments and agencies are usually less specialized: 55 per cent of all departments are active in all four regulatory tasks, whereas the largest proportion of agencies (41 per cent) is active in three tasks. Agencies are most active in monitoring and least active in rule-making. Ministerial departments and collegiate boards are mostly active in rule-making. With respect to the explanatory factors, economic regulation counts the most organizations. Social regulation is the second largest group, followed by general legal regulation. Regarding the level of government, a large majority of bodies are associated with the federal level.

Table 4.2 shows how many organizations each level has per policy field. The most proliferated policy field is economic affairs. When collegiate boards are excluded, 60 departments and agencies are active in this field. Further analysis showed that the most proliferated category of economic affairs is 'labour market and employment law' (ten organizations). The percentages reveal that one level rarely has the full authority over a certain policy field. We find only two fields that are exclusively allocated to one level: Defence is *purely federal* and education is *purely regional*. In all other policy fields competencies are shared by the federal and regional level. Social protection appears *dominantly federal*: 79 per cent of all bodies are federal. Conversely, social sectors such as 'housing', 'culture', and social protection are *dominantly regional*. Environmental protection is almost evenly *shared by both levels* and will be characterized

Table 4.2 Distribution of policy fields over levels of government (COFO6) (%, rounded off)

	Federal	Regional	Private self-regulation	N = 100%
General public services	75	25		45
Defence	100			2
Public order and safety	87	4	8	23
Economic affairs	66	15	19	120
Environmental protection	48	45	7	29
Housing and community amenities	33	67		12
Health	69	19	12	68
Recreation, culture and religion	20	80		30
Education		89	11	9
Social protection	79	21		28

by complex task divisions (e.g. economic affairs, environmental protection, health). Private bodies are mainly active in economic affairs, as well as some social policy fields (e.g. health, education, environmental protection).

Table 4.2 demonstrates how policy fields are shared, to some extent, by the federal and regional level. This is contrary to what we expected, since Belgium is, at least formally, considered to be a dual federal system where competencies on specific domains are exclusively allocated to one governmental level. Since most policy domains are shared to some extent, one would expect more mutual learning and isomorphic pressures between the federal and regional governmental level, leading to more similarities in regulatory style and organization. This would call for a reformulation of the hypotheses on level of government (H4 to H6).

These results could be relevant for the practice of regulatory reform. Negative effects of fragmentation, such as duplication and 'blind spots', are likely to occur in policy fields that have a high number of regulatory bodies, especially when these bodies belong to multiple levels of government. For instance, the potential for duplication will be high when multiple bodies are involved in the same regulatory task. A further analysis of the regime for the field 'regulation of the labour market' showed that six federal and one regional organizations are responsible for monitoring the employment of foreigners. Until recently, these organizations performed their inspections separately, leading to many complaints of businesses regarding administrative costs (Dienst Wetsmatiging 2008).

4.6.2   Hypotheses testing

To answer the second research question, we used ordinal logistic regression. This allows us to test the effect of explanatory factors (i.e. regulatory area, level of administration) on categorical dependent variables when the categories of the dependent variable can be ranked. A test for multicollinearity showed no problems in our data (VIF < 2; tolerance > 0.40). The results are presented in Table 4.3. For any given factor, parameter estimates are calculated for all but one category (i.e. reference category). Since the regulatory area has three categories, estimates are shown for two categories, with 'general-legal regulation' as the reference category. The 'Model Chi-Square' tests are likelihood ratio tests of the *overall model*. For vertical specialization and general task specialization, the model fits well. However, for regulatory task specialization, the model fit and the variance explained are very poor (Nagelkerke Pseudo-R^2: .028). Next, we will discuss the effect of each factor separately.

4.6.2.1 Regulatory area

Table 4.3 shows that there is a significant effect of the regulatory area on the legal status of regulatory bodies. For multinomial factors, positive coefficients mean a likelihood of higher scores on the dependent. Hence, bodies in economic regulation are more likely to score high on legal status (positive coefficient of the parameter estimate). They are significantly more insulated than bodies in general legal regulation (reference category). Social regulation scores low on vertical specialization but there is no significant difference with general legal regulation. Regarding general task specialization and regulatory task specialization, we find no significant differences. The standard ordinal regression only allows the comparison of two categories with the reference category. In order to compare economic and social regulation, we tested additional 'contrast statements', as shown in Table 4.4. Economic

Table 4.3 Ordinal logistic regression

	Legal status			General task specialization			Regulatory task specialization		
	Est.	SE	P	Est.	SE	P	Est.	SE	P
Economic*	0.804	0.355	0.024	−0.607	0.332	0.068	0.454	0.303	0.134
Social*	−0.285	0.385	0.460	0.665	0.367	0.070	0.181	0.346	0.600
Federal	1.628	0.283	0.000	−1.375	0.269	0.000	−0.317	0.148	0.032
N	264			275			272		
Model Chi-Square	48.661		0.000	45.252		0.000	7.259		0.064
Nagelkerke	0.189			0.177			0.028		

Note: * Reference category is General Legal.

Table 4.4 Additional contrast statements*

	Legal status			General task specialization			Regulatory task specialization		
	Est.	SE	P	Est.	SE	p	Est.	SE	P
Economic versus Social	0.391	0.114	0.001	−0.462	0.096	0.000	0.214	0.164	0.147

Note: *Contrast statement tested using the glm command with /lmatrix in SPSS 16.0.

bodies are significantly more insulated than social bodies and have significantly less general tasks. However, there is no significant difference between the three regulatory areas under study regarding the extent of regulatory task specialization, measured by the number of regulatory tasks.

In sum, we find support for the credible commitment hypothesis H1 that economic regulation will be more often performed by organizations that are more insulated from politicians. Regarding other general tasks besides regulation, economic bodies are more specialized than social bodies but not more than general legal bodies. Therefore, H2 is only partially confirmed. Finally, there are no significant differences between the regulatory areas under study with respect to the number of regulatory tasks, which means that H3 is rejected.

4.6.2.2   *Level of government*

Table 4.3 shows that the level of government has a significant effect on the extent of specialization. The coefficient for the federal level is positive, which means it delegates significantly more than the regional level. Regarding the general tasks, other than regulation, federal regulators are more specialized than regional bodies. Federal regulators are also more specialized in a few regulatory tasks than bodies on the regional level. In sum, we see significant differences between different levels, confirming H4, H5 and H6. This is surprising, since the descriptive analyses had shown that most policy domains are shared between the federal and regional governmental level.

4.7   Discussion

4.7.1   Descriptive research question

The data corroborates the idea that regulation is performed by highly-specialized, multi-actor and multi-level constellations. Delegation to autonomous forms of organizations is quite common. If we operationalize regimes as a bundle of four tasks, we find that most actors perform one or two regulatory tasks. Competencies are also dispersed across multiple levels of government. Considering that Belgium has a dual federal structure, we find more sharing than expected. The absence of concurrent competencies means that all legislative and executive authority for a certain competence is allocated to one level. Apparently, it does not preclude that some policy fields are only partially transferred and shared by both levels (Kovziridze 2001; Swenden and Jans 2006). Negative effects of fragmentation are likely to occur in policy fields with a high number of regulators and where many bodies are active in the same task. In those fields, extensive co-ordination will be necessary, especially when both levels have their own legislative and executive competencies.

4.7.2   Explanatory research question

4.7.2.1   *Regulatory area*

Credible commitment has previously been tested by comparing sectors on the extent of delegation to agencies. However, some studies have found poor support for this thesis (Roness *et al.* 2007; Lægreid *et al.* 2008; Yesilkagit and Christensen forthcoming). Following the call of Elgie and McMenamin (2005, 548), our study included a wider set of organizations than agencies alone. The data suggests that forms where regulatees are directly involved (i.e. boards and private organizations) could also serve to insulate tasks from politicians and increase credibility. Delegating tasks to organizational forms that are further away from government is done more frequently for economic regulation than for social and general legal regulation (see also Hajnal, Chapter 3, in this volume). Moreover, compared to regulators in other areas, economic regulators combine fewer other tasks with their regulatory tasks, making them more single-purpose, as advocated by NPM and liberalization doctrines (Brown *et al.* 2006).

However, looking at vertical specialization alone provides an incomplete picture of the mandate of regulators. Assuming that fragmentation reduces the power of single organizations by making them interdependent and by creating checks and balances, we hypothesized that spreading tasks is an additional mechanism to increase credibility. However, we found no significant differences between economic and other regulators in terms of the number of regulatory tasks performed.

Consequently, instead of leading to higher fragmentation, credible commitment requirements seem to imply the creation of independent bodies that combine multiple regulatory tasks. Independent bodies with a larger role in the regulatory process may be more autonomous than bodies that are active in only a few tasks, since they are not depending on other bodies for decision-making input. International organizations, like the World Bank, OECD, and the European Commission, encourage the establishment of strong regulators, combining features of organizational autonomy (vertical specialization), a single purpose (no other general tasks) and of a large regulatory mandate (combining norm setting, monitoring, enforcement) (Brown *et al.* 2006). However, it should be noted that the variation in the number of regulatory tasks explained by our model is very low.

4.7.2.2 Level of government

The federal and the regional levels differ strongly in regard to how they organize the regulatory function. The federal level delegates competencies more frequently to autonomous bodies. Specifically, it uses a high number of boards and commissions where regulatees are involved. However, these bodies have a limited mandate, as they perform less general and less regulatory tasks. Considering that both levels are active in the same policy fields, these findings are somewhat counterintuitive.

One explanation may be that, even though multiple levels of government are active in the same policy field, they may each specialize in different tasks. In certain federalist settings, the task of the higher level is to avoid that lower levels develop competing norms. The federal level will then be responsible for securing the harmonization of rules, through the development and enforcement of equal standards (i.e. rule-making and monitoring), whereas the implementation of those rules (i.e. licensing) is usually left to the lower level (Geradin and McCahery 2004; OECD 2005b). To the extent that different tasks are allocated to different organizational forms, this task specialization may also result in a different extent of delegation to autonomous bodies between levels of government. In sum, isomorphism could perhaps be observed more when organizations are active in the same (regulatory) task, rather than in the same policy field.

A second explanation refers to the specific consociational features of the Belgian federal polity, most notably the feature of power-sharing and mutual vetoes of different groups. First, although competences are exclusively allocated to one level, the regions are strongly involved in federal policy-making. Since competencies are fragmented across levels, complex problems can only be solved when all levels co-ordinate intensely with each other. Several federal laws also require the government to involve or hear the regions when their interests are affected (Swenden and Jans 2006). Even if a policy issue is a strictly federal competence, consultation is deemed necessary to maintain consensus between the Flemish- and French-speaking language groups (Deschouwer 2006). The large number of collegiate boards at the federal level could then serve as a forum that brings together members of the different regions and language groups. A second form of power-sharing at the federal level is the integration of social partners (i.e. interest groups representing employers and employees) in policy-making bodies and in governing boards of agencies. The presence of these partners in regulatory boards and governing boards allows the state to mobilize more resources and rally support for policy initiatives (Hemerijck and Visser 2000: 230). The distribution of policy fields over levels of government, as shown in Table 4.2, suggests that those sectors where corporatism will be particularly prominent (e.g. social security, economic affairs) are still mainly a federal competence (see also Cantillon *et al.* 2006). Both explanations may help to understand why the federal government organizes regulatory tasks at a larger organizational distance than the regional level.

These findings imply that governments may deliberately choose to disperse tasks to a wide range of actors because it increases support for new initiatives. This somewhat contradicts the recent attention given to the negative effects of fragmentation, as expressed in large-scale programmes for 'better regulation' and the reduction of the number of regulators in several European countries.

4.8 Conclusion

This chapter analyzed the specialization and fragmentation of regulatory bodies in Belgium. The recent interest for 'better regulation' reforms suggests that fragmentation has negative effects. Descriptive statistics showed some evidence of both vertical specialization (i.e. delegation) and horizontal (task) specialization. The extent of specialization differs significantly between areas or sectors of regulation. Economic regulators seem to have a relatively large regulatory mandate, calling for a refinement of the credible commitment hypothesis. Furthermore, regulators on different levels of government differ strongly from each other regarding their organizational autonomy and the scope of their regulatory mandate. We can conclude that distinguishing between different levels and areas is useful and that different styles of regulation may be observed, for instance with respect to the importance placed on the consultation with the regulatees.

Part II
Autonomy and Control

5
Policy and Management Autonomy of Federal Agencies in Germany

Tobias Bach[1]

5.1 Introduction

This chapter focuses on the autonomy of federal agencies in Germany in relation to their parent ministries. The academic debate on agencies has been strongly influenced by the practitioner's model of agencification, which proposes high levels of management autonomy in combination with performance contracting as main ingredients for improving administrative effectiveness and efficiency (Pollitt *et al.* 2004; Talbot 2004). However, numerous studies show that the ideal-type agency is hard to find in reality (Pollitt *et al.* 2004; Verschuere 2007; Roness *et al.* 2008; Verhoest *et al.* 2010). Also, it soon became apparent that agencies and other types of autonomous public organizations have existed for a long time in many countries (Hood and Schuppert 1988; Bouckaert and Peters 2004; Wettenhall 2005). This is also the case in Germany, where federal agencies have a long history going back to the second half of the 19th century. This research takes the agencification debate as its point of departure and examines the autonomy of federal agencies from different theoretical perspectives.

The first purpose of this study is to present empirical findings from a comprehensive survey of federal agencies in Germany as part of the COBRA research network. The federal administration is an excellent case for studying agency autonomy in the context of a typical *Rechtsstaat* administrative system dominated by traditional ways of managing public organizations such as hierarchical coordination, input-orientation, and rule-bound decision-making. In contrast to many local governments which have implemented management reforms, the federal administration followed a reform trajectory of maintaining that only resulted in gradual changes (Pollitt and Bouckaert 2004; Schröter 2007; Bach and

Jann 2009). Hence, the assumption is that federal agencies are quite the opposite of the practitioner's model and generally perceive low levels of autonomy. Also, several studies show that an agency's formal–legal type frequently does not correspond to perceived levels of organizational autonomy (Verhoest *et al.* 2004a; Lægreid, Roness and Rubecksen 2006; Yesilkagit and van Thiel 2008). This chapter asks whether this is also the case in the context of a highly legalistic and rule-dominated administrative system.

The second purpose of this chapter is to elaborate on different dimensions of agency autonomy, with a special focus on policy development autonomy. Autonomy is a relational concept, i.e. an actor's autonomy depends on other actors that may grant or withdraw this autonomy (Lægreid *et al.* 2006). Here, the focus is on the relationship between agencies and their parent ministries. Also, autonomy is a multi-dimensional concept (Bouckaert and Peters 2004; Verhoest *et al.* 2004a). For public sector organizations in general, one can broadly distinguish between management autonomy and policy autonomy (Verhoest *et al.* 2010). Here, management autonomy is operationalized as the agencies' authority to take decisions regarding their resources or input factors. The empirical analysis focuses on human resources management (HRM) and financial management. In contrast, policy autonomy is related to the core task of the organization, such as monitoring environmental pollution or paying social security benefits. Very often, this term is used for bureaucratic discretion in the implementation of policy programmes (Verhoest *et al.* 2004a; Lægreid *et al.* 2006; Roness *et al.* 2008). Throughout this chapter, this notion of policy autonomy is termed implementation autonomy. Another type of policy autonomy is the involvement of agencies in initiating and developing policies (Elder and Page 1998; Yesilkagit and van Thiel 2008; Verschuere 2009). This involvement may take different forms, such as preparing bills, providing statistical data or writing expert reports. These activities are referred to as policy development autonomy. With its focus on management autonomy and performance, the debate on agencification has mostly neglected both dimensions of policy autonomy, especially the second dimension.

The research questions are the following: (1) How much autonomy do federal agencies have in practice? (2) How can differences in organizational autonomy be explained? Does perceived autonomy correspond to formal levels of agency autonomy? What other factors play a role in determining perceived levels of agency autonomy?

This chapter is structured as follows: first, the politico-administrative context is presented, together with the most relevant agency types.

Secondly, several hypotheses regarding the relationship between structural-instrumental and task-specific variables and organizational autonomy are developed. Thirdly, data collection and methodology are presented, followed by the empirical results. The chapter ends with a discussion of the findings and concluding remarks.

5.2 The politico-administrative context

Germany is a federal state with a parliamentary, multi-party system of government. There is a functional division of labour between the federal and state levels, according to which the states implement most federal legislation, and in which the state governments participate in federal law-making via the *Bundesrat*, the second chamber of parliament. The origins of the federal administration trace back to the first imperial authorities of the 1870s. It is rather small compared to the state and local levels of government, and federal agencies generally do not have their own regional and local offices (Bach and Jann 2009).

The minister's parliamentary accountability strongly affects the relationship between federal agencies and the ministerial bureaucracy. With very few exceptions, agencies are fully answerable to their parent ministries, which may include ministerial instructions in individual cases. Also, each minister independently conducts the affairs of his ministerial portfolio, yet within the political guidelines set by the chancellor and the cabinet's decisions. In practice, the principle of departmental sovereignty dominates everyday policy-making and is jealously guarded by ministers and ministerial bureaucracy alike (Mayntz and Scharpf 1975).

Germany is a typical example for the *Rechtsstaat* or rule-of-law administrative tradition (Benz and Goetz 1996; Wollmann 2000). In this tradition, the principle of legality is highly valued, according to which each administrative action requires a codified legal basis, usually a statutory law. The genuine role of the administration is to apply law to individual cases, whereas the parliament's role is to select among policy alternatives. Another characteristic feature of the *Rechtsstaat* tradition is a highly specialized body of administrative law ensuring comprehensive individual rights of appeal against administrative acts. Therefore, legal skills and training are highly valued in the public sector. Finally, the public sector is heavily regulated by a large number of statutory laws and secondary legislation and specific collective agreements for public employees (Schröter 2007). Thus, ensuring the legality of administrative actions is generally valued higher than efficiency and effectiveness. However, the tension between the rule-of-law-principle and effective administration is

92 *Autonomy and Control*

usually eased by informal decision-making procedures and 'a good deal of pragmatism and informal flexibility' (Benz and Goetz 1996: 16).

There are two basic types of public-law based organizations within the federal administration, namely the direct administration, which is legally part of the state, and the indirect administration, which has its own legal personality. The direct administration consists of the ministries and all other organizations operating under full ministerial oversight. Here, a distinction is made between legal oversight, concerning only administrative affairs and functional oversight which includes instruction rights in policy matters (Bach and Jann 2009). As a rule, indirect administrative bodies are more remote from political control. They are subject to legal, but not to functional oversight (Loeser 1994). Also, financial management and staff regulations uniformly apply to the direct administration, whereas indirect administrative organizations may be granted higher levels of financial and human resources management autonomy (Döhler 2007).

In sum, the form of affiliation has important consequences for formal autonomy, accountability, and control. In 2008, the direct administration counted about 100 agencies at either national or regional level (Bach and Jann 2009). All of these were included in the total population for the survey, except for some recently restructured agencies, resulting in a total sample of 90 direct administrative agencies. Most indirect administrative agencies are not subject to legal oversight by a ministry. Therefore, only indirect agencies under ministerial supervision (n = 32) were included in the survey.

5.3   Theoretical approach

In addition to describing levels of policy and management autonomy, this research aims at explaining the observed variation in the dependent variables. To this end, the survey data are analysed both from a structural-instrumental and a task-specific perspective, which offer quite different explanations for organizational autonomy (Verhoest *et al.* 2010). Thus, following the strategy of contrasting different theories, their relative explanatory power will be assessed in the analysis (Roness 2009).

5.3.1   A structural–instrumental perspective

The structural–instrumental perspective focuses on the effects of formal rules and regulations, organizational structure and organizational capacity on decision-making in and between organizations (Egeberg 1999; Lægreid *et al.* 2006): how public organizations are organized, what formal goals they have, and what rules they have to follow will affect how much autonomy they have.

According to this perspective, the perceived autonomy of an organization should reflect its formal autonomy, and particularly so in the context of a rule-of-law administrative system. In terms of formal autonomy, direct administrative organizations are closer to the ministries compared to the indirect administration which has its own legal personality. As a consequence, direct administrative agencies are potentially subject to more ministerial control (e.g. when it comes to implementation), but potentially also have better access to policy decisions in the ministry than indirect administrative agencies.[2] In addition, the indirect administration is characterized by the involvement of societal actors in its decision-making structures, allowing for high autonomy in policy implementation (Loeser 1994). Also, the various internal public sector regulations fully apply to the direct administration, whereas the indirect administration may have higher degrees of management autonomy. Thus, the first hypothesis regarding form of affiliation can be formulated as follows:

H1 – Indirect administrative organizations perceive lower levels of policy development autonomy, but higher levels of management autonomy and implementation autonomy compared to direct administrative organizations.

Another structural–instrumental factor that strongly affects the formal relationship between ministries and agencies is the type of oversight exercised by the ministry (Döhler 2007). Functional oversight implies full ministerial instruction rights and full answerability of the agency to any request made by the ministry, whereas functional oversight is much more restricted. Although the exercise of functional oversight is usually associated with the indirect administration, there are several indirect administrative organizations that are subject to functional oversight despite having a legal personality on their own.

H2 – Organizations that are subject to legal oversight only perceive lower levels of policy development autonomy, but higher levels of implementation autonomy and management autonomy compared to organizations that are subject to functional oversight.

The structural capacity for decision-making is another structural-instrumental factor likely to affect organizational autonomy (Egeberg 1999). All other things being equal, the more agencies that are connected to a ministry, the lower the ministry's oversight capacity towards its agencies because of limited resources for attention. However, the total number of agencies per ministry is a rather imprecise measure of the ministries' relative oversight capacity. A better measure which takes into account the relative size of ministries and agencies is the ratio of staff numbers between parent ministry and its agencies. This leads to the following hypothesis:

H3 – The higher the oversight capacity of the parent ministry in relation to its subordinated bodies, the lower the organizations' perceived levels of policy autonomy and management autonomy.

Finally, agency size, which can be measured terms of staff numbers, is likely to affect agency autonomy, too. This variable is a proxy for structural capacity devoted to the performance of a given task. Also, large organizations are more likely to build up their own expertise based on experiences gained from policy implementation. Finally, all other things being equal, the larger an organization, the greater the difficulties of the parent ministry to control the organization (Verhoest *et al.* 2010). To conclude, the following hypothesis can be formulated:

H4 – The higher the structural capacity of an organization (i.e. the more staff it employs), the higher its perceived policy autonomy and management autonomy.

5.3.2 A task-specific perspective

If the head of a public organization were to deliver a speech on his organization, he would probably mention the organization's form of affiliation and staff numbers and maybe say something about the organization's formal relationship with the parent ministry. However, he will spend most of the time talking about what the organization actually does. This is the core of the task-specific perspective, according to which characteristics of the primary task of a public organization strongly affect its internal management and its stakeholder relations (Wilson 1989; Pollitt *et al.* 2004; Verhoest *et al.* 2010).

James Q. Wilson (1989) classifies public organizations based on the observability and measurability of outputs and outcomes of an organization, from which he develops four ideal-types, each being confronted with characteristic management problems. A major lesson from this typology is that there is no single best way of managing public organizations

(Pollitt *et al.* 2004). The extent to which outputs and outcomes are observable and measurable affects how well elected politicians and generalist bureaucrats in the parent ministry understand what an organization actually does and whether it does a good job. It is much easier to grasp and control production organizations where both outputs and outcomes are easily observable (e.g. tax collection) in contrast to procedural organizations which have an observable output but no observable or measurable outcome (e.g. health promotion).

An alternative way to classify public organizations is according to activities (Bouckaert and Peters 2004; Verhoest *et al.* 2010). Although a perfect match with the aforementioned types is not possible, it can be argued that organizations with service delivery tasks come closest to a production organization with allegedly higher levels of implementation and managerial autonomy (Verhoest *et al.* 2010). Thus, the following hypothesis can be formulated:

> H5 – Organizations having service functions perceive higher levels of implementation and management autonomy compared to organizations with other functions.

Another important type of activity is regulation. According to the functional logic of credible commitment, politicians deliberately create independent regulatory agencies with high levels of policy implementation autonomy in order to create policy stability beyond electoral terms (Majone 1997a). The legitimacy of regulatory agencies then relies on transparent and participatory modes of decision, high levels of expertise and professionalism, and a clear definition of stable policy objectives, rather than on political majorities (see Yesilkagit and Christensen 2009 for an overview of political explanations of agency autonomy). Finally, regulatory agencies are expected to operate at considerable distance from parent departments, but supposedly provide a lot of relevant expertise for policy development:

> H6 – Organizations having regulatory functions perceive higher degrees of policy autonomy and management autonomy compared to organizations with other functions.

Whether the activities of an agency are directed towards the administration itself or external actors is likely to affect agency autonomy, too. Administration is probably a more stable and predictable target group compared to private companies. Thus, following the basic tenet of contingency theory that the decision-making of an organization reflects key characteristics of its environment (Scott and Davis 2006), organizations with external target groups will have more management autonomy.

> H7 – Organizations having the administration itself as its target group will perceive low levels of management autonomy, whereas organizations having external parties as their target group will perceive high levels of management autonomy.

Political salience is frequently referred to as highly relevant for agency autonomy (Judge, Hogwood and McVicar 1997; Pollitt 2006; Verhoest *et al.* 2010). Among others, this rather elusive concept has been operationalized as budget and staff size, the extent of direct contact with citizens, policy area, and the number of parliamentary questions. In this research, the perceived level of parliamentary attention towards an agency serves as a proxy for political salience. The expectation is that highly politically salient agencies perceive lower levels of autonomy than agencies with a low political profile.

> H8 – The higher the political salience of an organization, the lower its perceived policy and management autonomy.

Finally, whether an agency generates income in addition to budget appropriations is also considered as an important task characteristic (Verhoest *et al.* 2004a; Pollitt 2006; Verhoest *et al.* 2010). The higher the share of income generated by an agency, the smaller its dependence on the parent ministry for its overall revenues. Here, additional revenues are operationalized as the percentage share of incomes via user fees in the agencies' annual budget:

> H9 – The higher the share of additional revenues in the total budget of an organization, the higher its perceived management autonomy.

The next section summarizes the research methodology.

5.4   Methodology

The analysis is based on a survey that was conducted in 2008 among all 122 federal public-law organizations operating under ministerial oversight. The questionnaire was an adaptation of similar surveys conducted in several countries (see the chapters on Hong Kong, Italy and Flanders in this volume) and addressed directly to the president or managing director, together with a short description of the project. The sample comprises national organizations with and without regional or local units, as well as regional organizations directly reporting to a ministry.

In total, 73 agencies returned the questionnaire. The overall response rate is 60 per cent, while response rates of the different forms are 58 per cent for direct administrative agencies and 66 per cent for indirect administrative agencies. As a result, the direct administration is slightly underrepresented in the dataset compared to its share in the total population. When it comes to ministry affiliation, no major deviations regarding ministry affiliation between sample and total population can be found.

5.5 How much policy and management autonomy?

In terms of policy development autonomy, the survey included several questions on activities that are usually understood as key functions of the ministerial bureaucracy. The respondents were asked whether these activities are typically performed by the ministry, the organization, or both. The data show that the ministries are generally perceived as main actors for policy development and evaluation, although several organizations report rather high levels of policy development autonomy (Table 5.1). These findings are in line with empirical observations on the pivotal role of ministerial bureaucracies in policy formulation (Mayntz

Table 5.1 Policy development autonomy (%)

	Only by ministry	Mostly by ministry	Ministry and agency	Mostly by agency	Only by agency	Does not apply	N
Evaluation and feed-back regarding policy effectiveness	10	26	30	12	4	18	73
Formulation of regulations and guidelines	16	32	15	22	1	14	73
Supporting political initiatives	18	38	20	8	–	15	73
Commenting on draft laws or decrees from other ministries	25	44	8	8	–	14	72
Formulating of draft laws or decrees	29	40	12	7	–	12	73

and Scharpf 1975). The respondents perceive the highest levels of policy development autonomy for the evaluation of policy programmes and the formulation of guidelines and regulations. Most importantly, these are the only activities for which some organizations report either high or very high autonomy. Yet most organizations perceive rather low levels of autonomy when it comes to the formulation of laws and governmental decrees or commenting on drafts from other ministries.

For further analysis, the five items were recoded into binary variables (1 = medium, high or very high levels of autonomy, 0 = low or very low levels of autonomy) from which a summative index of policy development autonomy was constructed. The index ranges from zero to five. Most organizations have an index value of either zero (32 per cent) or one (26 per cent), 32 per cent score two or three, whereas only few organizations reach index values of four or five (9.8 per cent).[3]

The survey also included several items measuring policy implementation autonomy. Answer categories ranged from very high implementation autonomy ('the organization takes most of the decisions itself, the parent ministry is not involved in the decision-making process and sets no restrictions') to low ('the parent ministry takes most of the decisions, independently of the organization') or very low implementation autonomy ('neither the parent ministry, nor the organization decides on this matter, since the involved legislation leaves no room for discretion on that matter'). A large majority of the respondents perceives either very high or high levels of implementation autonomy across all items. Almost seventy per cent of the respondents decide alone or with only minor involvement of the ministry on how they carry out their core tasks and set priorities, whereas the remaining agencies take most decisions after consultation or under explicit conditions set by the ministry. When it comes to the exact delineation of the organizations' target group, about 50 per cent of the respondents perceive very high or high levels of autonomy, whereas 40 per cent report intermediate levels of autonomy. For the selection of policy instruments, the picture is similar.

For the explanatory analysis, all items were recoded into binary variables (1 = very high or high autonomy, 0 = all other values) from which a summative index of implementation autonomy was constructed. The index ranges from zero to three.[4] Most organizations (40 per cent) have the highest index value, 18 per cent have index values of one or two, respectively, whereas 24 per cent score zero.

Table 5.2 summarizes the descriptive findings on strategic and operational HRM autonomy, i.e. whether an organization can take decisions in the field of human resources management without the approval or

Table 5.2   Strategic and operational HRM autonomy (%)

	For all staff	For most staff	For some staff	For no staff at all	N
Strategic HRM autonomy					
General criteria for recruitment	32	48	4	16	73
Criteria for staff evaluation	37	12	3	48	73
Criteria and conditions for staff promotion	21	33	6	40	72
Criteria and procedure for staff reduction	24	21	10	45	71
Level of salaries	8	18	–	74	73
Operational HRM autonomy					
Evaluation of a single employee	63	36	–	1	73
Dismissal of a single employee	35	51	8	6	72
Recruiting a new staff member	27	55	6	12	73
Promotion of a single employee	23	56	6	15	73
Wage supplement for a single employee	34	36	10	21	73

involvement of the parent ministry. Here, a distinction is made between strategic HRM autonomy, which comprises general decisions such as guidelines and standard operating procedures, and operational HRM autonomy, which is about day-to-day decisions regarding individual staff members (Verhoest *et al.* 2004a; Lægreid *et al.* 2006).

With regard to strategic aspects, most organizations perceive high or very high autonomy for the general criteria of recruitment. For the general criteria of staff evaluation, conditions for promotion, and staff reduction, the picture is more mixed. Finally, almost three quarters of the responding organizations perceive no strategic autonomy at all with regard to the level of salaries.

For operational HRM autonomy, the general picture is very different. Here, virtually all respondents perceive very high or high autonomy for evaluating individual staff. Also, the majority of organizations perceive high levels of autonomy for all other items measuring operational HRM autonomy. In sum, the respondents generally perceive considerably more operational HRM autonomy than strategic HRM autonomy. This finding is supported by similar research on public sector organizations in other countries (McGauran *et al.* 2005; Lægreid *et al.* 2006). Also, both for strategic and operational HRM management, only few organizations report having autonomy only 'for some staff', which indicates high levels of uniformity within the organizations regarding the management of human resources.

For the explanatory analysis, two summative indices were constructed, after recoding the items into binary variables (1 = for all staff or for most staff, 0 = for some staff or for no staff). The indices range between zero and five. In terms of strategic HRM autonomy, most organizations (24 per cent) have a moderate index value of three, whereas 17 per cent have the lowest and 16 per cent the highest possible value.[5] In contrast, 58 per cent score five on operational HRM autonomy, and another 18 per cent have an index value of four, whereas no organization scores zero on the operational HRM autonomy index.[6]

Table 5.3 summarizes the results for financial management autonomy. For all items, the respondents were asked to what extent the organization can take financial decisions independently of the parent ministry. The most obvious finding is that the majority of the respondents either

Table 5.3   Financial management autonomy (%)

	To a very large extent	To a large extent	To some extent	To a small extent	Not at all	Does not apply	N
Fix prices for services or products	18	17	20	13	3	30	71
Transfer of funds between personnel, running costs and investments	20	17	17	10	7	28	69
Transfer of funds between personnel and running costs	24	16	18	13	7	22	68
Transfer of funds to the following budgetary year	18	16	28	13	12	13	68
Fix the level of tariffs and charges	6	10	16	14	16	39	71

answered 'does not apply' or 'not at all' across all items. Here, the data seem to reflect the formal budgetary procedure, in which the budget is approved by parliament. This includes decisions on a more flexible financial management such as transferring funds between budget items or across budgetary years. However, most organizations have at least some autonomy with regard to transferring funds to the next budgetary year or between personnel and running costs. These measures were part of a reform in 1997 which increased budgetary flexibility, but left the basic features of the traditional line-item budgetary system unchanged (Schröter 2007). In sum, the data show that most organizations perceive rather low levels of financial autonomy, with some exceptions. Thus, despite the very detailed and cumbersome budgetary laws and regulations, there clearly is some variation as to how the traditional input-based financial management of the federal administration is put into practice.

For the explanatory analysis, all items were recoded into binary variables (1 = very high or high autonomy, 0 = all other values) from which a summative index of financial management autonomy was constructed. The index ranges from zero to five.[7] The majority (39 per cent) has an index value of zero, and 25 per cent score three on the financial management index.

5.6   Bivariate and multivariate analyses

This section addresses the relationships between the independent and the dependent variables, thus testing the hypotheses regarding structural-instrumental and task-specific organizational characteristics. First, bivariate correlations are tested, followed by multivariate linear regression in order to asses the relative explanatory power of the independent variables.[8] Table 5.4 shows that structural-instrumental features make some difference for management autonomy, but very little for policy autonomy. There is no linear relationship between form of affiliation and the indices measuring policy autonomy. However, in line with H1, indirect administrative organizations perceive higher levels of strategic HRM autonomy and financial management autonomy than direct administrative organizations.[9]

In contrast, type of oversight positively correlates with implementation autonomy, but not with management autonomy. Agencies that are subject to legal oversight only perceive more implementation autonomy than organizations that are subject to functional oversight which encompasses all aspects of policy implementation. Thus, H2 has limited support in the correlations analysis.

Table 5.4 Bivariate correlations (Pearson's R)

	Policy autonomy		Management autonomy		
	Policy development autonomy	Implementation autonomy	Strategic HRM autonomy	Operational HRM autonomy	Financial management autonomy
Form of affiliation	-0.11	0.21	0.29*	0.05	0.30*
Type of oversight	-0.06	0.36**	0.08	-0.20	0.14
Oversight capacity	0.01	-0.06	0.16	0.01	-0.10
Structural capacity	0.02	-0.24	-0.33**	-0.16	-0.08
Service provision					
• main task	–	0.17	0.06	0.05	0.25*
• secondary task	–	-0.40**	0.02	-0.02	-0.19
Regulation					
• main task	-0.13	-0.13	-0.26*	-0.13	-0.36**
• secondary task	0.26*	0.02	-0.04	-0.06	0.10
Target group					
• internal	–	–	-0.24*	-0.15	-0.08
• external	–	–	0.27*	0.37**	0.10
Political salience	0.30*	-0.26*	0.02	0.08	-0.11
Income via fees (%)	–	–	0.25*	0.07	0.03

Notes: * significant at 0.05-level (two-tailed); ** significant at 0.01-level (two-tailed).

Turning to the oversight capacity of the parent ministry, which is a relative measure of the total number of staff in the parent ministry and all subordinated organizations, no correlations with either policy or management autonomy are found. Thus, H3 has to be refuted.

The agencies' structural capacity correlates negatively with strategic HRM autonomy, which is the opposite of H4. Large organizations perceive themselves to have lower levels of strategic HRM autonomy than small organizations.

When it comes to task-specific variables, the overall picture is rather mixed, too. Organizations with service provision as their main task perceive themselves to have higher levels of financial management autonomy than organizations with other tasks, which is in line with H5. However, those organizations having service provision as their secondary task perceive lower levels of policy implementation autonomy than organizations having other secondary tasks.

Agencies having mainly regulatory functions perceive lower levels of financial management autonomy and strategic HRM autonomy than agencies with other main functions, which is the opposite of H6. In terms of policy autonomy, only those agencies with regulation as secondary task perceive higher levels of policy development autonomy than agencies with other secondary functions, as expected according to H6. This suggests that the combination with other functions rather than the regulatory function as such makes a difference for an agency's policy development autonomy.

The bivariate analysis seems to confirm the hypothesis on the effect of the target group on management autonomy (H7). The more the activities of an agency address other parts of the administration, the lower its strategic management autonomy. In contrast, the more an agency reports having external target groups (i.e. private companies), the higher its perceived strategic and operational HRM autonomy.

In this research, the political salience of an agency is measured as its perceived level of parliamentary attention. In contrast to the expectations formulated in H8, political salience does not matter for management autonomy. The findings on policy autonomy are inconclusive with regard to the theoretical expectations, too. As expected, highly politically salient agencies perceive lower levels of policy implementation autonomy. In contrast, they perceive higher levels of policy development autonomy than organizations which are less exposed to the parliamentary spotlight, which does not support the hypothesis.

Finally, the hypothesis on the relationship between an agency's share of income via fees and its perceived management autonomy gets only weak support in the correlations analysis (H9). This variable positively correlates with strategic HRM autonomy, but there is no correlation with operational HRM autonomy. Most importantly, organizations with large shares of income via fees do not perceive higher levels of financial management autonomy than organizations with low shares of additional incomes.

Let's turn to the results of the multivariate regression analyses (Table 5.5), where only statistically significant bivariate correlations are included. The overall picture is that the independent variables explain only little variation in the dependent variables. Also, several independent variables loose their explanatory power if other independent variables are controlled for.

In terms of structural-instrumental explanations, only form of affiliation (H1) and type of oversight (H2) have a significant effect on financial management autonomy and implementation autonomy, respectively. The significant relationship between form of affiliation and strategic

Table 5.5   Summary of ordinary least square regressions, standardized beta coefficients

	Political autonomy		Management autonomy	
	Policy development autonomy	Implementation autonomy	Strategic HRM autonomy	Financial management autonomy
Form of affiliation	–	–	0.22	0.26*
Type of oversight	–	0.26*	–	–
Oversight capacity	–	–	–	–
Structural capacity	–	–	−0.14	–
Service provision				
• main task	–	–	–	0.03
• secondary task	–	−0.33**	–	–
Regulation				
• main task	–	–	−0.26	−0.31*
• secondary task	0.25*	–	–	–
Target group				
• internal	–	–	−0.09	–
• external	–	–	0.25	–
Political salience	0.26*	−0.16	–	–
Income via fees	–	–	0.10	–
Multiple R	0.39	0.52	0.55	0.45
Adjusted R	0.12	0.24	0.22	0.16
F-value	5.93	7.43	3.73	5.13
Significance	0.00	0.00	0.00	0.00
N	71	64	58	66

Notes: * significant at 0.05-level; ** significant at 0.01-level; – not included in the model.

HRM autonomy disappears in the regression model. Thus, only form of affiliation matters for managerial autonomy, whereas type of oversight only makes a difference for policy autonomy. Thus, H1 gets limited support for management autonomy, but not for policy autonomy, and H2 is confirmed only for implementation autonomy.

According to H4, agencies with relatively more structural capacity should display higher levels of autonomy. The bivariate analysis shows a negative correlation between structural capacity and strategic HRM autonomy. However, this relationship disappears if other independent variables are controlled for, including form of affiliation. A possible explanation could be that most large agencies are direct administrative organizations which generally perceive lower levels of strategic HRM autonomy than indirect administrative agencies (although not significant in the regression model).

The task-specific explanations also receive only weak support in the regression models. The directions of the relationships are similar to the findings reported above, including those running counter to the expected directions. Yet, the relationship between service provision as a main task and financial management autonomy disappears if controlled for other relevant independent variables (H5). Also, similar to the bivariate analysis, the relationship between service provision and implementation autonomy is not in line with H5. In sum, H5 is not supported.

In terms of the effect of regulatory functions on management autonomy, the empirical findings are the exact opposite of what was expected. There is an independent effect of regulation as main task on financial autonomy when controlling for form of affiliation and service provision as main task. Thus, regulatory agencies do not have more managerial autonomy than agencies with other main functions (H6). However, H6 gets support for policy development autonomy, yet only for organizations having regulation as a secondary function.

The remaining hypotheses also have no support when other relevant independent variables are controlled for. There is no independent effect of target group on strategic HRM autonomy in the regression model, as suggested by H7. Also, the negative relationship between political salience and implementation autonomy disappears in the regression model, whereas there still is a positive effect of political salience on policy development autonomy. In sum, H8 is not supported. Finally, the positive relationship between the share of additional income in the agency budget and strategic HRM autonomy disappears when controlling for other independent variables.

5.7   Discussion

This research contributes to the literature on agency autonomy in several ways. First, it supplements previous findings on the relationship between formal autonomy and perceived autonomy. A number of empirical studies show that organizations with a higher level of formal autonomy do not necessarily perceive higher levels of autonomy (Verhoest *et al.* 2004a; Lægreid *et al.* 2006; Yesilkagit and van Thiel 2008). In the present analysis, form of affiliation makes a difference for financial management autonomy and strategic HRM autonomy (but without any significant effect on the latter in the multivariate model). Thus – albeit to a limited extent – the findings suggest that indirect administrative agencies perceive higher levels of management autonomy than direct administrative agencies. However, no relationship between form of affiliation and perceived policy autonomy can be observed. In contrast, type of oversight by the ministry as another measure of formal autonomy makes a difference for implementation autonomy, but not for management autonomy. In sum, formal autonomy has an independent effect on the perceived autonomy of federal agencies. A possible direction for further research on the relationship between formal and perceived autonomy would be to explore variation in perceived autonomy among sub-types of form of affiliation.

Secondly, the empirical results confirm the conceptual distinction between policy autonomy and management autonomy. A correlation analysis between the independent variables shows no connection between policy development autonomy and the other independent variables, but some statistically significant correlations between implementation autonomy and management autonomy (not reported in the analysis). In addition, no independent variable affects both policy and management autonomy at the same time. Overall, only few explanatory factors in the present analysis count for policy development autonomy. Among others, the nature of the policy programme under consideration and the agency's policy development capacity could provide better explanations for policy development autonomy (Verschuere 2009), but these factors are difficult to measure via organizational surveys.

Also, in contrast to the theoretical expectations, agencies perceiving high levels of political salience report high levels of policy development autonomy. The involvement of federal agencies in policy design largely depends on the willingness of the ministerial bureaucracy (Elder and Page 1998). Thus, the empirical findings suggest that parent departments are more likely to include agencies attracting a lot of parliamentary attention into policy development activities. Future research should explore why some agencies are more tightly integrated into policy decisions, whereas others operate at a greater distance from both parliament and parent ministry.

Thirdly, the explanatory power of both theoretical perspectives is rather low, especially if other variables are controlled for in the multivariate models. Having said that, the analysis reveals some statistically significant correlations. Interestingly, task-specific variables explain more variation in policy autonomy than structural-instrumental factors. On the contrary, both structural-instrumental and task-specific explanations make a difference for management autonomy. Again, this supports the claim that policy and management autonomy are clearly distinct concepts. Also, the findings suggest that using several theoretical approaches at the same time is an appropriate strategy for studying a complex and multi-dimensional phenomenon like agency autonomy (Pollitt *et al.* 2004; Roness 2009).

Fourthly, federal agencies generally perceive high levels implementation autonomy, but comparatively low levels of management autonomy, except for individual decisions on personnel. An earlier study found that ministerial control mostly focuses on purely administrative aspects, and much less on agency performance (Welz 1988). These results are supported by survey data on the frequency of ministerial intervention by which agency decisions were either changed or annulled (not reported in the analysis). More than 70 per cent of the respondents report a low or very low frequency of hierarchical instructions. On the contrary, more than 55 per cent of the agencies report high or very high levels of constraints on managerial decisions by personnel and budget laws and regulations. How can this divergence between high levels of perceived implementation autonomy (and few ministerial interventions) and low levels of perceived managerial autonomy (and high levels of perceived red tape) be explained?

An initial explanation relates to the method of measuring implementation autonomy as the extent to which the ministry is directly or indirectly involved in taking decisions related to policy implementation (or intervening by giving instruction). This indicator may not reflect the whole picture of the complex interplay between ministerial control and agency autonomy. Earlier studies argue that hierarchical interventions are only used in the event of obvious implementation deficits and major conflicts (Welz 1988; Döhler 2007). Agency officials prefer to avoid hierarchical intervention and hence try to anticipate the ministry's position, which is a well-known mechanism from the study of decision-making within the ministerial bureaucracy (Mayntz and Scharpf 1975). In sum, a very frequent use of hierarchical interventions would undermine the effectiveness of ministerial oversight. As a consequence, the level of implementation autonomy reported by the agency may exaggerate the actual autonomy because the ministry's position is anticipated by agency officials.

The characteristic administrative system with a strong rule-of-law tradition may also explain the striking divergence between implementation and management autonomy of federal agencies. In this tradition, the legal basis of an agency, which defines its policy objectives and instruments, is considered sufficient to ensure a well-performing and accountable administration (Döhler 2007). Administrative performance is taken for granted as long as the principle of legality is followed. At first sight, the combination of high implementation autonomy and low levels of managerial autonomy is typical for countries with a rule-of-law tradition, such as Germany and Flanders. However, similar patterns can also be observed in the case of Ireland, which has a very different administrative tradition (Verhoest *et al.* 2010). Thus, further research should more explicitly connect the empirical findings on agency autonomy to country-specific trajectories of public sector reform (Pollitt and Bouckaert 2004; Verhoest *et al.* 2010). Further, in order to draw robust conclusions on typical patterns of agency autonomy within the context of a typical *Rechtsstaat*, more internationally comparative research on the interrelations between different dimensions of agency autonomy in countries having similar administrative tradition is needed.

Fifthly, several studies suggest that ministry-agency relations differ among parent ministries (Gains 2004; BRH 2005; Döhler 2007) and even among otherwise similar agencies having the same parent ministry (Pehle 1998). In view of the high importance of the departmental principle for governing federal agencies, ministry affiliation may have a stronger effect than either structural-instrumental or task-specific features, which would explain the low levels of explained variation in the dependent variables. Also, although the analysis shows that form of affiliation makes a difference for management autonomy, there is no correlation between form of affiliation and the perceived level of constraints by internal public sector regulations (not reported in the analysis). In addition, no correlation between perceived levels of internal regulation and management autonomy can be found. An answer to this puzzle could be that public sector regulations are not applied uniformly among all federal agencies. According to interview data, the ministries have a substantial influence on how internal regulations are applied in practice. In other words, it is not the regulation *per se* that puts constraints on the agencies, but whether the ministries grant budgetary freedoms or autonomy in appointing personnel (e.g. by reserving the right to hire new agency staff for positions above a certain pay level). Here, further investigations should focus on differences in perceived levels of autonomy and internal red tape between agencies having the same parent ministry.

5.8 Conclusion

The major aim of this chapter was to describe and explain the autonomy of federal agencies in Germany, which is considered as a typical case of a rule-of-law administrative system. It finds that the formal autonomy of federal agencies has some effect on perceived levels of autonomy. Also, it shows that federal agencies perceive high degrees of implementation autonomy, despite the prevailing normative principle of a highly legalistic bureaucracy. In contrast, federal agencies perceive rather low levels of financial management autonomy, especially within the direct administration, and high levels of internal red tape. Finally, although the agencies generally consider the ministerial bureaucracy as key actor when it comes to policy formulation, they also report various degrees of involvement in policy design. The discussion on the findings also pointed out several directions for further research, which will shed more light on the effect of context factors such as country or ministry affiliation on agency autonomy and the relationship between policy autonomy and management autonomy.

Notes

1. I would like to thank Morten Egeberg, Birgitta Niklasson, Jon Pierre, Christoph Reichard, and the editors of this volume for their very useful comments on earlier versions of this chapter, and Markus Seyfried for his invaluable help with the data analysis.
2. Egeberg (1999) makes a similar argument with regards to differences between ministerial departments and agencies.
3. Cronbach's Alpha = 0.643.
4. Cronbach's Alpha = 0.784.
5. Cronbach's Alpha = 0.754.
6. Cronbach's Alpha = 0.698.
7. Cronbach's Alpha = 0.743.
8. For the analysis, interval scaling of the items in the questionnaire is assumed.

9. The correlation analysis has also been performed using other summative indices, generally leading to similar results as in the analysis reported in this chapter. However, if the index of operational HRM autonomy is constructed by including only those items indicating very high autonomy or by including all values, the correlation with form of affiliation is positive and statistically significant.

6
Explaining Autonomy in Public Agencies: The Case of Hong Kong

Martin Painter, John P. Burns and Wai-Hang Yee[1]

6.1 Introduction

Questions about organizational autonomy have been prominent in recent public administration reform discourse and, accordingly, have become of increased interest to public administration researchers (Verhoest *et al.* 2004a). As well as recent developments and debates, such as discussion about the benefits of New Public Management (NPM) style 'autonomization' and 'agencification',[2] there has been a long-standing focus within public administration on the effects of organizational form on effectiveness, notably in the voluminous literature on 'public corporations' and 'statutory bodies', which are designed to give them some degree of legal and operational autonomy (Scott and Thynne 2006). Our interest here is in explaining variation in the autonomy of organizations measured in terms of the perceptions of their senior management. We base our argument on a survey conducted in Hong Kong in 2007 of the perceptions of the chief executives of public agencies and the autonomy they exercised.[3]

6.2 Theoretical considerations

We follow Verhoest *et al.* (2004) in viewing autonomy in two dimensions: first, as the level of decision-making competencies of an agency and second, as freedom from constraints on the use of those competencies. The first dimension inquires into the question 'decisions about what?' and arrives at a distinction between policy autonomy and managerial autonomy and, within the latter, between autonomy over financial and personnel management. Policy autonomy is viewed purely in terms of agency policy, or policy about matters that are directly relevant to the operations of the agency. Most of our analysis in this chapter is based on the allocation of decision-making competencies, i.e. the extent to which a lower level body has the power to make different decisions. But we also look at some aspects of 'exemption from constraints', such as the extent to which agency managers may be subject to direct *ad hoc* intervention in various internal operational matters.

In this paper, our starting point is a structural-instrumental perspective on organizations. This approach sees organizations as instruments and emphasizes the importance of organizations' formal structure; the autonomy possessed hence is largely related to the best way to achieve organizational goals (Lægreid *et al.* 2005b; Christensen *et al.* 2007). In the analysis of organizational decision-making, this perspective highlights the importance of the distribution of roles and functions between levels in a hierarchy and among agencies. It owes much to the writings of Luther Gulick (1937), who spelt out a series of principles about the way organizations are structured. Once things get too complicated for a small group to handle collegially, tasks get delegated and become specialized. Fundamental is the division of labour, or the manner of *horizontal specialization*, coupled with a system of coordination and control, or *vertical specialization*. Vertical specialization involves delegation of authority with accompanying supervision or oversight, that is, varying levels of autonomy.

A second perspective, which suggests a different set of propositions about what shapes autonomy, focuses on task: certain types of task may best be undertaken through particular organizational forms. The underlying presumption is similar to the previous approach: organizational form is a rational adaptation to organizational purpose. One argument is that the nature of the task brings organizations into direct contact with different 'technical environments', requiring specific forms of organizational structure (Thompson 1967). Government-owned commercial undertakings, for example, are said to need managerial flexibility to negotiate successfully with other market actors (this is the basis for the traditional 'theory of the public corporation' (Chester 1953)). Another argument along these lines is that tasks whose output is more measurable can be more easily delegated while still being monitored, leading to more autonomy (Wilson 1989). Looking at another task-specific variable, when tasks have high 'political salience' or a high 'political controversy quotient' (Peres 1968) a different set of considerations may be in the minds of the controllers – for example, reserving the power to intervene on seemingly routine matters of detail when they arouse public controversy (Pollitt *et al.* 2004).

Logics such as these concerning allocating types of functions or activities to different organizational forms within the machinery of government are rarely hard and fast. Often, there are conflicting considerations. For example, some tasks when autonomy may seem appropriate – like child protection, because it involves high levels of professionalization, privacy concerns and so on – are also controversial and subject to frequent political intervention. Despite such ambiguities, task-specific rationales are commonly deployed in deciding whether some government organizations are tightly controlled and others are not. In Hong Kong, some semi-independent bodies dealing with civil liberties such as the Equal Opportunities Commission and the Office of the Privacy Commissioner for Personal Data were set up in that form primarily because of 'the need to assure the public that their activities would have a degree of independence from government' (Scott 2003: 260); the 'editorial independence' of Radio Television Hong Kong (RTHK), the local public broadcaster, has been a principal consideration underlying discussions on 'corporatization' of the broadcaster (Cheung 1997; Legislative Council Secretariat 2005).

Based on these two broad perspectives – structural-instrumental and task-specific – we will investigate some possible reasons for different grants of autonomy to Hong Kong government bodies. First, we explore a basic proposition about structure, namely that formal–legal status is an important determinant of autonomy. Within the Hong Kong system of government, as in most others, a fundamental distinction within the hierarchy of organizations is between departmental and non-departmental bodies. The latter, existing under a variety of names and forms (Scott 2005), are separated out from the 'departmental system' and given distinct organizational identities ('authority', 'board' 'commission' and so on).

Our first proposition (P1) is that *non-departmental bodies have more autonomy than departmental bodies*. In the course of investigating this proposition, we also explore the possibility that finer distinctions between different types of non-departmental bodies might add to our understanding of the relationships between structure and autonomy. Some non-departmental bodies have 'corporate' governance structures, for example a board. Members of the board may be governmental members or drawn from important stakeholder groups or they may be selected from the general community for their expertise. Such boards will likely inject their own considerations into management and policy decisions, thereby potentially diluting the strength of top-down control of the agency (Egeberg 1994; Christensen and Yesilkagit 2006: 208). We investigate the proposition (P2) that *bodies with governing boards have more autonomy than bodies without governing boards.* In addition, we explore whether or not different kinds of non-departmental bodies which customarily have boards, such as public companies, have more autonomy or not.

Turning to the task-specific approach, rational choice theorists using a 'principal-agent' approach argue that measurable, homogeneous tasks with clearly specified objectives can be more readily delegated to agents with less risk of poor results because they are more easily monitored by principals (Jensen and Meckling 1976; Wilson 1989). Thus, organizations undertaking simple public service delivery tasks like refuse collection can be given more autonomy than those undertaking more complex tasks like policy formulation. Drawing on these ideas, our third proposition (P3) is that *organizations concerned primarily with service delivery have more autonomy than organizations undertaking other kinds of tasks.*

Our fourth proposition is concerned with another set of ideas about how task affects autonomy. It is often argued that regulatory bodies should enjoy higher levels of perceived autonomy than other government bodies in order that they can make consistent decisions and win the trust of market actors, who demand predictability (Wettenhall 1968). Again from a rational choice perspective, autonomy is seen as a solution to the 'credible commitment problem': no incumbent government can assure stakeholders that its decisions about regulations that affect their business will have more than a very short 'shelf-life', because a new 'principal' might come to power at any time and shift course; hence, legislatures agree to delegate a function such as industry regulation to an independent regulator (Moe 1989; Horn 1995). From this perspective, we arrive at (P4): *bodies that have regulation as their primary tasks have greater autonomy than bodies with other primary tasks.*

Our fifth proposition takes a 'different cut' on the effects of task on autonomy by exploring political salience. One of the difficulties with using political salience as a task-related constant is that political controversies come and go somewhat unpredictably – today's 'hot issue' for politicians is tomorrow's dull administrative backwater. Leaving this complication aside for the moment, our fifth proposition (P5) is that *organizations in charge of more controversial tasks have less autonomy than organizations with less controversial tasks.*

Our sixth proposition explores another dimension of task – the policy field in which a task is located. A familiar distinction between redistributive, regulative and distributive policies provides a starting point (Lowi 1964). Redistributive policies such as economic policy and taxation bring onto the agenda big issues of class politics that potentially affect everyone. Regulative issues are more sectional and involve smaller circles of special interest group politics. Distributive issues concern matters that are even narrower in impact and may often be dealt with case by case through administrative discretion.[4] We would expect that in the more all-encompassing political domain of redistributive issues, the more reason there would be for governments to control an agency's operations. From this starting point, we suggest the following proposition concerning policy fields and autonomy: (P6) *Organizations in policy fields which are redistributive will have lower levels of autonomy than those in other policy fields.*

Before proceeding with the analysis, including discussion of how we operationalize the independent and dependent variables, we first outline the historical and institutional contexts of the Hong Kong case.

6.3 The case of Hong Kong

Hong Kong remained a British Colony ruled by a Governor appointed from London until 1997, when it became a Special Administrative Region of China. Under the Basic Law, agreed following discussions between Britain and China, the central government in Beijing appoints the Chief Executive and major officials of the government. A Legislative Council is formed by a combination of geographic constituency elections under universal franchise and elections by restricted franchise from so-called 'functional constituencies'. Hong Kong has its own legal system and police, its own tax system and it is fully responsible for its own budget. Despite enjoying the military protection of the national government, it pays no direct financial levy, nor does it receive any direct subvention from the central government. In nearly all matters concerning internal machinery of government, subject to the provisions of the Basic Law and to the checks and balances of the Legislative Council and the judiciary, the Hong Kong government enjoys full autonomy (see Miners 1998; Scott 2005).

The structure of the Hong Kong government has often been depicted as highly consolidated and relatively centralized, due to the existence of a unified civil service run by a relatively small, centrally managed administrative elite (Miners 1998; Burns 2004; Scott 2005). The executive branch in Hong Kong is chiefly composed of the Chief Executive, who is head of the Government; the Government Secretariat, comprising 14 policy bureaux each headed by a 'Secretary'; and the Executive Council, chaired by the Chief Executive and comprising the secretaries plus a group of appointed prominent Hong Kong citizens. The secretaries are equivalent to ministers and are personally appointed by the Chief Executive.[5] Beneath each policy bureau (which we consider to be the 'ministerial' core control agency) is a variety of government executive bodies (e.g. department, agency, authority, commission, government-owned company and so forth). For example, the Secretary for Commerce and Economic Development is the political head of the Bureau of the same name. Within his portfolio and under the oversight of the Bureau is a wide array of executive bodies including Trade and Industry Department; Hong Kong Observatory; Post Office; Innovation and Technology Commission; Intellectual Property Department; Radio Television Hong Kong; Office of the Government Chief Information Officer; Office of the Telecommunications Authority (who is in charge of a 'Department'); and Invest Hong Kong.

Prior to the 1980s, by most accounts the operations of departments and most other administrative agencies were subject to tight hierarchical control by the Colonial/Government Secretariat, headed by the Colonial/Chief Secretary who was deputy to the Governor and the official head of the civil service. Within the Secretariat, the Finance Branch kept departmental spending on a tight rein and held effective veto power over policy initiatives (Miners 1998: 112; Cheung 1999: 239). Many issues of departmental staffing and management were regularly passed up to be resolved by the Secretariat, creating a top-heavy and overloaded system of decision-making and management. Following a review in 1973 (McKinsey 1973), reorganization was undertaken with the intention of strengthening central policy capacity via a new structure of two resource branches (finance and personnel) and six policy branches, each under a Secretary. All posts in this system were held by civil servants until 2002.

The 1980s saw the beginning of gradual devolution of some financial and human resource decisions making from the centre (that is, Finance Branch) to departments (Cheung 2006a). Although the level of autonomy delegated was not high, the direction for decentralization of decisions to departments as a result of the McKinsey review was made quite clear and was further consolidated and rationalized through succeeding measures under the influence of NPM, in both financial and personnel administration (Sankey 1993, 1995, 2001; Burns 1994; Cheung 2006b). An important initiative in the 1990s was the transformation of a small number of departments into 'trading funds', which were accounting entities established by law to provide services on a commercial or quasi-commercial basis with the objective of recovering costs. Trading funds, mostly government monopolies, were deliberately structured to possess more dimensions of financial, managerial and operational autonomy than other departments but continued to employ staff on the unified civil service terms (Finance Branch 1995).

In the case of statutory corporations and other non-departmental bodies the picture is ambiguous and heterogeneous and has been subject to change over time. The departmental form has proved highly flexible (for example, as already pointed out the trading funds are departments; and some devolution of personnel management has gone ahead in both departmental and non-departmental bodies). While many non-departmental bodies, statutory corporations and public companies have been set up under the general rubric of reaping the efficiency benefits of greater autonomy, there are counter-examples such as a new 'department', Invest Hong Kong, set up in 2002 to engage with business and spearhead Hong Kong's efforts to attract inward investment.[6]

It has been argued that the attitude of the Hong Kong government towards public bodies of all kinds is that centralization and control are more important than organizational autonomy, particularly after Hong Kong's retrocession to China in 1997, which resulted in a high burden of expectations emanating from Beijing for close administrative and political control (Scott 2005). The government has activated its weapons of control whenever it perceives the need, regardless of organizational form. For example, the government sought tighter control over the Hospital Authority after the outbreak of SARS in 2003 (Caulfield and Liu 2006); the first two Ombudsmen and a chair of the Equal Opportunities Commission did not have their contracts renewed, the general assumption being that this was because they were too tough on the government (Cooray 2000; Burns 2004); and the Government has apparently sought to maintain control over policy and key management decisions in some non-departmental bodies, such as the Airport Authority (Cheung 2006c).

In sum, in Hong Kong as in other jurisdictions there are ambiguities and contradictions in observable patterns of structural differentiation, control and autonomy among public agencies. Against this background of puzzles and ambiguities, our empirical analysis takes a closer look at the degree, variety and some of the determinants of autonomy in Hong Kong's government bodies.

6.4 Method

In 2007 we surveyed the chief executives of departmental and non-departmental public bodies in Hong Kong, seeking their views on a variety of dimensions of autonomy and control in their agencies. The target population was identified according to a basic definition: a government 'body' for our purposes has some structural differentiation from other organizations, some capacity for autonomous decision-making and exhibits continuity of existence; it performs a public function, has some personnel and financial resources, was created by and funded at least in part by government, and was under some degree of administrative scrutiny by government.[7] We excluded the 14 policy bureaux, as these are the principal controlling agencies (or 'ministries'), but we included all government departments, which operate as executive bodies. Of the 'non-departmental' government-related and quasi-government bodies, we included all those that had the above features.[8] The total population thereby identified was 111 government bodies. An on-line survey was conducted between August and October 2007, with a response rate of 57 per cent (63 completed questionnaires).[9] Chief executives were contacted and asked either to fill in the survey themselves or to nominate an officer with the knowledge and authority to act for him or her. We understand from individual feedback that most chose to do it themselves or, if not, to check the responses before the survey was submitted. In the following sections, we turn to our findings.

6.5   Varieties of autonomy

In the survey, a series of questions probed perceptions of managerial and policy autonomy. Three aspects of managerial autonomy were measured. First, on 'strategic personnel autonomy' (SPA), questions were asked about whether the organization could set policies 'without interference' on such things as the level of salaries, staff numbers and ways of appointing personnel; second, on 'operational personnel autonomy' (OPA), questions were asked about what flexibility the organization had about wages, promotions, staff evaluation and appointments/dismissals with regard to dealing with individual employees (all staff, some staff or none); and third, with regard to 'financial management autonomy' (FMA), respondents were asked whether they could raise loans, set charges for services, shift money between different budget heads and so on. Scores were given (1, 0) for 'yes' or 'no' answers and an overall index (between 0 and 1) for each measure was computed. A composite measure of 'managerial autonomy' (MA) was computed by aggregating the three indexes. Two aspects of policy autonomy were measured. 'Strategic policy autonomy' (SPOA) was measured by asking respondents whether they set organizational goals on their own; following consultation with political and administrative leaders; together with the leaders; by leaders after the organization had been consulted; or by leaders alone. 'Operational policy autonomy' (OPOA) had two dimensions: whether organizations can choose the policy instruments they deploy, and whether they can direct their efforts to target groups of their own choosing. Again, these two indexes resulted in a score from 0 to1 (low to high).

The survey findings indicate that public bodies in Hong Kong perceive that they enjoy varying degrees of different types of autonomy (Table 6.1). One finding is that there is high heterogeneity among public bodies in the autonomy they enjoy, with high standard deviations around the mean in several categories. Given a tradition of relatively tight financial controls, we were not surprised to note that respondents reported on average quite a low level of financial management autonomy (mean = 0.45). In the Hong Kong system budgets are managed by Controlling Officers, the Permanent Secretaries located in the policy bureaux. Although policy Secretaries use budget envelops, which gives the policy bureau considerable flexibility to deploy resources, this practice apparently did not lead chief executives of departments to perceive that they had very much control over their own finances. However, the recent decentralization of personnel administration seems to be reflected in the relatively high reported level of operational personnel autonomy (mean = 0.65).

More surprisingly, the survey reveals that government bodies perceived that they possessed a high level of policy autonomy, particularly in the case of 'strategic policy autonomy' (mean = 0.81). This

Table 6.1   Varieties of autonomy

Variable	Mean	Standard deviation	Median	Min	Max	N
Managerial Autonomy (MA)	0.54	0.263	0.52	0.07	1	59
Strategic Personnel Autonomy (SPA)	0.53	0.386	0.57	0	1	59
Operational Personnel Autonomy (OPA)	0.65	0.276	0.60	0.13	1	59
Financial Management Autonomy (FMA)	0.45	0.256	0.42	0	1	61
Strategic Policy Autonomy (SPOA)	0.81	0.235	1	0	1	59
Operational Policy Autonomy (OPOA)	0.61	0.288	0.67	0	1	60

could mean that Lam's (2005) argument is correct – namely that due to information asymmetry departments (and presumably some non-departmental bodies as well) had considerable control over policy. Lam observed that before the handover of sovereignty in 1997:

> Many powers and authorities were written in laws and ordinances to be exercised by heads of department. The policy secretaries and the bureaux might give advice and requests, but the heads [of departments] ultimately decided what they were going to do. Departments controlled most financial resources in policy programmes. ...[T]he problem of information asymmetries was tremendous ....The department heads could sabotage the initiatives of the policy secretaries easily through delays and information manipulation. (Lam 2005: 640)

Alternatively, our finding on strategic policy autonomy could reflect the fact that departments are a major source of policy options and policy development and that there is considerable information sharing between departments and bureaus – that is, departments and bureaus are inter-dependent and must cooperate (see Waterman and Meier 1998). We lean towards the second explanation. Frequent networking and the career paths of senior civil servants reinforce cooperation. In the case of food safety policy, for example, the Food and Health Bureau relies on the Food and Environmental Hygiene Department (FEHD) for food safety policy development. The Head of FEHD is a former deputy to the Permanent Secretary for food safety, with intimate knowledge of the food safety policy domain and great expertise in this area. He has ready access to the Permanent Secretary and the policy Secretary. Accordingly, we might understand why a chief executive of a department like FEHD would perceive that he has considerable autonomy in strategic policy development.

6.6   Structure and autonomy

As already spelt out, the main focus of this chapter is to investigate some of the factors underlying these patterns of perceived autonomy with a specific focus on structure and task. Our first two propositions concern structure, namely whether the organization is a departmental body or not (P1), and whether it is governed by a board (P2). We divided the organizations which responded to our survey into two categories according to their name – departments and others – and labelled this variable 'vertical specialization' (department 0; non-department 1). In the survey, we asked our respondents whether their organization had a board and, if

Table 6.2   Structure and autonomy (gamma coefficients)

Variable	Vertical specialization	Governing board
Managerial autonomy	0.890**	0.709**
Strategic policy autonomy	0.155	0.071
Operational policy autonomy	0.678**	0.369*

Note: * Correlation is significant at the 0.05 level; ** correlation is significant at the 0.01 level.

so, whether it had formal decisions making authorities. This variable is labelled 'governing board' (no board 0; board 1). Bivariate analysis was undertaken to explore correlations between these independent variables and measures of autonomy (see Table 6.2).[10]

As we might expect, non-departmental status is positively correlated with managerial autonomy and with operational policy autonomy and in this respect P1 is confirmed. However, the non-departmental form is not associated with higher levels of strategic policy autonomy. It seems that all types of body perceive they have similar (high) levels of strategic policy autonomy. In line with our earlier observations on policy autonomy, it is important to note that traditionally most non-departmental bodies as well as departments have been staffed by civil servants, including their senior management. That is, if our interpretation is correct, the top officials of many non-departmental bodies would feel as close to strategic policy-making as their departmental counterparts. The findings on boards (P2) are not quite so clear. It seems that having a board is associated with managerial autonomy but that this feature is only a weak predictor of policy autonomy.

As well as the data on departmental forms from our survey, we also explored further distinctions and categorizations within our population of government bodies. Both departmental and non-departmental bodies in Hong Kong can be further categorized into different structural subtypes (for example, as mentioned earlier, some departments are set up as 'trading funds'; and non-departmental bodies include both those created by ordinance or statute and those set up by executive decision). We classified the 111 organizations in our survey using a version of such categories developed by Scott (2005), slightly modified for our purposes (see Table 6.3). Confirming our earlier finding, departmental bodies have on average less autonomy except in the case of strategic policy autonomy. Consistent with previous research (Huque *et al.* 1999; Cheung 2001), trading funds have significantly more financial management autonomy (but no more personnel autonomy) than departments,[11] while among

Table 6.3 Autonomy and organizational type (mean)

	Managerial autonomy	Strategic personnel autonomy	Operational personnel autonomy	Financial management autonomy	Strategic policy autonomy	Operational policy autonomy
1. Department (n = 25)	0.35	0.31	0.45	0.29	0.81	0.48
2. Trading fund department (n = 5)	0.38	0.32	0.31	0.50	0.81	0.46
3. Non-department executive bodies (n = 3)	0.75	0.76	0.86	0.59	0.82	0.75
4. Not-for-profit subvented statutory body (n = 10)	0.75	0.80	0.92	0.43	0.81	0.80
5. Not-for-profit non-subvented body (n = 9)	0.78	0.75	0.89	0.70	0.94	0.73
6. Partially commercial entity (n = 5)	0.71	0.77	0.80	0.55	0.80	0.60
7. Commercially viable entity (n = 4)	0.88	0.96	0.92	0.75	0.88	0.75

non-departmental bodies only not-for-profits and independent commercial entities have levels of financial management autonomy above
the norm. Although there is some variation in strategic policy autonomy, with not-for-profits and fully commercial entities reporting the
highest autonomy, their values are high in all cases. This can perhaps be
explained by the dominant role the civil service has played and continues to play in Hong Kong's public bodies. Departments and trading fund
departments are led by civil servants. Retired civil servants head many of
the other bodies considered in Table 6.3. Given that the political executive is staffed mostly by retired civil servants it is not surprising that their
colleagues also perceive that they have great strategic policy autonomy.

We remarked from observation of Table 6.1 that there is considerable
heterogeneity in the overall population. This is also the case within
some of the categories. Figures 6.1 and 6.2 present a cluster analysis,
plotting formal legal status using the Scott definitions against two
dimensions of autonomy: managerial autonomy and strategic policy
autonomy.[12] On the vertical axis, departments are located at the bottom
and private or publicly-listed companies are at the top – that is, the level

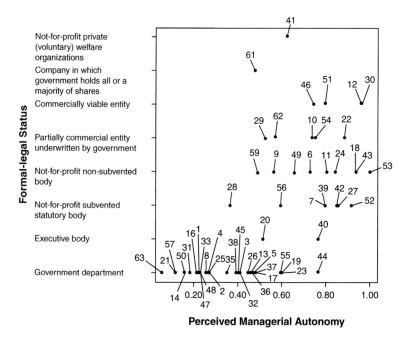

Figure 6.1 Formal–legal status and managerial autonomy

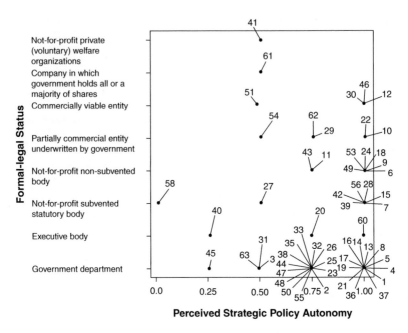

Figure 6.2   Formal–legal status and strategic policy autonomy

of independence according to the formal classification increases along the vertical axis. On the horizontal axis, public bodies with higher perceived autonomy in its different forms appear on the right hand side of the graph.

The fact that the top left-hand corner in each Figure is empty is a reflection of our finding that by and large the legal–structural form of Hong Kong public bodies is not a bad predictor of how much autonomy they enjoy. However, the number and pattern of departures from the norm are also striking. In Figure 6.1, we see that departments do cluster at the bottom left hand corner on managerial autonomy, but that non-departmental bodies are a much less predictable group, scattered widely on the diagram with no clear pattern. From Figure 6.2, we can see that there are a number of outliers among both departmental and non-departmental bodies who deny they have high levels of strategic policy autonomy, with no clear pattern among the latter according to sub-type. In sum, while the proposition that organizational form is positively related to perceived levels of autonomy holds broadly true in Hong Kong, there is a good deal of heterogeneity and some interesting departures from the norm.

6.7   Task and autonomy

We next turn to investigate the effects of task on the autonomy of Hong Kong government bodies. In the survey, organizations were asked about their primary and secondary tasks and were given five options: policy formulation; regulation; other kinds of exercise of public authority; provision of public services; and commercial activities. We assigned bodies to two categories – 'regulation' and 'public service delivery' if they nominated either as a primary task. The answers to this question provide the two variables 'public service delivery' and 'regulation' in Table 6.4.

As to the third variable in Table 6.4, 'political salience', respondents were asked which, and to what extent, 'external sources' influenced decisions concerning direction and strategy. The 'external sources' were listed as follows: Legislative Council; Central (China) Government; mainland sub-national; local district councils; Audit Commission; regulatory bodies; client groups in society; interest groups; advisory bodies; mass media; the public; and major corporations. Respondents could nominate 'to a large extent' (1); 'to a certain extent' (0.5); and 'not' (0). The degree of political salience of the task of the organization was calculated by taking the sum of the scores. We assume that a perception that these external political actors are important signals the existence of relatively high level of community and political interest in a body's activities. In this situation, political leaders are more likely to see the activities of these bodies as being politically salient.

Our findings (Table 6.4) do not support either (P3) or (P4). That is, we find no support for the notion that those organizations with either public service delivery or regulation as their stated primary task enjoy higher levels of perceived managerial or policy autonomy than other public bodies. Indeed, having public service delivery as the primary task is significantly correlated with low levels of perceived operational policy autonomy

Table 6.4   Task and autonomy

Variable	Public service delivery	Regulation	Political salience
Managerial autonomy	−0.325	0.060	(−0.289*)
Strategic policy autonomy	−0.332	0.304	(−0.098)
Operational policy autonomy	−0.598**	−0.023	(−0.370**)

Note: Gamma correlations are shown for public service delivery and regulation; Pearson's r is shown for political salience. * Correlation is significant at the 0.05 level; ** correlation is significant at the 0.01 level.

in our survey population. As to political salience, (P5) is supported by the finding of a significant negative correlation with operational policy autonomy, while there is a weak negative correlation with managerial autonomy. It seems that organizations with tasks that have a relatively high level of political salience have less autonomy to make both policy and managerial decisions about their administrative operations (although this finding does not also hold for strategic policy autonomy).

In attempting to interpret these findings, we find some clues in further analysis of the data. Tables 6.2 and 6.4 only show the relationships between the independent and dependent variables. Bivariate analysis of associations among all the variables also shows some significant correlations between our independent variables. In particular, we find that there is a significant positive correlation between political salience and public service delivery (gamma correlation 0.509 at 0.01 level) and a significant negative correlation between political salience and vertical specialization (gamma correlation –0.675 at 0.01 level). That is, Hong Kong governments keep public service delivery agencies within the departmental fold and one of the reasons seems to be that their tasks are often politically more sensitive. In the case of bodies describing their primary task as regulation, there are no significant relationships among these variables.

Why have Hong Kong governments *not* been particularly concerned to demonstrate the 'independence' of bodies undertaking regulatory tasks by giving them more autonomy? Regulatory organizations can be found in a variety of guises in Hong Kong, ranging from departments (such as the FEHD which licenses restaurants and regulates food safety) to more independent agencies such as the Hong Kong Monetary Authority (HKMA) and the Securities and Futures Commission (SFC). The latter do have more autonomous personnel policies (they do not employ civil servants) and have their own funding sources (the HKMA from the Exchange Fund and the SFC from duty on stocks and futures transactions). They have considerable policy autonomy in practice, making policy together with the Financial Secretary and the Secretary for Financial Services and the Treasury. That is, there are some 'classic' independent regulatory bodies in Hong Kong, but it is just as likely that regulation is done in a department.

Perhaps because of the historical character of Hong Kong as an 'administrative state', 'politicization' of regulatory decisions is viewed as less of an issue because elected politicians have never been in charge. Still, the political executive seeks to exercise direct influence over the direction of regulatory policy (and even its details) in such areas as telecommunications (Painter and Wong 2007). But there would seem to be a high level of general trust that the executive will not 'politicize' regulatory decisions to the disadvantage of major stakeholders. Perhaps this reflects Hong Kong's consensual style of government-business relations in which the Hong Kong government makes great efforts to consult all stakeholders through a complex array of advisory bodies. It also possibly reflects a high level of trust in Hong Kong's independent judiciary and in the government's long tradition of abiding by the rule of law. Again in the case of telecommunications, the regulator and other actors pointed to the high incidence of litigation over regulatory decisions as a strong safeguard of neutrality (Painter and Wong 2007). Whatever the reasons, modern fashion, which insists that such bodies as telecommunications regulators must be autonomous, has had limited impact in Hong Kong.[13]

To this point, we have discussed task-related explanations for autonomy in terms of three variables: service delivery, regulation and political salience. Political salience turned out to have a quite powerful effect on autonomy, making it deserving of more attention. We operationalized political salience by equating it with perceptions of high levels of external influence. Turning to (P6) on policy field, the categories used for assigning the government bodies in our population to different policy fields correspond to the functional groupings of the government's policy bureau, providing a somewhat blunt but at least unambiguous sorting device (Table 6.5). We suggest that two portfolio areas – first, Economic Development and Labour and second, Financial Services (which includes taxation) – are the most likely to bring up redistributive issues which have high political salience and hence would have less organizational autonomy.

Table 6.5 shows no clear pattern to support (P6). For example, Financial Service organizations enjoy rather more (not less) operational policy

Table 6.5 Managerial autonomy and operational policy autonomy by policy domain (mean)

	Managerial autonomy	Operational policy autonomy
Environment, Transport and Works	0.43	0.54
Home Affairs	0.58	0.73
Housing, Planning and Lands	0.72	0.65
Security	0.36	0.52
Commerce, Industry and Technology	0.59	0.61
Economic Development and Labor	0.47	0.58
Financial Services	0.56	0.71

autonomy than most, although not markedly so. Nevertheless, on managerial autonomy in particular there is considerable variation across policy fields, the lowest being in Security and the highest in Housing, Planning and Lands. There is a broadly similar pattern for operational policy autonomy. Given these differences, how can we interpret the findings? Earlier, we suggested some contextual explanations for the lack of independent regulatory agencies in Hong Kong. Going further along such lines, are there some particular features of Hong Kong government and politics that would account for some of the variations demonstrated in Table 6.5?

Agencies in the field of Housing, Planning and Lands were perceived to be granted high degrees of managerial and operational policy autonomy, probably reflecting the technical nature of their task, which government officials at all levels have traditionally seen in largely engineering terms. Accordingly the departments and agencies in this domain perceive they have a high level of managerial and operational autonomy to get on with the 'apolitical' business of building public housing and providing for more land. This may appear surprising, as these issues can in other contexts be highly divisive and controversial (and increasingly are becoming so in Hong Kong). In view of such contextual features, more detailed analysis through case studies would seem called for.

At the other end of the spectrum, senior security officials (such as police, immigration, correctional services and fire services) perceive that they have less managerial and operational policy autonomy than officials in other policy domains. Hong Kong's colonial legacy, which has included serious anti-government riots encouraged by Cultural Revolutionaries in China that were only put down by the police (in 1967), has encouraged the political executive to maintain tight control over security in the territory (Scott 1989). Evidence of this is the large size of the security apparatus in Hong Kong compared to its population (Burns 2004). Recent developments such as anti-terrorism measures and a range of complex border issues have further heightened political interest in the security services. Close oversight of the security apparatus would thus not be surprising.

This is only part of the picture, however. Historically, some of the discipline services have claimed and won some important measures of independence due to their 'special nature'. They are highly professionalized and have strong staff associations and they have sometimes acted militantly. On certain key issues, security agencies have extracted considerable concessions about terms and conditions of service. For example, the police objected to the tight scrutiny they perceived they were under when the Independent Commission Against Corruption was set up in 1973 (the police rioted then) and more recently in 2001. Government granted an amnesty to police officers for corruption offences committed before the ICAC was set up and more recently nominated a security services insider (former Director of Immigration Ambrose SK Lee) first to head the ICAC in 2002 and then to the post of Secretary for Security to better liaise with the ICAC in 2003. In addition, the police have persuaded government to set up special staff relations machinery (the Police Force Council) and pay review machinery for the police (they have a separate pay scale from the rest of the security services, which have separate scales from the rest of the civil service) (Burns 2004). Moreover, police maladministration is not generally subject to Ombudsman review (see Ombudsman 2007). Rather, a special Complaints Against the Police Office has been set up to handle public complaints, which are all investigated by the police itself.[14] Finally, the security services were able to exempt themselves from certain reforms that the government applied to the rest of the civil service through special provisions (such as the introduction of employment contracts for the security services that lengthened the probation period from three to six years) (Burns 2004; Scott 2005). In sum, if we look more closely at particular cases, such as the police, we will get a more nuanced picture of the manner in which history and circumstance affects perceptions, as well as how autonomy in particular respects might be conceded in a context of generalized tight control.

6.8   Conclusion

This paper has explored the nature of autonomy in Hong Kong government bodies and has revealed some important features. The single clearest conclusion is that, while acknowledging the potential explanatory power of other perspectives, formal status (whether or not a government body is structured in formal or legal terms to be close to or distant from the 'core' of government) does predict the degree of autonomy enjoyed by government bodies as measured in our survey. Second, disaggregating these bodies into finer-grained structural categories provides some support for the proposition that on some aspects of autonomy (notably, financial management autonomy) structural features still matter. At the same time the considerable heterogeneity found within various structural categories does draw our attention to other explanatory factors. These findings are broadly consistent with others from parallel COBRA studies using a similar survey instrument: in Flanders the hypothesis that bodies with a more independent formal legal status would experience higher autonomy was found to be largely but *not* strongly supported (particularly in the case of managerial and policy autonomy) (Verhoest *et al.* 2004a: 111); and in Norway, the relationship between structural features and autonomy held up only in the case of financial management autonomy (Lægreid *et al.* 2005b: 22–3).[15]

An important finding was that managers generally perceive that they have relatively high levels of autonomy on strategic policy goal setting: we suggest that this partly reflects the cooperative nature of policy-making among senior officials between departmental bodies and their respective policy bureaux. But when it comes to personnel and financial management issues, hierarchical control (not cooperation) is more evident. This seems to suggest that what matters critically to the leaders and controllers of Hong Kong's administrative state – who, in the past, were mostly civil servants – is (not surprisingly) keeping a tight hold on administrative relations between the government and the public. This claim finds support from the relationship found between political salience, a task-related feature, and the perceived degree of autonomy: the more an organization reported influence from groups in the society on its decisions, the less managerial autonomy it experienced from its political and/or administrative superiors.

In exploring other task-related features, we found some relationships between task or policy domain and autonomy. Some task-related arguments do seem to have influenced how governments make decisions about structure. In Hong Kong, bodies that perform public service delivery tasks are more likely to take the departmental form. They also perceive that they have relatively low levels of control over operational policy matters. Interestingly, we found no evidence that regulatory tasks are more likely to be given to non-departmental bodies, nor that bodies that primarily do regulatory tasks enjoy any more autonomy. Hong Kong governments, in granting or allowing autonomy to administrative public bodies, are not particularly swayed by contemporary orthodoxies in favour of the 'independent regulatory agency'. This finding is consistent with a similar result in the case of Norway, another jurisdiction where NPM has received a mixed reception (Lægreid *et al.* 2008b). Given that there has not been a strong trend in Hong Kong towards converting departments into non-departmental bodies in recent years, the strong correlation between non-departmental status and high managerial autonomy is more probably a product of earlier developments, not something that has blown in with the winds of fashion.

Of course, there remain unanswered questions. There are further variables to be explored other than those related to formal structure and nature of task (for example, cultural variables). For these purposes other analytical tools not deployed in this paper, such as (at one end of the spectrum) multivariate analysis and (at the other end) detailed case studies, should be able to take the analysis further.

Notes

1. Research for this publication was funded by the Hong Kong Research Grants Council with a Competitive Earmarked Grant Project No CityU 1440/06H: 'Autonomy, Control and Performance in Hong Kong Government Bodies'. Sam Pang, Senior Research Associate, City University of Hong Kong, provided invaluable research assistance and oversaw the conduct of the survey. Bram Verschuere of the Faculty of Business and Public Administration, University College Ghent visited Hong Kong in February 2007 and clarified for us key questions about the COBRA conceptual framework, while also assisting in the adaptation of the questionnaire. The on-line platform for the survey was provided by our COBRA colleagues at the University of Leuven, whom we thank for the facility provided.
2. For a discussion of this and related concepts, see Pollitt *et al.* (2004).
3. For details of the survey see below.
4. A potential weakness of this categorization, if used to characterize whole policy sectors, is that it ignores the common observation that the same issue can generate considerable conflict and deep division at one point in time, but not another. Moreover, within a single sector, issues of all three types could occur.
5. The formal identification of the role of Bureau Chief as a 'political' one (akin to a minister) did not occur until July 2002, when Chief Executive Tung Chee Hwa introduced the so-called 'Principal Officials Accountability System'.
6. Contrast the Hong Kong Tourism Board, which was created as a statutory body to market and promote Hong Kong as a world class tourist destination.
7. This definition of the population was designed to conform to the COBRA template for which the study was conducted. See http://www.publicmanagement-cobra.org/ (Comparative Public Organization Data Base for Research and Analysis) for an introduction to the survey goals and design.
8. Accordingly we excluded a very large number of purely advisory and consultative bodies, with no separate budget and no decision-making powers. In addition, we excluded the local district councils.
9. The population of 111 bodies comprised 55 departments and 56 non-departmental bodies. Of the respondents, 31 were departments and 32 were non-departmental bodies.
10. The composite variable 'Managerial Autonomy' is used throughout this chapter rather than its separate components.
11. Eight of these bodies currently exist, of which four responded to our survey.
12. This technique was used by Verhoest *et al.* (2004a).
13. It should be noted, however, that the telecommunications regulator as an 'authority' does have certain independent powers of the kind many officers

have traditionally enjoyed in other fields, such as the ombudsman, police commissioner and civil service commissioner; however, the agency is a department and the regulator is a civil servant.

14. The Independent Police Complaints Council, composed of non-police officers, oversees the police handling of complaints against it.

15. These studies were explicitly restricted to 'non-departmental' agencies, unlike the Hong Kong survey.

7
Determinants of Result-based Control in Italian Agencies

Dario Barbieri, Paolo Fedele, Davide Galli
and Edoardo Ongaro[1]

7.1   Introduction

Explaining the form of public sector organizations, and ultimately the decision-making behaviour of public sector organizations as the key dependent variable, is a major contribution that organizational theory has to offer to the study of the public sector. In this chapter, we investigate the characteristics of the relationships between agencies and their parent administration in the Italian central government. The study, rooted in organizational theory, adopts different theoretical angles, at first a 'cultural-normative' approach mainly embedded in a logic of appropriateness perspective (March and Olsen 1996, 1994, 1989), then an approach focused on instrumental rationality mainly embedded in a logic of consequences perspective (for an overview of different streams in organization theory for the study of the public sector, see Christensen *et al.* 2007).

Governments in many countries have established semi-autonomous single-purpose organizations (OECD 2002a), to which we refer as public agencies, and Italy has been no exception in this respect (Ongaro 2008 and 2006). How to wield the control function towards agencies has become a prominent area of research in public management. Many studies address the topic of control as a 'systemic' issue, as the notion of control has been related to the way the relationships among various actors are coordinated in order to achieve a common public goal (Kaufmann 1986). Other studies deal with the concept of control as an inter-organizational coordination tool (Klijn 2005; Narad 2006; Verhoest *et al.* 2007b). Other authors have explored control as an accountability-related theme (Mulgan 2000; Gregory 2003; Bovens *et al.* 2008) or even more generally as a central issue in public administration and public management reform (Kettl 2000; Romzek 2000).

As a starting point, we may assume that there are two broad modalities whereby control of agencies is exercised: *ex ante* controls and *ex post* controls. *Ex ante* controls (Wirth 1986; Thompson 1993; Verhoest *et al.* 2004b) refer to a broad set of mechanisms ranging from the appointment of the director general/CEO and the members of the board to the definition of rules and standards by the parent organization to which the agency has to comply (constraining the behaviour in order to steer the agency towards the outputs desired by the parent administration). This perspective refers both to the formal-structural aspects of the ministry-agency relationship (Egeberg 2003) and to other forms of control that can be read (also) through the lens of the theory of clans (Ouchi 1980) – whereby control is pursued through the selection and appointment of top executives having clannish relations (in the sense clarified by Ouchi) with the 'political master' in the parent administration.

The second perspective is based on the assumption that the 'parent' administration can steer and control 'its' agency by setting the goals it is expected to pursue and controlling *ex post* their achievement. This second perspective largely refers to the management control and performance management literature (Bouckaert and van Dooren 2003; Lægreid *et al.* 2006a; Moynihan 2006a; Bouckaert and Halligan 2008) and has important roots in the notion of 'Management by Objectives and Results', which, following many other authors, we define as a performance management concept that 'entails a redoubled attempt to operationalize goals for government and to use these goals more actively both in choosing between alternative actions and in evaluating results' (Christensen *et al.* 2007, 89). *Ex post* control, or result based control, concerns the assignment of goals to the agency and the assessment of their achievement by the parent administration, as well as the possible execution of sanctions or attribution of rewards associated to the degree of achievement of goals. The complex nature of the relationships between the parent administration and the agency based on a performance management logic has recently been studied with reference to the autonomy-control balance (Verschuere 2007; Barbieri and Ongaro 2008) or as an indicator of 'NPMness' of such relationships (Verhoest *et al.* 2004a; Verschuere and Barbieri 2009).

This chapter addresses the research question of what are the determinants of result-based forms of control. The analysis is focused on the *ex post* result control for three main reasons: the already extensive literature on *ex ante* control instruments on Italian agencies, which contrasts with the absence of any systematic investigation of the determinants of result-based controls; the chance to compare the findings on the impact of the selected independent variables (age, staff size, budget size, type of task and policy field) with investigations performed in other countries (see this book, and in the range of recent works on the topic the contributions by Lægreid *et al.* 2006; Verschuere 2007); the opportunity to empirically investigate the degree of implementation of a major public management reform that occurred in Italy in 1999, that had the declared goal of introducing forms of result-based control in the Italian public sector. In the study of the determinants of result-based control, we have at first considered that the forms of control between the agency and the parent administration may be determined by institutionalization processes that unfold over time under the influence of certain factors. We assume both ministries and agencies to be institutionalized organizations and we investigate their relationship on the basis of factors that may affect the organizational form of their relationship. Factors like age, size, type of task executed, and the policy field in which the agency and the ministry operate have been considered.

A supplement of investigation was required, however, since the statistical analysis did not provide conclusive evidence about the influence such factors may have on the form of control. We then adopted a different perspective, and considered the reform processes that occurred in Italy over the last two decades (Ongaro 2009). In the range of a number of reform programmes that were launched during that period in Italy, one can be singled out as regards the area of the organizational form of central government agencies and the agency-ministry relationship: in fact, in 1999 a comprehensive reform of the central government prescribed, within the framework of a general re-organization of state administrations, the establishment of a number of new agencies patterned on a well-identified model, which can be easily recognized in the UK 'Next Steps' model of public agency. Though it is beyond the scope of this chapter to investigate the policy process that led to the enactment of this reform programme, for the purposes of this work we may consider that a well-specified model of public agency, centred on result-based control, was intentionally introduced in the Italian central administration. From a hierarchically oriented instrumental perspective on reform (Christensen *et al.* 2007, chapters two and seven), we may quite straightforwardly state that the executive government at the higher level forced the introduction of a new organizational form in the Italian central public administration. What have been the effects of this reform on *ex post* controls in the relationship between agencies and their parent administration? Has this new organizational form, and particularly the type of result-based control which is a central component of it, institutionalized over time? As illustrated in closer detail later in this chapter, this reform has led to establishing a set of agencies that can be singled out of the overall population of the investigated central government agencies because of their high level of result-control. However, the reform has apparently not been 'institutionalized' and the broader population of Italian central government agencies (encompassing those agencies established subsequently to the 1999 reform) displays a level of result-based control markedly different from that of the agencies established by the 1999 reform.

The chapter is structured as follows: at first, an overview of the recent reform process in Italy is presented, with a specific focus on the 1999 reform; then, the hypotheses are outlined and the overall research design is described and the variables operationalized; data analysis is carried out; the findings are discussed and concluding remarks end the work.

7.2   The reform processes of the 1990s and public agencies

The establishment of agencies for carrying out public functions is not a novelty in the Italian context. Over the last century, in fact, many arm-length organizations have been created, through different acts and during different reform waves; the establishment of such bodies has occurred, however, without a deliberate strategy based on agencies as an organizational model for the public sector (Sepe *et al.* 2003). The number of agencies has however increased remarkably over the last decade and a half, a period of profound transformations of the Italian public sector (Ongaro and Valotti 2008; Ongaro forthcoming, 2009 and 2008). A major reform of the organization of the central government was enacted in 1999, through two legislative decrees. This reform can be considered a 'watershed' event: it was probably the first deliberate attempt to introduce a comprehensive reform of the organization of the central administration in the Italian administrative history (Sepe *et al.* 2003). Since the unification in the 19th century, in fact, there seems to be continuity in the formal organizational models, notwithstanding the transformations that occurred to the public sector in terms of size and role in the economy.

The reform package prescribed the merger of certain ministries and the re-organization of their internal lines of control along the so-called 'departmental' model, a sort of divisional model, in the terminology of

Mintzberg (1983). Concerning the subject of this chapter, the reform prescribed the establishment of eleven executive agencies, that were to operate in different policy sectors (Barbieri 2006; Ongaro 2006; Fedele *et al.* 2007). These agencies were explicitly inspired by the UK Next Steps' experience (Greer 1994 and 1992) and the so-called tripod model (Pollitt *et al.* 2004), stressing the importance of managerial autonomy and *ex post* result-based control. The large majority of the designed agencies were the result of a structural disaggregation, i.e. an internal unit of the ministries, specialized on a given area, was transformed into an 'agency'. The new organizations enjoyed a certain degree of managerial autonomy for what concerns financial and personnel management, although within the general regulation of central administrations. The provisions of the reform law were particularly innovative, in the landscape of the Italian public sector, as regards the approach to steering and control: the reform introduced a performance contract between the minister and the agency as a key component of the ministry–agency relationship. Though problematically from a legal–juridical standpoint, from an organizational point of view this agreement can be interpreted as a contract.

According to the reform act, this contract should, first of all, specify agency goals and the expected results with reference to a given period of time. The law states that the statute of each agency will prescribe 'the definition, through a convention that has to be stipulated between the minister and the director of the agency, of the goals specifically attributed to the latter, within the scope of the mission assigned by the law to the agency'. The definition of the funds to be allocated to the agency will also occur through the convention, as will the results to be achieved in a given time frame, as well as the modalities for 'verification of the results of the management of the agency'. The convention will also specify the 'strategies for the improvement of services' as well as 'the modalities whereby the ministry will be ensured the knowledge about the managerial factors of the agency, like its organizational design, the business processes, and the use of resources' (Point e. of Article 8 of Legislative Decree 300/99). Besides the highly legalistic style adopted by the text of the reform, the novelty represented by such prescriptions in the Italian system was quite substantial, since the regulation through a convention of the allocation of resources, and their connection with 'measured' targets represented something quite unusual. The provision of a 'performance contract' however was not the only component of the steering and control model envisaged by 1999 reform. The ministry retains formal powers of supervision on the agencies and can issue guidelines and directives. Furthermore, the ministry plays a substantive role in defining the statutes of the newly created organization as well as in the appointment of the director of the agency.

The implementation of the 1999 reform, however, was rather problematic. Four fiscal agencies were established in 2001, all operating in the policy field of the former finance ministry. These organizations are the only ones that were actually established under the frame of the decree 300 and fully correspond from a formal point of view to the design model it prescribed. Certain other agencies, although prescribed by the reform act, were established through *ad hoc* single acts by posterior government coalitions; still other agencies were closed down before they could even start their activities and never became operative. In the remainder of the chapter, we will refer to the four fiscal agencies as the '1999 agencies', since they are the only ones to have been formally shaped by the model designed by the reform embodied in the decree 300/99.

7.3   Theoretical background and hypotheses

Determinants of the shape of agencies have been analysed under many theoretical perspectives (Pollitt and Talbot 2004). One mainstream approach (Pollitt 2006; Lægreid *et al.* 2008) looks for the determinants of agency shape, its autonomy and the related forms of steering and control in certain agency-specific features which contribute, over time, to shape the ministry-agency deal. Such factors are, in broad terms, the structure of agencies, the organizational culture of agencies, and the primary task performed by the agency. In the present paragraph, based on this theoretical classification, a group of hypotheses is formulated with regard to result control in Italian public agencies.

The first perspective considered here is the structural instrumental one. This vision assumes that the formal organizational features influence the way autonomy and control are regarded by supervising bodies, as well as by the agency itself. The variable here considered is agency size in terms of staff, as an indicator of structural capacity (Egeberg 2003; Verschuere 2006; Lægreid *et al.* 2008b). Large staff agencies have more administrative capacity, i.e. the potential of elaborating information (Brambilla *et al.* 1999) and delivering outputs (Painter and Pierre 2005). Moreover, larger staff means more resources and stronger expertise that can eventually lead to higher power in the face of the supervising authority. As a reaction to this state of affairs, key agents in the ministry could be concerned about the risks associated to the potential autonomy of large agencies, such as loss of power and control over the agency by the same ministry. Consequently, when staff size increases, key agents in the ministry (intended as rational actors) could be willing to play a more active role in target-setting and monitoring results, in order to reduce information asymmetry and goal incongruence. This hypothesis is based on one major assumption: that autonomy, on one hand, and steering and control, on the other hand, are *distinct* dimensions that are however *closely interconnected* in the sense that enhanced autonomy triggers the activation of enhanced forms of control in order to restore a balance between autonomy and control. At the root of this balance lies the perspective of the ministry-agency deal being continuously adjusted in a dynamic way (under the assumption that officials in the agency pursue greater autonomy, and officials in the ministry pursue higher control). The hypothesis is then:

H1. Result control by supervising ministry is stronger in large staff agencies.

The second perspective focuses on how organizational culture can affect behaviour within organizations. Public organizations, in this specific case ministries and agencies, are not only formally designed structures, but also value-bearing institutions. The ministry-agency deal, consequently, will be influenced by the informal norms and values developed over time in the organizations under analysis. Finding a good measure of culture is not an easy task: agency age is here considered as a potential indicator of stronger organizational culture. It could be reasonably argued that older organizations have a stronger identity than newly created ones. A distinct organizational culture (Schein 1985) can develop over time. Consequently, older agencies are potentially more 'infused with values' (Selznick 1957) than newly created ones. An organization with a strong identity and an 'autonomous' culture tend to resist the pressures from external actors; when applied to agencies, this means that older agencies may, in a broad sense, better resist the oversight and the scrutiny by the parent ministry. Older agencies, consequently, could more effectively try to weaken the principal's supervision. Assuming again the perspective of the dynamic balance between autonomy and control, key agents in the parent administration could be willing to play a more active role in target-setting and monitoring results in order to reduce information asymmetry and goal incongruence and the related risks in term of cheating and loss of power. The hypothesis is then:

H2. Result control by supervising ministry is stronger in older agencies.

The third perspective focuses on task features as a key explanatory factor of the ministry-agency deal (Pollitt 2006; Lægreid *et al.* 2008b). The underlying assumption is that the nature of the task influences the type of scrutiny the ministry can perform. Task features can potentially matter in different ways (Pollitt 2006). First of all, some activities produce observable outputs and outcomes, or outputs that can be easily measured, while others are more difficult to observe, measure and standardise (Wilson 1989). Activities of the first type (for example, the services delivered by ICE, Agency for the Development of Export, that provides information and technical assistance for companies operating abroad) can more easily be monitored than activities of the second type (for example, those of the National Aviation Security Agency, that issues authorizations and regulates the behaviour of carriers in the field of air transportation). In the first case, it is easier to specify goals, performance measures and targets as well as recollect data for performance evaluation than it is in the second case. Broadly speaking, service production is an activity of the first type, while issuing and/or enforcing regulation can be considered a task of the second kind. Organizations which perform activities of the first kind will more easily undergo a stronger influence by politicians and supervising authorities through target-setting and performance measurement systems. Consequently, the hypothesis is:

H3. Result control is stronger in agencies whose primary task is service delivery.

The second relevant task-related variable is political salience (Krause 2003; Pollitt 2006). An issue or a policy area where the agency operates is salient if it is of relevance for public opinion and interest groups and it is often in the spotlight. If the agency performs a task which is politically salient, it is more likely that control by supervising authorities will be tighter. If the agency's task concerns non-controversial issues, politicians will be less worried of the consequences of the agency's behaviour and control will be looser. Policy area can be classified according to different criteria, making the picture quite complex; here we will cut the

Gordian knot and distinguish only two groups: economic policy area and other policy areas. Since economic issues, that often touch upon powerful organized interests (Gilardi 2006), are usually in the spotlight, the hypothesis is:

> H4. Result control is stronger in agencies within the economic fields than in agencies operating in all other fields

The third task-related variable which is deemed to be influential on the steering and control of agency is budget size. Budget size can be considered as a component of political salience. It can be reasonably assumed, in fact, that big state organizations (in the terms of the weight of their budget) are under strict scrutiny by governments because their course of action can massively affect the overall state budget (Pollitt 2006). Small budget agencies, on the contrary, cannot produce relevant consequences in terms of public expenditure and so they are more likely to be kept out of this strict control. Consequently, it may be argued that politicians will impose a complex set of indicators to keep big budget agencies controlled and constantly monitor their outputs and outcomes. The hypothesis is thus:

> H5. Result control is stronger in large budget agencies.

Before we proceed to hypotheses testing, the overall research design is outlined, a task to which we turn in the next section.

7.4 The overall research design

The analysis has focused on agencies at the central (national) level of government. The population is made up of only those bodies presenting the characteristic of being the only ones in the public landscape to exercise a given (range of) public function(s). To identify the units of the population, on the one hand the list of public bodies included in the 'consolidated' state budget has been considered, excluding all those that do not have the property of being single organizations in the Italian public system. The web page of all the ministries have been surveyed, in order to identify other bodies that, though not included in the consolidated state budget, do exercise a public function and are situated at arm's length from the ministry. No juridical classification has been adopted: the list includes departmental bodies, public law agencies, as well as private law entities such as some state-owned companies. Institutional-organizational features have been the basis for the definition of the subject of analysis. The final list included 57 agencies. Respondents were 40, the response rate has been 70 per cent.

Data have been collected through a survey conducted over the period October–December 2006, adapting to the Italian setting the methodology developed by the international research network named 'COBRA' (www.publicmanagement-cobra.org/survey). Data collection has occurred through a questionnaire, featuring two sets of closed-ended questions:

- first set: basic features of agencies and environment;
- second set: mechanisms of steering and control of the agencies.

The questionnaire has been sent to the CEO/General Director of all the agencies included in the population with an invitation letter jointly signed by the Italian department of public administration that financed the project, and SDA Bocconi School of Management. Each agency was requested to identify the function of the respondent, if different from the CEO/General Director (answers to the questionnaire have in all instances been validated by the CEO/General Director, in order to reach an appreciable level of uniformity in the interpretation of the answers).

The analysis is based on five independent variables: the age of the agency, its budget and staff size, the task performed and the policy field in which the agency operates. For statistical reasons all the five variables have been clustered as discrete variables. The age variable has been clustered in two clusters (pre-1999 and post-1999 as date of establishment). Budget and staff size have been clustered in three clusters (budget size: zero–10, 10–50, and above 50 million euros; staff size: zero–50, 50–500, above 500 employees). Concerning task, agencies have been clustered as performing operative and regulative tasks; the policy field has been clustered in economic policy and other fields. The dependent variable utilized as the indicator of the intensity of result-control on agencies is the Result Control Index (RCINDEX – see Verschuere and Barbieri 2009). It represents a five step result control process including: (1) setting organizational goals (2) specifying indicators for measuring the organizational results (3) measuring the organizational results (4) evaluating of the organizational results (5) issuing sanctions and/or rewards in case of poor/good results. Using those five steps it is possible to create an index, following a 'cumulative' logic (Verschuere 2007): the assumption behind this index is that an agency can be controlled in one step of the cycle by the parent ministry only if it is controlled also in the previous step.[2] What matters is not whether one agency is controlled at one or more steps of the process but if there is a cumulative (and progressive) presence of the parent ministry in the cycle. For completeness of analysis, also the un-weighted index has been considered and an analysis of the gamma correlation of the dimensions composing the RCINDEX computed (Table 7.1).

The RCINDEX is operationalized in the questionnaire by asking the respondent if result control is specified in a steering document, agreed upon between the agency and the ministry. If there is a steering document (first phase of the result-result control cycle) then the respondent is asked to specify (a) if a document setting the goals exist (GOALDOC) (b) if the organizational goals are set by the same organization (GOAL) (c) if there are indicators for measuring the organizational results (IND) (d) if there is the actual measurement of the organizational results (MEANS) (e) if there is an evaluation of the organizational results (EVAL) (f) if sanctions and/ or rewards in case of poor/good results are issued (SB). This leads to the RCINDEX. In case no goals are documented the score of the index is 'zero'. If the goals are documented, but they are specified by other actor than the organization the score is '0.16'. If the organization is involved in the goal setting (assumed that the goals are documented), the score is '0.33'. If the previous steps of the cycle have been satisfied and indicators to measure results exist, the value is '0.50'. If, in addition, these results are measured, the score is '0.67'. The evaluation of these results by the oversight authorities raises the score to '0.83'. If mechanisms of rewards or sanctions in case of good/poor results exist, the final score is 'one' (maximum value). The un-weighted index is the result of the sum of the six dimensions divided by six.

It may be noted that the RCINDEX is conceptually more articulated than what prescribed by the design of the 1999 reform; however, one can logically argue that if goals have to be specifically attributed to the agency (Point e. of Article eight of Law 300/99 – see section 7.2), then goals must be documented. More problematic is deriving from the provisions of the law any assumption about whether the agency is involved in goal setting – although the fact that the convention is 'stipulated between the ministry and the agency' seems to give leeway to the consideration that both parties should have a role. As regards the measurement of results, the reform law prescribed that 'verification of the results of the agency' has to be carried out. It is a logical connection that an evaluation should then be carried out, before rewards or sanctions are delivered. That the allocation of funds be an integral part of the convention is prescribed by the law, although the causal connection with results can only be deducted from the general framework of the law.

In order to calculate the relationship between the independent variables and the weighted and un-weighted RCINDEX (dependent variable), the Mann-Whitney U Test[3] (for age, task and policy field) and the Kruskal-Wallis Test[4] (for budget size and staff size) have been performed. As a further analysis, the mean (and also minimum, maximum and standard deviation) of the (weighted and un-weighted) RCINDEX scores in the overall population and in two clusters (pre and post 1999 reform agencies, including or not the fiscal agencies created in 2001) have been calculated.

7.5   Data analysis

7.5.1   Result control in Italian agencies: descriptive results

First of all, a cross tabulation of the RCINDEX dimensions has been calculated (summed up by Gamma measure) in order to assess the strength of their relationships. The results are summarized in Table 7.1.

Data suggest a positive correlation between the existence of a document in which the goals are set, the setting of the goals by the same organization and the presence of indicators. The evaluation of the results, the presence of indicators and the measurement of the results are also positively correlated. There is a significant correlation between the measurement on the one hand and the presence of sanctions and rewards on the other hand. Surprisingly, there is no significant relationship between the specification of the results and all the other dimensions (with the exception of the existence of the document and a border significant correlation between specification of the results and the presence of rewards and sanctions). It is worth highlighting also the absence of significant correlation between evaluation and the presence of rewards and sanctions.

Table 7.1   Gamma correlations of the RCINDEX dimensions (N = 40)

	GOALDOC	GOAL	IND	MEANS	EVAL
GOAL	0.78*				
IND	0.43*	0.07			
MEANS	0.08	0.04	0.45*		
EVAL	0.22	−0.12	0.51**	0.34**	
SB	0.34	0.30	0.19	0.50*	0.01

Notes: * Gamma correlation is significant at the 0.05 level;
** Gamma correlation is significant at the 0.01 level.

On one side, the results of the gamma correlation may indicate that some factors of incoherence may exist in the implementation of the *ex post* control processes in the Italian agencies, in particular for what concerns the application of mechanisms of rewards and punishment as a consequence of a good/bad performance of the agency. On the other side, the positive correlation between the existence of indicators, measurement, and evaluation may reveal a (partially) coherent design of the *ex post* control process, but only loosely coupled with the result specification as well as sanction and rewards.

7.5.2 Result control in agencies: explanatory results

The significance of the correlation between the independent variables and both the weighted and the un-weighted RCINDEX has been tested using the Mann-Whitney U Test and the Kruskal-Wallis Test. The results are summarized in Tables 7.2 and 7.3.

The results of the Mann-Whitney U Test (for age, task and policy field) and Kruskal-Wallis Test (for budget and staff size), computed on the whole population, do not show appreciable results in terms of explaining the variation of the extent to which result control components (as measured through the RCINDEX) are in operation as a consequence of variations of the selected independent variables.

Table 7.2 Mann-Whitney U test on the RCINDEX (differences between old and young agencies, between agencies with operative and regulative tasks, and between agencies operating in economic and other policy fields)

	RCINDEX (Weighted)	RCINDEX (Un-weighted)
AGE		
Pre 1999 (mean rank)	20.42	18.68
Post 1999 (mean rank)	20.63	23.53
Mann-Whitney U	185.5	142.0
Sig.	0.95	0.19
TASK		
OPE (mean rank)	21.64	21.64
REG (mean rank)	17.50	17.50
Mann-Whitney U	126.5	126.5
Sig.	0.32	0.32
POLICY FIELD		
Economic (mean rank)	25.21	24.54
Other (mean rank)	18.48	18.77
Mann-Whitney U	111.5	119.5
Sig.	0.84	0.14

Table 7.3 Kruskal-Wallis test (SPSS) on the RCINDEX (differences between bigger (budget and staff size) agencies)

	RCINDEX	RCINDEX (Un-weighted)
Budget		
0–10 Mil. Euro (mean rank)	19.75	20.65
10–50 Mil. Euro (mean rank)	15.09	16.19
>50 Mil. Euro (mean rank)	20.82	21.12
Kruskal-Wallis Chi-Square	2.21	2.14
Sig.	0.33	0.24
Staff		
0–50 staff (mean rank)	13.50	12.01
50–500 (mean rank)	17.63	18.98
>500 (mean rank)	21.20	20.75
Kruskal-Wallis Chi-Square	2.48	2.89
Sig.	0.28	0.32

7.5.3 Result control in agencies: the impact of the 1999 reforms

Given the poor explanatory power of the independent variables, the task of elaborating some purposeful descriptive statistics has been under-taken. Knowledge of the context provided a cue: given the stated goal of the 1999 reform to introduce a form of result-based control for the newly established public agencies, it has been deemed worth exploring the differences between the cluster of agencies established before 1999 and those established after 1999, with an additional distinction between the agencies directly stemming from the provisions of the 1999 decree and those that did not. All the dimensions of the RCINDEX have been computed (see Tables 7.4, 7.5 and 7.6). Agencies have been clustered into two groups, depending on their date of establishment (pre and post 1999 – including or not the fiscal agencies that were established after the 1999 reform). Table 7.7, showing the frequencies of the scores of the RCINDEX, is also presented.

The results show that the un-weighted RCINDEX is always higher, in all the clusters considered, than the weighted RCINDEX. *Ex post* 1999 agencies present higher levels of RCINDEX (weighted and un-weighted) than the pre 1999 agencies, even if the latter show a lower level of un-weighted RCINDEX when disaggregating the fiscal agencies from the cluster. The impact of the four fiscal agencies established by the 1999 reform is indeed relevant and induces a relevant shift in the value of both the weighted and the un-weighted RCINDEX. Concerning the mean values and the frequency of the items, sanctions and rewards are

Table 7.4 Results of descriptive statistics – RCINDEX and its dimensions (N and mean values)

	GOALDOC (goals are documented)	GOAL (goals are specified by the same organization)	IND (indicators to measure results exist)	MEANS (results are measures)	EVAL (results are evaluated by oversight authority)	SB (sanctions and rewards exist)	RC INDEX (unweighted)	RC INDEX (weighted)
All Agencies (N)	40	33	20	18	15	26		
(Mean value)	1.00	0.83	0.50	0.45	0.38	0.65	0.63	0.48
Pre '99 (N)	25	21	11	10	7	15		
(Mean value)	1.00	0.84	0.44	0.40	0.28	0.60	0.59	0.46
Post '99 (N)	15	12	9	8	8	11		
(Mean value)	1.00	0.80	0.60	0.53	0.53	0.73	0.70	0.50
Post '99 without fiscal agencies (N)	11	9	5	4	4	7		
(Mean value)	1.00	0.82	0.45	0.36	0.36	0.64	0.61	0.39

Table 7.5 Results of descriptive statistics – RCINDEX and its dimensions (% of the items)

		GOALDOC (goals are documented)	GOAL (goals are specified by the same organization)	IND (indicators to measure results exist)	MEANS (results are measures)	EVAL (results are evaluated by oversight authority)	SB (sanctions and rewards exist)
All agencies	Yes	100	83	50	45	38	65
	No	0	27	50	55	62	35
Pre-1999	Yes	100	84	44	40	28	60
	No	0	16	66	60	72	40
Post-1999	Yes	100	80	60	53	53	73
	No	0	20	40	47	47	27
Post-1999 (without fiscal agencies)	Yes	100	82	45	36	36	64
	No	0	18	55	64	64	36

Table 7.6 Results of descriptive statistics – RCINDEX weighted and un-weighted (details)

All agencies (Valid N = 40)	RCINDEX Min. (unweighted)	RCINDEX Max. (unweighted)	RCINDEX Standard Deviation (unweighted)	RCINDEX Min. (weighted)	RCINDEX Max. (weighted)	RCINDEX Standard Deviation (weighted)
All Agencies (N)	40.00	40.00	40.00	40.00	40.00	40.00
All Agencies	0.16	1.00	0.30	0.16	1.00	0.40
Pre-1999 (N)	25.00	25.00	25.00	25.00	25.00	25.00
Pre-1999	0.16	1.00	0.20	0.16	1.00	0.25
Pos-1999 (N)	15.00	15.00	15.00	15.00	15.00	15.00
Post-1999	0.33	1.00	0.15	0.16	1.00	0.32
Post-1999 without fiscal agencies (N)	11.00	11.00	40.00	11.00	11.00	40.00
Post-1999 without fiscal agencies	0.33	1.00	0.11	0.16	1.00	0.20

Table 7.7 Results of descriptive statistics – scores of RCINDEX weighted and un-weighted

	RCI	0%	0,16	0,33	0,5	0,67	0,83	1
All agencies	Weighted	0	20	37.50	15	7.50	2.5	17.50
	Un-weighted	0	2.50	20	25	17.50	17.50	17.50
Pre-1999	Weighted	0	16	42	12	12	4	12
	Un-weighted	0	4	23	23	19	15	16
Post-1999	Weighted	0	27	27	19	0	0	27
	Un-weighted	0	0	13	27	13	20	27
Post-1999	Weighted	0	27	36	27	0	0	10
(without	Un-weighted	0	0	18	36	18	18	10
fiscal								
agencies)								

always higher, in all clusters considered, than the measurement and the evaluation dimensions, and in some instances also higher than the other dimensions. To conclude, goals are always documented, but the agencies are not always involved in the specification of the goals. It is important to underline that the results of the descriptive statistics are coherent with the analysis of the gamma correlations of the RCINDEX dimensions. The distinction between weighted and un-weighted RCINDEX, not relevant in the case of the explanatory analysis, influences the results of the descriptive analysis: the cumulative nature of the weighted RCINDEX absorbs the effect of the outlier dimension 'presence of sanctions and rewards' but this does not happen in the case of the un-weighted index.

7.6   Discussion and conclusion

What considerations can be drawn from the analysis of data? As a first point, it emerges from the statistical analysis that it is not possible to state whether there is any influence of age, size, task or policy on result-control. The only partial exception in this respect regards the policy field, about which it appears that agencies operating in the economic policy field are indeed more controlled than other agencies, thus providing partial confirmation to hypothesis four. Besides this (border significant) finding, it seems that searching for the determinants of the agency shape in factors like age, staff or budget size, or the task performed is not conducive to explaining the extent to which *ex post* result-control will be employed.

Other considerations emerge from the clustering of agencies produced by using as watershed event the 1999 reform. Fully-fledged result control appears to be employed only in the case of the four agencies that were established as a direct effect of the 1999 reform. But this cluster represents an outlier in the overall picture of Italian central agencies: the value of the result-control index is 0.63 (un-weighted) and 0.48 (weighted) for the overall population. Interestingly, if we partition the population of agencies and we consider the agencies established before 1999 and those established after 1999 (that is, we exclude from the population the agencies established by the 1999 reform and partition the remainder on the basis of the alleged watershed nature of this event), we discover that agencies established *before* 1999 have a weighed result-control index which is superior to the index of the post-1999 agencies excluding the fiscal agencies (0.46 vs 0.39); as regards the unweighted result-control index, in this case the post-1999 agencies have an only slightly superior value (0.61 vs 0.59 of the agencies established before 1999); agencies established after 1999 excluding the fiscal agencies have both weighed and un-weighed result-control index inferior to the overall population.

We have dwelled a bit upon the details of the RCI of the different clusters because they point to one interesting finding: the reform of executive agencies carried out in 1999 and inspired by the UK 'Next Steps' reform programme seems to have left a mark only on a specific subset of agencies (the fiscal agencies); the 1999 reform has *not* determined any significant shift in the pattern of control of Italian agencies. 'Traditional' control arrangements have remained in operation – which does not mean that there is no overall consistency in the system of controls: as previously observed, the positive correlation between the existence of indicators, measurement, and evaluation may reveal a (partially) coherent design of the *ex post* system of control, although such components are not at all or only loosely coupled with components like result specification and sanction and rewards. But what emerges is that the 1999 reform has been only limitedly implemented, and has not marked any change in the pattern of agency control adopted in the Italian public sector. This may add confidence to investigations rooted in the perspective of historical institutionalism that tend to put emphasis on continuity or small changes, that only at some critical junctures or because of the triggering of specific mechanisms may lead to major changes – whilst in general persistence of administrative styles is the norm.

What lessons can be drawn from this investigation of agencies in Italy for the study of the phenomenon of agencies more broadly? We will stress one point: the importance of 'contextual' knowledge about the processes of public management reform in the country where the study on agencies is conducted. Agencies are sometimes the product of long-term historical processes and the layering of a multiplicity of interventions on the configuration of the public sector in a country. On other occasions, however, they are the intentional product of reform programmes that are shaped by relatively well-specified ideas and models about how they should function: this has been the case especially during the last two and a half decades of 'global' public management reform during which many ambitious, broad-scope reform programmes have been launched in many countries.

Models about how public agencies should function may have different origins: they may be the result of instrumentally rational assessment and selection of alternatives, or they may be 'organizational myths' spreading internationally and well received by policy-makers and practitioners in one country looking for the legitimacy deriving from the introduction of 'modern' organizational arrangements in the public sector of their country.[5] However, independently of their origins, what matters for the purposes of our study is that such reforms may be very specific as concerns one or more of the factors employed in the study of agency form. As regards age, they may have occurred recently or late in time; they may regard only 'large' or only 'small' size agencies;[6] they may target agencies in one or a few specific policy fields or be government-wide and cross-cutting policy sectors in scope;[7] they may regard agencies performing one specific type of task or at the opposite all or most agencies independently of the type of task performed; and, of course, they may regard only a small portion of the overall population of agencies or a large part of it.[8]

As regards the analysis conducted in this and in many other chapters of this book, this means that contingent reforms may affect in specific ways the relations one can find between the chosen independent variables and the amount of result control. Thus, in order to interpret findings, a good understanding of the local context is necessary. True is that '[I]t is important to distinguish between reform and change in public organizations [...] change is often a gradual process in organizations [...] Indeed, many gradual changes have no background in reforms' (Christensen *et al.* 2007, pp. 122–3), but these reform programmes may have an influence on the configuration of the public sector in the given country, and this should be taken into account when interpreting the findings of statistical analysis on the influence of factors like age, size, task and policy on the form of agencies and their relationship with the parent administration.

These final remarks are a cautionary tale about drawing too easily conclusions about the influence of general factors like age, size, task, or policy on agency form. It is also a source of alternative lenses through which to study the phenomenon of agencies in one country: knowledge about the history of reform processes in the country may provide valuable indications for a more thorough interpretation of evidence about agency shape in a given country. The two approaches should ultimately be combined, and may powerfully benefit from large-scope cross-national research work.

Notes

1. Dario Barbieri and Edoardo Ongaro are both from Università Bocconi and SDA School of Management; Paolo Fedele is from Udine University; Davide Galli is consultant at Business Integration Partners.

   The chapter is the joint work of the authors: however, in the final writing the first section has been written by Edoardo Ongaro; the second section has been written by Paolo Fedele; the subsequent section has been written by Dario Barbieri and Paolo Fedele; the fourth section has been written by Dario Barbieri and Davide Galli; the fifth section and the Annex have been written by Dario Barbieri; the final section has been written by Edoardo Ongaro.

   This work has been made possible by the participation of the Authors to the COST Action 'IS0601 CRIPO'.

2. The weighted index is constructed following the idea that an agency can be controlled by the parent ministry in one step of the index only if it was controlled also in the previous step. For example, it would not make sense if the goals are set by the same agency and there is an external evaluation or if this evaluation is made when measures do not exist. The weighted index aims to measure the cumulative presence of the steps in the RCI cycle. On the contrary, the unweighted index does not consider the step in which the agency is controlled: the rational behind this index is the fact that there are steps of the result control index cycle in which the agency is controlled. As a consequence, the value of the unweighted RCI is the results of summing up of the values of the different steps, divided by the number of the steps, not considering if there is a logical control cycle behind the construction of the RCI.

3. The Mann-Whitney Test is a nonparametric test used to determine whether the means of two populations are equal.

4. The Kruskal-Wallis Test is a non-parametric test and it is an n-sample extension of the two-sample Mann–Whitney test. It tests the null hypothesis that the n sampled populations have the same distribution function.

5. A point which is to be further explored as concerns the events that led to the 1999 reform in Italy: if the influence, at least in terms of inspiration, of ideas and the experience of the British 'Next Steps' reform on the reform process in Italy is undoubted, the exact extent and the concatenation of mechanisms through which policy transfer occurred is a field ripe for scholarly investigation.

6. In Italy for example the 1999 reform regarded only agencies large in both budget and staff.
7. In Italy the reform turned out to apply only to agencies operating in the sector of fiscal policy.
8. The 1999 reform regarded only a small portion of central government agencies.

Part III
Performance and Results

8
The Long-run Performance of Decentralized Agencies in Québec

Marie-Ève Quenneville, Claude Laurin and Nicole Thibodeau[1]

8.1 Introduction

In this study, we examine the performance of autonomous agencies in the province of Québec following administrative decentralization and the concurrent implementation of Results-based Management (RBM).[2] Facing heavy fiscal and political pressures, during the mid 1990s, Québec's authorities followed in the wave of 'New Public Management' (NPM) and post NPM government reforms of Western economies over the last twenty some years (Borins 2002). Emphasizing autonomy and performance-based as opposed to process-based management of the traditional public administration, these reforms focus on service delivery and efficiency (Pollitt & Talbot 2004; Verhoest *et al.* 2004a). More specifically, Québec has created agencies that are under an integrated RBM programme including agency performance agreements, strategic plans, performance reports and responsibility to parliamentarians along with RBM integration in civil servants performance evaluations.

Such a programme is intended to facilitate management and provide public servants with the incentive and the ability to innovate and work towards performance goals, and thus potentially lead to stated objectives. However, important factors may mitigate against the success of such an effort, including the difficulty to effectively implement such a wide scale reform, the government's ability to commit to actual decentralization and impediments to managers effectively using the performance measurement system for monitoring and decision-making. Other mitigating factors include difficulties in measuring performance in government as well as questions on the potential value of decentralization in this sector. Indeed, in highlighting the different dimensions and levels of accountability such as operational versus policy-making,

Verhoest *et al.* (2004) and Lægreid *et al.* (2006) raise important questions about the effectiveness of decentralization.

While the NPM literature is extremely rich and descriptive, empirical evidence of its association with reported performance is scarce (Boyne 2003; Pollitt 2004a). The NPM literature and the more recent study of agencification nonetheless cast doubt on the value of such reforms as a broad solution in any context. Similarly, Vining and Weimer (2005) argue that RBM is an idealistic concept and that its value has not been demonstrated. However, few studies examine 'objective' performance results – outputs, outcomes, efficiency and quality indicators – that the so-called reforms are supposed to improve.

The study of Québec agencies offers a rich opportunity to examine the reported performance associated with enhanced administrative autonomy and RBM. First, Québec leaders have had the chance to observe and to learn from other experiences, such as New Zealand's or the United Kingdom's as well as other federal and provincial reforms in Canada (Borins 2002). Second, and more importantly, Québec's effort, formalized in 2001 with the adoption of '*La Loi sur l'Administration Publique*' (or LAP; see Côté 2006), has survived many elections, including a change in the ruling party. Furthermore, it appears to be in full application and going strong seven years following the critical adoption of the LAP and thirteen years after the initial creation of agencies (Gouvernement du Québec 2005). Such long lasting reforms are perhaps not unique but contrast with numerous other government reforms in North America that were criticized for petering out for lack of leadership (Cooper and Ogata 2005), for being more for show than of substance (March and Olsen 1983) or due to the ebb and flow of political waves (Light 1997).

We ask: 'Has the reported performance of decentralized agencies improved with the decentralization of managerial autonomy and result-based control as part of the LAP reform in 2001?' We also explore why agencies show variations in performance. To do this, we analyse output, efficiency, financial and quality performance indicators from fiscal year 2002 to 2007 of 16 of the 18 agencies in operation during this period of time. We collected a variety of financial, workload and output data reported by agencies in their annual reports, from fiscal year (FY) 2002 or from the year of each agency's inception to its last reporting fiscal period (2007). Although our results indicate that average annual financial performance across agencies clearly improved over this period, and although agency specific costs show substantial decrease, output and productivity did not change. The few agencies that track complaints and delays report substantial improvement, while results on customer satisfaction and quality performance targets are mixed. Examination of cross agency performance across all dimensions suggests that decentralization to agencies may be more valuable in some circumstances than others and/ or that some agencies may have had more latitude and made better use of RBM.

8.2 Québec's reform

In 1995, the Québec government created the first *Unités Autonomes de Services* (UAS), equivalent to the UK's decentralized agencies. Somewhat disorganized and loosely planned, this first attempt at decentralization yielded mixed results (VGQ 1998). In 2001, the government pursued its effort by adopting the LAP. A much more serious and formal attempt at reforming its public sector, and specifically in decentralizing agencies to improve performance through RBM (VGQ 1998), the law mandated agencies and departments to define a mission along with specific actions and performance metrics in a strategic annual plan to be submitted to and monitored by elected representatives (Côté 2006). Under the law, eight UAS were transformed into formal agencies while five new agencies were created, thus decentralizing the administration of select activities such as tax collections and student loans to 'autonomous' agencies. This decentralization was intended to make operations more flexible, thus more responsive to citizen demands and more efficient (VGQ 1998, 2004). To address the coordination and incentive problems that come with greater decentralization, the government mandated that RBM be integrated and acted upon with performance agreements between agencies and the government and through subsequent annual reports to be monitored by parliamentarians.

At the time of creation each agency negotiated an agreement with the government through the treasury council, including a strategic plan that it intended to implement in exchange for increased autonomy in managing financial and human resources. While the level of autonomy granted varies across agencies, agency operations are conducted under fewer restrictions than they were under the previous regime, whether these operations were conducted in a UAS or in a department (Aubert *et al.* 2005). For example, agency managers may have negotiated increased discretion in the allocation of financial resources within their agency, including the right to carry over unused budget allocations to following years. Under some restrictions, agencies were also allowed to spend excess revenue for discretionary expenses. In terms of human resources, some agency managers were allowed to implement some form of incentive-based compensation and were no longer subject to government restrictions for their hiring process.

In the following section, we discuss reasons why decentralization with RBM could lead to the intended improvements in service delivery and efficiency in the province of Québec and reasons why they may not. We then briefly review other studies on government reforms and then proceed with a description of methodology and data, followed by the analysis and discussion of results.

8.3   Theoretical and empirical background

Economic theory does not provide a clear prediction on the association of performance with decentralization and the RBM implemented in Quebec agencies. On the one hand, agency and public choice theorists could argue that narrowing the task domain of managers through agencies and enhancing their accountability will reduce information asymmetry. However, decentralization may not be warranted. Furthermore, there are other limitations particular to the public sector: measurement of results, learning to manage performance as well as constraints on the use of incentives. Nonetheless, the empirical evidence is mixed, with some studies showing promise for decentralization when it is warranted or aligned with an effective RBM that is used in decision-making and to allocate resources and rewards. We next discuss some of these issues and why we may expect the reform to have to improve on service delivery and efficiency.

8.3.1   The pros and cons of administrative decentralization

While Bilodeau *et al.* (2007) observe that corporatization in Canadian governmental agencies is associated with an increase in performance on most metrics examined, and in spite of the agencification trend (Verhoest *et al.* 2004a), it is not clear that decentralization of activities is necessarily appropriate throughout the public sector. Managerialists argue that enlarging managerial autonomy enables public organizations to innovate. More dynamic and innovative public organizations may better be able to perform on key dimensions such as productivity and the quality and relevance of service to users (Verhoest *et al.* 2007a). Thus, delegation of authorities to lower levels should be particularly valuable in highly specialized and competitive environments such as the healthcare or high-tech industries where local specific knowledge is more valuable and outweighs the monitoring costs entailed by decentralization (Brickley *et al.* 1995).

Centralization and process control has long been the model adopted by government. Centralized management implies less management discretion and thus facilitates monitoring, reduces the risk that unsanctioned actions are taken and provides economies of scale (Pollitt 2005). While decentralization calls for incentive rewards, these are not well perceived in the public sector and government regulation often severely constrains the ability to use them. As a result, managerial autonomy may be more difficult to monitor in the public sector and leave more opportunity for rent seeking (Vining and Weimer 2005). Furthermore, without the discipline of product competition, decentralization may foster corruption associated with the monopoly powers of decentralized agencies that operate like small businesses (Meier and Hill 2005).

8.3.2   The pros and cons of RBM

Whether or not it is deemed appropriate, autonomy increases the need for accountability and incentive mechanisms to motivate and guide managers towards organizational objectives (Pollitt 2005). Indeed, weak accountability, lack of strategic direction and poor monitoring of results have often been invoked as the cause of various financial crises leading to 1980s reforms in government (Hood 1991). RBM is implemented to solve this problem. It provides the information structure, through planning and feedback on relevant performance metrics (Hood 1991). This structure should help various constituents, including parliamentarians and government managers, to assess the cost, the output and ultimately the outcome of actions taken by members of various government entities. Monitoring outputs and outcomes rather than processes is supposedly designed to hold public sector managers accountable for the results of their actions, correcting one of the major weaknesses of 'old style' bureaucratic public management (Hood 1991). As Boukaert and Halligan (2008) and Van Dooren and Van de Walle (2008)'s detailed reviews reveal, such monitoring is not so new and the effectiveness of this approach in government is coming into question, as governments that report outcomes and output cannot seem to make effective use of it in resource allocation.

The effectiveness of RBM though depends on a number of factors including civil servants' ability to influence performance on chosen metrics through their actions. Indeed, as Pearce and Perry's (1983) study of merit pay in the Federal government and Wildavsky's (1984) account of Management by Objectives suggest, the effectiveness of RBM on civil servants' motivation and their ability to act will depend on the former as well as on the government's commitment to actually incorporate the RBM metrics in performance evaluations, promotions and pay decisions, as well as resource allocation decisions. Government reforms may be implemented 'for show' and lack the commitment to full integration within the organization (March and Olsen 1983; Lægreid *et al.* 2006). Indeed, other studies have shown that reforms implemented with a lack of accountability measures, or with no clearly demonstrated usefulness of measures, are not acted upon effectively by civil servants (e.g., Cavalluzzo and Ittner 2004). Finally, and just as important, is the choice of metrics; the degree of congruence between performance metrics and strategic objectives will determine the extent to which good performance on chosen metrics translates into value for the citizens, i.e., increases service quality and improves efficiency in delivery. Public sector entities face particular measurement constraints due to specialized services or lack of competition for their services.

Power (2005) argues that performance measurement may become an end in itself. When reforms come as a result of a crisis (such as in the UK), reformers may put too much emphasis on accountability, creating an 'audit explosion'. As a result, the growth of auditing can lead to a decline in organizational trust as it creates an excessive preoccupation with representations of performance and the associated games that are played at the expense of public service quality. Indeed: '... if accountability is pursued too harshly, public managers may therefore learn the wrong thing, they learn to avoid risk taking, to pass the buck and to shield themselves against potential mistakes and criticism' (Behn 2003, 11). Finally, given the lack of experience with a performance measurement driven system, even motivated managers may have to go through a learning curve to identify informative and available measures and how to utilize them effectively.

The preceding discussion underscores the difficulty in assessing the performance of government organizations which have multiple goals and constituents and the difficulty in motivating and coordinating effort towards desired outcomes (Shapiro 2005). In their study, Heckman *et al.* (1997) report that 'the short-run performance measures that are used ... are either uncorrelated with or negatively correlated with net value added, especially in the long run' and that civil servants game the performance standards to maximize their center's performance. Indeed, as they state, it may be 'unreasonable to expect that externally imposed performance standards can solve the problems of governance and direct activity toward socially productive goals in bureaucracies that serve many masters with conflicting or ill-defined goals'.

Recent research does nonetheless suggest that increased operational autonomy along with RBM can lead to concrete, value-added performance improvement, when supported by strong commitment by governing bodies and integrated in decision-making (Verhoest *et al.* 2004a; Verhoest 2005; Verhoest *et al.* 2007a). For example, Thibodeau *et al.* (2007) examined the Veterans Health Administration's decentralization of operations with an integrated RBM-type performance structure through performance contracts and reporting aligned with strategic objectives. Their results suggest that such a programme can lead to economically significant cost per patient reductions with improvements in service quality and access, though not without some gaming of performance measurement. The Veterans hospital system early experience suggests that, with continued commitment, decentralization with concurrent performance incentives is possible in a large organization facing private sector competition, operating in a highly specialized and evolving environment where local knowledge may be particularly valuable and where market competition provides discipline (Thibodeau *et al.* 2007). Nonetheless, as follow-up research on the VHA reveals, government commitment to effective wide-ranging decentralization is difficult, and part of that may be due to the highly political nature of government operations, to the high scrutiny of certain government operations and to the responsibility that managers ultimately bear for their actions.

8.3.3 Québec's reform versus the pros and cons of decentralization and RBM

Our initial assessment of Québec's reform suggests that the government's commitment was strong enough to have an impact on the performance of decentralized agencies. The strategic plan adopted by each agency suggests that the degree of autonomy allowed to decentralized agencies is strong. However, it appears to vary across agencies, with some agency leaders complaining, for example, of lack of flexibility in hiring procedures. Nonetheless, agencies are allowed some discretion in spending certain categories of unused funds (Gouvernement du Québec 1999).

A notable feature of Québec's LAP is that agency managers and department deputy ministers are accountable directly to parliament through performance agreements. Furthermore, the level of monitoring and follow-up on performance reports by the parliamentarians initially suggests that accountability is taken seriously by the government. Accounts of parliamentary discussions and auditor reports suggest that parliamentarians and the auditor general are paying more than lip service to the performance documents; deputy ministers and agency managers have to answer very detailed questions on performance targets and results from parliamentarians who, with the help of the auditor general's office, seem to scrutinize the performance agreements and subsequent performance reports (e.g., see CPAP 2001). While these discussions may be just a show by the parliamentarians, such accountability is an important shift in behaviour and suggests that RBM is being used for control and decisions.

As for incentives, Québec's reform specifically mandates that agency performance metrics be incorporated in employee performance evaluations. Also, the auditor general's office certifies that agencies adhere to this mandate in its value for money audits. Another source of incentives comes from added revenue that agencies may collect and keep or from less stringent budget constraints. Finally, perhaps recognizing the importance of measurability in RBM, the Québec government apparently targeted the decentralization to government operations directly involved with citizens and that are measurable (VGQ 1998). Such commitment to decentralization, accountability and incentives, at least on the surface, suggests that the Québec government is determined to improve the efficiency and quality of service delivery.

If flexibility and monitoring are indeed integrated and functioning as described and decentralization is warranted for those agencies, we may observe systematic improvements in performance across the agencies. However, if, as other studies of government reforms have observed, reforms are 'for show' rather than effectively implemented, then, all else being equal, we may not observe improvements.

We analyse performance on four dimensions of service delivery: output, productivity, financial and quality. We document the evolution of a large set of performance indicators over time, from 2001 up to the latest year of reporting. We use the 2001 LAP as the critical event date as the LAP legislation formally introduced the agencies and mandated the RBM-based accountability framework under which they would operate. Therefore, starting on that year, the results reported by the agencies are generated under a formally reformed administrative framework.

We next describe more specifically our data, sample agencies and methodology followed by results and conclusion.

8.4　Methodology

Data collection proceeded in three steps: (1) sample identification, (2) data extraction, and (3) long-term performance scorecard.

8.4.1 Sample

First, we identified all the agencies for which we could obtain a stream of at least four annual reports, starting with fiscal year (FY) ending 31 March 2002, and proceeded to obtain these reports. The first three columns of Table 8.1 show the year of creation, total FTEEs (Full-Time Employment Equivalents) and the annual budget for each of the 16 agencies in our sample.

8.4.2 Data extraction

We then extracted performance data from each agency's annual performance report, from fiscal 2001 up until the last report available (FY 2006 or FY 2007). We first categorized the measures into the following four categories: output, productivity, financial, and quality. We then reclassified these data into two main categories which we use for our analysis: *(1) neutral indicators* and *(2) agency specific indicators*. Neutral indicators are reported by each agency. *Agency specific indicators* typically vary across agencies as they are tailored to each agency's *mission* and are part of the annual performance contract that each agency negotiates with the government. We next describe each of the four categories followed by a description of how we constructed the metrics.

8.4.2.1 *Output*

Increasing responsiveness to citizens is one of the key objectives behind the creation of autonomous agencies. Agencies are expected to make services available to a wider array of citizens, including those with limited access due to regional or other constraints, to improve service delivery and to alter their menu of services in response to consumer demand where necessary. The RBM process implemented in the reform supports this effort by focusing attention on service delivery rather than processes and by providing feedback on performance. However, the lack of competition for most of the services offered by agencies may constrain the effectiveness of this process. Improvements in service delivery may be observed through increases in the volume and in the variety of services provided by each agency as well as in the quality of service. For our performance scorecard we focus on volume and quality (discussed below). We use *output* in reference to the volume of each of the services provided by an agency. There is one output measure for each service. We identify the output of the service that is most directly linked to the agencies' mission for the set of neutral indicators. The remaining output measures are included in the agency specific indicators.

Table 8.1 Descriptive statistics and neutral indicators' index values for 2007

Agency	Descriptive statistics			Primary output (+)	Productivity (+)	Financial		
	Year of creation	Total FTEEs	Annual budget (in 000)			Total revenue (+)	Revenue/ Cost (+)	Average unit cost (−)
AFE	1997	344	19,500	1.077	1.045	–	–	1.045
BIA	2001	141	9,394	0.656	0.546	0.793	0.807	1.498
CARRA	1995	441	40,400	1.303	1.182	1.254	1.032	0.932
CCQ	1995	30	2,183	1.021	1.059	0.955	1.110	0.843
CEAEQ	1997	107	10,446	0.930	1.002	0.954	1.062	0.966
CEH	2001	175	12,761	–	–	2.284	1.480	–
CGER	1997	410	53,482	1.100	0.944	1.280	0.996	1.163
CPF (2006)	1995	1,079	80,500	0.931	0.798	1.384	1.314	1.132
CR	2001	238	12,700	0.952	1.268	–	–	0.836
CSQ	2001	30	4,567	0.434	0.448	1.211	1.017	2.743
EQ	1998	4,484	292,700	0.980	0.702	–	–	0.961
LSJML	1996	137	9,723	1.358	1.218	2.488	2.336	0.785
RC	2001	43	5,365	1.703	2.020	1.585	1.288	0.723
RRQ	1997	1,121	144,900	1.160	1.056	–	–	1.015
SAG	1995	162	57,773	1.039	1.122	0.874	0.996	0.845
SR (2006)	2001	5,671	151,464	0.860	1.093	–	–	0.872
Geometric mean				0.991	0.975	1.281*	1.173*	1.026
% in the expected direction				8/15 53%	10/15 67%	7/11 64%	8/11 73%	9/15 60%
Average annual change				0.14%	−0.29%	5.13%	3.35%	0.75%

Note: This table presents standardized performance results for each agency on each of the five performance dimensions in the neutral indicators. Performance is calculated as the ratio of the value of the measure at the end of the period divided by the ratio of the measure in the base year, FY 2002. * indicates that the mean is different from 1 (95% confidence level, Wilcoxon Signed Rank Test).

Table 8.2 Description of agencies

1. *Aide financière aux études (AFE):* Manages student financial aid programmes.
2. *Bureau des infractions et amendes (BIA):* Ensures the follow-up of citations and the collection of overdue fines and legal costs imposed by a judgment.
3. *Commission administrative des régimes de retraite et d'assurances (CARRA):* Administers pension plans for the Québec government and provides related expertise.
4. *Centre de conservation du Québec (CCQ):* Provides professional restoration services and expertise to museums and other institutions engaged in conservation.
5. *Centre d'expertise en analyse environnementale du Québec (CEAEQ):* Provides environmental analyses to support the availability, quality and continuity of expertise for environmental protection and resource conservation.
6. *Centre d'expertise hydrique du Québec (CEH):* Manages the provincial water network ensuring the safety, equity and sustainable development of water supplies.
7. *Centre de gestion de l'équipement roulant (CGER):* Operates and maintains the Québec government's fleet of vehicles and motorized equipment.
8. *Centre de perception fiscale (CPF):* Recovers fiscal and other debts owed to Revenue Québec.
9. *Centre de recouvrement (CR):* Collects amounts owed to the Health and Social Services Ministry.
10. *Centre de signalisation (CSQ):* Manages road signalization throughout Québec.
11. *Emploi-Québec (EQ):* Provides employment related services to individuals and organizations to develop the workforce and to reduce unemployment in Québec.
12. *Laboratoire de sciences judiciaires et de médecine légale (LSJML):* Provides forensic expertise for police or legal investigations and certifies the integrity of lottery terminals.
13. *Régie du cinéma (RC):* Manages the motion picture rating system and related distribution fees within the province. Also classifies and approves films for distribution in movie theaters and home video outlets.
14. *Régie des rentes du Québec (RRQ):* Administers the Québec Pension Plan and the Family Benefits Programme and offers counselling on other compensation and benefits.
15. *Service aérien gouvernemental (SAG):* Manages and operates government owned aircrafts.
16. *Sécurité du revenu (SR):* Manages financial aid to individuals and families.

8.4.2.2 Productivity

Improving productivity, that is, increasing the amount of services delivered, while using the least amount of resources, is another important goal of this reform enforced through the annual performance contracts. As discussed in section 8.2, decision authority varies across agencies. Some agencies may be more limited than others in their ability to manage

labor, their primary resource, and thus may not be able to influence productivity significantly. To the extent that agency managers have effective
decision authority over labor and that there is room for improvement,
all else being equal, we should observe an increase in productivity across
agencies following the LAP.

In the set of neutral indicators, we measure an agency's productivity as
the ratio of primary output volume to an agency's number of full-time
employee equivalents (FTEEs). Some agencies also track and report their
own measure of productivity. We include performance on these agency
specific measures of productivity in the set of agency specific indicators.

8.4.2.3   Financial

Government entities, by definition, do not exist to make a profit but to
provide services. Studies of financial performance in government thus
typically look at expenditures (Boyne 2003). However, the creation of
agencies targeted government services that could be specifically isolated
and that, very often, were performed in exchange for some form of revenue (e.g., collection agencies, aerial services).[3] Hence, it makes sense to
examine the change in revenues and in revenues versus costs following
agency creation. Total revenue, cost savings, the ratio of revenues to
operating costs or the difference between revenues and operating costs
may be key performance metrics under RBM, particularly for the agencies that are allowed to keep revenue surpluses (Bilodeau *et al.* 2007).

We examine total revenues generated, the ratio of revenues to operating costs along with the average cost per primary output in the set
of neutral indicators. Some agencies also report performance on other
financial indicators related to revenue or budget surplus and cost savings.
We aggregate and analyse the latter under agency specific indicators.

8.4.2.4   Quality

Many critics of RBM argue that too much emphasis on financial indicators can lead to the deterioration of the quality of the services. However,
improving service delivery is a central object of Québec's initiative.
Agencies thus have incorporated a variety of process and output or outcome quality metrics to guide and to motivate their employees. These
metrics vary across agencies. However, a number of agencies track some
measure of customer satisfaction, number of complaints, wait times
and/or response time and have preset targets on these measures (e.g.
number of times services are provided within a certain amount of time).
We thus extracted and analyse performance on these four dimensions of
quality under agency specific metrics, i.e.: (1) meeting a specific target,

(2) customer satisfaction, (3) delivery time or delays, and (4) number of customer complaints.

8.4.3 Long-term performance scorecard

We used standardized values of each indicator to aggregate and compare results across agencies and over time, following a standard methodology (Bilodeau *et al.* 2007). For each agency, we built two long-term performance scorecards of annual standardized performance: *(1) neutral indicators,* and *(2) agency specific indicators.* We then calculated the annual change in the value of the index and the annual change over the period for each indicator in each agency. For agency specific indicators, we first calculated the average value of the index across multiple indicators in one category for each year.

8.5 Results

8.5.1 Cross-sectional performance

We present two tables summarizing the performance of agencies from FY 2002 to FY 2006 or 2007 and examine the within agency performance over time, across the sets of *neutral* (Table 8.1) and *agency specific* (Table 8.3) indicators. We then examine more closely differences in performance across agencies (Table 8.4) and characteristics of those agencies.

8.5.1.1 Neutral indicators

Columns 4–8 of Table 8.3 show the end of period value of the performance index for each agency for each *neutral indicator*: primarily output, productivity and three financial indicators. Visual inspection, confirmed by statistical tests, reveals that, on average, agencies did not significantly improve in terms of output or productivity or on reductions in average unit cost. However, total revenue and revenue over cost measure reveals economically and statistically significant improvements across all agencies. The average end values across agencies are 1.281 and 1.173 respectively (significantly different from 1, 95 per cent confidence interval, Wilcoxon Signed Rank Test). The bottom line of Table 8.1 reveals that the average annual increase on these two dimensions was 5.1 per cent and 3.4 per cent, respectively.[4]

Interestingly, the results reveal that although average output remained stable, average revenue increased by 28.1 per cent over the period of 2002 to 2007. This can happen if, for instance, agencies decided to charge higher tariffs for their services, a scenario that becomes even

170

Table 8.3 Agency specific indicators – end value (2007) of index by agency

| Agency | Productivity (+) | Financial | | Quality | | | |
		(Surplus) (+)	(Cost) (-)	Meeting target (+)	Customer satisfaction (+)	Delays (-)	Complaints (-)
AFE	–	1.045	–	–	0.888	0.323	–
BIA	0.632	1.116	0.573	–	–	–	–
CARRA	–	–	1.233	1.195	–	0.822	–
CCQ	1.065	–	0.805	–	1.031	–	–
CEAEQ	1.250	1.028	0.942	–	–	–	–
CGER	0.990	1.161	0.893	0.757	–	–	–
CPF (2006)	1.026	–	0.952	1.050	–	0.299	–
CR	1.076	–	0.518	1.400	–	–	0.578
RC	–	–	–	1.023	–	–	–
RRQ	–	1.440	–	0.999	–	–	0.500
SAG	–	–	–	0.961	–	–	–
SR (2006)	–	0.949	–	–	–	0.894	–
Geometric mean	0.986	1.113	0.814	1.039	0.957	0.516*	0.538
Proportion improved	4/6 67%	5/6 83%	6/7 86%	4/7 57%	1/2 50%	4/4 100%	2/2 100%
Average annual change	0.31%	2.94%	-2.63%	0.81%	0.02%	-7.69%	-9.20%

Note: This table presents standardized performance for each agency on the agency-specific indicators. Performance is calculated as the ratio of the value of the measure at the end of the period, divided by the ratio of the measure in the base year FY 2002. * indicates that the mean is different from 1 (90% confidence level, Wilcoxon Signed Rank Test).

more conceivable given that most agencies are in a monopolistic position. These aggregate results do not reveal a systematic improvement in efficiency, output or productivity, as purportedly aimed by the reform. They are consistent with agencies managing a financial crisis.

Table 8.3 shows the value of the indexes at the end of the period by agency and across years for the *agency specific indicators*. When an agency reports more than one indicator in a category, we aggregate the agency's indicators in that category for each year and then compute the average across years for the agency.

8.5.1.2 *Agency specific indicators*

While only six agencies report measures during the whole period, the results for *agency specific* productivity indicators are consistent with those on primary output (Table 8.1). Two out of three agencies have improved while the growth rate (geometric mean) is below 1, revealing lack of overall improvement and high variability. The results on agency specific financial surplus are also consistent with those on neutral indicators on revenues. Of the six agencies reporting, 83 per cent are increasing, with the average result being slightly less than the average increase in revenues in Table 8.1.

However, agency specific cost indicators show an average reduction of 18.6 per cent, much higher than the 2.6 per cent average increase in unit cost from Table 8.1. Each agency reports better results on the agency specific indicators. This difference may reflect an inappropriate selection of cost measures on our part and/or errors or differences in methodology or calculation. They may also reflect real improvement on selected performance drivers of cost measures by each agency. Another potential explanation that we cannot discard without further investigation is that agencies game the system by choosing to report mostly those cost indicators that they know are improving.

While we only have data on quality indicators from a few agencies for the full time period, the results are interesting. First, a thin majority of agencies report improvements in meeting their quality targets. While this result is highly dependent on how attainable the target is, this indicator at least reveals that eight agencies have tracked and managed quality targets over our reported period. Only two agencies tracked customer satisfaction during the length of the period, with AFE reporting an 11 per cent decline and CCQ remaining relatively stable (3 per cent increase). Finally, although few of them do so, all of the agencies that measure delays or complaints show substantial improvements with an average decline of almost 50 per cent. Although these results do not allow us to formally conclude about quality, they suggest that observed systematic revenue increases and cost reductions across agencies during our period of study were likely not reached at the expense of quality. For the most part, the management of quality indicators, though limited, is yielding positive outcomes.

In sum we observe that, all else being equal, on average, agencies have not increased output or productivity but were able to generate increases in revenue and generate surplus. Also, while agency specific measures are even more indicative, on average agencies were able to achieve cost savings in their operations. Agencies that report on delays or complaints have significantly improved on those dimensions. However, there are some agencies that appear to be doing relatively well on all the dimensions during our period of study while others are not. In the following section, we examine cross agency variability in performance and potential explanations.

8.5.1.3   *Agency specific performance*

To examine differences in agency specific performance across all dimensions, we adopt a heuristic approach. We first rank agencies in quartiles using their relative performance on each of the indicators for which we have data for at least eight reporting agencies. We then group the agencies together based on average quartile rankings across indicators. These results are shown in Table 8.4 and described below. We then attempt to identify the similar characteristics of agencies within groups and those that differ across to identify the characteristics of better performers versus those of agencies that lag.

The quartile rankings reveal that LSJML, RC and CR (group 1) performed better than their peers across almost all dimensions for which we have a performance indicator. Their average quartile ranking varies from 1 to 1.67. In the second group, we find RRQ, CARRA and CCQ, with an average quartile ranking ranging from 2 to 2.17. The third group is comprised of six agencies, including SR, the largest agency in terms of FTEEs, with an average quartile ranking ranging from 2.50 to and 2.83. Finally, EQ, BIA and CSQ comprise the last group with an average quartile ranking of 3 or above.[5]

The top performers (group 1) include small agencies (less than 250 FTEEs) with a very clear mission statement and with primary tasks oriented towards providing services (Lægreid *et al.* 2008a). These agencies have autonomous revenues that increase as a direct function of their output. In short, these agencies are in a situation where they can basically operate like small private ventures.

Table 8.4 Quartile ranking of agencies across select performance indicators

Rank	Agency	Output	Productivity	Revenues	Revenues/ costs	Average unit cost	Financial (cost)	Average quartile ranking
1	LSJML	1	1	1	1	1	1	1.00
	CR	3	1			1	1	1.50
	RC	1	1	1	2	1	4	1.67
2	RRQ	1	2			3		2.00
	CCQ	2	2	3	2	1	2	2.00
	CARRA	1	1	2	3	2	4	2.17
3	CPF	3	3	2	1	3	3	2.50
	SAG	2	2	3	4	2		2.60
	AFE	2	3			3		2.67
	CGER	2	3	2	3	4	2	2.67
	SR	4	2			2		2.67
	CEAEQ	3	3	3	2	3	3	2.83
4	EQ	3	4			2		3.00
	BIA	4	4	4	4	4	1	3.50
	CSQ	4	4	4	3	4		3.80

Note: This table presents the quartile ranking of each agency on five neutral indicators and one agency specific indicator (financial (cost)). Each neutral agency specific indicator was selected for which there was data from at least eight agencies. For each indicator, the quartile rank 1 was attributed to the 25% highest performers, quartile rank 2 to the next 25% and so on. Then agencies were ranked in descending order on each indicator. The last column shows the agency's average quartile ranking across the measures for which there was data. CEH was omitted because of insufficient data.

The second group is comprised again of agencies with a clear mission statement and nonconflicting objectives. The CCQ is quite similar to the agencies found in the first group, in terms of size, autonomy and mission. While RRQ and CARRA are much larger, they both have very specific missions related to portfolio management, and thus key performance indicators will be financial. Furthermore, their autonomy is constrained as the agency must follow a conservative portfolio management strategy to ensure the safeguard of assets under management that belong to Quebec citizens. These agencies also have the distinction of being the oldest, dating back to 1995, and so likely have more experience in performance management.

The last two groups include large agencies such as EQ, SR and CPF, each with more than one thousand FTEEs. A closer look at this group reveals agencies such as AFE, EQ and SR with mission statements that are unstable over time. For example, in a recent survey of performance indicators used by decentralized agencies in Québec, Bégin-Lafontaine (2008) found that due to the confusion related to their mission statements, AFE and EQ have changed their strategic plan and altered their set of performance indicators almost every year since their creation. Given their social role, agencies such as AFE, EQ and SR, that all deal with financial aid of some sort, are also more prone to political intervention. Similarly, among all the agencies in our sample, CEAQ has the most expanded mission statement.[6] Only a small portion of its revenue comes from autonomous sources. As the proportion of autonomous revenues decrease over time, the agency basically relies on government financing and thus is prone to government intervention. The remaining agencies in group 3 could also be classified has having a relatively low level of autonomy. CPF is large and is endowed with strict operational procedures. Smaller in size, SAG and CGER are basically serving other governmental organizations and, as such, do not have a clear autonomous revenue source or incentives from external customers.

Finally, among the poor performers (group 4), we find agencies that experienced severe problems during the period of study. Most of CSQ's poor performance results are driven by a severe drop in output that occurred in the first post-LAP year. Although output production is stable from year 2 to 5, indexed cumulative results remain negative at the end of the period covered in this study.[7] As for BIA, results are fairly stable until FY 2006, when it was hit by an employee strike. The agency has not been able to recover during the two remaining years covered in this study.

We attempted to identify *ex post*, discriminating agency characteristics based on a qualitative and informal approach. It appears that small service providing agencies with a clear mission statement that is stable over time with managerial autonomy perform better than their peers. These results echo those of Lægreid *et al.* (2008a) who report that size, the level of autonomy and the nature of the primary tasks matter for performance evaluation. Concepts like autonomy and mission stability are undoubtedly hard to measure and further analysis is needed to further ascertain these conjectures.

8.6   Conclusion

This study examined the association of performance of agencies subjected to an RBM programme following the LAP across multiple dimensions from FY 2002 to 2008. Limitations include the absence of data prior to the reform or of data to capture external macroeconomic factors. We also do not attempt to predict the performance that could have been without the decentralization. Nonetheless, this preliminary but detailed examination of reported performance across such a large number of agencies and over such a long period time provides some interesting insights and paths for further investigation.

Our cross-sectional analysis suggests that agencies may have focused more on revenue and cost areas than on productivity or quality. On average, agencies report substantial and statistically significant increases in revenue and revenue over cost indicators. However, average reported performance on output, productivity and cost (neutral indicators) is relatively stable during this period. This suggests that agencies would have increased revenues through an increase in fees, an approach which is not the pure intent of new public management. We do observe quite substantial cost reductions for agency specific indicators, a result that prompts further investigation. Overall, these results are not surprising considering that financial crisis is one of the drivers behind Quebec's reform. Results for quality, though limited, suggest at least that increases in revenue were not at the expense of quality and if anything, those that have been tracking delays and complaints have substantially reduced them.

The absence of improvement in the ratio of primary output to FTEEs may also suggest that many agencies were very productive prior to the reform. Alternatively, it may be that, in spite of appearances, agencies have little 'effective' control over human resources and thus are not able to reduce manpower. Finding no systematic increase in output and productivity throughout this period may merely reflect market demand and the possibility that those agencies were highly productive prior to the reform. The data used in this study does not allow us to discriminate between these possibilities; however, further investigation is warranted.

Consistent with findings by Lægreid *et al.* (2008a) in their analysis of a similar programme in Norway, there may also be a learning factor. Agencies that report financial measures often were reporting and managing these measures prior to the LAP as those were key metrics. Managers are used to managing these aspects of operations and understand the actions that need to be taken. Furthermore, a financial crisis would have prompted agencies and parliamentarians to focus on financial metrics. The focus on productivity and quality is a relatively newer phenomenon; many agencies are still learning to manage them and to identify the performance drivers of service quality.

Analysis of agency specific performance reveals that agencies operating in conditions similar to those of small private ventures – a clear and nonconflicting mission statement coupled with greater autonomy – perform better than larger, more constrained agencies pursuing a large number of potentially conflicting objectives. These results suggest that some agencies are better at managing than others, may be better suited for decentralization, or may have been attributed more latitude.

Notes

1. Support for this research was provided by the Centre sur la productivité et la prospérité (HEC Montréal) and the Willamette University Center for Governance and Public Policy Research. We are very grateful for the assistance of Estelle Kamau and Louisette Thibodeau.
2. Administrative decentralization consists in devolving competencies to nonelected administrative bodies as opposed to political autonomy, the delegation of authority to other elected levels of government. See Verhoest *et al.* 2004a.
3. All but three agencies considered in this study generate revenues that are a function of their output. In contrast to many other governmental organizations in Québec, agencies use a form of accrual accounting to report revenues and costs in the annual report.
4. Similarly, unreported analyses of cross agency annual performance reveal an index standard value for revenues and revenues to cost ratio that is significantly different from 1 for most years covered in this study (based on Wilcoxon Signed Rank Tests), suggesting that agencies were able to generate more revenue and surplus in most years.
5. Because it reports only two performance indicators, CEH was excluded from this analysis.
6. The mission statement covers close to one full page, compared to a few lines for most other agencies.
7. The CSQ was fully privatized in April 2009.

9
Comparing Impacts of Modes of Governance

Marieke van Genugten

9.1 Introduction

For about three decades now, the provision of public services has been undergoing a process of intense change. Privatization has occurred, markets have been opened to competition, and entirely new regulatory regimes and administrations have been created. Generally speaking, the efficiency of these institutional changes is difficult to assess (Walsh 1995). Furthermore, claims that contracting out leads to greater efficiency have been shown to be invalid (Boyne 1998). Moreover, in most studies transaction costs remain undiscussed, while they appear to be assuming an increasingly important part in the debate (Hodge 2000).

From the viewpoint of Transaction Cost Economics (TCE), a minimization of transaction costs is to be expected when there is a match between the attributes of a transaction and the attributes of a governance structure. However, in reality we observe a wide variety of modes of governance in respect of public services. The question is whether this has an impact on the efficiency of these public governance structures. In this chapter we compare the transaction costs of different modes of governance at the Dutch local government level. The local level offers excellent opportunities to study one type of public service under alternative institutional arrangements. We have conducted a comparative case study, comparing a variety of governance structures related to the provision of a particular public service, household waste collection. Under the Environmental Management Act, Dutch local authorities are responsible for collecting household waste. Municipalities, however, are free to decide whether to provide the service in-house or contract it out. As a consequence, there is a wide variety of governance structures, which affords a satisfactory opportunity to apply the comparative institutional analysis that TCE prescribes.

This chapter makes a dual contribution. First, many researchers have already shown the relevance of TCE in the context of public service provision (for a review see Van Genugten 2008). This has been done within the TCE literature (see for example Dixit 1996; Williamson 1999; Ménard and Saussier 2002) and also within the public administration literature, which takes a transaction cost-based view of local government privatization decisions (see for example Moe 1984; Frant 1991; Horn 1995; Lane 1995; Sclar 2000; Dollery 2001; Warner and Hebdon 2001; Brown and Potoski 2003; Walls 2005). While these studies mainly focus on explaining the choice of particular governance structures, we are interested in the question whether alignment between governance structures and transactions really matters for efficiency. Secondly, this study aims to contribute to the body of knowledge on the relative efficiency of different modes of governance in terms of transaction costs.

The outline of this chapter is as follows. In the next section we start by discussing local government reform in the Netherlands. In the third section we discuss the way in which public sector transactions and governance structures are aligned. Next, in the fourth section, we introduce our research method, which is a comparative case study, and the way in which efficiency is operationalized. Following this, in the fifth section, we present the results of our empirical study, consisting of an identification of alignment with regard to the public service of household waste collection and our findings regarding the efficiency of alternative governance structures. In the sixth section we end with a discussion of our findings.

9.2   Local government reforms in the Netherlands

In this chapter we study transaction costs of modes of governance by comparing different modes of governance at the Dutch local government level. This level has witnessed many reforms. First, major reforms concerning local public management have been implemented. From the early post-War period until the present, different organizational models have been implemented, one after the other (Hendriks and Tops 2003). In the early post-War period, virtually all municipalities had a uniform, traditional bureaucratic structure. Under the influence of new public management we now find a diversity of municipal internal organization structures. Secondly, other kinds of administrative reforms were implemented in the 1980s and 1990s, such as privatization and competitive tendering, while bureaus have been given more freedom to manage. An important argument for implementing these changes has been to separate policy and administration so that politicians, policy-makers and policy implementers can concentrate on their core business (Van Thiel 2004a). This move was related to the discussion of what could be viewed as the essential tasks of municipalities. The total number of tasks was growing rapidly and, to prevent overload, it was held that tasks that were not genuinely public in character should not be performed by local governments. Other motives were to improve the efficiency of policy implementation and to reduce costs as an answer to the need to achieve cutbacks and enhance the quality of customer service (Van Thiel 2004a). The expectation was that the market could perform some of the tasks more efficiently and effectively (Ter Bogt 2003). Against this background, a variety of governance structures came into being. The spectrum of local governance structures now ranges from public bureau to external autonomization – inter-municipal cooperation and public company – to contracting out. In the fields of education and social welfare services, municipalities are reluctant to decentralize, autonomize or privatize (Van Thiel 2004a). The preferred form is often the public bureau. In addition, local governments are showing a tendency to use the second and third forms, particularly in the fields of culture, health, utilities, sports, recreation and waste collection, which is the public service analysed here.

9.3   Transaction Cost Economics

TCE studies the way contracting partners protect themselves against *hazards* that are inherent in exchange relationships. All hazards can be attributed to two behavioural assumptions: bounded rationality and opportunism. The way protection is established is by designing and organizing appropriate governance structures. The suitability of a specific governance structure depends on the characteristics of the exchange relationship and is related to the extent to which transaction costs can be reduced.

TCE's basic proposition is that economic institutions are created to economize on transaction costs (Williamson 1985: 17). In that respect, the core of the analysis consists of weighing the costs of planning, adaptability, and monitoring of an activity under alternative governance structures. The *discriminating alignment hypothesis* adopts an efficiency point of view to address the governance structure that is most suitable to support transactions of a given kind. The hypothesis gives expression to a matching principle stating that 'transactions, which differ in their attributes, are aligned with governance structures, which differ in their cost and competence' (Williamson,1999: 312). This means that characteristics of the transaction should ideally match with characteristics of the governance structure. The method of analysis is a comparative institutional analysis in which only feasible alternative governance structures should be compared.

9.3.1   Public sector transactions

The core concern of public sector transactions is the delivery of public services. Following Savas (2000), we distinguish between the roles of three basic participants involved in the delivery of a public service: the service consumer, the service producer and the service provider. The *consumer* (i.e. citizen) obtains a service directly. The *producer* delivers the service directly to the consumer; a producer can be a government unit or a private company. In this chapter producers can take any of these forms. The service *provider* assigns the producer to the consumer, that is, selects producers that actually serve the consumers. Here the service provider is a local authority.

We define the public sector transaction as the exchange relationship between service provider and service producer. The content of this typical relationship is formed by, on the one hand, the objective of local government to promote the public interest and, on the other hand, the objective of the service producer to obtain the right to deliver a public service to consumers. This third party, the consumer, is not a partner in the exchange relationship, but the consumer's opinion and behaviour have a considerable influence on the relationship between the service provider and service producer. An additional aspect is the emphasis on the public interest. Often it is difficult to define exactly what the public interest is, let alone measure it. This has implications for the attributes of the public sector transaction.

To Williamson (1985), the transaction is characterized by three attributes: asset specificity, uncertainty and frequency. *Asset specificity* mainly involves physical and human asset specificity. It refers to the question whether or not specific investments are required to produce some good or service. Specific investments apply to the production of one service but are very difficult to adapt to the production of other services. *Uncertainty* refers to two aspects, namely, behavioural and environmental uncertainty. Behavioural uncertainty, which refers to the measure of uncertainty facing the service provider, i.e. the government, regarding the behaviour of the service producers, depends on the measurability of the service and probity hazards of a public service. Environmental uncertainty – that is, the predictability of the environment in which the contract is to be executed – refers to a variety of factors. We distinguish between the public causing uncertainty, the political process and the rate of technological change for each service, and demands from higher levels of government and policy imposed on the local government level. The *frequency* of transactions in the public sector is often high because public service provision is a recurrent responsibility of governments. The three attributes discussed here cause contractual hazards. In light of the resulting transaction costs involved, efforts to minimize these contractual hazards gain in importance (Richman and Boerner 2006). Safeguards against the contractual hazards at issue can be described as mechanisms to provide mutual security to the contracting parties (Bréchemier and Saussier 2001). They generate trust and permit adaptations to unforeseen contingencies. The safeguards can take various forms, leading to a spectrum of public sector governance structures.

9.3.2   Public sector governance structures

The spectrum of public sector governance structures is characterized by the fact that the government is one of the partners in the exchange relationship. The government can be viewed as an 'entrepreneur' who must take decisions on whether to make or buy public goods or services. This means that the government is responsible for deciding whether to keep the delivery of certain goods and services in its own hands (make), to contract out to a private firm (buy), or to choose some intermediate governance structure. At the local level, we distinguish between municipal service, contracting out to a private company, and public company.

A *municipal service* is any distinct part of the municipal organization. A unit of this kind can be more or less independent. The government 'makes' (provides) the public service itself. The roles of service provider and producer coincide. Taking into account the characteristics Williamson (1999) distinguishes, the municipal service scores low on *incentive intensity* and high on *administrative support*. This is a consequence of the fact that municipal services are part of the internal organization of the municipality and, therefore, are subject to hierarchical control. The *duration* of the relationship is quasi-permanent. The period of time involved is indeterminate, but municipal authorities can decide at some point to privatize the municipal service. The *degree of completeness* in case of a municipal service is low. Subsequent readjustments within a series of transactions are effected through fiat. They can be made without the need to consult or revise agreements between contracting partners. *Disputes* are *settled* without recourse to the judicial system. They will be resolved internally, by hierarchy 'operating as its own court of appeal'

(Williamson, 1991: 274). *Enforcement* takes place on the basis of hierarchical authority. All in all, this means that the measure of adaptation in this mode of governance can be characterized by a low level of *adaptive autonomy* and a high level of *adaptive integrity*.

In case of *contracting out*, activities are most often conducted by private organizations, but local government is still engaged in the activities as principal (Ter Bogt 2003). In that case, the local government contracts with a private organization to perform the tasks. In this mode of governance, government buys the production of public services from an external organization. Service provider and producer are different organizations. Contracting out scores high on *incentive intensity* and low-to-average on *administrative support*. Incentive intensity is high compared to the other modes of governance in that governments put the production of a service out to tender. Usually, the lowest bidder gets the award. With regard to administrative support, partners to the contract hold regular consultations and there are often additional enforcement procedures, such as monitoring arrangements. Contract law can be characterized in terms of four factors. Contracts differ in *duration*, but are generally short-term for a fixed number of years. With regard to *degree of completeness*, contracts can be characterized as very complete. Every aspect of the production of the public service, such as quantity and quality, is meticulously specified in the contract. The contract governing the exchange is seen as fixed, and if performance according to specification fails, damages can be claimed. Readjustments only take place in periods between two transaction agreements. *Dispute settlement* takes place through third party involvement such as arbitration and court orders. Finally, *enforcement procedures* consist of monitoring arrangements and reporting duties. In conclusion, the measure of adaptation in this mode of governance can be characterized by a high level of *adaptive autonomy* and a low-to-average level of *adaptive integrity*.

Public companies are separate organizations, at arm's length from the local administration. In general, this means that the elected politicians' direct control of certain tasks or activities diminishes (Ter Bogt 2003). Usually, the company performs a well-defined public task (Ter Bogt 2003) which is laid down in a charter. Local authorities are shareholders of the company and at the same time, as principals, they have a long-term contractual relationship with the public company as their agent. This mode of governance is one in which government buys the production of a public service from a separate organization. Service provider and producer are different organizations. This mode does have hierarchical elements, however. Public companies constitute long-term contractual relationships that preserve autonomy but provide added safeguards, because parties to the contract are multilaterally dependent. This involves a low-to-average level of *incentive intensity* and an average level of *administrative support*. The level of administrative support is viewed as average because governments have crucial powers by virtue of their shareholding. For example, they have powers to appoint and discharge the members of the Executive Board and the Supervisory Board of the public company and to influence the main lines of its strategic policy. The level of incentive intensity is low-to-average. Piece-rate systems and hourly wages can be used and partners to the project receive rent dividend. With regard to contract law, the contracts tend to be more long-lasting than relationships resulting from contracting out. Often they are even of indeterminate *duration*. Governments can only withdraw from them by paying a fine. The *degree of completeness* can be scored as average. Aspects of the production of the public service, such as quantity, quality and price, are specified in the contract. In comparison with contracting out, contracts are more incomplete due to their longer duration. Over the long run, the formal arrangements tend to reflect real conditions less and less adequately. Regular readjustments are required, typically by renegotiation of the original agreement. *Dispute settlement* takes the form of third party dispute settlement (arbitration or court order). Finally, *enforcement procedures* resemble procedures used in contracting out public services. Enforcement procedures mainly consist of monitoring and reporting. Consequently, the measure of adaptation in these modes of governance can be typified by a low-to-average level of *adaptive autonomy* and an average level of *adaptive integrity*.

9.3.3   Public sector alignment

Characteristics of the transaction should ideally match characteristics of the governance structure. Following TCE-based reasoning in the private sector (Williamson 1979; David and Han 2004), we infer the conditions under which an alignment can be said to exist between public transactions and public governance structures, comparable to an alignment in the private sector (see Van Genugten 2008). The main conclusions are that transactions conducted under a low level of uncertainty demand additional safeguards in case the level of asset specificity increases. Safeguards are strengthened by moving from contracting out, to public company, and finally to municipal service. A low level of asset specificity demands a level of safeguard typical of contracting out, while transactions with a high level of asset specificity demand the stronger safeguards of a municipal service. If transactions are conducted under conditions leading to a moderate level of uncertainty, contracting out is most efficient in case of nonspecific investments. This is also expected with regard to transactions characterized by a moderate level of uncertainty and mixed asset specificity, since in case of bilateral contracting, negotiations about adaptations are not excessively costly. Public companies, then, are unsuitable, due to high costs of negotiating about adaptations, while municipal services offer a higher and therefore costlier level of safeguard than required. Transactions either conducted under conditions with a high level of uncertainty or characterized by a high level of asset specificity require a level of adaptation and safeguards which are typical of a municipal service.

9.4 Method

Theory predicts that aligning transactions and governance structures leads to a transaction cost economizing result. Most of the empirical studies in TCE do not address this prediction but try to explain contractual choices that have actually been made. The empirical findings of these studies are broadly supportive of transaction cost propositions (see, for example, Richman and Boerner 2006). Empirical research to date supports the view that transaction cost considerations influence organizational choices and that the theory is therefore a useful tool for understanding and explaining the choice among organizational alternatives (Masten 1993). These studies show that contractual choices correspond to what the theory predicts and infer from this that these choices must have been efficient, which is to say that transaction costs must have been minimized. But they rarely provide hard evidence in support of this conclusion by showing how much is lost by going from the best to the next best institutional arrangement (Joskow 1991). A subsequent step would be to connect observed 'misalignment' – identified on the basis of the theory's predictions – with observed performances, which is done in 'second generation TCE' research (Yvrande-Billon and Saussier 2005).

9.4.1 Comparative case study

Following the relatively small number of prior studies in second generation TCE, we attempt to test directly the impact of alignment. To that end, we formulate one main proposition. This proposition has the form of a prediction to the effect that agreement between transactions and governance structures will lead to a transaction cost economizing result. This prediction is the core of the empirical study. To test this prediction we analyse the transaction cost-economizing result of *one* single type of transaction – the collection of household waste – under alternative modes of governance. The empirical study to address this issue is a comparative case study (or focused comparison approach (Denters and Mossberger 2006)). An important advantage of a comparative case study is that it offers opportunities to sort out the effects of different explanatory factors (Denters and Mossberger 2006). The processes and mechanisms that lead to a relationship between alignment and an efficient result can be made visible.

In this case study, municipalities are the units of analysis. The independent variable is alignment, which is constructed on the basis of matching two components, attributes of transactions and attributes of governance structures, while the dependent variable is the transaction cost economizing result in terms of the types and relative level of transaction costs.

We selected eight municipalities that participated in the benchmark of SenterNovem (a bureau of the Dutch Ministry of Economic Affairs) in 2005 and 2006. All of them are highly urbanized, use fixed fees and are characterized by one of the three modes of governance distinguished in the previous section. Three of them provide household waste collection as a municipal service, two municipalities contract out to a private firm and the other three municipalities organize household waste collection in a public company of which they are one of the shareholders. Data collection was based on formal documents, such as contracts, shareholders' agreements, municipal regulations and waste plans. Furthermore, we used semi-structured interviews with key persons: municipal officials involved in waste collection in a particular municipality; managers in the private and public companies; and in the municipal organization providing the service.

9.4.2 Operationalization of efficiency

To test the main proposition, we analysed the transaction cost economizing result (i.e. efficiency) regarding the provision of household waste collection under the three alternative modes of governance.

Transaction costs are notoriously difficult to measure and cannot be calculated exactly. Many hazards of exchange are either implicit or latent in the transaction. Others, while manifest, are often difficult to quantify (Masten *et al.* 1991). As Kähkönen (2005) observes, evaluation of a non-measurable phenomenon requires a different way of comparing advantages and disadvantages. It seems that detecting such a different, qualitative, way may be more valuable than persistently conducting econometric analyses to evaluate efficiency, as is often done in TCE. To tackle the problem of comparing efficiency we make use of such a qualitative method of assessing the types and relative levels of transaction costs under different governance structures. To that end it is useful to distinguish between two types of transaction costs: direct costs and costs of friction. Rindfleisch and Heide (1997) relate these costs directly to asset specificity, environmental uncertainty and behavioural uncertainty. Direct costs are the costs of mitigating the contractual hazards of asset specificity, environmental uncertainty and behavioural uncertainty. Costs of friction are the costs of failures to mitigate these contractual hazards (Table 9.1). By focusing on direct costs, as well as costs of friction, we heed Williamson's warning that 'our understanding of complex economic organization awaits more concerted study of the sources and mitigation of friction' (Williamson 1996: 87).

To assess the relative levels and types of transaction costs, we make use of the work of Commons (1924), which forms an important inspiration for Williamson's work (Van Genugten 2008). We study direct costs and costs of friction with the aid of Commons' concept of *working rules*. The working rules of a governance structure constitute the legislation its participants must observe in dealing with each other and with others. Working rules determine the rights, duties and liberties of participants and the extent to which the rights of third parties need to be respected. They form the constraints that determine the interaction between actors in a governance structure. By studying the working rules

Table 9.1 Sources and types of transaction costs (based on Rindfleisch and Heide 1997)

	Asset specificity	*Environmental uncertainty*	*Behavioural uncertainty*
Sources of transaction costs	safeguarding	safeguarding and adaptation	performance definition and evaluation
Direct costs	costs of crafting safeguards	communication, negotiation and coordination costs, and costs of crafting safeguards	specification and measurement costs
Costs of friction	failure to invest in productive assets	maladaptation, failure to adapt	productivity losses through effort adjustments and bad performance

underlying governance structures we are, to a certain extent, able to analyse the direct costs of governance structures that are chosen by municipalities, since these rules tell us how activities take place. We analyse
not only duties and rights, but also how they are dealt with and what
the ex-post effects are on the contracting parties and their relationship
(Walsh 1995; Dow 1987). Costly frictions are produced when the working rules of the governance structure fail to mitigate the hazards of asset
specificity and environmental and behavioural uncertainty attached to
a particular public sector transaction.

The relative levels of direct costs as well as costs of friction are tracked
on the basis of an analysis of the working rules of the governance structures. In our analysis of working rules we focus, first of all, on 'black
letter rules' that are part of actual legal behaviour, the social practices.
Besides these black letter rules we analyse rules that are not laid down
in agreements, but that are of vital importance in the relationships
between contracting partners. Think of social norms and customs, for
example. We track both types of working rules in two separate ways.
Here we distinguish between 'law in books' and 'law in action' (Pound
1910). First, we analyse 'law in books', that is, rules and agreements
that are laid down in, for example, Organization Ordinances, Service
Level Agreements (SLA), Specifications and Shareholders' Agreements,
provided that they are also 'law in action'. Secondly, we analyse 'law in
action' which cannot be found in 'law in books'. These rules are tracked
based on interviews with key persons. A next step is to gain insight into
the frictions that arise in the different governance structures when working rules fail to mitigate the hazards of asset specificity and uncertainty.
These are also tracked on the basis of the interviews with key persons.
This leads to a picture of types and relative levels of direct costs and
costs of friction. In this way we are able to assess the relative level of
efficiency of the different governance structures. It should be noted
that it is not our aim to quantify these direct costs and costs of friction.
We only compare the relative level of these costs in terms of none, low,
average or high transaction costs (as is common usage in qualitative
research (King, Keohane, and Verba 1994).

9.5   Results

The starting point of the empirical analysis is how the public sector
transaction of household waste collection is aligned with public sector
governance structures. Therefore, we first consider the attributes of the
transaction of collecting household waste and characterize the public

governance structures in which the eight municipalities have organized waste collection. Following this, we identify alignments between the two and present our findings with regard to the main proposition.

9.5.1   Alignment in household waste collection

In the pertinent literature, waste collection is often characterized as a relatively simple public service with a moderate level of asset specificity (Domberger and Jensen 1997; Brown and Potoski 2003). These characterizations often lack any in-depth analysis of the attributes of the transaction of household waste collection. We used the interviews in our case study as an opportunity to ask respondents to rank waste collection on the basis of the attributes distinguished in the third section.

With regard to asset specificity, we distinguish between investments in physical objects and in people. Most investments in physical objects are only suitable for the collection of household waste. The depreciation period of waste collection vehicles, for example, is eight years and waste collection companies therefore have to be assured of the exclusive right to collect waste in a particular municipality for a relatively long period. In addition, every municipality has its own household waste collection infrastructure, requiring ever different methods of collection with regard to different types of waste. Investments in people are not very specific, although employees have specific knowledge of the districts and municipalities in which they work, which can only be obtained by learning-by-doing. This leads to the conclusion that the collection of household waste is not idiosyncratic, while it clearly demands some measure of specific investment. We therefore qualify the asset specificity of waste collection as mixed.

In ranking uncertainty, we distinguish between behavioural and environmental uncertainty. We defined behavioural uncertainty in terms of service measurability and the hazard of probity. The provision of household waste collection is not a sovereign transaction and it is precisely for this reason that we do not have to consider probity. We therefore restrict our discussion of behavioural uncertainty to service measurability. Waste collection itself is easy to measure in terms of production norms and environmental performance. This is not the case when the quality of service delivery is concerned – an issue that is important to local authorities – because waste collection is a visible public service. The most important problems are the definition and measurement of quality requirements. Intervening contracting difficulties are the behaviour of residents and quality monitoring. Based on these considerations, the measurability of waste collection can be rated as very difficult. Environmental uncertainty is related to the political sensitivity of the transaction and the political and technological changes to which it is subject. Regarding the political sensitivity of waste collection, our conclusion is that in normal circumstances it is not politically sensitive. The normal course of events relating to the collection of waste is not politically loaded. However, disruptions of the public service of household waste collection are extremely politically sensitive. The current threat of such disruptions preoccupies local authorities and the municipal council. Furthermore, the collection of waste has an important symbolic function because it is a visible public service. In that sense it is moderately politically sensitive. In combination with the political developments and technological changes waste collection goes through, the environmental uncertainty can be characterized as moderately uncertain. All in all, this means a moderate-to-high level of uncertainty. The frequency of the transaction with regard to the provision of household waste collection is high.

Given the former characterizations of local governance structures and of the transaction of household waste collection, we are now able to formulate when alignment occurs according to TCE. Alignment, again, is the case when the chosen governance structures fit the characteristics of the transaction. The main predictions with regard to alignment and misalignment are formulated in the third section. With mixed specific investments and a moderate to high level of uncertainty, the matching governance structures are contracting out and/or municipal service. Since we were not able to classify the uncertainty of the transaction as either moderately uncertain or highly uncertain, we are not able to choose definitely in favour of contracting out or municipal service. Recall, however, Williamson's analysis of transactions with mixed specific investments and increasing uncertainty. In such cases, contracting out and municipal services provide a better alignment than public companies, because in the case of public companies readjustments cannot be made bilaterally (as is the case with contracting out) or by fiat (as within a municipal service). With public companies mutual consent is required among municipalities and between the different municipalities and the public company. This will take too much time. If in a public company readjustments to disturbances are negotiated laboriously, only to be rendered obsolete by the next disturbance requiring a further round of negotiations, failures of readjustment are predictable. The conclusion we draw is that the public company is a misaligned mode of governance in case of the provision of household waste collection and that contracting out and municipal service are both aligned modes of governance.

9.5.2 Transaction costs of alternative modes of governance

The efficiency of alternative modes of governance in terms of transaction costs is determined on the basis of an analysis of direct costs and costs of friction. The types and levels of these costs can be determined in a comparative analysis, that is, as relative cost levels.

As an apparent answer to costs related to asset specificity, all municipalities, irrespective of the mode of governance, own parts of the collection infrastructure. They own at least collection means, such as wheelie bins and dumpsters. In addition, municipalities with a municipal service also own collection vehicles and hire personnel. This entails a higher level of direct costs of bureaucracy as a consequence of the numbers of management staff and the burdens flowing from collective labour agreements for municipal officials and support staff. The difference is not very large, because the municipalities do not have a large staff charged with managing the department. Most municipalities have a waste department managed by a head of department assisted by a policy advisor, team managers and coordinators. The other municipalities have to write contracts and negotiate them. To that end they employ roughly two municipal officials. Consequently, the level of direct costs in municipal services can be characterized as high, while the level of costs in contracting out and public companies is average. The costs of friction are of a different kind in each mode of governance. The costs of friction of the municipal services and contracting out modes as a consequence of failures to invest are little or none, while the costs of failures of this kind are larger in public companies. This is a result of the fact that shareholders in the company, who have to consent to investments, do not always do so. Public companies therefore have a low level of costs of friction.

Regarding environmental uncertainty, communication, coordination and negotiation lead to direct costs. With municipal services the emphasis lies on communication and coordination between the municipal executive, the head of the department and employees collecting the waste. This takes place through hierarchical lines on a regular basis. The level of these direct costs is not significantly different from the costs in the two other governance structures. In the latter two cases too, the emphasis lies on communication and coordination. However, in addition they require negotiation because adjustments to the contract have to be agreed and cannot be imposed, as with a municipal service. In cases of contracting out, communication and negotiation take place in the framework of the relationships between the waste department and the municipal executive and the waste department and the private company, respectively. Public companies are characterized by an additional relationship, namely that among shareholders of the public company. This leads to a higher level of direct costs. Therefore, we characterize the level of direct costs of municipal services as low, of contracting out as average, while the level of direct costs of public companies is high. Both contracting out and public companies cause costs of friction as a result of either the adjustments to the contract or the disadvantages attached to their omission. In the case of public companies, these frictions are the more severe because parties are involved in a multilateral relationship rather than a bilateral one, as in the case of contracting out. Consequently, municipal services have few or no costs of friction, while contracting out and public companies are characterized respectively by a low and average level of costs of friction.

Behavioural uncertainty demands performance definition and evaluation. In the contracting out modes the level of direct costs is high in comparison to the other governance modes. Frictions do exist but they are marginal, because parties have submitted themselves to a very comprehensive contract underlying their bilateral relationship. In the case of public companies, contracts are incomplete and evaluation and monitoring are only marginal. The direct costs are therefore lower than with contracting out. However, costs of friction are higher due to insufficient control and means of enforcement. It is therefore inevitable that malperformance will occur. With municipal services, the direct costs are higher than with public companies, but lower than with contracting out. Performance evaluation by the municipal executive occurs a few times a year. Assessment of the actual collection of waste is done by team managers as part of their daily work. Costs of frictions are due to malperformance as a consequence of a lack of well-defined performance indicators. This is compensated to some extent by the practice of solving problems without indicating who is to blame for causing them. Costs of friction therefore exist, but are not as high as with public companies. Summing up, we characterize the level of direct costs of municipal services as average, of contracting out as high, and of public companies as low. The level of costs of friction in municipal services is low, in contracting out it is little or none, while it is average in public companies.

When we compare the types and levels of costs of the three modes of governance, we find that the level of transaction costs in the governance structure of public companies is highest, followed by contracting out and, finally, municipal service. When we compare these relative levels of transaction costs with our proposition – a prediction to the effect that agreement between transactions and governance structures will lead to a transaction cost-economizing result – we find support for this proposition. We concluded that the public company is the misaligned mode of governance for the provision of household waste collection and that both contracting out and municipal service are aligned modes of governance for this kind of transactions. In our analysis in this section we have seen that the public company is the governance structure with the highest relative level of transaction costs, which agrees with the above conclusion. Our case study confirms the prediction that agreement between transactions and governance structures will lead to a transaction cost-economizing result, while misalignment will lead to a higher level of transaction costs.

9.6   Discussion

Our comparative case study in which we analysed the efficiency in terms of transaction costs of alternative modes of governance has led to the conclusion that public companies are misaligned governance structures in the case of household waste collection. This misalignment does indeed lead to a higher level of transaction costs as TCE predicts. What does this mean for the governance structure of public companies and for the provision of public services in general? This study does not support the conclusion that the misaligned mode public company would in all cases be unsuitable in the public sector. However, if a specific transaction exhibits the attributes that also characterize the provision of household waste collection, public companies may be expected to be relatively less efficient than forms of contracting out to a private company and municipal services.

Particularly striking is the finding that uncertainty, especially environmental uncertainty, plays such an important role. It is our expectation that the importance of the attribute of uncertainty is not restricted to the public service of local household waste collection but can be established with regard to other public services too. If even a rather straightforward public service such as household waste collection is surrounded by a considerable measure of uncertainty, we expect a multitude of transactions concerning the provision of other public services to be even far more uncertain. This raises the fundamental question whether hybrid modes of governance, such as public companies, are, from a transaction cost-economizing perspective, actually suitable modes of governance for the provision of public services. Hybrid modes of governance more often than not include more than two parties as partners to the contracting relationship. The resulting multi-partite relationships make it relatively expensive to adapt to changing circumstances. In terms of transaction costs the consequence is a higher cost level owing to the need for more consultation, coordination and negotiation. In terms of costs of friction the hazards of maladaptation increase considerably.

An important element in this study is our measurement of transaction costs. These costs are often left undiscussed, but they are an increasingly important area of the debate (Hodge 2000). One of the reasons that these costs are not well researched (Hodge 2000) is that they are difficult to measure (Masten *et al.* 1991). In comparing transaction costs we have emphasized the distinction between direct costs and the costs of friction. Costs of friction are even more difficult to determine than direct costs. They have been determined based on formal documents and interviews with key persons. Although conclusions based on such sources have to be treated with care, given the subjective elements attached to the method combined with an inherent lack of precision, to our knowledge these types of costs have not often been measured before. In that respect, this should be viewed as a first step.

A final aspect that should be discussed here is so-called 'second generation' TCE research (Yvrande-Billon and Saussier 2005), to which our study purports to make a contribution. It addresses the issue of the critical relationships between aligning transactions and governance structures leading to a transaction cost-economizing result. Most empirical studies do not pay attention to these predictions but try to explain choices for particular governance structures that have actually been made. TCE, therefore, is in need of evidence that supplements the assumption that aligning transactions and governance structures leads to a transaction cost-economizing result. Second generation TCE research attempts to provide this supplementary evidence by connecting observed misalignment – identified on the basis of the theory's predictions – with observed transaction costs. These studies are still limited in number and scope, but they suggest that modes of governance do indeed have significant impacts on efficiency, and that alignment matters. This chapter has contributed to the evidence, broadening the scope of this line of research by analysing a hitherto unexplored type of public service, the provision of household waste collection.

In future work two issues deserve special attention. First, original TCE makes use of a compact way of classifying transactions and governance structures. This is an important requisite in formulating predictions about alignment and misalignment. In our study we followed the same reasoning as Williamson followed in the original TCE, distinguishing between three broad modes of public governance. In practice, though, the spectrum of public governance structures is much more pluriform. A challenge for further research is to extend TCE so it can also capture these differentiations. Secondly, this study points out that the attribute of uncertainty – specifically, the attribute of environmental uncertainty – is important in finding a solution for the problem of aligning transactions and governance structures in the public sector. It is very probable that governments cannot afford to enter into multi-partite relationships, which makes it relatively expensive to adapt to changing circumstances. While private sector analyses of alignment often pay little specific attention to the attribute of uncertainty, it is required that public sector analyses pay extensive and operational attention to this attribute, which gives expression to the special nature of the provision of public services.

10
Are Regulatory Agencies Delivering What They Promise?

Martino Maggetti

10.1 Introduction

The wave of re-regulation in Western Europe has been sustained by policy-makers for more than two decades in order to correct market failures, to increase the allocative capacity of markets, and to promote the use of specialized knowledge in the policy process (Majone 1994; Majone 1996; Majone 2001a). Numerous independent regulatory agencies (IRAs) were created, such as telecommunication authorities, banking commissions, and competition agencies, to which a great deal of public authority has been delegated. Two main official rationales for delegation exist: on the one hand, the increasing need for policy credibility through independence from politicians; and, on the other, the aspiration of enhancing decision-making efficiency through expertise (Majone 1996; Majone 2001c). Policy *credibility* can be defined as the expectation that an announced policy will be properly carried out (Drazen and Masson 1994), so as to create credible policy commitments *vis-à-vis* stakeholders (e.g. foreign investors), consumers, and citizens (Shepsle 1991). Credibility is considered a crucial condition for solving the time-inconsistency problem related to the political cycle (Kydland and Prescott 1977; Barro and Gordon 1983). Decision-making *efficiency* designates the resource-saving implementation of predetermined goals (Blühdorn 2006). Accordingly, the purpose of delegation is to reduce decision-making costs by taking advantage of an agency's expertise, while avoiding the enactment of policies different from those preferred by the political decision-makers (Epstein and O'Halloran 1999; Bendor, Glazer, and Hammond 2001; Majone 2001c).

Therefore, the delegation of regulatory competencies to IRAs is frequently interpreted, namely by new public management (NPM) advocates, as a technocratic instrument for the management of increasingly complex societies – where the imperatives deriving from an 'internationalized economy' and a 'risk society' require quick adaptations, certainty, and informed answers. The explanatory power of this functionalist and normative perspective is, however, limited, as there is cumulative evidence for the relevance of non-functional factors driving the establishment of independent regulators, drawing from organizational theory and sociological institutionalism (Christensen and Yesilkagit 2006). Processes of learning and isomorphism and strategies for coping with political uncertainty and blame shifting are frequently highlighted (Gilardi 2002; Thatcher and Stone Sweet 2002; Gilardi 2008). Above all, the establishment of independent regulatory agencies in Western Europe followed a syndrome of diffusion: governments made decisions interdependently according to an emulation process wherein the symbolic properties of IRAs appeared to be more important than the functions they would perform (Gilardi 2005a).

Yet the official goals of delegation in terms of credibility and efficiency represent a relevant analytical benchmark in the context of this study, which, instead of examining *why* agencies are created, deals with the *consequences* of delegating public authority to independent regulatory agencies. A growing literature exists, with reference to the unintended consequences of agencification, that underscores the unintentional effects, the delays, and the frequent implementation problems occurring in public sector reforms (McGowan and Wallace 1996; Pollitt and Bouckaert 2004); the varying effects of regulatory reforms on diverse political and administrative systems, which are shaped by phenomena of path-dependence and frequently reinterpreted by national actors according to a 'logic of appropriateness' (Hood, Rothstein, and Baldwin 2001; Peters 2001; Pollitt, Tablot, Caufield, and Smullen 2004; Christensen and Yesilkagit 2005; Christensen and Lægreid 2006); and the increasing importance of IRAs, which are opening the decision-making process while constituting the 'third force' in the regulatory state, together with elected politicians and regulated industries (Thatcher 2002b; Gehring 2004; Coen and Thatcher 2005; Thatcher 2005).

However, very few studies focus on the question of whether IRAs can really deliver what they promise, in terms of credibility and efficiency, with a systematic comparative empirical perspective. The evidence of the supposed benefits in terms of improved regulatory performances is still 'very patchy', and at the same time the convergence towards this model seems to hide a variety of actual practices (Pollitt, Bathgate, Caulfield, Smullen, and Talbot 2001). The rare studies examining agencies' performances (Talbot 2004; Verhoest 2005; Yamamoto 2006), while helpful for building detailed country-specific knowledge, have hardly led to general clear-cut results; and above all they do not focus on agencies that are formally independent from elected politicians, which represent the trickiest cases, both from the point of view of the potential legitimacy deficit and pertaining to the puzzle of combining autonomy with efficiency gains (Majone 1999; Majone 2001a; Majone 2001b).

The main reasons for the persistent uncertainty about the consequences of agencification can be briefly summarized with the following three points. First, it is difficult to develop a measurement of the IRAs' impact because their constitutional goals are varied, mixed, broad, and often ambiguous (Chun and Rainey 2005). Second, the concept of regulatory quality has to be considered empirically sensitive to the subjective understandings of the different actors involved, implying unrelenting difficulties in reaching a general agreement on its assessment (Papadopoulos 2003; Radaelli and De Francesco 2007). Third, the verification of the causal connections between the regulatory action of IRAs and the broad outcomes in the whole society implies a 'micro-macro' transition that involves serious attribution problems (March and Sutton 1997). In order to contribute to this discussion and to circumvent the aforementioned problems, this chapter deals with a specific type of regulatory outcome – that is, agencies' media reputation for credibility and efficiency. The research question is as follows: can IRAs, though created for symbolic purposes, deliver what they promise in terms of media reputation for credibility and efficiency?

In the next section, I will show the relevance of conceptualizing the reputation of agencies through the analysis of media coverage. Then, I will illustrate my theoretical expectations. In the methodological section I will present the logic of the comparison and the operationalization of the selected variables, as well as the limitations of this approach. The results of the comparative analysis follow.

10.2 The agencies' media reputation for credibility and efficiency

To begin with, it is self-evident that agencies' *credibility* is in the eye of the beholder; credibility exists when the stakeholders and the public at large believe in the proper implementation of the announced policies and make choices relying upon these anticipations (Brabazon 2000). Credibility in practice cannot be simply deduced from the structure of delegation, contrary to what mainstream theories of credible commitments seem to assume. Instead, organizational credibility is necessarily reputational: it is built over time through interaction with the larger environment (Mahon and Wartick 2003). Previous empirical research on organizational credibility has dealt mainly with central banks' credibility by means of survey inquiries about individual perceptions of central bankers (Blinder 1999) and private sector economists (Waller and de Haan 2004). Here, another line of attack is proposed – the analysis of reputation through media coverage – so as to minimize the potential bias derived from the subjective self-evaluation of organizational credibility, and from the social valorization of the current 'best practices' incorporated into the shared beliefs of the international policy community (Wilks 2007).

The media represent a point of view that is socially relevant. A large body of research indicates that media do guide opinion formation, especially when they cover issues that are less well known or considered as very technical (Zaller 1992; Bryant and Zillmann 2002). One can draw a parallel with empirical studies of firm credibility in business management literature. It is widely accepted that media-provided information affects the credibility of firms and thus investors' behaviour, influencing in turn their performances, such as price rate and stock turnover (Pollock and Rindova 2003). The media constitute, in fact, a crucial element of the process of contagion that proceeds from the level of individual cognition to the level of social propagation and back to that of individual cognition again, transmitting the image of the corporation through an informal network and eventually affecting credibility (Balboni 2008). Similarly, we can assume that the agencies' media reputation for credibility represents a very important outcome, which could have a crucial impact on the perceptions of the public and the relevant stakeholders, promoting confidence in policy commitments and potentially improving regulatory performances. It is worth noting, however, that the scope of this chapter is limited to the assessment of media reputation, leaving aside the question of its wider impact.

Next, with the following two points, I shall argue that the media reputation for *efficiency* is another indirect but crucial outcome of delegation to IRAs. First, organizational reputation is an essential characteristic of IRAs that largely influences the effectiveness of their regulatory action – that is, the factual delivery of their intended outcomes (Blühdorn 2006). Organizational reputation allows agencies to build networks and coalitions, to exert political influence, to increase their room for manoeuvre *vis-à-vis* the elected politicians, and to reinforce their position before those being regulated (Carpenter 2001). Specifically, a reputation for efficiency is instrumental in gaining support from interest groups concerned with regulatory reforms (Krause and Douglas 2005). In this context, the media provide a forum for debate and dissemination of information, recording evaluations, reducing information asymmetry, and influencing the opinion of stakeholders (Deephouse 2000).

Second, the media perform a fire-alarm function (McCubbins *et al.* 1987), representing a venue for policymakers for the appraisal of regulatory outcomes. As the political principals suffer from a structural informational disadvantage *vis-à-vis* the regulatory agencies, they must rely on external sources of information to monitor whether the agency is acting according to the predefined notion of 'public interest', before eventually deciding upon engaging in – costly – political oversight activities (Hopenhayn and Lohmann 1996). Media coverage constitutes an important 'linkage mechanism' between regulatory agencies and policy-makers (Waterman *et al.* 1998; Waterman and Rouse 1999; Carpenter 2002). Concretely, the press, which is the most important channel of communication for the bureaucracy and its most critical observer (Lee 1999), plays a key role in communicating policy ideas and framing issues (Coglianese and Howard 1998), being at the same time politically relevant and affecting the setting of the political agenda since decision-makers, for instrumental reasons, look also for (regulatory) policies that reflect the so-called public opinion (Stimson *et al.* 1994).

10.3   Symbolic delegation in practice

As mentioned in the introduction, the delegation of regulatory competencies to IRAs is deemed to follow two main functional logics (Majone 1994; Majone 1996; Majone 2001c). On the one hand, delegating powers to IRAs should promote the *credibility* of regulatory policies, *vis-à-vis* stakeholders, by enhancing the time-consistency of policy commitments, given the expected independence of agencies from elected politicians. On the other hand, the delegation of powers is expected to foster decision-making *efficiency* by reducing decision-making costs, based on the assumption that agencies are faster and more proficient than democratic institutions in producing policy outputs in favour of the 'public interest'.

Yet cumulative evidence indicates that the forces behind the delegation to independent regulators follow less instrumental rationales (Gilardi 2005a; Levi-Faur 2005; Jordana *et al.* 2007; Gilardi 2008). Specifically, IRAs were established in Western Europe through a process of international emulation, 'where the symbolic properties of independent regulators mattered more than the functions they performed' (Gilardi 2005a). Following Gilardi, on the one hand, this organizational model is becoming 'taken for granted' as the preformatted solution in search of a given regulatory problem. On the other, IRAs represent a socially valued organizational model that is likely to undergo a process of symbolic imitation for its supposed legitimacy gains from the point of view of policy-makers. In this sense, the diffusion of IRAs follows a strategy for building techno-cratic legitimacy (Radaelli 2000), rather than a rational learning process. The pursuit of credibility and efficiency through independence from politicians is a myth celebrated by policy-makers, which IRAs perpetu-ate to gain, in turn, organizational legitimacy (Meyer and Rowan 1977; Brown 1994). As a consequence, when IRAs were created, the expecta-tions for their performances were very low (Thatcher 2005).

Following a new institutionalist perspective, symbolic politics may, however, have a direct impact on implementation, regulatory practices, and behaviour (Braithwaite and Drahos 2000; Christensen and Lægreid 2003). Crucially, although regulatory reforms are brought into being from symbols, rituals and interpretation (Hood 1998; Christensen and Lægreid 2006), the rhetorical dimension of decision-making might have substantial consequences (March 1984; Brunsson 1989; Christensen and Lægreid 2003; Pollitt and Bouckaert 2004) so that institutions, although established according to phenomena of symbolic diffusion, once in place, 'take on a life of their own' (Pollack 1996). Therefore, regulators that were established according to a 'social logic of delegation' (McNamara 2002) could still become more successful than what was expected, delivering the official goals of delegation as 'a more or less unintended' by-product (Wilks and Bartle 2002).

These theoretical expectations about IRAs' credibility and efficiency should have empirically observable implications for their media repu-tation. The media coverage of agencies' regulatory action is expected to incorporate an evaluation of their credibility: prior evidence shows that media go beyond coverage of scandals, and, however selective, the media cover regulations when they have a direct effect on everyday life, describe problems that could be improved, or take policy in new direc-tions; in addition to credibility, the media are also expected to cover the regulatory action of IRAs with regard to their efficiency, framing it as a typical issue of general interest that could be relevant for the public (Coglianese and Howard 1998).

10.4   Methodology

10.4.1   Case selection and the logic of comparison

Following the idea that 'one strategy for explanation (...) would be to select administrative systems that differ most and, from the research into those systems, develop propositions that appear to hold true regardless of the vast differences that may exist among the research locales' (Peters 2004), the examination of IRAs' media reputation for credibility and efficiency requires a 'most different systems design'. I needed two cases that shared a high level of *de facto* independence from politicians – as effective delegation is a necessary precondition for the analysis – but that ideally diverged in all the other conditions that might influence the outcomes. Agencies' de facto independence from elected politicians could be assessed using my own survey-based dataset (Maggetti 2007), in which this variable is conceived as the synthesis of two components (i.e. the self-determination of agencies' preferences and the autonomy of their activity of regulation).

The analysis required, to begin with, ensuring the comparability of the selected cases; a number of variables displaying extreme values across cases; and two distinct dependent variables – to be measured in the next section, that is, their media reputations for credibility and for efficiency. According to this logic, two IRAs that are factually independent from the politicians were compared: the British Competition Commission (CC) and the Swiss Competition Commission (ComCo). In fact, since the functionalist logic of delegation should be particularly strong for economic and business regulation, I focused on the regulation of competition, to maximize the chances of obtaining positive outcomes of credibility and efficiency (Christensen and Yesilkagit 2006). Competition policy is a politically salient regulatory issue for electorally sensitive politicians, who are likely to be more concerned about the level of credibility and efficiency (Elgie and McMenamin 2005). In addition, I selected a sufficiently long time period to avoid potential bias due to contingent phenomena (the years 2006–2007), wherein a similar crucial issue was examined in both countries – that is, high concentration in the grocery market. Finally, the agencies' organizational models are equivalent: a structurally disaggregated public sector body with regulatory competencies, disposing from its own budget, defined as a legal entity by public law, with a management board headed by an appointed chairperson, and with its own secretariat in charge of the day-to-day regulatory routine.

Then, as required by the 'most different systems design' logic, I examined two politico-administrative systems that are exceedingly dissimilar. The British political system, despite some recent trends towards the devolution of political competencies, is considered as the ideal-type of the majoritarian polity (Dunleavy and Margetts 2001). The electoral system gives to each major political party the opportunity to contend for governmental offices, with no need for grand coalitions. The political power is concentrated in the hands of the party in government, while the other plays the role of the opposition. Once a candidate is in office, there are few political and institutional checks and balances, so the government is certain to rely on its majority in government to pass its legislative programmes and to make and implement decisions (Norris 2001; Armingeon 2002). According to a pluralist model, interest groups usually lobby the parliament, the administration, and the government for promoting the most favourable legislation, but they are not steadily integrated into the core of the policy-making process. The Anglo-Saxon style of public administration traditionally emphasizes management rather than legalism in the performance of public tasks, a contractualist and market-oriented logic, and a career-based professionalized civil service system (Peters 2004). The NPM reforms implied, on the one hand, the reinforcement of market-oriented structures and the creation of quangos, semi-public organizations, and semi-autonomous agencies responsible for operational management (Hood 1991). At the same time a tendency emerged towards the centralization of control and the use of performance assessment and oversight procedures (Knill 1998; Moran 2003). In this context, the British independent regulatory agencies, and especially the CC, enjoy a high level of formal independence, are considered as exemplary by international peers, and dispose from more human and financial resources than other domestic regulators (GCR 2006; Maggetti 2007; Wilks 2007).

The Swiss political system, conversely, typically displays a consensual model, traditionally showing a multi-party concordance government. The decision-making process is open, inclusive, and strongly shaped by the pre-parliamentary phase, where expert committees play a crucial role and the political parties, the interest groups, and the cantons are extensively consulted by the federal administration (Papadopoulos 2008). The participation of organized interests in policy formulation and collective negotiations is institutionalized, according to neo-corporatist logic (Armingeon 2002; Katzenstein 2003). The parliamentary veto power is reinforced by the electoral formula of proportional representation and by balanced bicameralism. Other crucial features characterizing the political system are the instruments of direct democracy and the fragmentation of the party system (Kriesi and Jegen 2001). The presence of a decentralized federalism guarantees considerable political autonomy to the cantons and the capacity for them to crucially shape the implementation of federal policies (Braun 2003). According to the federal structure and the related principle of subsidiarity, political competencies are entrusted to the lowest possible level, especially regarding implementation. In addition to this vertical dimension, the fragmentation of the system is horizontally increased by frequent reliance upon non-professional administrators, extra-parliamentary commissions, and quasi-state organs (Varone 2007). The NPM was introduced in order to impose a greater degree of responsibility and to evaluate the results of public actions. However, it produced contradictory injunctions to civil servants, resulting in an increased 'institutional selfishness and one-purpose specialization' that produced even increased fragmentation, lack of cooperation, and poor coordination (Emery and Giauque 2003; Widmer and Neuenschwander 2004). In this context, the Swiss ComCo, like other agencies, suffers from a lack of human and financial resources, is comparatively less independent from the regulated industries, and is frequently criticized by international experts for its supposed lack of effectiveness (OECD 2005a; GCR 2006; Maggetti 2007).

10.4.2   Content analysis of media coverage

My strategy was to examine the so-called quality or broadsheet press. Quality newspapers are indeed considered as determinant because they are influential on other media, thus directly or indirectly also influencing the mass audience (Coglianese and Howard 1998). It is, in fact, widely recognized that the elite press reaches a much larger segment of citizens by determining issues and perspectives for the news coverage of all types of media (Kepplinger *et al.* 2004). In addition, it should be noted that the perceived quality of information determines the magnitude of its effect on the prior beliefs of readers (Gentzkow and Shapiro 2006). Editorials and commentaries are particularly important in shaping the symbolic environment, although they are unfortunately quite neglected in media coverage studies (Voltmer and Eilders 2003). In fact, they become more and more essential as they respond to the people's need for orientation (Voltmer 1998), especially concerning 'non-obtrusive' issues, such as the action of regulatory agencies, that cannot be experienced in everyday life (Lang and Lang 1984). Moreover, they are the place where the media's own positions are most openly and legitimately expressed (Eilders 2000; Eilders 2002). Therefore, a focus on editorials, comments, and interviews would allow me to examine press articles that expressed an explicit evaluation of the agency in a transparent and direct manner.

Nevertheless, at least three problems existed in adopting this approach. First, the press is not a neutral channel that evaluates agencies' performance with perfect objectivity. On the contrary, politicians and representatives of organized interests can try to use the press strategically in order to sustain their points of view. The press also functions according to a partially autonomous logic, following commercial and/or ideological goals. Therefore, the media are neither neutral evaluators reflecting reality, nor mere channels of communication for political actors. They are indeed involved in the process of constructing reality, and they impose their read of the story (Swanson 1981; Mazzoleni 1987; Altheide and Snow 1988). Secondly, news coverage tends to be cyclical in nature, with coverage that peaks around important events, and then suddenly disappears from the news agenda. Similarly, media are selective: the newspapers do not cover everything agencies do, but they focus on those regulatory issues that have the most direct impact on the public (Coglianese and Howard 1998). Thirdly, the press tends to have a negative bias towards politics. Political news, when explicitly evaluative, is usually negative in tone (Kepplinger and Weißbecker 1991; Lee 1999; Clark 2005).

To put it simply, the solution adopted for this chapter was to consider the aforementioned flaws as constant across cases because of the comparability of the structure of the media field. Then it was possible to compare the relative variations across countries per time period, using an ordinal scale, while also highlighting the different targets of media criticisms. In addition, although media are sometimes in alliance with political parties, competition issues do not fit into the usual left–right continuum; therefore, media position is an open empirical question.

10.4.3   Operationalization and assessment

How do media evaluate independent regulatory agencies and their regulatory action? A reputation measure can be created. For each newspaper, each article that mentioned the investigated agency corresponded to an observation, and it was preliminarily coded as an editorial ('e'), a comment ('c'), or an interview ('i'), along with the date of publication (years 2006–2007). News items, where the agency was marginally cited, and ordinary articles, where the journalist referred to the agency without any judgment or comment, were excluded from the sample. Then, the coder considered each article according to the explicit evaluation of two distinct elements: the credibility and the efficiency of the related agency. Each element was appreciated through four facets. The related criteria referred to a number of empirical indicators of organizational reputation, which were derived and adapted from different streams of literature dealing with organizational credibility and efficiency (Peters *et al.* Covello, and McCallum 1997; Brunetti, Kisunko, and Weder 1998; Blinder 1999; Deephouse 2000; Maeda and Miyahara 2003; Blühdorn 2006; de Jonge *et al.* 2007; Kim, Bach, and Clelland 2007; Radaelli and De Francesco 2007) (see Table 10.1).

Table 10.1 Criteria for evaluating agencies' reputation

	Criteria	*Evaluation*
Credibility	1. Autonomy from elected politicians 2. Predictability of decisions 3. Status of board members 4. Autonomy from the regulatees	• Negative (−) • Neutral (0) • Positive (+)
Efficiency	1. Public good–oriented action 2. Uniqueness of the solution 3. Capability 4. Cost-benefit gains	

Concretely, the code for each single criterion was assigned on a three-point scale by considering whether the article referred explicitly to that criterion in a positive, negative, or neutral tone (i.e. no evaluation present; not all editorials were clearly evaluative; some were characterized by a neutral and diagnostic tone). A positive reference to one criterion corresponded to the code '1', a negative evaluation corresponded to '−1', and a neutral evaluation to '0'. In turn, each element was nominally appreciated as positive, negative, or neutral according to the positive, negative, or neutral value of the sum of the four criteria defining that element.

10.5   The empirical analysis

10.5.1   Data

Data sources are as follows:

> Case 1: United Kingdom, 'UK' (325 articles): *The Daily Telegraph* (63 articles), *The Financial Times* (70 articles), *The Guardian* (62 articles), *The Independent* (64 articles), *The Times* (66 articles).
> Case 2: Switzerland, 'CH' (214 articles) : *24 Heures* (11 articles), *Basler Zeitung* (28 articles), *Der Bund* (23 articles), *Neue Zuercher Zeitung* (54 articles), *Tages Anzeiger* (55 articles), *Le Temps* (31 articles), *Tribune de Genève* (12 articles).

Before the analysis, the consistency of the coding procedure was examined through the recoding of a random sample of articles by another researcher so as to determine the intercoder reliability with Krippendorff's Alpha (Krippendorff 2004), using the SPSS macro developed by Hayes (Hayes and Krippendorff 2007). The result was a satisfactory level of intercoder reliability that was representative of the population at 95%: KALPHA: = .7194.

10.5.2   Results

It appears that in both cases the element that received the most intensive media coverage by far was 'efficiency': among all articles referring to credibility or efficiency, 88 per cent evaluated the efficiency of the British CC and 85 per cent evaluated the efficiency of the Swiss ComCo. The first figure presents the results in an aggregated manner. Some crucial findings can be highlighted. First, according to media coverage, credibility was considered positive and significantly higher for the British Competition Commission (i.e. a differential of +5 percentage points) than for the Swiss Competition Commission (–8, i.e., negative). Conversely, the British CC was not reputed to be significantly more efficient than the Swiss ComCo. Indeed, the tone of the evaluation of the agencies' efficiency was almost identical in the UK and in Switzerland: in both cases, negative articles were significantly more frequent than positive ones. The differential between positive and negative cases was about –19 percentage points in the UK and –16 in Switzerland. Overall, we had 38 per cent negative and 19 per cent positive evaluations in the UK, and 37 per cent and 21 per cent , respectively, in Switzerland;

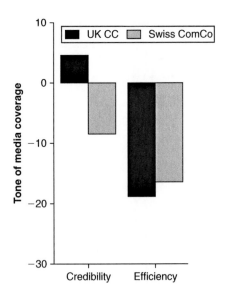

Figure 10.1 Difference between positive and negative evaluations (aggregate percentages)

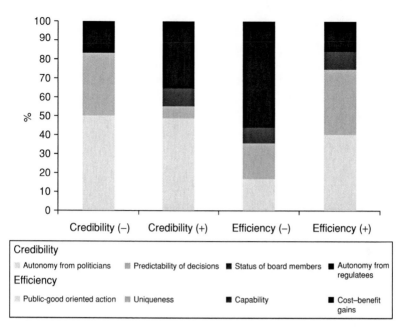

Figure 10.2 Contribution of each criterion to the reputation for credibility and efficiency (British CC)

hence the CC was evaluated slightly worse according to this dimension. Figures 10.2 and 10.3 illustrate the relevance of each criterion of the coding for the aggregated reputation for credibility and efficiency, respectively. Concerning the British Competition Commission, the analysis showed that the positive evaluation of credibility was principally due to a perception of the CC as largely separated from politicians and from organized interests. Conversely, the negative reputation for efficiency stemmed largely from a harmful evaluation of cost-benefit gains. Pertaining to the Swiss Competition Commission, it appears that the negative evaluation of credibility was almost entirely due to the perception of non-autonomy from those being regulated, whereas its perceived weak efficiency derived principally from a negative evaluation of capabilities, i.e. human and financial resources, and from the perception of low cost-benefit gains.

10.5.3 Discussion

The decision to delegate public authority to the British Competition Commission clearly had a large symbolic and rhetorical component: the agency was 'established with ambitious goals but with [relatively]

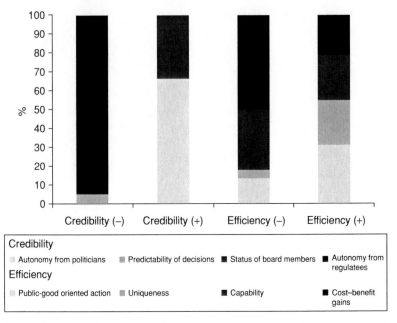

Figure 10.3   Contribution of each criterion to the reputation for credibility and efficiency (Swiss ComCo)

modest resources, with conformist staffing and with hidden limitations on their independence', and the focus on the very general task of 'defending a competitive market economy' permitted *inter alia* the avoidance of more stringent legislation (Wilks and Bartle 2002). However, it appears from the empirical analysis that the British CC benefits from an excellent media reputation for credibility in practice. To be precise, the agency is considered as autonomous both from elected politicians and from the regulated industries. This finding is clearly in line with the literature that assumes that symbolic reforms may also have substantial effects in practice (Christensen and Lægreid 2003; Pollitt and Bouckaert 2004).

At the same time, the empirical analysis shows that the Swiss Competition Commission has a poor media reputation for credibility, while benefiting from factual independence from politicians. This result suggests that effective delegation is insufficient to create credible commitments, and that the translation of symbolic elements into actual practices is likely to be crucially shaped by actors that hold positions of structural power in the regulatory state, such as the regulated industries. Indeed, the criterion of 'autonomy from the regulatees' has the most negative impact on the reputation for credibility of the Swiss ComCo, configuring another potential necessary (although not sufficient) condition for credibility.

From a theoretical point of view, the finding about the insufficiency of agencies' factual independence from politicians for guaranteeing credibility challenges a crucial argument of much research on the functioning of IRAs: pure principal-agent models, mainstream theories of bureaucratic delegation, and, above all, the economic literature on credible commitments (Kydland and Prescott 1977; Barro and Gordon 1983; Shepsle 1991; Cukierman *et al.* 1992). The existence of credible commitments cannot be simply deduced either from the formal structure of delegation (as predicted), or from its effective implementation in terms of de facto independence from politicians (more interestingly). The relationship between the agencies and the regulatees should be treated not as an exogenous factor that can alter the equilibrium of the principal–agent framework, but rather must be fully integrated into the model, conceiving IRAs as intermediary organizations (Braun 1993). Agencies are the focal point that mediates the double interaction between politicians and the regulated industries wherein each relationship may influence the other.

On the other hand, the empirical results about the effect of symbolic delegation on the agencies' media reputation for efficiency deserve special attention. Even in the very promising case of the British Competition Commission, the reputation for efficiency is clearly negative. This finding defies the New Public Management ambition of enhancing both administrative autonomy through agencification and decision-making efficiency by combining delegation with the application of ex-ante, ex-post and procedural controls. In line with the literature highlighting the more general problems of implementing NPM reforms (Aucoin 1990; Hood 1991; Pollitt 1995; Rhodes 1996; Barzelay 2001; Christensen and Lægreid 2001; Pollitt and Bouckaert 2004), it is confirmed that 'turning symbols into practice is not an easy task to do' (Christensen and Lægreid 2003).

10.6   Conclusion

The establishment of formally independent regulatory agencies in Western Europe has followed a process of diffusion, which was driven more by mechanisms of symbolic emulation than by processes of rational learning (Gilardi 2005a). As a result, especially in competition regulation, IRAs were expected to limit themselves to a mere passive, symbolic defence of a 'competitive market economy' (Wilks and Bartle 2002; Thatcher 2005). However, according to a new institutional perspective, once in place, agencies created for symbolic reasons are expected to have an actual impact on regulatory practices. Therefore, it is relevant to ask whether and to what extent IRAs really can deliver what they promise, adopting the official goals of delegation as an analytical benchmark: the increase of policy credibility (through independence) and the enhancement of decision-making efficiency (through expertise) (Majone 2001). In order to contribute to this debate, and given the difficulty of the direct measurement of regulatory performances, the present study suggested focusing on the reputation of agencies in the media. Thus, two 'most different' cases were examined in terms of their reputation for credibility and efficiency, the British Competition Commission and the Swiss Competition Commission, through a content analysis of the major national newspapers during the years 2006–2007.

The empirical analysis highlights, first, that although IRAs may have been created for symbolic reasons, they can become active and can benefit from a media reputation for credibility, as the case of the British Competition Commission (CC) illustrates. In addition, this paper demonstrates that the effective independence of agencies from elected politicians – entailing a broad delegation of regulatory competencies, extensive discretion *vis-à-vis* the elected politicians, and freedom from ex-post controls – is insufficient to secure credible commitments. In fact, the case of the Swiss Competition Commission (ComCo) shows that perceived autonomy from the regulated industries is another plausibly necessary condition. Second, even in the very favourable case of the British Competition Commission, the evaluation of efficiency is negative, supporting the criticisms towards the NPM's ambition of reconciling bureaucratic autonomy with decision-making efficiency gains.

11
Performance of Public Sector Organizations: Do Managerial Tools Matter?

Koen Verhoest, Bram Verschuere, Falke Meyers and Andrew Sulle

11.1 Introduction

The influence of management on the performance of public sector organizations has regained academic interest with the rise of the *'management matters' thesis*, itself inspired to a large extent by the doctrines of 'managerialism' and the 'New Public Management'. These doctrines advocate the adoption of private managerial tools (e.g. Hood 1991; Osborne and Gaebler 1992) within public sector organizations in order to increase their efficiency, effectiveness, and quality of service delivery. The amount of empirical evidence on the influence of *managerial styles and strategies* on organizational performance has been growing rapidly, but the contextual factors remain very unclear. Besides, not much is known about the influence of specific *managerial tools* on performance of public sector organizations. Finally, studies in this area mainly focus on governments as a whole rather than on individual public sector organizations.

This chapter tries to contribute to the existing literature on the link between management and performance by amending some of the shortcomings listed in general public management research and agencification research. The possible influence of specific managerial tools on the performance of public sector organizations will be explored while specific contextual factors are controlled. In this paper, we first discuss the relevant literature and theories in order to construct our theoretical model. Secondly we elaborate on the measurement of concepts and the methodology we use. Next, we present the results of our empirical research, which relies on survey data from Flemish public sector organizations. Finally, we will discuss the relevance and implications of the research results for theory, practice, and for future research.

11.2   A short literature review

Traditionally, the literature on performance of public sector organizations has mainly focused on the constraints and stimuli posed by external factors, such as the rule of law and specific contingencies (Boyne and Walker 2005). One popular approach is the focus on the performance-enhancing influence of private versus public ownership (see e.g. the relative efficiency studies in the '80s or the privatization debate, like Dunsire *et al.* 1991; Willner and Parker 2002). Next to that, some authors focus on organizational variables, like the internal organizational management (Brewer and Selden 2000; Hill and Lynn 2005; Forbes and Lynn 2005).

There is a rapidly growing body of empirical evidence on the influence of management on the performance of public organizations, which shows that 'management does indeed matter' (e.g. Ingraham *et al.* 2003; O'Toole and Meier 2003; Boyne 2004; Nicholson-Crotty and O'Toole 2004; Moynihan and Pandey 2005). This is probably a valid statement, but nonetheless the contemporary empirical evidence is eligible to, at least, four kinds of flaws: the nebulous management terminology, the absence of knowledge about relevant covariates, the elusive concept of performance, and the lack of theoretical underpinnings. In this chapter, we will try to address these flaws.

First, management is a somewhat elusive term that covers several issues, such as the impact of frontline supervisory management (Brewer 2005), managerial successions (Hill 2005), managerial quality (Meier and O'Toole 2002), and human resources management systems (Donahue *et al.* 2000). In this respect, Forbes and Lynn (2005) make a useful analytical distinction between administrative structures, managerial tools, and management values and strategies in order to describe the concept of public management. They argue that most empirical studies focus on the latter dimensions of public management rather than on the dimension of 'managerial tools'. This article focuses on the influence of managerial tools, but uses managerial quality (i.e. values and strategies) as a control variable. The sets of managerial tools discussed here are frequently referred to as *management systems* or *management capacity* (e.g. Ingraham *et al.* 2003). In many publications, management capacity is used as a dependent variable (e.g. Joyce and Sieg 2000; Ingraham and Moynihan 2001). Only a few studies link specific management capacity with measures of performance (e.g. Selden and Moynihan 2000; Selden and Sowa 2004). Most studies on management systems focus on systems and instruments within central, state, or local governments as a whole. Much less has been published about the internal use of managerial tools within individual public organizations and the effects on the performance of these organizations. In this chapter, we use perceptual survey data from Flemish public sector organizations to study the link between managerial tools and organizational performance. We focus on an extended set of managerial tools, which are all linked to specific managerial subsystems (e.g. financial management or performance management).

A second flaw, next to the nebulous management terminology, is that, although there seems to be cumulating evidence about the positive influence of management on performance, less is known about the exact conditions and contingencies that affect this influence (Boyne *et al.* 2005). Therefore, we will include several covariates in our models based on theoretical insights and empirical results of existing studies.

The third flaw lies within the concept of *performance*, which is widely recognized as being multi-dimensional. As Boyne *et al.* (2005: 634) state: 'managerial aspects seem to matter for some dimensions of performance, but not all'. Probably the most comprehensive notion of performance is elaborated by Heffron (1989), grouping 35 criteria into five approaches of performance in the public sector: the goal approach, human resources approach, internal process approach, systems approach, and political approach. As the use of an overly broad concept of performance may hamper clear interpretation of empirical findings and is not manageable in the scope of one chapter, we focus on performance related to the goal approach mentioned by Heffron (1989) and the NPM-doctrine in general. Hence, focus in this chapter is on efficiency, effectiveness, and quality of service delivery.

A last flaw of performance studies is a lack of theoretical underpinnings, which help to select the relevant control variables or covariates that should be included in models (for exceptions see the discussion in Boyne 2003; Forbes and Lynn 2005). Most studies start with the assertion that management should matter, but this assertion mostly is not built upon a clear theoretical framework. In the next section of this chapter, we will use economic neo-institutional theories to give a broader theoretical underpinning to the model that will be developed. Additionally, we formulate a counter-hypothesis grounded in sociological institutionalism. This counter-hypothesis states that, even when conditions for performance-enhancing effects are fulfilled, managerial tools do not necessarily have an effect on performance, because of e.g. the decoupling of managerial tools from the actual work procedures.

11.3   A rational choice model

A lot of normative literature in the field of private and public man-agement takes a positive stance towards the adoption of managerial tools (cf. Hood 1991; Pollitt 1995). Some authors, who advocated NPM approaches, suggested that the use of managerial tools can be a condi-tion for better organizational results (Naschold 1996; Kastelein 1990). However, doctrines of 'managerialism' are mainly practitioner-oriented, and their theoretical foundations are not always solid or without inter-nal conflicts (see e.g. Aucoin 1990 on the conflicting theoretical and normative theories underlying the New Public Management). At the level of broader theoretical frameworks, the economic neo-institutional theories, such as principal-agent and property rights theory, can be use-ful. From this perspective, the use of internal managerial tools is consid-ered a rational choice by utility maximizing actors in order to enhance their performance. Principal agent theory concentrates on institutions within a specific framework of contractual relations between principal and agent, with goal incongruence and information asymmetry as cen-tral themes (Pratt and Zeckhauser 1991). Goal conflict and information asymmetry can lead to adverse selection (*ex ante*), moral hazard (*ex post*), and – in policy settings – to a subversive or deviant policy execution (Waterman and Meier 1998; Van Thiel 2001; Verhoest 2005), or, alterna-tively stated, to a lower performance with respect to the principal's goals in general. Three kinds of mechanisms can be used to avoid these prob-lems and to increase the performance of the agent: monitoring, bonding (in the form of *ex ante* guarantees or contract limitations), and incen-tives and risk turnover (Jensen and Meckling 1976; Verhoest 2005).

In the context of public sector organizations, three important principal-agent relationships can be distinguished. First, inside the agencies a principal-agent relationship exists between senior management and the lower organizational levels. Second, the government can be considered the principal of the public sector organization. A third principal-agent relationship can be distinguished with the user or customer of the serv-ices of the public sector organizations as the principal. In all of these principal-agent relationships, goal differentiation and information asymmetry are assumed present.

The managerial tools under study in this chapter can be considered as either bonding mechanisms or monitoring and risk sharing mechanisms that reduce information asymmetry and goal conflicts. On the one hand, they can be viewed as control instruments that are used by senior management in relation to lower organizational units (e.g. the internal control of organizational units regarding objectives and results) in order to reduce opportunistic behaviour. On the other hand, managerial tools can play a role in the external principal-agent relationships of the public sector organization with the government or with its customers. Managerial tools can be used by the public sector organization as a guarantee (bonding) towards its external principals in order to ensure them *ex ante* that the organization will achieve high standards of performance (e.g. the use of quality management systems like Balanced Score Card or ISO norms). Moreover, some of the instruments enable these external principals to monitor the performance of the public sector organization *ex post* (e.g. the use of quality standards for production and/or service delivery in the agency). Based on agency theory, we expect that *the presence of managerial tools will increase the performance of public sector organizations.* This is because the senior management will use these instruments in order to avoid agency problems and agency loss within the organization. Additionally, these instruments may reduce agency problems in the external principal–agent relationships with government and users.

At this stage, our theoretical framework is rather simplistic because it does not take into account possible contextual factors. Therefore, we will refine it by controlling for five relevant variables, identified in the literature. First, in several empirical studies managerial quality was shown to have a direct effect on performance of public sector organizations (e.g. Meier and O'Toole 2002; Boyne 2003) and should be included in the model as a covariate. Managerial quality can also be regarded as a precondition for the effective use of managerial tools. One may assume that the use of managerial tools will especially affect performance when high quality managers use them as tools.

Second, resources are a quite consistent determinant for organizational performance in the public sector (Boyne 2003). Moreover, within agency theory it is acknowledged that the principal must have the resources to use the necessary managerial tools in an effective way. In our model, we will use one indicator of resources, i.e. number of staff. This is also a measure of organizational size, and one could assume that bigger organizations with more staff will find it easier to attract specialized expertise. In addition to having a direct influence on organizational performance, 'number of staff' also may have an intervening influence on the relationship between managerial tools and performance. We assume in this chapter that staff number is an appropriate proxy for the operational budget, given that staff is the most important production factor for public sector organizations and, hence, the ratio of capital on labor is quite constant across such organizations.

Third, several agency research studies point at flexibility as a variable with a direct positive influence on organizational performance, although the empirical findings are still inconclusive (see for an overview of such studies, Verhoest *et al.* 2004a; Pollitt 2004). According to agency theory, the agent needs some capacity for autonomous decision-making concerning the use of resources, i.e. managerial autonomy (for full definition see Verhoest *et al.* 2004a), in order to fulfil the principals' goals in the most optimal way. Likewise, in order to use managerial tools optimally in decision-making processes, the public sector organization needs to have sufficient flexibility or managerial autonomy. Therefore, flexibility can have both a direct and/or an indirect influence on performance. In this study we will use a rough proxy for flexibility or managerial autonomy, i.e. the 'legal type of organization', ranging from core-departments, public law agencies, and private law agencies (cf infra) and suggesting an increasing level of managerial autonomy. This proxy for managerial autonomy has been used frequently in agency research (see for a discussion Verhoest *et al.* 2004a). For the specific sample of the Flemish agencies used in this study, there is a strong positive correlation between level of managerial autonomy and form of affiliation. The 'legal type of organization' as a variable can have a positive influence, not only because of increasing flexibility, but also because of increasing incentives to perform well. Both agency theory and property right theory state that actors are motivated to perform well to the extent that they are considered 'residual claimants'. When moving to legal types further away from the government, agency boards or heads can increasingly be considered as residual claimants, hence their incentives to perform well and to use appropriate managerial tools increase. Property rights theory leads to a somewhat similar assumption (Furubotn and Pejovich 1974). The more property rights are centralized in one actor, the more this actor will be encouraged to perform in an efficient way. In public law agencies and, even more articulated, in private law agencies, more property rights would be allocated to agency heads and/or boards, in contradiction to core-departments.

Fourth, rational choice economics also refer to specific task characteristics, in particular, the tangibility of tasks or the measurability of its results, as a condition for performance. A principal can measure the results of tangible tasks more easily than the results of intangible tasks. Hence, the agent can be controlled more strictly when executing tangible tasks (instead of intangible tasks). Some studies have found an influence of task related features on performance (e.g. Brewer and Selden 2000). As most managerial tools rely on some performance information, they can be used more easily and effectively in the case of tangible tasks, compared to organizations with less tangible tasks.

Finally, in the model of Brewer and Selden (2000; see also Boyne 2003), organizational culture proved to be a determinant of performance of public organizations. The New Public Management doctrine advocates an organizational culture with a strong emphasis on goal achievement and customer satisfaction. According to this doctrine, such an organizational culture will encourage the adoption and use of modern managerial tools, which are inspired by the private sector. It also allows for managerial autonomy while strictly controlling for results and quality (Osborne and Gaebler 1993; Pollitt 1995). Therefore, we expect that managerial tools will be more effectively used in organizations with a goal-oriented or customer-oriented culture, than in organizations where such a culture is less dominant. Likewise, bureaucratic organizational culture stresses the importance of detail, through standardized procedures, emphasis on compliance to rules and regulations, and close supervision of policy implementation. In organizations with such a detail-oriented culture we expect that managerial tools, which match a result-oriented logic, would be less effectively used compared to organizations with no detail-oriented culture.

Taking into account these covariates, we can construct a more refined theoretical model (see figure 1). The mere presence of managerial tools as such might not be sufficient to cause an increase in performance. The managerial tools need to be used effectively. One could assume that the effective use of the available instruments is determined by the covariates in the model. The organization may need a management of a high quality, enough resources, enough flexibility and incentives, as well as the appropriate organization culture – or at least some of these elements – in order to use the managerial tools in an effective way (see figure 1). Based on the economic neo-institutional theory, we can formulate the following hypothesis:

> H1: The use of managerial tools will lead to better performance. This effect is intermediated by the quality of management, the available resources, the managerial flexibility, the available incentives, and the organizational culture.

In this chapter we will first check to what extent the individual managerial tools have an influence on performance (A), and second, to what extent the control variables have a direct effect on performance (B). In the last step, the variables with a significant direct influence on

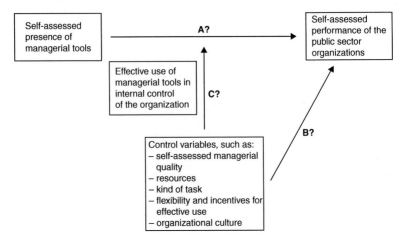

Figure 11.1   Theoretical model based on rational choice theories

performance (C) will be controlled in order to test the indirect effect of control variables on the relationship between the use of managerial tools and the performance of the organization. In the next sections, we will test the theoretical model in Figure 11.1, but first, we will formulate a counter-hypothesis, based on a competing theoretical framework.

11.4   A sociological institutionalist based counter-hypothesis

Our theoretical model seems less valid when we take another theoretical stance. The starting point for the developed model was the rational choice framework. However, when we take into account another theoretical framework, more specifically, sociological neo-institutionalism, the presence of management tools need not be perceived as a predictor of a better performance of public organizations. In contrast to a 'logic of consequence' prominent in the rational choice neo-institutionalism, the sociological neo-institutionalism suggests a 'logic of appropriateness' (March and Olsen 1996).

For sociological neo-institutionalist scholars studying organizations and their behaviour, the latter are not expected to show predominantly instrumental behaviour that responds to functional needs: Organizational structures and instruments may actually be decoupled from the organizations' missions, and an efficiency-maximizing strategy is not anticipated (Meyer and Rowan 1977). Formal organizational structures are supposed to exist mainly because of some form of external legitimacy (Meyer and Rowan 1977). Likewise, new organizational practices are believed to be primarily introduced because they enhance the social legitimacy of the organization or its participants (Hall and Taylor 1996). Similarly, Christensen *et al.* (2007: 59) state that socially constructed 'myths' of organizational structures are *'recipes for how to design an organization'*. Likewise, many management tools, like Total Quality Management, act like 'superstandards' (Christensen *et al.* 2007). From this point of view, it is possible that management tools are adopted because of specific isomorphic pressures in order to obtain and maintain legitimacy and/or to reduce uncertainty. Instead of interpreting the presence or absence of management tools as rational choices made by utility maximizing actors, it may be that whether or not these techniques are used is the result of specific isomorphic pressures.

Three mechanisms for institutional isomorphic change are suggested by DiMaggio and Powell (1983): mimetic, coercive, and normative mechanisms. More specifically, mimetic isomorphism suggests that organizations tend to take example from other organizations in their field that are perceived as being successful, in those instances where there is uncertainty in the relation between means and ends or where measurement of organizational outputs is weak or imprecise (DiMaggio and Powell 1983). Coercive isomorphism can occur through a common legal environment of a public sector organization or through its large dependence of financial and other resources (DiMaggio and Powell 1983). The legal environment affects organizational structures and instruments in public sector organizations because of all kinds of requirements that ensure eligibility for the receipt of governmental contracts or funds (DiMaggio and Powell 1983). Moreover, DiMaggio and Powell (1983) expect organizations to copy the behaviour (e.g. whether or not management tools are used) of the organizations they depend to a large extent on for resources, in order to safeguard those resources. Lastly, organizations may react to normative isomorphic pressures stemming from professionalism and prevailing doctrines, such as NPM, which are spread by international organizations, consultancy, media, and training providers (Christensen *et al.* 2007: 64–5). One can assume that, particularly in the public sector, organizations will face at least one or several forms of isomorphic pressure: in many cases, measurement of outputs is difficult, resource dependence is high, and normative pressure from all kinds of actors, disseminating fashionable recipes is overtly present since the 1980s. In a study of management tools in Norwegian agencies, Lægreid *et al.* (2007: 405) explain the extensive dispersion of some tools by referring to a combination of coercive and mimetic pressures, the latter stemming from informal 'soft' rules introduced as standards and guidelines.

Moreover, the sociological neo-institutional perspective emphasizes that structures and instruments are used mainly as 'symbols for enhancing organizational efficacy' (Christensen *et al.* 2007: 59). Popular concepts, such as management tools, are often too vague or unsophisticated to deal with the complexities of an organizations' task or are not in line with basic values. Consequently, although such management tools are adopted because they are considered by the environment as 'modern' and 'up-to-date' recipes, they function mainly as window-dressing. Such management tools are decoupled from actual practice in the organization and do not affect internal routines and decision-making procedures (Meyer and Rowan 1977). Hence, sociological institutionalism warns against an overly optimistic view on management tools and considers it to be likely that there is a lack of a link between the mere presence of management tools, their effective use in the internal decision-making, and control of the public sector organization and its performance. Therefore, we formulate a counter-hypothesis based on sociological institutionalism:

> H1': The use of managerial tools does not necessarily lead to better performance because of decoupling. This effect is not influenced by the quality of management, the available resources, the managerial flexibility, available incentives, and the organizational culture.

11.5 Methodological issues

In this section, we will discuss our research design: the survey, respondents, and operationalization of the main concepts. Furthermore, the analyses performed in order to study the relationship between managerial tools and performance will be elaborated.

11.5.1 Survey and respondents

We merged data from two similar surveys, conducted respectively in 2002–2003 and 2004–2005 (see annex 1 for more information). The survey population consisted of four different groups of Flemish public sector organizations. To date, the Flemish public sector exists of a number of concentric circles, with its core the Departments and Administrations that are hierarchically structured under the responsible ministers. The other circles are at a larger distance from this core, meaning that the organizations that belong to these circles have some levels of autonomy

Table 11.1 Four different legal types of Flemish public organizations

- *Type 1*: Core government organizations that are part of the legal person of the Flemish community, and that are in the budget of the core department to which they belong (N = 24 on a total population of 41)
- *Type 2*: Departmental agencies with their own budget (some managerial discretion) without governing board, and, in most cases, without their own legal personality (N = 19 on a total population of 40)
- *Type 3*: Public law agencies with their own budget, a public law legal personality and a governing board (N = 29 on a total population of 34).
- *Type 4*: Private law agencies with their own budget, a private law legal personality, and a governing board (N = 52 on a total population of 120)

vis-à-vis the political and administrative principals (they are at an *arm's length* of the core government). The surveys represent data from 124 Flemish public sector organizations varying from departments to departmental agencies to private law agencies. Four legal types of public sector organizations can be distinguished (see Table 11.1). However, the total number of cases included in the analyses will range between 86 and 91, due to missing values.

The first survey focused mainly on organizations from types 1 to 3; while the second survey focused solely on the type 4 organizations.

11.5.2 Operationalization of the main concepts

The two surveys both dealt with specific variables that are relevant for the research question in this chapter. The sets of managerial tools, central in this study, are frequently referred to as management systems or management capacity. We distinguish between four management subsystems based on existing subdivisions in the literature (e.g. Pollitt 1995; Ingraham *et al.* 2003; Flynn 2002): financial management, performance management, human resources management, and quality management. For each subsystem, we identified a number of important managerial tools, which are proclaimed as good practice by NPM literature (Naschold 1989; Pollitt 1995) (see Table 11.2). For each of the public sector organizations, the respondents were asked to report for each instrument whether it was used and to what extent it was used. Table 11.2 reports the frequency of the managerial tools, which is used in one model which is developed further in the paper.

The operationalization of the dependent variable 'performance', in this chapter, is limited to efficiency, effectiveness, and quality of products and services. In our study, respondents were asked to rate the effectiveness (the degree to which the desired societal impact and results are

Table 11.2 Operationalization and frequencies concerning use of managerial tools by agencies for the model on the dependent variable 'effectiveness' (in absolute numbers; N = 91)

Managerial tool	Model re: Effectiveness		
	No	Some extent	Large extent
Financial management			
Internal result-based allocation of resources to organizational units	22	39	30
Development of a cost calculation system	36	35	20
Human resources management			
Extended internal management autonomy for lower organizational units	33	42	16
Development of a results driven HRM	27	38	26
Performance management			
Internal steering of organizational units on objectives and results	9	40	42
Development of an internal reporting and evaluation system to enable board and management to assess results	11	37	43
Use of a multi-year planning	10	27	52
Quality management			
Use of quality standards*	38	53	
Use of customer surveys*	20	71	
Use of quality management systems*	50	41	
Use of internal units that monitor quality in the organization*	40	51	

Note: * these variables are dichotomous (yes–no).

achieved given the objectives of the organization), efficiency (the degree to which the desired outputs are achieved with a minimal amount of resources), and quality of products and services (e.g. number of trains that arrive in time, care for the public domain, etc.) of their organization on a 10-point scale.

Next to efficiency, effectiveness, and quality of products and services, Heffron (1989) suggested quality of management also be added to the framework. In Heffron's framework, quality of management can be situated in the internal process approach of performance. In our theoretical model (cf. supra), we expect the quality of management to be an important intervening variable. In the survey, respondents could rate the quality of management (which can be observed through the actions of the managers, and the status of the managers in the eyes of the subordinates) on a 1–10 scale.

Table 11.3 Frequencies of dependent variables (after re-calculation of the 1–10 scale into a 6 point scale) (in absolute numbers)

Variable	Values						Mean	SD
	1	*2*	*3*	*4*	*5*	*6*		
Efficiency	8	14	25	32	10	1	3.27	1.16
Effectiveness	3	10	31	34	11	2	3.51	1.03
Quality of products and services	1	3	18	39	22	3	4.01	0.93

As the survey was directed to the senior management of the public sector organizations, the performance variables, as well as the other variables about quality of management and organizational culture, are based on self-perception and self-assessment. This operationalization may lead to a response bias (e.g. systematic overestimation). Indeed, the variance of the variables on performance and quality of management within the lower range of values is limited. Almost all of the original scores ranged from 5–10 on a scale of 10. Since there is still enough variation in the remaining 6-point scales, we consider these variables to be useful if we focus our analysis on the variance within these 'medium to high' scores. Hence, in order to increase the discriminating nature of the variables, we have recoded the dependent variables (see Table 11.3) and the 'quality of management' variable to a 6-point scale.

Other covariates, integrated in our model, are:

1. The organizational resources, operationalized as the number of staff (FTE) working in the organization.
2. The legal type of the organizations with three values distinguishing between core government organizations (type 1), public law agencies (including departmental agencies type 2 and type 3), and private law agencies (type 4) (cf. Table 11.2).
3. The organizational task as a covariate with a distinction in tangible (public service delivery, industrial and commercial services) and intangible (policy formulation, regulation-scrutiny-control, public authority, coordination of policy sector) tasks.
4. The organizational culture, for which operationalization we used the dimensional approach of Tepeci (2001). The dimension of valuing customers and quality of service delivery consists of the measures of quality of service delivery, valuing customers, relations with customers and giving customers what they expect. The dimension of the goal-oriented culture consists of the measures of task accomplishment,

224 Performance and Results

Table 11.4 Size of samples and means of most important covariates for the model on the dependent variable 'effectiveness' (in absolute numbers)

Dataset	Covariate	N	Mean	SD
Model re: Effectiveness	Quality of management	91	3.52	1.06
	Customer oriented culture*	91	5.72	0.92
	Detail oriented culture*	87	5.02	1.04
	Result oriented culture*	91	5.82	0.82

Note: * These variables were measured on a 7-point scale.

working hard, goal orientedness, and commitment to accomplish set targets. The dimension of detail oriented culture consists of the measures of detail orientedness, attention to detail, precision, and accuracy. Respondents were asked to rate, on a 1–7 scale, how characteristic the aforementioned cultural features are for their organizations (1 = very uncharacteristic 7 = very characteristic). The mean scores for each dimension are used as the cultural indices.

Table 11.4 reports the frequence of the most important covariates for one model which is developed further in the chapter.

11.6 Managerial tools and performance: empirical evidence from Flemish agencies

In order to test for the link between managerial tools and performance and the influence of possible intervening variables we conducted ordinal regression analyses. For each individual managerial tool, we looked at the influence on efficiency, effectiveness, and quality of products and services with separate regression analyses. Before we entered the suggested covariates in the regression models, we computed bivariate correlations in order to explore the link between each individual variable and the dependent variables. The management tools as independent variables that showed a significant correlation with the dependent variable(s) were retained for ordinal regression analyses. The management tools that proved to be significant determinants of performance in these analyses were preserved for the final regression models. These final regression models thus consisted of individual managerial tools and the covariates that proved to be significant in bivariate correlations. In the following parts, results of these analyses are discussed separately for each dependent variable (efficiency, effectiveness, and quality of services and products).

11.7 Influence of managerial tools on efficiency

Ordinal regression analyses with the individual managerial tools as independent variables and efficiency as the dependent variable show that only the 'internal result-based allocation of resources to organizational units' on the one hand, and 'extended internal management autonomy for lower organizational units' on the other hand have a significant influence. The question now is whether this influence remains significant in case we control for specific conditions by putting covariates in the model. In order to assess which of the covariates suggested in our theoretical model (cf. supra) have a significant direct influence on efficiency, we first computed some bivariate correlations. These correlations reveal that only customer oriented culture, detail oriented culture, result oriented culture, and quality of management have a significant relation with efficiency When put together in an ordinal regression model, only the quality of management proves to be a significant determinant of efficiency. The final regression models thus respectively consist out of internal allocation of resources on the basis of results and the extended management autonomy for lower organizational units, both in combination with the quality of management. Table 11.5

Table 11.5 Final regression models for testing influence of managerial tools and other intervening variables on efficiency (N = 90)

Model	Nagelkerke	Estimate	Wald	p
Quality of management, Internal result-based resource allocation	0.508	• Quality of management: 1.685	39.304	0.000
		• Internal result-based resource allocation to a large extent: 1.115	3.755	0.053
		• Internal result-based resource allocation to some extent: 0.323	0.385	0.535
Quality of management, Extended internal management autonomy for lower organizational units	0.508	• Quality of management: 1.685	39.244	0.000
		• Extended internal management autonomy to a large extent: −0.750	1.545	0.214
		• Extended internal management autonomy to some extent: 0.516	0.452	0.254

gives an overview of the results of these regression analyses. In the table, only the results of the models with the managerial tools that were significant in the first analysis are included.

These results show that none of the managerial tools has a significant ($p < 0.05$) influence on efficiency when controlled for quality of management. One managerial tool, 'internal result-based allocation of resources' has a p-value of 0.053, which is a borderline significance. However, when looking at the percentage of explained variance, in none of the models does this percentage increase substantively, compared to the model with quality of management as the only independent variable. These results points to a limited explanatory power of the managerial tools. It can thus be concluded, based on the results of the statistical analyses, that quality of management largely mitigates the direct effect of 'internal result-based allocation of resources' on efficiency. Moreover, 'quality of management' as a variable overrules the independent effect of the variable 'extended management autonomy for lower organizational units'.

11.8   Influence of managerial tools on effectiveness

The second dependent variable to test is the effectiveness or the degree to which the desired societal impact and results are achieved given the objectives of the organization. Similar to the analysis with efficiency as a dependent variable, 'internal result-based allocation of resources' has a significant positive effect on the individual ordinal regression analyses without covariates. Two other managerial tools also seem to be significant determinants of organizational effectiveness: 'the use of internal reporting and evaluation systems to enable board and management to assess results' and 'the use of cost calculation systems' have positive effects. After the computation of the bivariate correlations between the theoretically suggested covariates and effectiveness, the variables 'result oriented culture' and 'quality of management' were retained for the regression analysis. Again, as was the case with efficiency as a dependent variable, only the quality of management proves to have a significant influence in the covariates regression model. Based on these results, the quality of management is the only suggested covariate that will be put in the final regression models. Table 11.6 reveals that the individual relations between managerial tools and efficiency change when quality of management is added to the regression model. Again, in the table, only the results of the models with the managerial tools that were significant in the first analysis are included.

Table 11.6 Final regression models for testing influence of managerial tools and other intervening variables on effectiveness (N = 91)

Model	Nagelkerke	Estimate	Wald	p
Quality of management, Internal result-based resource allocation	0.384	• Quality of management: 1.279	28.342	0.000
		• Internal result-based resource allocation to a large extent: 1.096	3.721	0.054
		• Internal result-based resource allocation to some extent: 0.597	1.329	0.249
Quality of management, Internal reporting and evaluation systems	.380	• Quality of management: 1.343	32.215	0.000
		• Internal reporting and evaluation systems to a large extent: 1.106	2.879	0.090
		• Internal reporting and evaluation systems to some extent: 1.021	2.393	0.122
Quality of management, Cost calculation systems	.402	• Quality of management: 1.358	32.470	0.000
		• Development of cost calculation systems to a large extent: 1.020	3.510	0.061
		• Development of cost calculation systems to some extent: − 0.360	0.639	0.424

In this final model, none of the managerial tools has a significant ($p < 0.05$) influence on effectiveness when controlled for quality of management. The variable 'internal result-based allocation of resources' again shows a borderline significance. When comparing the amounts of variances explained by the covariate model and the amount of variance explained when a managerial tool is added to the model, there are no substantive gains. These results show that the quality of management is an important determinant of organizational effectiveness and that this variable has a strong mitigating effect on the relation between managerial tools and effectiveness.

11.9   Influence on quality of services and products

When quality of services and products is used as dependent variable in ordinal regression analyses with the individual managerial tools, no single tool has a significant influence. This is a somewhat surprising finding because we would expect the use of managerial tools, especially the ones in the subsystem of quality management, to have some effect on the quality of services and products. Bivariate correlations between the expected covariates and the quality of services are similar to the correlations between these covariates and the other two dependent variables (efficiency and effectiveness). Customer oriented culture, result oriented culture, and the quality of management are retained for the covariates regression model. Also added to this model is detail oriented culture because this variable too showed a significant correlation with the quality of services and products.

Manual backwards elimination leads to a model where only the quality of management (Estimate = 1.004, Wald = 18.371, p = 0.000) and result oriented culture (Estimate = 1.127, Wald = 15.161, p = 0.000) are significant determinants of the quality of services and products (Nagelkerke = 0.396, N = 86). Because no single managerial tool has a significant influence on the quality of services and products (cf. supra), a combined final model will not be developed here.

11.10   Main findings and discussion

In the following paragraphs, we discuss the findings and their implications at empirical level, theoretical and methodological level.

11.10.1   Empirical findings and implications

Figure 11.2 tries to present in a schematic way the main empirical findings on the relationship of managerial tools and other variables on self-assessed performance of the public sector organizations included in our research.

Figure 11.2 shows that only the use of some managerial tools seems to be associated with a higher organizational performance, in terms of efficiency and effectiveness. In the bivariate correlations and regression models without the covariates, organizations that internally allocate resources to subunits on the basis of results report both higher efficiency and effectiveness than organizations where there is no or only little result-based resource allocation. Similarly, efficiency further seems to be enhanced by delegating more managerial autonomy to lower levels of management. Organizations with well-developed internal systems for reporting and evaluating performance and for cost-calculation report higher levels of effectiveness. All these managerial tools listed here are quite central to the NPM-idea of result control of public organizations: senior management set

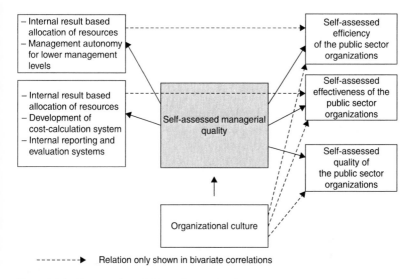

Figure 11.2 Empirical model based on ordinal regression analyses

goals to lower management, who receives extended managerial autonomy and flexibility. Funding of organizational divisions is based on their set goals and achieved results. Cost calculation systems set the prices per output and control costs. Lower management reports their performance through internal reporting and evaluating systems.

Together, these systems form a coherent package for result control, and hence, the associations found are quite easy to explain. Moreover, one could see these results as support for the theoretical model, based on principal agent theory: *some managerial tools increase the performance of public sector organizations.* These instruments can help the senior management to overcome internal principal-agent problems and to avoid opportunistic behaviour from lower levels. Moreover, senior management signals its trustworthiness and good intentions to the external principal (i.e. bonding) by using these instruments. However, the story is much more nuanced than that.

First, it is quite surprising other managerial tools that are also strongly linked to result control, such as result oriented HRM or internal steering of subunits on objectives or results, do not show significant relations with efficiency or effectiveness. Apparently, internal steering on results is much more wide-spread in Flemish public sector organizations and does not differentiate as much between these organizations, compared to the more advanced result control tools that do show significant relations.

Moreover, none of the quality management tools in our study show a significant value in the tests with the self-reported quality of services and products. This contradicts the base line in all quality management handbooks.

Secondly, bivariate correlations and simple regression models of the covariates point at the relevance of organizational culture: an organizational culture oriented towards results and to customers is associated with higher values of self-reported performance. Again, these empirical findings are consistent with NPM literature, rational principal-agent models, and some recent empirical studies (Brewer and Selden 2000; Boyne 2003). However, nowadays detail-oriented organizational culture is in a NPM mindset not really considered as being synonymous to high-performing organizations; it is more associated with the Weberian idea of procedural correctness. Surprisingly, none of the other covariates, except for quality of management, has any impact on self-reported performance. Organizational resources – measured by number of staff, the measurability of task, and legal type of the organization as a proxy for flexibility and incentives – do not affect the reported performance directly or indirectly by enhancing the use of managerial tools. These are rather contra-intuitive findings. They imply for example that in Flanders core departmental organizations are not perceiving themselves as being poorer performers (in terms of efficiency, effectiveness, or quality of services delivered), compared to arm's length agencies. However, recent agencification programmes that are pursued in many OECD countries assume that such organizations are 'better performers' because they are closer to citizens and have more managerial flexibility, etc. (OECD 2002a).

Thirdly and most importantly, *it all seems to boil down to the quality of management.* When we control for quality of management as a covariate, the influence of managerial tools on self-reported performance disappears (or at best, is borderline-significant). In our research, quality of management appeared to be the variable with the most important and direct influence on performance. Organizations which report to have a relatively higher quality of management also report relatively-higher performance, and vice versa. This finding supports the 'management matters' literature and aligns with the findings from studies like that of Meier and O'Toole (2002), who state that managerial quality has a direct effect on performance of public sector organizations. The quality of management also seems to play an important intervening role in the relation between managerial tools and performance. This should not surprise us. In the end, it is the quality of management that determines if and how a managerial tool is used. In this way, managers and their actions also determine whether and how a managerial tool is actually used in the decision-making of the public sector organizations, and, as a consequence, has an influence on the organizational performance. Still, it is at least amazing that this variable turns out to be so dominant in our empirical findings. This would imply that when public sector organizations looks for new managerial tools to increase their performance, it should first invest in management development, securing high quality of management.

11.10.2 Theoretical implications

What are the implications of these findings for our hypotheses and theoretical frameworks?

Some managerial tools do seem to be associated with high self-reported performance, although this influence disappears largely when controlling for quality of management. In case of these managerial tools, our rational choice model helps to some extent to explain their influence. Referring to the full rational choice model, we have developed, we can conclude that only a small minority of the variables that were assumed to have an effect on organizational performance did indeed show to be statistically significant determinants.

As many of the managerial tools do not have a direct influence on reported performance, one could question whether the sociological neo-institutional theoretical framework is not more equipped to explain these findings, compared to the rational choice model we developed. As Lægreid *et al.* (2007, see also Osborne 1998, Verhoest *et al.* 2007a) asserted, the introduction of managerial tools (and other innovations) by public sector organizations has more a symbolic function in order to strengthen their social legitimacy. In such a situation, managerial tools may be lying on the 'surface' of the organization, but they are decoupled from actual practices. Though they are formally present, these managerial tools are not actually used in organizational routines and decision-making.

Managers play the most crucial role, and they decide whether or not to actually use the managerial tools in their decision-making and guidance.

11.10.3 Methodological considerations and implications

However, there could also be more methodological explanations for our limited findings with regard to the intervening effects of quality of management and managerial tools on performance. The data, used in the analyses, were based on subjective survey data, with the senior manager of the public sector organizations reporting his perceptions.

This may have led to response biases, but we tried to control for them as much as possible. As we already reported, there was originally a low variance in the values for the performance variables, which we countered by reducing the measurement scale and increasing the discriminative power of the measurement. Concepts of performance, culture and management of quality were clearly defined in the survey. However, it remains striking that performance and quality of management seem to be regarded as very closely related (or even the same) concepts by the respondents. It may be hard for respondents to distinguish properly between the quality of managerial action, its cultural environment, and its outcomes in terms of efficiency, effectiveness and product quality.

Furthermore, for this chapter, our starting point for analysis was the individual effects of separate managerial tools. It is possible that when certain managerial tools are used in combination, they interact together and in this way they are able to affect organizational performance.

It would also be interesting to study whether a more refined and complete measurement of covariates, like resources and flexibility would show any effect.

Therefore, future research on this topic would need to complement perceptual survey data, by more qualitative research strategies, where document analysis and interviews are combined in multiple case study design.

Part IV
Post-NPM and Whole-of-Government: Increased Complexity

12
Post-NPM Responses to Disaggregation Through Coordinating Horizontally and Integrating Governance

John Halligan

12.1 Introduction

As a result of decentring and the proliferation of central government agencies public sectors have become characterized by fragmentation, lack of coherence and attenuated central control. It is generally accepted that that the injunctions to disaggregate and devolve under the influence of new public management (NPM) maxims fuelled the movement towards distributed governance. In the post-NPM era there has been a counter-movement towards reintegrating the fragmented state by focusing on government as a whole and joining up the parts through horizontal (and vertical) coordination. Two processes are at work: countering the limitations of NPM and the search for balance between decentralized modes of operating and central needs for direction and control.

The chapter examines the different types of horizontal coordination and integration, and their significance and impacts. The experience of Anglo-Saxon countries is drawn on, in particular Australia, because of its focus on several modes of coordination.

12.2 Disaggregation and decentralization

The expansion of agencies under the more flexible regimes and fashions of NPM are well documented (Pollitt and Talbot 2004). For the purposes of contextualising the conditions produced under NPM it is necessary to fill in the other elements that decentralized the state. There was a greater reliance on expanded use of specialized agencies, reliance on third parties for services, and 'devolution' of responsibilities to line departments and other organizations.

In examining these questions, two caveats are relevant. First, there have been wide variations in the propensity to agencify with some countries adopting a systemic approach, while others followed a more selective strategy. In New Zealand, arguably the system most disaggregated vertically and horizontally following NPM reform, the results of fragmentation were stark. Apart from the proliferation of public organizations, the Minister for State Services observed that departments compete against each other to hire the same staff, sometimes to the detriment of the government overall: 'Some sectors ... require major co-ordination from the centre that soaks up resources. There's an absence of ... feedback on whether policies actually work – because the policy advisors work in a department other than the delivery one and the connections between operations and advice aren't established ... [I]n a fragmented system the centre needs to be strong. But – paradoxically ... the centre has been struggling for definition' (T. Mallard, quoted in Boston and Eichbaum 2007: 152).

Australia choose not to agencify systemically like New Zealand and the United Kingdom, but did create Centrelink as a multi functional delivery agency (Halligan 2008b), and there was still a flowering of mainly small appendages. The head of public service proclaimed the dangers of 'bureaucratic proliferation' with departments of state employing only 22 per cent of public sector employees – most working in approximately 180 agencies, many with statutory independence (Shergold 2004a).

Secondly, there are debates about how much power is actually relinquished by allowing delivery to go down and out. Certainly for Anglo-Saxon countries the centre of government remained relatively strong (see Richards 2008); but hollowing out raised questions of capacity, coherence, control and performance. The interpretation of the configuration of the machinery of government has implications for how the sequencing is handled: are NPM and post-NPM to be used as models, characterization of phases or as simply chronological developments?

12.3   Modes of coordination: traditional and new

Coordination has been a perennial consideration in system design, but now features more prominently in reform agendas (Verhoest and Bouckaert 2005; Peters 2006; Bouckaert *et al.* 2010), and particularly where movement away from disaggregation is pronounced and governments are seeking to reassert central direction in order to improve performance. The new significance of coordination reflects in part a rebalancing following 1990s new public management (Halligan 2006,

2007b). Much of the coordination has a traditional character, but it also seems to have acquired new characteristics and emphases.

Australia came late to new wave coordination with its emphasis on horizontal and whole-of-government. Earlier experiments had occurred at the federal level – and traditional coordination still existed – but they were not well articulated and strongly supported. The federal government's connecting government agenda was ambitious with high-level commitment to a multi-layered approach that included cultural change, and was encapsulated within a broader reform programme of integrated governance.

Australian coordination in the 2000s took three overlapping forms: traditional, experimentation with new modes of coordination (variations on joined up and horizontal government) and integrated governance. The boundaries were not always clear, and the official characterizations not necessarily helpful. Take for example the term 'whole-of-government', which is used by officials for a range of cross-service and inter-departmental activity, the emphasis partly depending on where the observer is located.

A traditional conception of coordination is 'a process in which two or more parties take one another into account for the purpose of bringing together their decisions and/or activities into harmonious or recipro-cal relation' (Kernaghan 1987: 263). Coordination may be represented as 'remedial activity', implying a more retrospective focus, reacting to disasters and responding to communications problems. It would be an overstatement to depict traditional approaches as retrospective and their contemporary counterparts as prospective, except the emphasis has moved more to the prospective. Another definition addresses pro-cedural and policy/functional coordination centred on central agencies (Painter 1987). The archetypal mechanisms of traditional coordination were the interdepartmental committee and central agency coordination through control of transactions.

Horizontal government approaches have developed in the last decade in public sector practice in order to promote inter-agency collaboration and cooperation in the pursuit of government policy goals (Bogdanor 2005). These approaches reflect both traditional coordination and new forms of organising, structuring, and coordinating that seek to connect distinct parts of the public sector. In Australia and internationally, such approaches represent an important break with conventional notions of public sector organising, and a response to dealing with complex public policy problems and operating in complex environments. A range of instruments reflecting horizontal and whole-of-government princi-ples have been resorted to in order to address the increasing number of wicked problems and other issues that cannot be handled within a functional department. The issues include climate change, obesity, indigenous disadvantage, land degradation (APSC 2007a), crime, immigration, poverty and national security.

These approaches have gained strong endorsement from governments in Australia and elsewhere with parallel developments in the United Kingdom (joined up government), Canada (horizontal government), the United States (networked government) and New Zealand (integrated government) (Bakvis and Juillet 2004; Kamarck 2004; 6 2005; Bogdanor 2005; Christensen and Lægreid 2007). Within these concepts and applications there are a range of meanings that vary between managing horizontal relationships in the sense of operating more at the inter-agency level to broader formulations that envisage integration of government operations.

Coordination and integration can be differentiated, but as distinctive elements (Verhoest and Bouckaert 2005). Or they can be regarded as clusters of activities on a spectrum in which coordination refers to fairly rudimentary activities that range from 'taking into account' to dialogue and joint planning, but stopping short of implementation; and integration refers to implementation through structures that range from joint working (defined as temporary collaboration) through alliances to unions (6 2005: 48–50).

Much of the recent reform agenda involves the third form of coordination, integrating governance (Halligan 2007b). Whereas the forms discussed above typically arise with regard to addressing specific problems, in this case the agenda relates more to addressing systemic weaknesses, and in particular the rebalancing of administrative machinery. This is multi-faceted and the dimensions involving coordination and integration are not necessarily congruent. They range from centrally driven policy and implementation processes to attempts to make horizontal interaction a routine part of agency management.

12.4   Integrating and rebalancing governance in Anglo-Saxon countries

This move to integrate was common across Anglo-Saxon countries, although predictably contextual factors played a significant part in how this was applied.

For Australia, the emergent model in the 2000s had several dimensions, which reflected several themes: implementation, coherence and whole-of-government and performance and responsiveness to government policy. The four dimensions were designed to draw together fundamental aspects of governance: resurrection of the central agency as a major actor with more direct influence over departments; whole-of-government as the new expression of a horizontal forms of coordination; central monitoring of implementation and delivery; and rationalization of the non-departmental sector. A centralising trend within the federal system has also been apparent within specific policy sectors, which has become comprehensive (Moran 2008). In combination these provide the basis for integrated governance (Halligan 2006).

These trends shifted the focus to some extent from the vertical towards the horizontal by emphasising cross-agency programmes and collaborative relationships as well as the individual agency. At the same time, vertical relationships receive reinforcement. The whole-of-government agenda also had a centralising element in as far as central agencies were driving policy directions systemically and across agencies. The result has been the tempering of devolution through strategic steering and management from the centre and a rebalancing of the positions of centre and line agencies.

There was also underlying elements of political control: improved financial information on a programme basis for ministers; strategic coordination under cabinet; controlling major policy agendas; organizational integration through abolition of bodies; and monitoring implementation of government policy down to the delivery level. The overall result provided greater potential for policy and programme control and integration using the conventional machinery of government – cabinet, central agencies and departments – as well as new mechanisms.

In New Zealand, system rebalancing and renewing public management outcomes became central. Several themes emerged in the 2000s covering capability, outcomes, integration and central agency roles within a philosophy supportive of the public sector. The Minister of State Services observed that 'the centre had been struggling for definition in the last ten years or so ... the SSC [State Services Commission] is still facing up to the nature of its role and DPMC [Department of the Prime Minister and Cabinet] is working fulltime with the co-ordination problems that come from a fragmented State sector' (quoted in Boston and Eichbaum 2007: 152).

Having failed to implement the Schick report (1996), New Zealand confronted the limitations of its model with the *Review of the Centre* (MAG 2002), which examined the public management system and its responsiveness to ministers and citizens. The report reflected standard views about the model's deficiencies (Boston *et al.* 1996; State Services Commission 1998; Scott 2001), concluding that the public management system provided a foundation to work from, but that significant shifts in emphasis were needed. Specific issues requiring attention were the products of fragmentation under an agency system: the need for integrating service delivery, cross-agency coordination, improvements to public service culture, and the need to augment central agency responsibilities.

As part of the reform agenda, there was rationalising and refining of systemic elements to align them with government goals; measures to readdress organizational fragmentation and coordination gaps; and vertical relationships were augmented by considerations about horizontal integration. The State Services Commissioner's powers were expanded to encompass the state sector with broader responsibilities for developing capability and providing leadership. This action was designed to enhance the effectiveness of the SSC within an expanded role in the state services.

A subsequent inquiry was undertaken on the core central agencies (Department of Prime Minister and Cabinet, State Services Commission and Treasury) and their role in managing state sector performance. Under the devolved system of public management, individual agencies were responsible for performance, but performance across the public sector performance was uneven and in some cases below acceptable standards. Central agencies were seen as having roles in aligning agencies and government goals, and leading on and ensuring high performance in the state sector, but their focus was insufficiently developed on a whole-of-government basis, and there was a lack of an integrated approach (Central Agencies Review 2006).

In Britain coordination and integration dimensions were apparent under Blair for a decade, and 'reconstituted Westminster' had been recognized (Bogdanor 2005; Richards and Smith 2006). The working through of the tensions between political control (or variants of the Westminster model) and administrative autonomy (variants of new public management) had demonstrated the dynamic interplay between contradictory reforms. One analysis saw a tendency for Anglo-Saxon systems to move from a Westminster model to a new public management model, but a more recent development (termed Westminster Model 2) saw the attempts to re-impose traditional mechanisms of control onto new public management systems of delivery (Richards and Smith 2006: 298). These features covered in particular political authority in the centre and re-imposition of central control using direct political control as well as regulation and targets (Richards 2008).

12.5   Dimensions of integrated governance

The tendencies across Australia and New Zealand have been strong with regard to a spectrum of relationships, which in summary involved a rebalancing of centre and line; a focus on performance around outcomes and improved delivery; a rationalization of public bodies; and a commitment to whole-of-government and integrating agendas at agency and service levels.

12.5.1   Resurrection of the central agency in coordination and integration

The reassertion of the centre was a strong element in both countries as central agency weaknesses were reversed by giving them greater capacity for leadership and direction. System maintenance is ever present where comprehensive reform is occurring and become particularly prominent in the 2000s. Adjustments were made to the overall system to correct misalignments, conflicts and low effectiveness. In both countries there has been significant rebalancing of the centre, new horizontal relationships, reform correction (u-turns in some cases) and realignments of different components. An overriding trend of the reform era – to devolve responsibilities to agencies – remains a features of the two systems, but they has been modified through horizontal management, and a more prominent role for central agencies in espousing and enforcing principles, monitoring performance and providing guidance.

Diminished central agencies – the Australian Public Service Commission and Department of Finance and Administration and the NZ State Services Commission – were reconstituted with stronger roles. The prime minister departments have also been enhanced, marginally in the case of New Zealand, but most clearly in Australia where the department has driven the whole-of-government agenda and has the undisputed directive role.

In terms of monitoring performance and values, a counter to the devolved environment was to seek greater public accountability through the legislative requirement of an annual report by the Australian Public Service Commissioner on the state of the public service. The Commission extended evaluation to include surveying employees and agencies, and to scrutinising more closely the institutionalization of values in public service organizations as part of the greater focus on evaluation and quality assurance (APSC 2006).

The Department of Finance's role and capacity to oversight financial management and information was enhanced, with a greater focus on departmental programmes, and an expansion of staff capacity in a shrunken department to provide the necessary advice for government.

Unlike the domination of New Zealand's Treasury in the first generation of reform, the State Services Commission began to articulate perspectives on public management towards the end of the 1990s (e.g. the roles of building expectations and promoting outcome evaluation: SSC 1999). It then acquired broader responsibilities from central agency strengthening (MAG 2002). The outcome of the Central Agencies Review (2006) has been to require a coordinated approach to the state services with the three central agencies (Prime Minister and Cabinet, State Services Commission and Treasury) jointly responsible for leading on the development goals (State Services Commission 2007).

As mentioned earlier, the State Services Commission acquired a new systemic focus across the state services and a wider role for the state services commissioner in enabling whole-of-government and central agency analysis of services. The development goals are reported as focusing on performance goals and monitoring across the state services. There is a concern with unifying the state services 'in essence, this is an opportunity to consider how the operation of the whole can be greater than the sum of its parts.' Legislation established a framework to encourage coherence, to improve overall performance, and to strengthen integration (Prebble 2005; Rennie 2008).

12.5.2 Vertical monitoring of programme delivery

Implementation has often been the neglected end of the policy spectrum. Under the market agenda, outsourcing, agents and specialized agencies were favoured for service delivery. Governments have reviewed internal constraints on implementation in response to public perceptions of the performance of delivery agencies. The solution was to extend central control to remove implementation blockages and delays. Following the experiment with the UK Delivery Unit an Australian Cabinet Implementation Unit was established in the Department of the Prime Minister and Cabinet to seek effectiveness in programme delivery by ensuring government policies and services were delivered on a timely and responsive basis.[1] It was depicted as a partnership with government agencies in producing systematic reform to the implementation of government policies, and to ensuring effective delivery. The implementation being monitored involved testing against reality the logic underlying policy decisions, the policy instruments and the resources allocated during the policy formulation (Shergold 2003).

The authority of cabinet was drawn on both as a 'gateway' and a 'checkpoint'. New proposals required appropriate details regarding implementation. Cabinet submissions with a risk element must address a delivery framework including milestones, impacts and governance. Second, adopted policy proposals required formal, detailed implementation plans. On the basis of these plans, progress was reported to the prime minister and cabinet against milestones in 'traffic light' format. The CIU reviews of policy initiatives that cross portfolio boundaries were seen to be requiring agency reflection on how to improve co-ordination.

A core principle of the 1980s was to require departments to manage as well as to provide policy advice. Under the market agenda of new public management, outsourcing, agents and specialized agencies were favoured for service delivery (e.g. Centrelink). The language of the mid-2000s became to enforce effective delivery as well as policy advice with the latter defined in terms of outcomes.

Around 200 policy implementations were monitored. The 'traffic light' report to the prime minister and cabinet was regarded as a powerful incentive for organizational learning for public servants. Cultural change was promoted around a project management approach employing a methodology designed to codify and think through the connections between policy objectives, inputs, outputs and outcomes, to expose underlying assumptions to questioning and to clarify risks and results (Shergold 2004b; Wanna 2006).

The New Zealand approach provides a contrast because central monitoring through a delivery unit was not a feature. The single-purpose agencies that had clearly specified outputs were accepted as producing efficient service delivery. Nevertheless, there has been a strong agenda around delivery and results and addressing solutions to silos through integrated service delivery, and this has been reinforced through an approach focused on six state sector development goals and the use of indicators to measure and monitor progress. The concern has been with unifying the state services 'to consider how the operation of the whole can be greater than the sum of its parts.' This legislation basis was designed to establish a framework that encouraged coherence, improved overall performance, and strengthened integration (Prebble 2005; State Services Commission 2007).

12.5.3   Re-aggregation and rationalizing public agencies

The partial reversal of the agencification trend is apparent internationally, but not as explicitly as the 're-aggregation' prevalent in the

Britain. 'From the large-scale disaggregation of the early 1990s policy seems to have almost completely reversed itself, in practice if not in rhetoric' (Talbot and Johnson 2006: 55–56). The merger of big agencies left numerous small agencies that account for a minority of civil servants. Yet broadly similar movements are underway reflecting a mood to review and tighten oversight through some restructuring and considerable rationalization of public bodies.

Both Australia and New Zealand have foresworn the chronic restructuring apparent at early stages of reform. New Zealand was always the country with most potential to roll back the multiplicity of specialized agencies organized around the functional principle. It was standard practice to critique the fragmentation for more than a decade. Yet the changes have been relatively modest and confined to restructuring within policy sectors, the most notable being the creation of a Ministry of Social Development (Boston and Eichbaum 2006; Gregory 2006).

The centre in New Zealand did however move 'to create and grasp more effective levers of control over crown entities that form part of the broader state services' (Gregory 2006: 153). In response to confusing arrangements for governance and problematic legislation, the Crown Entities Act 2004 established a framework for establishing and operating crown entities, of which there were over 3000, and clarified governance including accountability relationships between entities, board members, ministers and parliament. The state sector agencies category 'public service departments' dropped slightly (38 in 2000 to 35 in 2008). One conclusion is that 'the general movement of the pendulum towards widespread creation of new arms-length bodies may have stalled, and there now is a period of considerable restructuring together with consolidation of the governance regime. There is little evidence of a pendulum shift away for arms length bodies in New Zealand' (Gill 2008a: 10).

In Australia's case several agencies have been pulled in closer as part of the clarification of corporate governance templates discussed below. The most significant was the creation of a Department of Human Service as a small agency for strategically directing, coordinating and brokering improvements to the delivery of services and which incorporates under its umbrella six agencies, including Centrelink, discussed below.

An important strand of the model has involved the swing back to a more comprehensive ministerial department. The targeting of the broader public sector derived from election agenda and the commissioning of a review into the corporate governance of statutory authorities and office holders (Uhrig 2003; Wettenhall 2004). The post-Uhrig agenda was for ministerial departments to have tighter and more direct control over public agencies because of two issues: the extent of non-departmental organizations, and their governance. 'If implementation is to be driven hard it is important that there be clarity of purpose, powers and relationships between ministers, public servants and boards. Good governance depends upon transparency of authority, accountability and disclosure' (Shergold 2004a).

An agenda for enhancing the ministerial department through absorbing bodies or extending controls was given formal recognition in Australia through the Uhrig review into the corporate governance of statutory authorities and office holders. Departmentalization then occurred through absorbing statutory authorities and reclaiming control of agencies with hybrid boards that did not accord with corporate (and therefore private sector) governance prescriptions. The medium term result was a reduction in the number of agencies in the outer public sector (114 to 87 between 2003 and 2009) and an expansion in the number in the core public service (84 to 104).

Agendas for rationalising non-departmental organizations have also been apparent in other Anglo-Saxon systems (Christensen and Lægreid 2006). The Canadian government's response to the Gomery inquiry into the 'sponsorship scandal' was to address control over crown corporations and accountability in general (Aucoin 2007).

12.5.3.1 *Agencification, delivery integration and inter-agency coordination*

Centrelink has provided a case of a complex (multi-functional) agency that was political salient and budget significant, and which operated in an 'ambiguous environment' (Halligan 2007a). The ambiguity derived from how the functions were originally divided up, the scope for differing interpretations of relationships between the agency and departments, and the multiple models that entered into the calculations for the new agency. In essence a horizontal question (inter-agency failures in collaboration) was converted into a vertical question (defining the relationship in terms of purchaser and provider).

Centrelink was established as a one-stop-shop, multi-purpose delivery agency to deliver services to several purchasing departments, and therefore provided a case of agencification (of a distinctive type) and horizontal coordination of service delivery. Essentially, two separate networks of regional offices for social security and employment were brought together.

Structural reforms of government organization involving functional boundaries can still leave public officials with the problem of how to bridge vertical separation and horizontal divisions. In Centrelink's case, the basis for subsequent debates about the roles of purchasing department and provider agency were laid by embedding several models in its organizational imperatives. There remained issues about the separation of policy formation and implementation and how best to constitute a multi-purpose service delivery agency. On the vertical dimension, the limitations of basic purchaser–provider as the means for handling relationships were apparent. The advantages of the horizontal integration of welfare delivery can be realized more effectively through partnerships and alliances for delivering services for a range of clients (Halligan 2007a).

The position of Centrelink changed under the integrating governance agenda concerning agency governance and ministerial accountability, and rebalancing through reducing the levels of devolution. The impact of integrated governance on Centrelink was comprehensive. Centrelink came under a new parent department and within a new portfolio under a central agency. A Department of Human Services was created within the Finance portfolio with responsibility for six delivery agencies that operated under direct ministerial control and one advisory board.[2] The rationale was to improve the delivery of services within a whole-of-government approach by strengthening the vertical dimension (ministerial and departmental control) and horizontal dimension (delivery network across agencies within the portfolio) (Halligan 2008b).

12.5.4   Horizontal collaboration through whole-of-government

Australia and New Zealand came relatively late to new wave coordination, variously termed joined-up, horizontal, integrated governance and whole-of-government. New Zealand acquired an emphasis on 'horizontally-integrated, whole-of-government capacity and capability' and cross-agency collaboration (Prebble 2005; Boston and Eichbaum 2007: 34).

The Australian agenda was given high-level attention by the head of the public service, Peter Shergold. This is not to say that earlier experiments had not occurring at the federal (and state) level – and that traditional coordination was an integral layer of the governmental machinery – only that they were not well-articulated and strongly supported. The new whole-of-government conception was potentially ambitious with high-level commitment to a multi-layered approach that had at its core a focus on cultural change. Shergold (2004, 2005) regarded building a culture of collegiality and creativity as his primary objective. Horizontal governance was depicted as being located alongside vertical relationships and hierarchy.

Australia was how however slower to adopt a systematic approach to whole-of-government than Canada and the UK, which were pursuing these issues in the 1990s while Australia focused on management reform agendas. The environment created by these reforms emphasized devolution of responsibility to agency heads, with direct agency accountability through them, and the importance of each agency pursuing its own business and policy agenda. In the 2000s, the need to temper devolution with a broader, whole-of-government perspective permeated much government activity.

The shift was expressed in three ways. At the political level, the Prime Minister committed to a series of whole-of-government priorities for new policy-making that included national security, defence and counter-terrorism and other generally defined priorities such as sustainable environment, rural and regional affairs and work and family life (Howard 2002; Shergold 2004a). Traditional political coordination through cabinet were streamlined, including changes to processes aimed at strengthening its strategic leadership role (e.g. assigning more time in cabinet's programme to consideration of broader strategy and strategic issues, and giving more emphasis to following up decisions). The priorities were pursued through a range of coordinating or whole-of-government processes, including: cabinet and ministerial processes; the Council of Australian Governments (COAG) and Commonwealth/State arrangements (e.g. sustainable water management, land transport); inter-departmental task-forces (e.g. work and family life); integrated service delivery (e.g. stronger regions); and lead agency approaches (e.g. indigenous initiative).

The government's organizational response to the testing external environment experienced by Australia was mainly to build coordinating units within current structures, particularly within the Department of the Prime Minister and Cabinet. The whole-of-government approach to national coordination covered strategic and operational levels. There was a National Security Committee of Cabinet, a National Counter-Terrorism Committee (for intergovernmental coordination) and a National Security Division was created to coordinate and apply whole-of-government principles in national security focusing on border protection, counter-terrorism, defence, intelligence, law enforcement and security. The Department coordinates activities across the Australian Public Service as well as inter-governmentally.

Thirdly, the shift was officially expressed through an articulation of the elements in *Connecting Government* (Management Advisory Committee 2004), which indicated how to address issues about whole-of-government processes and structures, cultures, managing information, budgetary frameworks; and including different levels of policy advice, programme management and integrating service delivery. Whole-of-government was defined as 'agencies working across portfolio boundaries to achieve a shared goal and an integrated governance response to particular issues'. The conception was fairly inclusive for approaches may operate formally and informally, range from policy development through programme management to service delivery and cover the activities of coordinating departments (central agencies), integration (reducing the number of departments) and cooperative federalism (MAC 2004: 1, 6–7). There was an underlying rationalist conception suggesting that difficult policy problems and management questions can be laid out, solutions designed and challenges managed to produce improved problem solving, service delivery and performance.

The effectiveness of different approaches depends both on the complexity of the policy or programme task and the way it can be configured. In practice, there was a wide spectrum of experiments ranging from crisis management through to the challenges of coordinating the administration of indigenous programmes and services (Gray and Sanders 2006).

Of the several mechanisms, the interdepartmental committee (IDC) was a central component of traditional machinery, numbering as many as 180 IDCs, mainly between departments with responsibilities ranging from routine administration, and adjudication to policy. The policy IDCs (normally between 30 and 50), displayed two significant characteristics: operating as a collection of delegates who defended the interests of their department and 'the norm, and the practice of, of IDCs of searching for a consensus outcome' (Painter and Carey 1979: 62). IDCs retained a recognized presence, and their traditional roles were recognized, but they were no longer the main mode of cross-departmental coordination for programme design, review and management with new structural innovations emerging for strengthening collective and cross-portfolio coordination (MAC 2004).

Task forces originally rose to prominence as a means of avoiding the defects of IDCs and as short-term vehicles for giving focus to government agendas. The task force has become 'semi-formalized as a device to develop new policy or to deal with significant, urgent issues' (MAC 2004: 29). Whereas once task forces were distinguished informally from other cross-agency structures, the understanding is now consistently entrenched that 'a task force is a discrete, time-and-purpose limited unit responsible for producing a result in its own right'. Their capacity for operating independently from policy departments was strengthened by the Department of the Prime Minister and Cabinet being assigned administrative responsibility for them in many cases (Hamburger 2007).

Of the traditional mechanisms the cabinet (of ministers) and the central agencies were prominent. Task forces became relatively institutionalized and addressed significant issues, but only affected a relatively small proportion of Senior Executive Service/Executive Level public servants (13 per cent). Joint teams (regarded as longer lasting structures that blend functions across portfolios) accounted for 16 per cent. Membership of inter-departmental committees continued to be the most significant activity (22 per cent) (APSC 2006).

12.6   Explaining the rebalancing movement

Sustaining change over the long term is difficult because it involves multiple processes, alignments between components and traditional cycles of public administration. These complexities have meant that different types of process and organizational response have been apparent. It is also possible to distinguish both patterns that inevitably seem to prevail over the long term and other transient drivers that provide the circumstances and motive force in practice. The tensions between different forces and contradictory positions have been frequently recognized in public administration, particularly with regards to conflicts over distinctive values and swings between different structures (Aucoin 1990).

This can be seen first of all through cycles of public administration. One argument is that core values can be identified, which have been successively pursued over the long-term organization of government. The administrative history of the machinery of government in the United States is depicted as a succession of shifts between different dominant values (Kaufman 1956; Light 1997).

A second ineluctable tension in government is between the pressures for centralization and decentralization. Government management is inherently focused on central control and coordination as in other complex organizations. However, 'decentralization ... requires conscious and continuing efforts to tilt the organization in ways that contain, even resist, the natural tendency to reign in the power at the centre' (Aucoin and Bakvis 1988: 6). Explaining this further, the authors observe, based on the Canadian case, that centralization has been promoted in accordance with the combination of parliamentary and cabinet government by the two principles of individual responsibility and collective responsibility (Aucoin and Bakvis 1988: 13–14). With regard to the latter, cabinet acts as a centralising force because of its corporate character and by seeking high levels of policy coordination, integration of decision-making and implementation, and administrative policies that require compliance by the whole public service (Aucoin and Bakvis

1988: 14). Over the long term the tendency in Canada has been for the concentration of power at the centre (Savoie 1999).

The injunction to steer rather than row ignores the imperatives of central and national government and the need for control (Schick 2003). It does however point up the fundamental basis of national government and that ultimately the steering role will prevail.

In the reform era, other factors has been apparent, namely the greater focus on organization and design, and overall government management. This can be expressed through attention to how best to reconcile centralization and decentralization (Metcalfe and Richards 1987; Aucoin and Bakvis 1988). One argument is that centralization and decentralization are opposites that can only be brought into balance by some form of trade-off (Metcalfe and Richards 1987). If that tradeoff is not carefully thought through, or if government priorities change significantly, an imbalance arises.

One implication is that coordination and decentralising initiatives may be simultaneous. The relationship between specialization and coordination can take several forms and be divergent as well as complementary (Bouckaert *et al.* 2010).

What are the specific triggers that produce movement? The progression of reform is subject to conflicts among objectives and interruptions from external interventions as various political and global factors come into play (Aucoin 1990; Hood 1994; Pollitt and Bouckaert 2004). Both external and internal factors assist with explaining change.

Despite the different patterns of change between New Zealand and Australia – New Zealand's distinctive expression of new public management imposed rapidly whereas Australia's variant assumed a full-fledged version after over a decade of reform – they confronted broadly similar issues by the turn of the century. The unintended consequences of neo-liberal reforms provided substantial potential in the 2000s for corrective mechanisms and the recentring of operating principles and practice, but the explanations for this major shift were more complex. An examination of the internal and external explanations for such change provides insights into what promoted homogeneity and integration.

The internal factors were overshadowed by movement within the public management reform cycle as the excesses and limitations of NPM received corrective attention. Reflection on the results of an intense neo-liberal reform agenda produced refinements and revaluation of the worth of the public service under new leadership of central agencies that suited different agendas (Gregory 2006; Halligan 2006). The features of new public management – disaggregation, devolution, outsourcing, and multiple services providers – supported specialization but led to fragmentation and reinforced vertical structures (or silos). New Zealand's failure to correct well-known weaknesses was widely reported as unfinished business with the need 'to debug' the less successful elements and to make modifications that would allow further development and reform (Schick 1996; Boston *et al.* 1996; Scott 2001; Boston and Eichbaum 2006).

There were other complex domestic policy issues, such as climate change, the environment and security that required strategic and integrated government responses involving multiple agencies and levels of government. These were both intractable policy problems and issues experiencing bureaucratic blockages.

Underlying new directions were political control and performance issues. Governments that had driven neo-liberal reforms confronted their limitations and the contradictions of complex reform programmes. Governments internationally became concerned that political priorities were neither being sufficiently reflected in policy directions nor followed through effectively in programme implementation and delivery.

External pressures were originally fiscal in nature and economic factors (e.g. international competitiveness) remained a driver, but external threat emerged in the 2000s, in countries such as Australia where issues of security and terrorism dominated both the domestic and international landscape.[3] The threat of global terrorism and the challenges of counterterrorism, protection of borders and domestic security were regarded as having transformed Australian life and identity. For New Zealand, the impact of security and international developments were less direct and immediate, but insecurity issues have been represented as broadly comparable in the sense of protecting a country's national interests. A 'whole-of-insecurity' strategy was required to handle increasing complexity, economic and environmental threats and international obligations (Gregory 2006; Halligan 2006).

For these countries, the intensity of the reassertion of the centre resulted from system shortcomings as well as environmental uncertainty and threat. External threat is a powerful motivating force for inducing integration though central coordination and tighter control. The combination of internal and external factors led to the emergence of a more integrated approach to governance.

12.7   Significance of post-NPM coordination

Much of modern coordination is similar to traditional arrangements, but there is now a greater intensity and commitment to horizontal coordination and embedding inter-agency collaboration in the public service. At the same time there are several relationships in play each of which has horizontal and vertical dimensions.

The principle of 'function' is the universal basis for most central government organization. The key issue with whole-of-government is about refocusing agencies constituted around functional hierarchies into ones that routinely incorporate horizontal collaboration in their modes of operating. However, the question remains of 'how far vertical accountabilities can be sacrificed' (Scott 2008: 11).

Horizontal management and whole-of-government raise intriguing issues in organization design and behavioural challenges. The Australian agenda has been fairly ambitious and was located within the broader framework of integrating governance. This compatibility between the agenda and the framework ensured that inherent conflicts did not apply at that level and that there was political and bureaucratic drive and support. In the new public service, horizontal governance was located alongside vertical relationships and hierarchy. The need to develop a culture that supported collaboration was an integral element.

The obstacles to inculcating cultural change however have remained substantial. How do public servants incorporate whole-of-government operating principles into underlying assumptions that shape day-to-day work, and how do agencies substantiate claims about cultural change? The evidence from mid-2000 surveys was uneven. Most Senior Executive Service/Executive Level public servants had some form of direct dealings with other agencies, but 61 per cent of those surveyed had no structured engagement. The remainder were involved in task forces and IDCs and joint teams (Australian Public Service Commission 2006: 214; see also reports, 2003–2004 to 2006–2007).

Agency support for collaboration was quite strong according to public servants' perceptions of whether their agency encouraged a constructive approach to collaboration with public organizations, but the level of support appeared to be waning as the intensity of commitment to the agenda faded. Multi-agency forums had been represented as an indicator of change and commitment, yet public servants saw such forums as more focused on solving agency objectives compared to whole-of-government priorities. Of the indicators, high support for cross-boundary focus on outcome was the more promising.

Long-term change is unlikely without cultural change because pressures from functional established systems are too intense. The imperative of the functional principle and the rigidity of organizational boundaries have still loomed prominently. The official verdict is of lack of progress: 'Despite some successes ... the overall implementation of the Connecting Government report has been disappointing and the report does no appear to have had a fundamental impact on the approach that the APS [Australian Public Service] takes to its work' (APSC 2007b: 247).

Other relationships also compete for attention. The rise of the centre as expressed through the key central agencies is of heightened importance in countries like Australia and Canada. The concept of 'whole-of-government' from the perspective of the centre may be far removed from that at the level of inter-departmental activity and relationships. Balancing line department and central agency continues to be a challenging issue because of the need to reconcile coordination and empowerment (Peters and Savoie 1996).

12.8 Conclusion

The long-term significance whole-of-government is still being examined. As far as central agencies looking across government as a whole, their position is again consolidated. For horizontal management, the challenges are well known, and the rather mixed impact that these agendas have had in countries like the United Kingdom and Canada (Peters 2006), have been repeated in Australia and New Zealand. In a federal system like Australia, intergovernmental relations can play a more pronounced role because of the reliance on state government for delivery; whereas, in a relatively centralized unitary system like New Zealand, central government can be more self-contained for many purposes.

The level of horizontal management activity appears to have been expanded through a mixture of central agency push and shove using task forces, a reliance on traditional IDCs for some purposes, and some new interactive mechanisms (although until more systematic material is acquired the judgement must be qualified).[4]

The conventional wisdom became that horizontal relationships were simply to be incorporated into the routines of governance. Given the pressures of the functional principle and shifting relational priorities, the viability of this expectation in practice was problematic. There is of course no single formula for balancing agency requirements and whole-of-government imperatives. Maintaining balance is difficult. Imbalances can trigger further movement.

The overall commitment to horizontal and integrated governance remains, but a horizontal agenda requires a combination of leadership and incentives. Leadership at the public service level has been clear, if transient, but more attention needs to have been given to the incentives for agencies to engage systematically in horizontal collaborations. These types of relationship are otherwise too vulnerable to being trumped by the priority given to other relationships.

In the Australian context, there is a more significant medium term challenge. A new phase in modernising intergovernmental relations has commenced under a federal government that places a high emphasis on vertical relationships within the federation (i.e. between the federal and state governments[5]) (Moran 2008). While this can be interpreted as 'whole-of-government' or 'governments' they can hardly be conceptualized as horizontal. The drive within policy sectors, and overall, means that the reform priorities have become more complex. Perhaps a new horizon is unfolding that combines the vertical and horizontal in fresh ways.

Notes

1. In contrast to the UK Delivery Unit, the Implementation Unit employed public servants rather than political advisers and was integrated into the Department of the Prime Minister and Cabinet.
2. Six agencies deliver services and payments that account for over $90 billion and also include the Child Support Agency, Health Services Australia and Medicare Australia.
3. There were terrorist attacks in Bali and the Australian commitment of forces to the coalition of America and Britain in Iraq as well as the enduring impact of 9/11.
4. A research project at the University of Canberra is investigating the results of a whole of government agenda: http://www.canberra.edu.au/arc-wholegov/.
5. There are six states and two territories under the constitution. Intergovernmental reform was partly prompted by all nine jurisdictions being Labour governments.

13
Increased Complexity in Public Organizations – the Challenges of Combining NPM and Post-NPM

Tom Christensen and Per Lægreid

13.1 Introduction

Modern public organizations are complex and they seem to be becoming even more so. One reason for this is that modern democracies are institutionalizing administrative policies and are implementing different generations of modern public reforms at an increasing pace (Christensen and Lægreid 2007b). Reform efforts have resulted in a complex and multiple-layered system (Streeck and Thelen 2005), where certain elements of structure and culture have remained relatively stable, others have become strengthened and institutionalized, and others still have been reorganized, modified or deinstitutionalized (Røvik 1996).

The increased complexity of the structure and culture of public organizations may be seen as the result of instrumental organizational design, reflected in a consciously conceived structure (Egeberg 2003); equally it may be construed as the result of a long-term culturally oriented evolutionary process (Selznick 1957). However, increased complexity may also result from negotiation processes (Cyert and March 1963; March and Olsen 1983), or from pressure from the technical or institutional environment (Meyer and Rowan 1977; Christensen and Lægreid 2001b).

The results of increased structural and cultural complexity may in principle be diverse (Christensen and Lægreid 2007b). Complexity may indicate instrumentality and rationality. As societal and political–administrative problems and requirements become more complex, structure and culture must also become more complex. Complexity may also mean flexibility, because structural and cultural diversity enable a public organization to relate to different parts of its own organization and the environment in a variety of ways. Yet complexity may also imply organized chaos, where public leaders have problems coping with the demands and problems of using the structure and culture in systematic ways (March and Olsen 1976).

This chapter will discuss the processes, challenges and effects of complexity by focusing on the distinction between political and administrative control on the one hand, and institutional autonomy on the other, and relate this to NPM and post-NPM reforms. The NPM reform wave advanced the autonomy argument, stressing structural devolution and increased distance to executive politicians, while post-NPM reforms have revived the control and coordination aspects (Christensen *et al.* 2007d). The NPM reforms combined vertical specialization or structural devolution with extensive use of the principle of 'single-purpose organizations' or horizontal specialization, creating a fragmented system which, it was argued, catered to 'role purity' (Gregory 2001). Post-NPM reforms, which started in the late 1990s in some countries that had been NPM trailblazers, introduced a combination of a) vertical integration via stronger control measures and making more capacity available to the political executive, and b) more horizontal collaboration and coordination in the form of networks, teams, projects, etc. (Gregory 2003; Halligan 2006).

We address two main research questions: 1) What characterizes the new structural complexity and layering of NPM and post-NPM reforms in public organizations? 2) How might we analyse the development of this complexity? What is the role of the political and administrative leadership in this development, and to what extent do other factors come into play? The first question is addressed by giving a brief overview of the change from NPM reforms to post-NPM reforms followed by empirical data from four reform processes in Norway that increased complexity. The second question will be answered in a theoretical discussion using a transformative approach and by analysing the experience of balancing control and autonomy in NPM and post-NPM reform measures in the Norwegian reform process. We will conclude with some reflections on the implications and effects of the new complexity.

13.2   Complexity in public organizations

Structural complexity in public organizations may be measured according to some central dimensions. One is vertical specialization, another is horizontal specialization, and both dimensions have intra- and inter-organizational elements (Gulick 1937; Simon 1957; Egeberg 2003). Vertical intra-organizational specialization tells how the formal authority is distributed among levels. Strong vertical specialization means that the hierarchical controlling and coordinative power is widely divided among many leaders and levels. Vertical inter-organizational specialization focuses on the specialization among public organizations. Strong vertical specialization in this respect may be ministries with a lot of subordinate agencies, while weak specialization is indicating integrated ministries.

Horizontal intra-organizational specialization means internal specialization in public organizations, in different departments and divisions, according to principles Gulick (1937) labels purpose, process, clientele and geography. Strong horizontal specialization indicates division into several sub-units. Horizontal inter-organizational specialization focuses on specialization among public organizations on the same hierarchical level, like among agencies. Strong specialization means many such units. Combining these dimensions gives us an indication of the complexity in a system. The extremes here are strong vertical and horizontal specialization overall, meaning strong proliferation and fragmentation, and low specialization on both dimensions, meaning an integrated political–administrative system. We will not measure complexity very specific, but indicate through using the dimensions, in what direction four sectors or policy areas are moving.

Cultural complexity is also part of the equation, but less central in our analysis than structural complexity. It is also more difficult to grasp. Strong cultural complexity means that there is a variety of informal, cultural norms and values in and among public organizations. Weak cultural complexity means cultural homogeneity and integration; and that organizational members are very committed to the basic cultural norms and values (Selznick 1957; Krasner 1988; March and Olsen 1989).

13.3 NPM and post-NPM reforms: increasing complexity

When New Public Management was introduced in Australia and New Zealand in the early 1980s it was intended to be an alternative and a challenge to the 'old public administration', which was held to represent a centralized, integrated model of extensive government (Boston *et al.* 1996). The main message from the NPM entrepreneurs was that public sectors around the world not only needed to be scaled back, but also fundamentally restructured along the principles espoused by the private sector (Wright 1994). The structural model proposed was one of increased specialization and fragmentation, both vertically and horizontally (Christensen and Lægreid 2001a). Vertically, it was argued that structural devolution was the answer to central capacity problems, and would allow leaders to focus on more strategic questions, while leaving the choice of implementation instruments to officials on lower levels (Gregory 2001). The NPM-entrepreneurs argued that both control and autonomy would be improved by the reforms.

There were many new forms of structural devolution. One was to give traditional agencies more leeway (Christensen *et al.* 2007d). Other measures included establishing more regulatory agencies with strong autonomy, based on professional values (Pollitt *et al.* 2004); transforming public administration bodies into state-owned companies; giving state-owned enterprises a larger amount of autonomy (Spicer *et al.* 1996); and privatizing public activities related to services and the market. Adding to this has NPM been connected to increasing horizontal specialization, concerning more specialized roles. Taken together these NPM reform ideas produced a more fragmented public-sector model. They introduced more complexity, partly because elements from the 'old public administration' did not disappear, but were modified and combined with the NPM elements.

Studies of NPM have pointed to the fact that in reality it has constituted a complex and mixed bag of reform elements (Gregory 2003). Boston *et al.* (1996) showed that the underlying economic ideas of NPM reforms were both ambiguous and contradictory about how to organize the public sector. Some of the central ideas were related to theories on contracts. Over the last two decades of NPM it has become increasingly clear that devolution and deregulation have come to be coupled with re-regulation and more scrutiny and control (Christensen and Lægreid 2006). It is also quite easy to show that NPM in reality represents a lot of variety and complexity between and inside countries and policy sectors (Christensen and Lægreid 2001a; Pollitt and Bouckaert 2004). The overall trend has been in the direction of increased autonomy. This has created problems of political control.

When the first post-NPM measures emerged in Australia and New Zealand in the late 1990s, they could primarily be seen as a kind of reaction to the effects and implications of NPM-related reforms (Gregory 2003; Christensen and Lægreid 2007a; Halligan 2007b). Two types of challenges seemed to be important. One was the undermining of control and central capacity that NPM brought. Now it was time for the executive politicians to take back some of that control and increase their own capacity to solve cross-sectoral societal problems. The measures used were to vertically reintegrate some of the agencies and enterprises, either by dissolving some agencies and integrating their activities in the ministries, or by establishing more controls and constraints. Another measure was to strengthen overall administrative or political capacity close to the political executive (Halligan 2006).

The horizontal challenge was seen as even more important than the vertical, because a lot of specialized sectoral pillars or silos had been created that were seen as obstructing the solution of cross-sectoral problems (Pollitt 2003b). The NPM reforms' heavy promotion of the principle of 'single-purpose organizations' was perceived as negative, because it led to a lot of horizontal specialization and fragmentation and turf wars among competing public organizations. The political and administrative leadership in post-NPM countries like the UK, Australia and New Zealand came up with several new coordinative measures that were easier to implement than only reversing structural devolution: More collaboration was introduced in the central government apparatus, among both political and administrative leaders and across sectors. Cross-sectoral programs, projects and networks were established, and there were even some structural mergers (Gregory 2003; Halligan 2006). The political and administrative leadership also tried to combine the two main sets of measures, resulting in more control of the different types of cross-sectoral collaboration and coordination.

When the post-NPM reforms were introduced, the balance tipped back somewhat towards more control, but it did not restore the situation that had existed under the 'old public administration' (Christensen and Lægreid 2007d). This was partly due to the fact that changing some of the structural devolution was both politically and administratively difficult. Post-NPM plays out more along the horizontal dimension, with more structural and cultural integration, and has added to and modified the NPM reforms, making the system even more structurally and culturally complex. The development has been from simple integration (old public administration) through complex, fragmented and unbalanced complexity (NPM), to integrated and more balanced complexity concerning political control and autonomy (post-NPM).

13.4 Adding complexity by balancing control and autonomy – four reform cases

To take a closer look at the dynamics of transforming a civil service through modern reforms, we will describe and analyse briefly how control and autonomy were balanced in four Norwegian reforms that all led to more structural and cultural complexity. This involves studying how NPM-related reforms were partly transcended by post-NPM reform elements. We will first describe the main features of the background – motives and processes – related to the reforms, and then examine in more detail how the reforms are characterized by complexity, but a varied balance between autonomy and control, or between NPM and post-NPM elements.

13.4.1   The immigration administration reform

In 2001 a major reform of the central immigration administration took place in Norway. All responsibility for this policy field was gathered under the Ministry of Local Government and Regional Affairs, moving the regulatory role away from the Ministry of Justice and Police. The Norwegian Directorate of Immigration (NDI), established in 1988, was given more formal autonomy, and a new body was established with a lot of formal autonomy – the Immigration Appeals Board (IAB). The main motives behind the reform were to ease the capacity problems and burdens of the central political and administrative executive by hiving-off immigration cases, and it also involved a blame-avoidance component (Christensen *et al.* 2007b). After the reorganization, the political executives could no longer interfere in ordinary individual cases. Steering was to be done from a distance, via general policy directives, thus furthering professional autonomy.

When the new Conservative-Center government came to power in 2001 and was supposed to implement the reform, it soon became clear that the minister was not satisfied with a situation where she carried responsibility for many immigration cases but had her hands relatively tied in handling them (cf. Brunsson 1989). She therefore launched another, smaller-scale reorganization process. The aim of the process was to exert more control over the immigration administration. The new measures – giving more general policy instructions from the ministry, having more formal routines for informing the ministry and having a new large board inside IAB for handling 'positive' decisions – went into effect in 2005. The immigration division in the ministry was split into two, a regulatory and an integration part, and this change was also reflected in the NDI, which also split into one agency for regulation and one for integration and inclusion. In addition, the immigration units were moved to a new Ministry of Labour and Social Inclusion. Under the current Red-Green government the control measures have been tightened still further (Christensen *et al.* 2007b).

The 2001 reform was very much in NPM mode. The ministers behind the later reorganizations were, however, both motivated by post-NPM factors and control aspects. Given that they would eventually get the blame anyway, it was deemed better to try to regain political control over the cases. So instead of solving Brunsson's (1989) dilemma of control and autonomy in an autonomy direction they decided to respond to media pressure with more control.

Overall, this case shows a marked NPM-oriented structural devolution reform, which is difficult to reverse, also because it developed an autonomy-related culture both in NDI and IAB after 2001. The later efforts at reorganization and reasserting control do not seem to have reversed the main features of the first reform, so the message here is a balance in favour of autonomy. The main effect of constant reorganizations and increased complexity is that the political executive is struggling to control the implementation of laws and rules pertaining to immigration policy, even though it has increased its frame-steering.

13.4.2 The hospital reform

In 2002 responsibility for Norwegian hospitals was transferred from the counties to the central government. The reform centralized the ownership function, and the Ministry of Health was given the main responsibility, aided in administrative and oversight functions by two subordinate agencies. Five regional health enterprises with separate professional boards were established, comprising 33 local health enterprises overseeing 250 health institutions of different types. The official goals of the reform were to enhance coordination and utilize resources more efficiently through better control of the financial situation of the hospitals. The reform process was in many ways an entrepreneurial political effort by the responsible minister.

The NPM elements in the reform are rather evident. The hospitals were removed from the ordinary public administration and transformed into enterprises which were supposed to have great managerial autonomy. The post-NPM parts of the hospital reform are also rather evident. The most important one is that the central government, represented by the minister of health, took over the ownership function and established an ownership division in the ministry. This ownership function is, however, very much enacted through a performance-management system (NPM-related), where central targets are set, resources provided and results reported from regional and local enterprises. Another aspect of this centralization is that the ministry has more legitimacy when it has to take drastic measures, for example if there is a major crisis going on in the hospitals (Christensen *et al.* 2006b). A small part of the hospital reform was reversed when the new Red-Green government came to power in 2005, because it brought politicians back onto the boards of hospitals, i.e. a change with a post-NPM flavour but also decentralization features.

Summing up, the hospital reform introduced a rather complex combination of centralization, decentralization and commercialization into its formal structure and displayed features of both NPM and post-NPM reforms, also reflected in diverse cultural elements (Lægreid *et al.* 2005). Overall it tilted the steering of the hospitals more in the direction of centralization, but this was balanced out by the increased managerial autonomy of the hospitals. Overall the reform created more bureaucracy, more control and more reporting in the hospitals.

13.4.3   Reform of the regulatory agencies

In 2003 the Conservative-Center government proposed a regulatory agency reform. The proposal was inspired by the OECD model (Christensen and Lægreid 2007d) and had two main parts. One was a proposal for structural devolution, making the regulatory agencies more independent and making the role of a regulatory agency more specialized and unambiguous. Overall, it was proposed that there should be a principle of non-interference from political executives in single cases in the regulatory agency, and this was followed up by more detailed proposals for eight specific agencies. It was also proposed that the appeal cases should be moved out of the ministries. The second main element was to relocate the chosen regulatory agencies, i.e. move them out of Oslo. After a tug-of-war between the minority government and the opposition, particularly the Labour Party and the Socialist Left Party, a compromise was reached. The relocation part was agreed on, but it was decided that the main overall devolution principle should not be applied to all regulatory agencies and there should be no change for the appeal cases.

The minister behind the proposal supported the NPM principles concerning structural devolution. He argued that politicians, central administrative leaders, interest groups and ad hoc groups should stay away from single cases, and that the relocations should ensure this. Although he acted as a political entrepreneur he had to compromise. Post-NPM elements in this case were connected to two opposition parties. The Labour Party, which had gradually begun to accept NPM arguments from the 1980s onwards, was now starting slowly to think otherwise and was skeptical about the lack of political control and influence potentially involved in an overall reform implying structural devolution for all regulatory agencies. The Socialist Left Party was generally more against NPM.

The regulatory agency reform also implies increased complexity, since the aim of an unambiguous principle of structural devolution is obscured by the compromise reached, thereby also combining a traditional culture of control with a new culture of autonomy. Autonomy and control are combined, but the overall impression of the reform is that autonomy has gained the upper hand even if it is weaker than originally planned by the reform agents.

13.4.4 The welfare administration reform

This reform was initiated in 2001, approved in 2005, and after an interim period of a year, began to be implemented in 2006 in a process to last through 2010. The centerpiece of the reform is a merger of the employment administration, represented by the Directorate of Labour (DOL) and the National Insurance Administration (NIA), into one new labour and welfare agency, the NAV, represented on all levels (Christensen *et al.* 2007c). It was also decided that a new local frontline service should be organized – a one-stop shop – resulting from a new partnership between the NAV and locally based social services. This local partnership combined control and formalization with flexibility and variety.

The parliament (Storting) initiated the reform, something that is highly unusual, since most such initiatives normally come from the political and administrative executives. The initiative implied that the government should present the Storting with models embracing the principle of one institution or sector for labour and welfare, but the government was reluctant to do so for two years and tried throught the work of a public commission to convince the Storting that a fragmented solution was the best. The incoming minister in the merged Ministry for Labour and Social Affairs finally changed the course, however. He worked closely with the Storting to get a proposal accepted that implied a partial merger, leaving responsibility for social services to the local government but in a partnership with the merged central agencies.

Two of the three main goals of the reform, namely increased efficiency and increased user-friendliness, were connected to NPM. The efficiency would be enhanced by economies of scale. The goal of increased user-friendliness was primarily reflected in the new local partnership and the one-door policy, which was also related to the third goal of getting more people into the workforce, particularly multi-service users. NPM was also evident in the internal organization of the new central NAV agency, because a large provider unit, a 'agency withing an agency' was created, while the rest of the NAV agency was to become a kind of strategic purchaser (Askim *et al.* 2009). The whole new organization was also equipped with a performance-management system.

The main background to the reform as a whole was to coordinate a fragmented structure better, thus reflecting the post-NPM trend. The merger finally decided on was partial, since it did not fully include the social services; nevertheless, it was the largest sectoral merger ever undertaken in the

Norwegian central administration. So the holistic aspect of the reform was central, but a very challenging part is to unify three different professional cultures into a new NAV culture. The reform has probably tilted the balance more in the direction of central control and less local autonomy. A new and stronger ministry including all the relevant services has been established, as has a new and merged agency with a strong administrative apparatus. The new local partnership is potentially dominated by the NAV organization (Fimreite and Lægreid 2009).

13.4.5   The reforms compared

Comparing the four reforms with respect to the motives behind them and the conscious design undertaken by the political and administrative leadership shows a varied picture. Two of the reforms, the immigration reform and the regulation reform, aimed primarily to increase autonomy with a view to reducing capacity problems and introducing more strategic steering, while the hospital and welfare reforms aimed to enhance control and coordination.

Not one of the reforms uses a 'pure' set of principles taken from either NPM or post-NPM. Three of the reforms are designed by combining NPM and post-NPM reform elements in a complex mix, while the fourth one, the regulation reform, started with NPM but ended up as a compromise, implying complexity. In the two cases where post-NPM dominated the aims, the hospital and labour/welfare cases, formal vertical and horizontal reintegration or despecialization was used, blended with NPM instruments. In the cases where the main goals involved NPM-type measures, the immigration and regulation reform cases, the main reorganization measures are structural devolution, while the counter-moves are, respectively, stronger structural integrative measures and avoiding using structural devolution as an overall principle. There is also a tendency to try to modify the reforms after they have been decided on, which potentially increases complexity still further, as well as increasing tension between control and autonomy.

What is interesting about the mixed development described is that Norway lagged behind in adopting NPM (Olsen 1996) and embarked on it later then many other Western countries. But once reforms did start they rather soon became subject to the influence of post-NPM elements, so the most intensive NPM period was shorter than in many comparable Western countries. This is illustrated in two of the cases, the hospital reform and the labour/welfare reform; nevertheless, additional complexity and layering are also evident.

Table 13.1 Features of four reforms in the Norwegian central civil service

	Background and motives	NPM features	Post-NPM features	Main focus of (re)balancing	Perceived and potential effects
Immigration	Fewer executive capacity problems through structural evolution Blame-avoidance	IAB and NDI typical strong structural devolution	More central directives More formalization of procedures and information	Relatively more autonomy	Political executives struggle to control policy practice, but still get the blame
Hospitals	Strengthen control in general and increase spending control	Decentralization to commercial health enterprises, DRG system	Centralization and increased ministerial control Politicians back at the boards	Relatively more central control	More central control and getting the blame for negative effects; local autonomy
Regulatory agencies	Hive-off and create more central, strategic steering Increase distance to political executives	Structural devolution of selected agencies	Devolution not common principle Keeping appeals in the ministries	Relatively more autonomy	Less central political and administrative control Not professional objectivity, but negotiations
Labour and Welfare	More holistic organization furthering efficiency and user-friendliness and bringing more people into the work-force	Purchaser-provider split between NAV and NDU Performance-management system	Merger of two agencies and local partnership with a third service. Focus on coordination	Relatively more central control	More central control overall Struggle to get local partnerships to work according to main goals

Overall, a typical feature of the reforms analysed is that they score low on unambiguous organizational thinking, while the actor and influence pattern is either characterized by hierarchical steering and political entrepreneurs (in the hospital, regulatory and welfare reforms) or coalitions features (in the immigration and labour and welfare reforms, but also some in the regulation reform). Concerning organizational thinking, it came as a surprise when the autonomous immigration agencies gained a lot of influence, showing that expectations prior to the reform had been unrealistic. In the hospital reform, the complexity of the new system was underestimated. In the regulatory reform, the minister stood for wishful thinking and superstitious learning that was later difficult to implement. And effects of the local welfare offices was difficult to estimate.

In all cases, the political–administrative executives seemed to struggle to get the reforms to work and the effects and implications are difficult to judge. In all cases cultural complexity is also potentially obstructing of modifying expected effects, either because structural complexity furthers cultural complexity or because of tension between cultures that are developing or increasing confronted with each other.

13.5   Explaining increasing complexity

An important point of departure for understanding the complexity and layering of NPM and post-NPM reforms is that they are each rather complex in themselves. NPM is a mixed bag of economic organization theories and management theories that are to some extent inconsistent with one another (Boston *et al.* 1996). In addition, the actual implementation of NPM varies considerably from one country to another (Wright 1994; Pollitt and Bouckaert 2004). This variety and complexity are due partly to different national contexts, but also to cognitive problems among the executives in relating to the reform wave. Post-NPM is also a complex set of reform measures, some of which are also inconsistent, and they promise many things without having any very firm grounds for doing so (Christensen *et al.* 2007d). Like NPM it is a cognitive challenge for leaders.

13.5.1   A transformative approach

According to a transformative approach, the decision-making of public actors in reform processes is constrained and influenced by three sets of factors or contexts (Christensen and Lægreid 2001d and 2007d; Christensen *et al.* 2007a; 2007d). Structural and constitutional factors, related to an instrumental perspective, specify the structural and other formal constraints on leadership decisions, and come in a hierarchical and negotiative version (March and Olsen 1983). A cultural perspective specifies a second set of constraints. According to this perspective public organizations develop core informal norms and values gradually in an evolutionary process of institutionalization, leading to the formation of a distinct institutional culture (Selznick 1957). A third set of factors relates to an environmental perspective. According to Meyer and Rowan (1977), the technical environment is substantially about efficiency, production and exchange. The institutional environment may have a less instrumental character and be based more on tacit assumptions about what is an appropriate organizational structure, and internal culture (March and Olsen 1989; March 1994).

These three sets of factors or contexts, which both constrain and facilitate leaders' actions in reform processes, may be seen as analytically equal. Often, however, structural-hierarchical constraints will tend to have the upper hand in explaining decision-making behaviour. Many studies of national administrations and comparisons of administrations in different countries seem to indicate that leaders are not only formally designated to make the most important decisions in public organizations, but they do so in reality as well (Lægreid and Olsen 1978; Christensen and Lægreid 1998b; Egeberg 2003; Pollitt and Bouckaert 2004). In this chapter the importance of hierarchical steering is taken for granted, and other factors, like negotiative, cultural and environmental factors, will be discussed in terms of whether they limit or further potential hierarchical control in designing complexity and in balancing political control and autonomy.

13.5.2 The hierarchical design of complexity

The first question is to what extent and how political and administrative leaders may design complexity as a way of achieving a balance between control and autonomy. A simple answer is that this is seen as the most instrumental solution to the challenges confronting public organizations (March and Olsen 1983). Both the internal conditions and the external constraints may be so demanding and complex that the executive leadership will want to diversify the structure to try to cater to both control and institutional autonomy at the same time. So there may be congruence between complex constraints and complex structure or reforms.

Second, complexity may signal flexibility on the part of leaders. Complexity could mean a more loosely coupled organization (March and Olsen 1976), 'creating noise' in decision-making processes (Cohen and March 1974), or creating more opportunities and options (Brunsson 1989). Motives of this kind may result in leaders using myths and symbols to balance control and autonomy, pretending to some audiences that the control side is important, while others will hear the message of autonomy. Or control might be emphasized in certain periods, while autonomy is focused on in others (Brunsson 1989).

Third, scoring low on rational calculation might mean that complexity is a result of arbitrary processes. Leaders may wish to develop the public organization in a systematic way, but do not succeed in this endeavor because they lack the ability to see the connection between means and ends. This limited cognitive capacity could result in complexity in situations where there is a lot of reorganization or patch-work reform. Overall, more comprehensive reforms are the most difficult to design and control, while more narrow and partial ones are often more easily implemented (Wright 1994).

The process of developing complexity through modern reforms may take different paths in different countries, depending on what the political–administrative structures and traditions are, not to mention the environmental and temporal contexts. NPM trail-blazing countries like Australia, New Zealand and the UK all have Westminster-type systems, which means it is quite easy to get reforms decided on and pushed through parliament (Hood 1996). Hence the preconditions for hierarchical design seem to be fulfilled, at least on the control side. But executive leaders in those countries had general problems with rational calculation, partly because of the comprehensiveness of the reforms, but also because the underlying basis in economic theory was not solid enough (Boston *et al.* 1996).

What about the hierarchical design of complexity in the four Norwegian cases described? All cases show active ministers, some of them typical political entrepreneurs, trying to achieve a certain balance between control and autonomy. In all cases the main executive leadership was not firmly grounded concerning rational calculation concerning potential effects. In all cases the preferred solutions were also later modified, either because of rethinking or because another solution was forced upon them.

In the immigration case, the reform entrepreneurs focused on the advantages of autonomy for creating more capacity and avoiding blame, and the problems with control came as a surprise. The incoming minister in 2001 saw problems with exerting control and introduced some control measures without having any clear idea of what the consequences might be. Later on new layers of control were added, but still fell short by comparison with the basic autonomy elements in the model. In the hospital reform the minister produced a tactically clever final solution, but did not give many arguments for this model. In this respect he also struggled with cognitive problems. It was one thing to get the reform decided, but quite another to make it work in practice. The hospital steering model contains a lot of ambiguity concerning how much central ownership control there should be, what means should be used to exert it and over what issues – and with how much leeway for regional and local influence, based on commercial/economic values, and for the influence of professional groups in the hospitals.

In the regulatory reform case, the minister was quite convinced that he knew best, but the reform contained a lot of superstitious and unrealistic thinking and did not include much learning either from other countries' problems with regulatory reform or lessons from post-NPM efforts (Christensen and Lægreid 2007d). He also ran into problems of control. In the welfare reform case the political and administrative executives insisted for a long time on keeping the divided and fragmented structure, until a new minister came up with a new solution that was accepted by the parliament, so hierarchical control of the process was reinstated. But this was a complicated solution that lacked clarity concerning the possible effects.

13.5.3 Negotiations furthering complexity and influencing hierarchical design

If we further explore the control aspects, heterogeneity may be an explanatory factor for complexity. Heterogeneity inside government, diverse institutionally based interests and a tug-of-war between different leaders may create the background for organizational complexity (March and Olsen 1983). Heterogeneity may foster complexity through compromise, winning coalitions or 'sequential attention to goals and the quasi-solution of conflicts' (Cyert and March 1963). Structural complexity may reflect the wide range of different interests playing into a reform process. Central political and executive leaders could be the main proponents of control measures, while agency leaders may work hard to further autonomy measures.When the NPM reforms began, they were backed in many countries by a winning coalition of different actors (Gregory 2001). When the post-NPM reforms started to emerge, this coalition was partly dismantled and a new formed (Christensen *et al.* 2007d).

Negotiations are definitely an important element in increasing complexity in modern reforms. This characteristic is most typical in non-Westminster parliamentary systems or in presidential systems (Wright

1994). Overall, negotiations make reforms and their underlying systems more complex, because of the necessity of attending to different interests that have their attention focused on different parts of the reforms. One might say that when the post-NPM reforms started, the winning coalition and compromises behind NPM in many countries were renegotiated. Actors who had been skeptical when NPM started to gain influence swung back after seeing the consequences of the reforms and became part of a new winning coalition favouring post-NPM elements (Gregory 2003; Halligan 2006).

The organizational models in the four Norwegian cases analysed reflect this tendency toward negotiation and compromise. Often the new complex structures contain elements that are directly connected to a range of actors. In the immigration case, the winning coalition that had supported the autonomy model, firmly believing in devolution furthering central capacity, went over a few years later to supporting a more control-oriented model. In the hospital reform case, the minister managed to include most interests in the complex control-oriented solution, which endowed it with legitimacy, but later on there were problems getting the new structure to function, because it was to heterogeneous and complex. In the regulatory reform case the minister was forced into a compromise that made the regulatory agency system diverse rather than a standardized autonomy-oriented system. In the welfare reform process the incoming minister managed to resolve a stand-off between the executive and the parliament by garnering support for a compromise containing both control and autonomy elements. That compromise had its focal point in the local partnerships – an organizational form that tries to combine central hierarchical steering and standardization on the one hand, and local autonomy and considerations on the other.

13.5.4   Cultural complexity

How might complexity be related to cultural development? One answer might be that the cultural path and logic of appropriateness developed is complex, embracing a variety of informal norms and values, probably more complex, the older the public institution.

The cultural complexity of public organizations becomes rather evident when modern reforms are introduced, for NPM reforms represented a challenge to the traditional culture in the public sector (Christensen and Lægreid 2001d). Although the introduction of competition, performance systems and service-orientation under NPM challenged the culture of 'old public administration', the old rule-steering was still preserved, producing a kind of mixed administrative culture in many countries. When post-NPM reforms came along they tried to revive some of the traditional cultural norms and values, but more supplementing than replacing the NPM culture (Christensen and Lægreid 2008b, 2009). The challenge now was to culturally 'reprogram' civil servants to think more about control, coordination and common culture again. This increased the cultural complexity at the 'cultural cross-roads'.

The Norwegian reform cases also illustrate this increasing cultural complexity. When the central immigration administration was reorganized in 2001 it embarked on a new cultural path, involving autonomy for the professional groups handling the single cases (Christensen *et al.* 2007b). In the hospital reform case the new cultural path was a complex one, which tried to unite a centralized control culture, an efficiency-oriented culture driven by economists and a more traditional medical and caring culture. In the regulation case the minister attended to a new OECD-inspired regulatory culture, which was rather incompatible with the traditional ministerial one and it was only semi-implemented, leaving a complex cultural impression. The relocation of some regulatory agencies also builds into the equation regional and local norms and values.

The challenge of cultural change is greatest in the welfare reform, where the former employment service, which had been modernized and more consequence-oriented, was merged with a more traditional Weberian culture in the national insurance service in an attempt to create a new culture. Added to this was the challenge of including a third factor to the cultural equation – the locally based and discretionary-oriented social services.

13.5.5 The impact of the technical and institutional environment

How might the technical environment explain the development of more structural and cultural complexity in public organizations? First of all, the technical environment is diverse and possibly turbulent, which would create internal complexity (Scott and Davies 2006). Balancing control and autonomy could be the result of attending to different actors and institutions in the technical environment. Demands from the technical environment constitute one raison d'etre for NPM, for example when there is a crisis. This was the background to the reforms in New Zealand that began in 1984 (Boston *et al.* 1996; Aberbach and Christensen 2001; Gregory 2001). Another possibility is that a public organization will grow more complex because the demands on the organization from one or several outside sources have become more complex.

Reform myths coming from the institutional environment are in general believed to have the effect of making public organizations isomorphic, i.e. more similar in form, at least on the surface (Meyer and Rowan 1977). The argument behind this is that myths develop in the institutional environment and spread rather quickly to other populations of organizations, where they primarily function as 'window-dressing', creating an image of the organization that increases its legitimacy (Brunsson 1989). NPM was partly based on the myths that a large public sector was bad, and that structural devolution and differentiation were good. The complexity that NPM brought was also a complexity of ideas and ideology. When post-NPM came along a set of counter-myths gained support: namely, that an integrated public system was better than a fragmented one, that coordination was better than competition, that central capacity and standardization were better than institutional autonomy and variety (Christensen *et al.* 2007d). This created an even more complex system of ideas, because not all NPM ideas were deinstitutionalized, but continued to exist alongside post-NPM ideas.

Increased complexity may have something to do with public organizations imitating and combining institutional standards from different periods and types of reform (Lægreid *et al.* 2007). Complexity could also result from organizations combining different reform elements containing both control and autonomy measures (Røvik 2002). If we relate this to NPM and post-NPM reforms, complexity may result from a pragmatic adaptation to the two reform waves, whereby countries, sectors and organizations pick different institutional standards and combine them in a 'patch-work-like' way.

The influence of a combination of environmental factors is also evident in the Norwegian cases. Immigration reform was made necessary by changes in the technical environment, like an increasing number of refugees and asylum seekers and by ensuing capacity problems, but it was also accompanied by symbols of devolution. These symbols lost political support when the influx of immigrants continued to grow and become even more problematic, and instead control symbols began to prevail, particularly after some scandals and media pressure.

The background to the hospital reform was expensive hospitals and efficiency problems, combined with symbols of NPM (the enterprise model). The reform has not been seen as a success, so the symbols of enterprise have lost their attractiveness, particularly when huge budget deficits have characterized the hospitals year after year. This has increased the external pressure on the owner – the central government. In the regulation reform there was no obvious external crisis, but a minister catering to a lot of NPM rhetoric, and eventually also a lot of anti-NPM rhetoric emerged that resulted in a compromise.

The welfare reform was based on real problems in the technical environment, because too many people were on pension and social benefits, creating efficiency and other problems. When the reform finally was decided on, several symbols of unity and local partnership emerged, not always covering reality.

13.5.6 Hierarchical design modified

The hierarchical design of complexity may be both strengthened and modified by the contexts presented in the other supplementary perspectives. In the best of all worlds, political and administrative leaders will further a reform catering to a complex balance of control and autonomy and receive support from a variety of stakeholders, thus increasing its legitimacy and gaining access to supportive cultural norms, values and symbols that present the complex design as modern and good. At the other extreme, hierarchically based design of complexity may be marred in complex negotiations, come up against a resistant culture and unwilling professions and be challenged by counter-myths. All this may modify the original intentions of the executives. In fact, both NPM and post-NPM reforms seem to have these features.

What tends to happen in practice is that hierarchically controlled reform has less difficulty controlling the participants and more difficulty controlling the problems and solutions (Pollitt and Bouckaert 2004; Christensen and Lægreid 2001d and 2007d). Often heterogeneity is 'used' in favour of hierarchical control of reform processes, or compromises are struck that make it possible to stay the course. Leaders tend to have the upper hand in manipulating symbols, but this is not always sufficient to stop cultural resistance. Our cases show that executives often have problems either defining clearly what they would like to do, or in gaining insight into the effects of the reforms they are proposing, or else they may underestimate the cost of reforms, etc., something that seems generally to have happened with both NPM and post-NPM reforms. All this often makes it easier for other actors to enter into the negotiations and to further their interests and solutions, whether based on their structural position, culture and professional background, or on pressure from the environment.

13.6 Conclusion

Structural complexity in public organizations enables them to cope more easily with complex societal problems and heterogeneous interests and demands. Political and administrative leaders thus have a repertoire of responses to complex and diverse problems at their disposal. Culturally, complexity may indicate that a hybrid culture, catering to diverse traditions and sub-cultures, has developed, enabling organizations to be flexible in adapting to internal and external efforts to bring about change. Our cases show that complexity participate in deciding and implementing the reforms, but also in making them problematic to result in expected effects.

Increasing complexity results in control becoming more problematic for political and administrative leaders. Complexity means having a variety of actors and institutional norms and values to attend to, which may make it more difficult to influence 'local' activities and implementation. The more complexity, the more potential capacity and cognitive problems leaders will have, a problem that can be coped with by delegation, making administrative leaders more powerful. Political leaders have to divide their attention and process more information than before, while policy questions may become more technical and complicated, which makes politicians more reliant on experts. The down-side of complexity may be that it includes incompatible elements, leading to uncoordinated or countervailing actions and creating chaos or stale-mates (Boston *et al.* 1996). The ultimate question is whether it is possible for executive leaders to choose many roads at the same time, going in the direction of both control and autonomy, without getting lost or encountering problems. Our cases also illustrate the executive problems related to complexity. The immigration and regulatory agency cases show the executive struggling with control problems because of strong autonomy elements, while the hospital and welfare cases also show control problems, more because of counter-veiling tensions in the organization models used.

The four Norwegian cases analysed show diverse reform processes that are leading to complex solutions, that in different ways attend to a balance of autonomy elements from NPM reforms and control elements from post-NPM reforms. The complexity emerging is definitely reflecting the central elements from a transformative perspective: the hierarchical efforts of controlling the reforms processes, influence and partly modified by the elements of negotiations and heterogeneity, the complexity of cultural elements, the pressure from changing technical environments and the competing reform myths from the institutional environment. The problems of rational calculation are also evident in all cases.

The Norwegian cases also show that expected effects are problematic to fulfil for political and administrative leaders. In the immigration case the central executives are struggling to influence practice in the complex system, while the agency leaders and their civil servants complain about interference from above and shifting constraints. In the hospital reform case the overall performance of the complex system has not been good, as shown by accumulating deficits and strong tension between central control, enterprise autonomy and professional practice. Since the reform of regulatory agencies, central political and administrative control has been lost, and the new reformed practice is often characterized by ambiguity and negotiations. And relocation has resulted in a loss of professional competence. In the labour and welfare reform the overall performance of the new system has not lived up to expectations, so even though central control has been achieved, the local partnerships and offices are struggling to deliver on the main reform goals.

14
Organizing Public Sector Agencies: Challenges and Reflections

Koen Verhoest and Per Lægreid

14.1 Introduction

Over the past twenty years traditional public administration models in contemporary democracies have been under pressure from the New Public Management (NPM) movement. This book was inspired by the observation that these new trends are changing how public sector are organized all over the world. Specialization within large, monolithic bureaucracies has resulted in the establishment of single-purpose autonomous agencies and a proliferation of the administrative system, warranting changes in forms of control. According to the NPM doctrine, the ideal type of agency scores high on managerial autonomy and on *ex post* result control and low on policy autonomy and *ex ante* control. We have examined to what extent this ideal type can be found in practice and what the implications are of such an agency form. We have also addressed the post-NPM reforms, focusing on whole-of-government issues and the need to strengthen political control as well as on horizontal coordination within a fragmented state.

Public administrations have been, so to speak, smitten by agency fever (Pollitt *et al.* 2001), but we are also seeing parallel processes of decentralization and centralization and of regulation and de-regulation (Christensen and Lægreid 2006a). A central feature of these changes is that there is an unstable balance between autonomy and steering of the central agencies. Although governments are adapting to the new trends, there have still been few systematic academic studies of such changes and their implications for the functioning of the public sector. A characteristic feature of the current reforms is a lack of reliable and systematic knowledge about the effects and implications of alternative organizational forms.

This concluding chapter discusses the links between the main concepts of the book: proliferation and coordination, autonomy and control, and performance and results. The chapter elaborates on how complexity, proliferation, specialization, and coordination, as well as autonomy and control of agencies affect performance in different administrative systems. A main aim is to understand contemporary administrative reforms and public administration after New Public Management.

14.2   Main findings

14.2.1   Specialization and proliferation

The first part of the book brought together papers that addressed the following set of research questions: How much evidence is there of a straightforward process of increased specialization and organizational proliferation in central government? How can this specialization and proliferation be explained? To what extent has this proliferation resulted in coordination and control problems? The three chapters in this part addressed these questions in three different European political–administrative contexts: a Scandinavian welfare state (Norway), a continental federal state (Belgium), and a post-communist state (Hungary).

Descriptive findings. The Norwegian study of changing organizational forms reveals, first, that there have been a large number of structural changes in the state apparatus. Second, the authors find a significant decrease over time in the number of civil service organizations outside the ministries and an increase in the number of state-owned companies. Third, along the vertical dimension, specialization has been more widespread than de-specialization. Vertical specialization through corporatization is the most common form, but there are also several instances of agencification. Fourth, along the horizontal dimension we find a larger extent of de-specialization, primarily due to mergers or absorptions of existing organizations.

Fifth, the extent of change has been markedly lower from 2005 onwards, reflecting the skepticism of the Centre–Left government towards NPM. Finally, there are also several sector- and organization-specific differences. For example, there are centralizing elements in the hospital reform and the recent reorganization of the immigration administration and also the recent reform of the welfare administration in Norway was informed by 'whole-of-government' doctrines.

Like Norway, Hungary has also seen extensive structural changes in central government organizations. However, the changes seem to lack overall consistency in terms of their orientation: Both NPM elements and non-NPM related changes are present. In the Hungarian context the problematic field of agencification has tended to be conceptualized and explored not as a unidirectional and consistent pattern of administrative policy but as one often involving sharp reversals and opposing components. The majority of changes has been of a purely formal–legal character and lack any coherent administrative policy.

Both the Norwegian and the Hungarian findings reveal that reorganization is a very popular administrative reform tool, as observed by Peters (1988); but in contrast to Kaufman's (1976) statement that 'government organizations are immortal' authors find much more turbulent organizational life-cycles. The findings support Light's (1997) argument of 'tides of reform', especially in the Norwegian case, where the time-span is longer.

In *Flanders* we find that regulatory administration is rather complex. Rommel and associates reveal a proliferation of 265 regulatory bodies involving multiple sectors and levels of government. The data corroborate the idea that regulation is increasingly performed by highly-specialized multi-actor and multi-level constellations (Jordana and Sancho 2004). Delegation to autonomous forms of organization is most common. Most organizations perform one or two regulatory tasks, implying a fragmentation of regulatory chains across several organizations. Half of the bodies have other general tasks besides regulation and are multi-functional, instead of being single-purpose bodies. The extent of proliferation differs across areas, with the most proliferated regulatory area being economic affairs. Considering that Belgium has a dual federal structure, the authors find, surprisingly enough, that one level rarely has full authority over a given policy field. Their study points to resulting problems of coordination, lack of transparency, and high administrative burdens for regulatees.

Explanatory findings. Lægreid and associates' findings are in line with a transformative perspective in which international doctrines are modified by institutional and cultural values in the Norwegian political–administrative apparatus and by specific deliberative domestic action and choices. The general picture is not one of increased fragmentation and proliferation, but rather a movement of organizations further away from the central political authorities combined with mergers.

What we see is a combination of robustness in organizational forms and a large degree of turbulence and change activity within and across these forms. This produces, via a sedimentation process, a more complex structural anatomy involving a mixture of rather unstable vertical and horizontal specialization. These findings are in line with Pollitt's (2007) characterization of the Nordic states as neo-Weberian states or strong modernized states that have been able to combine old Weberian bureaucratic features, NPM doctrines, and post-NPM structural elements. The conclusion is that to understand the structural anatomy of the Norwegian state apparatus we need to combine explanatory factors related to external pressure from internationally dominant administrative doctrines and national features related to domestic political-administrative culture and instrumental choices made through an active administrative policy (Christensen and Lægreid 2007b).

The *Hungarian* data on regulatory agencies support the relevance of the credible commitment hypothesis; it is reasonable to assume that one of the motives driving politicians to grant (increased) autonomy to certain agencies is their desire to provide institutional guarantees for key external stakeholders against future intrusions into regulatory matters driven by short-term political motives.

Somewhat contradicting the functional logic of credible commitment, there is a peculiar and perverse relationship between agencies' de facto stability and their institutionally entrenched structural autonomy. The more institutionally well-protected an agency is, the higher the chance of politically intrusive restructuring affecting that autonomy. This finding contradicts the expectation that the more formal–legal autonomy an agency has, the stronger its resistance to political forces. Hajnal develops two alternative explanations. The first is related to the political significance of the organization regarding the possibilities for political appointees. The second refers to the perceived loss of central strategic control over autonomous bodies, resulting in reorganizations, which allows control to be regained by disabling their management.

A main finding in the Flanders case is that both regulatory area and governmental level explain the extent of and differences in task specialization and organizational proliferation. As with the Hungarian case, the credible commitment theory is partially supported, since regulatory actors in the economic area are relatively further away from government and more single-purpose. However, Rommel and associates find no significant differences between economic regulators and other areas in terms of the number of regulatory tasks performed. The design of regulatory bodies seems to be largely explained by the governmental level on which they were created. Large differences between regulators at the federal and regional levels are found, although both governmental levels are active in the same policy fields. The authors account for this by citing aspects of the polity and political–administrative history of Belgium.

The conclusion is that distinguishing between different levels and areas is useful to explain different organizational design of regulation.

Summing up, these findings reveal that there is no evidence of a straightforward process of increased specialization and organizational proliferation in central government. The processes are much more complex and we find parallel dual processes of vertical specialization and horizontal de-specialization as well as pendulum swings between agencification and de-agencification. In line with previous findings there is a rather loose coupling between administrative doctrines and actual changes (Lægreid and Roness 2003). In spite of a trend towards single purpose organizations as a dominating administrative doctrine, combining regulatory tasks with other tasks in the same agency is still widespread (see also Lægreid *et al.* 2006). Thus the NPM ideal of increased vertical specialization (structural devolution) and increased horizontal specialization (single-purpose organizations) has only partly been implemented. Furthermore, the agency form as a organizational model is characterized by great heterogeneity and diversity in both organizational features and type of tasks (Rubecksen 2009). That said, agencies are a prevalent organizational form in all three countries studied, and proliferation is a main feature. This is a bit surprising given the different starting points and different political–administrative context of the three counties. But we also see an editing and refining process, indicating that even if the same concepts and labelling of organizations are used in the different countries they can still embrace big differences in actual organizational forms (Røvik 1996). As observed also by a recent seven country-study, this organizational proliferation has brought about a new and increased need for coordination (see below; Bouckaert *et al.* 2010).

There is no single-factor explanation for the various specialization and proliferation trends. We have revealed differences between countries, administrative levels, and policy areas. External pressure, domestic administrative culture, and structure as well as deliberate choices by political and administrative executives all help to account for the processes of proliferation and specialization (Christensen and Lægreid 2007b).

14.2.2   Autonomy and control

According to NPM doctrine, increased task specialization and organizational proliferation optimally result in organizational forms with formal and *de facto* high levels of managerial autonomy and result control, but with low levels of policy autonomy and *ex ante* input-oriented control. The second part of the book brought together three papers focusing on the patterns of autonomy or control of agencies visible in countries with different political–administrative cultures: Germany, Hong Kong, and Italy. In addition, these contributions analysed whether different types of organizational affiliation affected the de facto autonomy and forms of control within the administrative system. It also asked what other factors besides organizational affiliation affect the perceived autonomy and control of public sector bodies.

Descriptive findings: With regard to autonomy, both the chapter on Germany and the one on Hong Kong support insights raised in recent agency literature. This may surprise us, since both countries have at first sight rather different political–administrative regimes, with Germany being a typical *Rechtsstaat* administrative system dominated by traditional ways of managing public organizations such as hierarchical coordination, input-orientation, and rule-bound decision-making, and Hong Kong, as a Special Administrative Region of China, having a highly consolidated and relatively centralized structure and rather ambiguous attitudes towards organizational autonomy and control. First, both country studies concur that autonomy is a multi-dimensional concept (see also Christensen 2001a; Verhoest *et al.* 2004a; Gilardi 2008), implying that levels of managerial autonomy and of policy autonomy may be combined in many different ways for organizations (Verschuere 2006). Moreover, in most cases both concepts seem to be explained by different sets of factors, as will be discussed in more depth below.

Second, despite the hierarchical administrative tradition in both countries, a majority of managers of all kinds of agencies perceived themselves to have high levels of bureaucratic discretion. This observed high level of discretion on policy matters seems to be a common empirical phenomenon in other countries with very different political–administrative cultures, such as Norway, Ireland, Flanders (Verhoest *et al.* 2010), Austria (Steigenberger and Hammerschmid 2009), and Lithuania (Nakrosis and Martinaitis 2009). For Germany, Bach refers to the persistent emphasis on government control of inputs, combined with anticipated behaviour of administrator. In Hong Kong, high levels of policy autonomy may be explained by information asymmetry, but also by interdependence and intensive networking between policy designing bureaus and implementing departments.

A third common observation for Germany and Hong Kong is that the diversity in levels of management autonomy is large between organizations, but also that managerial autonomy in general is more limited than policy autonomy. In particular, the extent of financial management autonomy is perceived to be low in both countries, owing to strict financial controls. As for autonomy regarding Human Resource Management issues, operational autonomy is rather widespread, but strategic autonomy is perceived to be much lower.

A last empirical finding in both countries, which is common to most recent agency studies, is that there is considerable divergence in levels of 'de facto' autonomy for organizations belonging to the same formal-legal type of agency (see also Verhoest *et al.* 2004a; Maggetti 2007). This latter empirical finding brings us to the question of the explanatory power of structural features, such as formal–legal status, in explaining the level of autonomy in the countries studied, which will be discussed in the following paragraphs.

The Italian country study shows that, contrary to what one would expect in a country with a rule-oriented political–administrative culture, a substantial share of Italian agencies have fairly elaborate result-control systems; it also suggests, however, that the components of these systems are often loosely coupled (see Lægreid *et al.* 2006 for similar findings for Norway). In line with its Napoleonic political–administrative culture, Italy seems to emphasize sanctions more than measurement and evaluation of results. Agencies created as a result of the 1999 reform showed complete result-control cycles, but agencies created several years later showed considerably lower levels of result control. This points to a lack of persisting effects of administrative reforms.

Explanatory findings: A central question in both the German and Hong Kong studies was whether formal–legal status, form of affiliation, and legal distance from government, which is central in the structural-instrumental perspective, affects perceived autonomy. Despite differences between agencies with a similar formal–legal status, most aspects of managerial autonomy in both countries still seemed to be positively and significantly related to the formal–legal distance from central government (see also Verhoest *et al.* 2004a; Verschuere 2006 on Flanders; Lonti 2005 on Canada; and Steigenberger and Hammerschmid 2009 on Austria). In Hong Kong organizational form also affects operational policy autonomy, whereas in Germany and other countries such a clear relationship is absent (see on Ireland and Flanders Verhoest *et al.* 2010; on Lithuania, Nakrosis and Martinaitis 2009; and on the Netherlands, Yesilkagit and van Thiel 2008). A recent study by Egeberg and Trondal (2009) convincingly shows that senior officials in Norwegian agencies do indeed seem to pay significantly less attention to signals from the political leadership compared with their counterparts in ministerial departments.

However, the relationship between formal–legal autonomy and actual autonomy is not a straightforward one. Other explanatory factors also shape de facto and perceived autonomy. The presence of a governing board, which is another structural feature, affects positively the extent of managerial autonomy and operational policy autonomy of public sector organizations in Hong Kong. A recent study of agencies in Norway, Ireland, and Flanders supports this claim in case of managerial autonomy (Verhoest *et al.* 2010). This latter study also found that large agencies had relatively more managerial autonomy than small agencies, a finding which is partially contradicted in the case of the German agencies (see Lonti 2005 for similar contradictory findings regarding Canada). Nevertheless, size seems to be important for autonomy, not only for the agency involved (Lægreid *et al.* 2008b), but also at the other side of the relationship. Egeberg and Trondal (2009) claim that bureaucratic autonomy in agencies is perceived to be lower when capacity at the parent department is high (for similar findings, see Verhoest *et al.* 2010). Structural factors like size do not help to explain the extent of result control in Italian agencies, but in a three-country study on Norway, Ireland, and Flanders, large agencies did have a greater degree of result control than small agencies. The latter study showed, moreover, that in the case of large agencies, a high degree of managerial autonomy was combined in some countries with high levels of result control.

In what is still generally considered to be the most influential study on agencies, Pollitt *et al.* (2004) explain the de facto autonomy and control of agencies in four countries in terms of both task characteristics and political–administrative culture, pointing to political salience, measurability, and complexity of the task at hand. Political salience also figures in the studies included in this book as an important variable; in Hong Kong, agencies' managerial autonomy seem to be negatively correlated with the saliency of their activities (for similar findings see Hogwood *et al.* 2000; Egeberg and Trondal 2009a; Verhoest *et al.* 2010) The reader may have noted that, surprisingly enough, the involvement of German agencies in policy design is nevertheless higher when they perform politically salient tasks. The nature of the task performed also plays a major role in Germany, with agencies with regulatory tasks reporting having less managerial autonomy than agencies with other tasks. Although credible commitment theory may have some explanatory power regarding the formal autonomy of agencies, this finding for German agencies casts doubt on the validity of credible commitment theory to explain de facto autonomy of agencies. This is confirmed by other studies, like those on Hong Kong, Ireland, Flanders, and Norway, where the regulatory nature of tasks did not seem to affect the autonomy of agencies directly (see also Verhoest *et al.* 2010). Agencies with easily measurable service delivery tasks reported less policy autonomy in

Hong Kong, whereas in the study on Norway, Flanders, and Ireland they reported more financial management autonomy (Verhoest *et al.* 2010).

Interestingly, both the Hong Kong study and the German study point to substantial differences in levels of autonomy for agencies across ministerial portfolios or policy domains. This might relate to the features of the tasks involved, but also to the legacies and traditions of control in certain policy fields (see also Gains 2004). Moreover, Bach's research suggests that deliberate actions by the parent ministry may diminish or strengthen the application of internal regulations on subordinate agencies. This issue of ministerial affiliation or policy domain path-dependencies merits more research in the future (e.g. van Thiel 2006).

Surprisingly, the study on result control in Italian agencies did not find any influence of type of task. Indeed, the absence of a direct influence of task characteristics, except for budget size, was confirmed in a recent three-country study (Verhoest *et al.* 2010). The authors of the Italian study explained the patterns of result control mainly by referring to the specificities of the reform trajectories within the Italian public administration: the actual implementation of the 1999 NPM-like reform was limited, indicating the entrenched nature of the existing administrative style. More generally, in line with the emphasis of Pollitt *et al.* (2004) on path-dependencies, Verhoest and associates (2010) assert in their study of Norwegian, Irish, and Flemish agencies that several country-level factors with respect to polity, political–administrative culture, and traditions as well as actor constellations have strong explanatory power when it comes to autonomy and control of agencies. The importance of cultural-historical explanations is also shown nicely by Yesilkagit and Christensen (2009).

In sum, the studies on autonomy and control of agencies in different countries point both to the multi-dimensionality of the concepts involved, and to the multi-dimensionality of their explanations. Formal–legal status and organizational forms only partially explain observed levels of de facto autonomy and control. Theoretical perspectives, emphasizing structural-instrumental, task-specific and environmental characteristics all have relevance for explaining de facto autonomy and control. Furthermore, the story becomes even more complex if we take into account that control affects autonomy in specific ways (Ebinger 2007; Roness *et al.* 2008; Yesilkagit and van Thiel 2008).

14.2.3   Performance and results

In the third part of the book, four contributions studied the impact of organizational form on the performance of public sector organizations.

NPM doctrines state that agency status, implying high levels of managerial autonomy, result control, and private sector-style internal management, will enhance the performance of public sector organizations. However, empirical evidence of such effects is rather patchy and overall results of studies are inconclusive. For example, Verhoest *et al.* (2004) review ten empirical studies, of which only half showed positive effects of formal or de facto autonomy on performance. A study of Japanese agencies by Yamamoto (2006) found that perceived change in operational autonomy resulted in reported increases in performance, but such effects were much less clear or absent for financial management autonomy, HRM autonomy, and organizational management autonomy.

More generally, within the recently developed series of papers on public sector management and performance in the Journal of Public Administration Research and Theory (see, for example, Boyne and Walker 2005), the limited number of studies with a focus on affiliated aspects of centralization of decision-making did not show univocal results either. Moynihan and Pandey (2005) find a negative impact of centralization on performance, while Andrews and others (2007) do not find an independent effect of centralization. In their review of nine centralization studies, the latter found that in five of the studies a clear negative correlation was found between centralization and performance (Andrews *et al.* 2007: 61, Table 1). Some more recent studies do show significant positive effects of autonomy and result control on agency characteristics that might be considered as preconditions for higher performance, such as innovative behaviour (Verhoest *et al.* 2007a) or the adoption of result-oriented management tools by agencies (Verhoest *et al.* 2010).

The majority of the studies reviewed above work with survey data and limited operationalizations of performance. The studies in this book used different operationalizations of performance and different data-gathering strategies, including objective measures of output quality by data series analysis (Chapter 8), transaction costs in eight case studies (Chapter 9); media reputation for credible commitment and decision-making efficiency (Chapter 10); and survey-based self-perceptions of efficiency, effectiveness, and quality (Chapter 11).

Descriptive findings: The performance review of sixteen agencies in Québec showed mixed results. For revenue and revenue-over-cost indicators, on average substantial and statistically significant increases were found. However, average reported performance in terms of output, productivity, and cost remained relatively stable during this period. There is, however, considerable variation as some agencies reveal large increases or decreases in average growth for both the pre- and post-reform periods.

This unequal pattern of performance changes with regard to the different dimensions of performance involved or across agencies, as has been noted to some extent in other evaluative studies, like Talbot's (2004) study of UK agencies, the recent evaluation review study of twenty-eight EU agencies (Euréval 2008), or a study on Thai agencies (Kim 2008).

In her theoretically driven study on the relative efficiency of different organizational forms for household waste-collection in eight Dutch municipalities, Van Genugten concludes that transaction costs are highest in the governance structure of public companies, followed by contracting out and, finally, municipal services.

The case studies of Maggetti (Chapter 10) show that the two main rationales for the delegation of powers from governments to formally independent regulatory agencies – the increase in policy credibility (through independence), and the enhancement of decision-making efficiency (through expertise) – are indeed hard to reconcile. The author examines the reputation of agencies in two contrasting cases, according to the criteria of credibility and efficiency. The case of the British Competition Commission illustrates that regulatory agencies, even when created for symbolic reasons, can become active and can benefit from a media reputation for credibility. But in both cases, the evaluation of efficiency is negative. The latter finding questions the NPM tenet that autonomy leads to performance improvement in terms of efficiency.

The chapter by Verhoest *et al.* shows that in the case of the 124 Flemish agencies the formal–legal organizational form does not correlate significantly with self-perceived performance. However, the study only focused on formal autonomy, not on perceived de facto autonomy (cf. Lonti 2005).

Explanatory findings: In the Dutch case (Chapter 9) the researcher explains the relative efficiency of different organizational forms by pointing to the mismatch between the governance structure of public companies and the transaction at stake, namely, waste collection. Transaction costs are much higher in this organizational form because of uncertainty aggravated by ownership by multiple shareholders and distance to the municipal authorities, implying the use of contractual relations.

Maggetti enriches the credible commitment theory with interesting insights, since he found that in order to secure credible commitments, effective independence of regulatory agencies from elected politicians – including the broad delegation of regulatory competencies, extensive discretion *vis-à-vis* elected politicians, and freedom from ex-post controls – needs to be complemented by perceived autonomy *vis-à-vis* the regulatees. Following this reasoning, autonomy of regulatory agencies emerges when political principals and the regulates are opposed and equally distant, that is, when agencies can successfully develop a 'functional antagonism' in front of the external actors (Braun 1993).

In Chapter 11 the authors point to some variables that may intervene in the causal relationship between autonomy and performance, and that also figure in recent agency-literature and empirical performance studies. These intervening variables suggest that the relationship between autonomy and performance is a contingent one (cf. Andrews *et al.* 2007). Some of these variables refer to deliberate actions by actors. Verhoest and associates found that the quality of management seems to matter most, supporting the 'management matters' literature (Moynihan and Pandey 2005).

Other variables, as found by Verhoest *et al.* (Chapter 11), refer more to a cultural-institutional theoretical perspective: An organizational culture oriented towards results and customers also correlates with higher self-perceived performance. In a similar vein, Lægreid *et al.* (2009) found that a result-oriented organizational culture fosters innovative behaviour. In management and performance studies, organizational culture is indeed cited as an important variable enhancing performance, alongside quality of management (see Moynihan and Pandey 2005).

Through an inductive analysis of well-performing and badly-performing agencies in Québec, Quenneville *et al.* suggest that agencies operating in conditions similar to those of small private ventures, with a clear and non-conflicting mission statement coupled with greater autonomy, perform better than larger, more constrained agencies pursuing a large number of potentially conflicting objectives. Whereas Quenneville and associates consider organizational size to be potentially important as a structural variable, Verhoest *et al.* do not find a direct relationship with self-perceived performance. Other studies find opposite effects (cf. Lonti 2005 and Kim 2008) on performance, or they find positive effects of size on the use of result-oriented management tools (Verhoest *et al.* 2010) and on innovative behaviour in the case of budget size (Lægreid *et al.* 2009).

Task-specific factors do not show significant correlations with performance in the Verhoest and associates' chapter, but other studies do see positive correlations with internal management and innovative behaviour (Lægreid *et al.* 2009; Verhoest *et al.* 2010). Quenneville *et al.* inductively point to the relevance of clear objectives for agencies, which is also mentioned in studies on performance effects of centralization (Moynihan and Pandey 2005). Other studies suggest that the extent of financial dependency of an agency on government budget allocation may play a role in explaining performance of agencies, but these studies come to contrasting conclusions (cf. Lonti 2005 versus Kim 2008 and Verhoest *et al.* 2010).

From part III of this book and the literature review above, it becomes increasingly clear that the effect of change in organizational form, enhanced autonomy, and control of agencies is not at all a straight-forward one. As noted in other literature (see, for example, Boyne and Walker 2005), the performance of public sector organizations seem to be contingent upon a complex interplay of variables, some of which refer to deliberate action of rationally behaving actors and some of which are structural, cultural-institutional, and task-specific in nature. The chapters in this book point to several such factors. Autonomy and control are only two of a potentially large number factors that will determine performance, and are most probably not sufficient conditions on their own. Even the question of whether increased autonomy and result control are insufficient but *necessary* conditions for enhancing performance has still not been fully answered.

14.2.4   Whole of Government: coordination and complexity

The last part of the book addresses the implications of 'Whole-of-Government' reforms. The question is to what degree they foster horizontal coordination and increased central control over a proliferated governmental apparatus. The authors try to ascertain whether these post-NPM reforms have replaced NPM reforms or whether they are supplementing them, producing increased complexity. One of the two chapters examines some of the NPM pioneers, focusing specifically on Australia. The other focuses on Norway, traditionally seen as a reluctant NPM reformer (Olsen 1996).

Descriptive findings: None of the recent Norwegian reforms studied uses a 'pure' set of principles taken from either NPM or post-NPM doctrines. Formal vertical and horizontal reintegration are used, blended with NPM instruments. A typical feature of the reforms analysed is that they score low on unambiguous organizational thinking, while the actor and influence pattern is either characterized by hierarchical steering and political entrepreneurs or by coalition features. The Norwegian case shows diverse reform processes leading to complex solutions. These solutions attend in different ways to a balance between autonomy elements from NPM reforms and control elements from post-NPM reforms. There is a layering and sedimentation process going on producing increased complexity. This is in line with the institutional turn in the study of organizational change (Pierson 2004; Streek and Thelen 2005; Olsen 2009).

In Australia, New Zealand, and the UK there has been a tendency towards integrated governance involving a rebalancing of centre and line; a focus on performance in terms of outcomes and improved delivery; a rationalization of public bodies; and a commitment to whole-of-government and integrating agendas. The following dimensions can be observed: reassertion of the central agency, vertical monitoring of programme delivery, re-aggregation of public agencies, delivery integration and inter-agency coordination, and horizontal coordination through whole-of-government (see also Halligan 2006; Christensen *et al.* 2007d).

Taken together the two chapters show that WG initiatives differ according to the starting points and administrative culture in different countries. But in both cases WG does not break with the past or fundamentally transform existing organizational modes. Rather it is a question of rebalancing the existing administrative systems without changing them in any fundamental way (Gregory 2006; Christensen and Lægreid 2007a). In this respect the reform processes echo earlier paths (Christensen and Yesilkagit 2006a).

Explanatory findings: The complexity emerging from the Norwegian case reflects the central elements of a transformative perspective: the hierarchical efforts of controlling the reform process, influenced and partly modified by elements of negotiation and heterogeneity; the complexity of cultural elements; the pressure from the changing technical environment; and competing reform myths from the institutional environment. The problems of rational calculation are also evident in all cases. The Norwegian case also shows that expected effects are problematic to fulfill for political and administrative leaders.

An examination of the internal and external explanations provides insights into what promoted homogeneity and integration in the case of Australia and New Zealand. The internal factors were overshadowed by movements within the public management reform cycle as the excesses and limitations of NPM received corrective attention. There were also other complex domestic policy issues linked to political control and performance that required strategic and integrated government responses.

External pressures were originally fiscal in nature and economic factors remained a driver, but in the 2000s an external threat emerged in countries such as Australia where issues of security and terrorism dominated the landscape. The intensity of the reassertion of the center resulted from system shortcomings as well as environmental uncertainty and threat perceptions. External threat is a powerful motivating force for inducing integration through central coordination and tighter control. The combination of internal and external factors led to the emergence of a more integrated approach to governance. The two case studies revealed that we need to combine instrumental features focusing on conscious organizational design by reform entrepreneurs with negotiations and external pressure from the institutional as well as the technical environment as well as constraints imposed by the cultural-institutional context in the various countries to understand the emergence and content of WG reforms (Christensen and Lægreid 2007a).

Summing up, the post-NPM 'Whole-of-Government' reforms imply an increased focus on integration, horizontal coordination, and enhanced political control (Pollitt 2003b). The emergence of post-NPM reforms can be understood as a combination of external pressure from the technical and institutional environments, learning from NPM reforms, and deliberate choices by political executives. This counter-reaction of increased central control and coordination to organizational proliferation has been observable not only in Norway, Australia, and New Zealand, but also in the UK, Sweden, and The Netherlands, as shown in a recent seven-country study (Bogdanor 2005; Bouckaert *et al.* 2010). Canada has also been a front-runner regarding WG initiatives (Bakvis and Juliett 2004), while other countries like Belgium, France, and the United States have shown less-pronounced reaction patterns. However, in all these countries external and internal pressures have questioned the effectiveness of a proliferated public sector. These include internationalization and Europeanization, security threats and crisis management needs, as well as a call for more integrated service delivery and holistic policies, e-government and regulatory reform initiatives, and the loss of a common civil service culture (Bouckaert *et al.* 2010; see also Bogdanor 2005). These post-NPM reforms have, however, not replaced the NPM reforms. Rather they can be seen as supplementary adjustments producing increased complexity in public sector organizations. Countries show complex combinations of organizational autonomy on some issues, increased centralized control, and network-like coordination mechanisms, alongside remnants of traditional hierarchical controls (Bouckaert *et al.* 2010).

14.3   Theoretical implications

In this book we have revealed that public sector organizations are in constant flux or permanently changing, adapting and being adapted. There is a lot of dynamic change going on resulting in increased complexity. Instead of regarding the administrative apparatuses as stable we claim that reforming the organizational pattern has become a routine (cf. Brunsson and Olsen 1993). That said, there is also a combination of flexibility and robustness in the way these organizations change (see Pollitt and Bouckaert 2009; Roness and Sætren 2009). On the one hand, the overall organizational forms show a lot of robustness, but on the other hand there have been major changes within each form and also a movement of organizations between different forms as well as a changing balance between the different organizational forms.

Another main finding is that we need to go beyond the formal categories and study actual autonomy and control in the 'living' organizations as opposed to formal and legal autonomy (Christensen and Lægreid 2007c). A third finding is that we see a combination of convergence and divergence in the change pattern. On the one hand there is convergence, in the sense that the agency form is very popular and that all countries now have central agencies. On the other hand there is divergence, meaning that there is considerable variation among countries regarding what they mean by an agency and also regarding the actual autonomy and control of agencies. Thus context matters and different countries start from different points.

Our argument is that administrative reforms are based a combination of different driving forces. Single-factor explanations such as the credible commitment theory face considerable problems when their claims are confronted with empirical data (see also Christensen, forthcoming). The same is the case when some of the major NPM doctrines face the practical world and the realities of empirical complexity in different political–administrative contexts (Ongaro 2009; Rubecksen 2009; Christensen and Lægreid, forthcoming). Thus, what we see in the diverse empirical realities are very much in contrast with ideas of 'generic' public management, 'global recipes' and simple models of administrative reforms. The organization of the public administration is becoming increasingly complex and multi-functional, with different organizational principles resulting from multiple factors working together in a complex mix (Olsen 2007b; Christensen and Lægreid 2008e; Egeberg and Trondal 2009b). Compound administrative reforms are multi-dimensional and represent 'mixed' orders and combinations of competing, inconsistent, and contradictory organizational principles and structures that co-exist and balance different interests and values (Olsen 2007: 13–14). Compound reforms assume that executive governance rests on the mobilization of multiple sets of institutions, actors, decision-making arenas, and norms, which we have labelled a transformative approach. Thus complementary approaches to reforms are more appropriate than either-or reforms in which one reform replaces the previous one. In a pluralistic society, with many criteria for success and different causal understandings, we have to go beyond the idea of a single organizational principle to understand how public organization functions and is reformed and to look at it as a composite process (Olsen 2005, 2007a).

Instead of assuming a linear development towards more and more NPM reform, or a cyclical development where tradition strikes back and reinstalls the old public administration, our argument is that we face a dialectical development in which the old public administration mixes with New Public Management and post-NPM features to produce new hybrid organizational forms (Christensen and Lægreid 2001a). Our understanding of institutional change in the case of administrative reform is a combination of robustness and flexibility. There is a kind of layering (Streeck and Thelen 2005) or sedimentation (Olsen 2008) process going on, implying that new reforms complement or supplement old reforms rather than replacing them. Old and new institutions co-exist and co-evolve even if they are founded on partly inconsistent principles. This means that NPM is by no means dead and has not simply been replaced by post-NPM reforms. Rather we see previous reforms being modified and adjusted through the addition of new and partly different reform measures. The result of such a process is not only increased complexity in the organization of the public sector but also increased turbulence because the trade-offs and balance between different principles tend to change over time, between countries, and across policy areas.

How to understand why this increased complexity occurs is, however, contested. Our argument is that we have to look for a composite and complex mixture of different driving forces. We cannot assume that reform agents have sufficient capability, cognitive capacity, and power to act as rational actors. Their behaviour is constrained by different contextual features. Instrumental theories need to be complemented by other theoretical perspectives (e.g. sociological or historical institutionalism) to explain actors' behaviour. While this may be dominated by the logic of consequence in some instances, under other conditions, the logic of appropriateness might prevail (March and Olsen 1998: 952–3; Pollitt *et al.* 2004: 250). This book has shown, for instance, that credible commitment logic may, at least partially and in some countries, play a role when agencies are created and their formal form chosen – especially in the case of regulatory agencies – but credible commitment seems much less relevant when explaining de facto autonomy of agencies and the way political principals deal with that autonomy (see also Verhoest *et al.* 2010).

Polity, culture, and environmental features are all important constraints on deliberate organizational design and actual functioning, but the still unsolved question is under what conditions each set of factors is most important and also how they work together and reinforce or counterbalance each other. There is no agreed-on empirical administrative theory specifying under which conditions one set of factors has greater explanatory power than others (Olsen 2007a).

There is, however, an increasing realization that administrative reforms offer no universal panacea; rather, they must be matched carefully with the needs, traditions, and resources of each political system (Olsen 2006; World Bank 2000). Reforms that do not take the historical institutional context into consideration tend to produce new reforms rather than increased performance. In this book we have argued that global prescriptions for administrative reforms have been interpreted and responded to differently depending on national and sector-specific institutional arrangements and historical traditions.

There is no agreed-on theory explaining how reforms happen that identifies the mechanisms and determinants of administrative reform and change. Indeed, this book has revealed that there is no one-factor explanation. To understand the complex relationships involved in the governance of public sector organizations, how they change, and what their effects are we need to blend and combine different theoretical approaches. It is generally difficult to establish a firm theoretical basis for institutional design. We do not believe in generic theories. Rather, what we need is middle-range theories that once again take account of context and historical and cultural constraints and that are able to clarify under which conditions one set of factor matters more than others and how their mutual influence can be understood.

A main challenge is to have theories that are consistent with the complex empirical realities of change and yet clarify the processes underlying the contextual details. We embrace the growing claim that context matters (March 2008), but there is still no good theory of context that specifies under what conditions different contexts matter (Pollitt 2003a).

14.4 Methodological implications

What we need more than anything else is to have more reliable and systematic empirical knowledge about the establishment, maintenance, and change of public sector organizations and agencies more specifically but also of the study of public management and administration more generally. There is a need to build comprehensive data bases covering changes over time as well as across countries, administrative levels, and policy areas with respect to how political–administrative organizations work in practice. Systematic mapping of formal organizational features is important, but we need to go beyond formal structures and to study actual autonomy, control, and coordination as well as performance. The subjective opinions and perceptions of the members of an organization are important but they must also be supplemented by more objective measures. When studying results and performance it is important to develop methodological approaches that go beyond the internal focus on efficiency and take account of an organization's relations with external stakeholders and citizens as well as the democratic implications.

There is a need for methodological approaches that allow for data triangulations that embrace qualitative as well as quantitative approaches, using a combination of case studies and surveys. Mapping exercises must be supplemented by comparative statistics and process data.

Based on the interpretation in this study of what is going on 'on the ground' in administrative systems it is our claim that we need a movement in the field of public administration away from studies of contrasts and succession of administrative paradigms, reform models and doctrines towards comprehensive empirical work on a large and systematic scale that are able to handle the complex empirical reality of public sector organizations.

The challenges for future research are first of all a need for more systematic comparative studies over time and across countries, administrative levels, and policy areas. What we need more than anything else is good data. There is also a need for more and better studies able to analyse the dynamics of reform and change by focusing on the processes and especially on the effects and implications of major structural reform programmes as well as day-to-day changes.

14.5   Practical implications

One implication is that reformers score higher on political control than on rational calculation. The Achilles heel in administrative reforms seems to be that reform actors have a limited understanding of the consequences and implications of their own reform initiatives. Results are something that they promise or expect but which they seldom have reliable knowledge about *ex ante*. Systematic evaluations of major structural change programmes are hard to come by and we cannot expect precise and operational lessons (Pollitt 2009). Reforms and administrative change are affected by ideology and international fashions which often have a weak evidence-based fundament. This is why reforms often look more attractive *ex ante* than *ex post* (Brunsson and Olsen 1993). Disappointment with the results of previous reforms tends to encourage new reforms. Hence the conclusion is that reform produces reform.

In situations with a weak understanding of the effects and implications of reform it might be wise to avoid major and controversial radical reforms based on big new ideas and to opt instead for more incremental change processes that enjoy high legitimacy among the reformers as well as the reformed (Olsen 1997). There is also a need to build feedback-loops and possibilities for experiential learning into the reform process so that adjustments can be made as reforms proceed.

Another practical implication is that rather than purifying a single model we need a repertoire of models for political–administrative institutions to understand the future challenges of public management, administration, and governance. The public administration is multifunctional and has to balance different values and goals. The modes of hierarchy, networks, and markets are normally not alternative but supplementary (Olsen 2006). Therefore, a main challenge is to understand how they can be combined and balanced. This requires an understanding of the diversity, complexity, and dynamics of the contemporary political–administrative system. We need better descriptions and analyses of the way people and organizations cooperate and better interpretations and explanations of the dynamics of organizational change.

Designers of public sector organizations have to be aware of the fundamental dialectical relations between basic organizational principles. When organizations are specialized based on one principle (e.g. purpose/sector), coordination needs will arise that involve other specialization principles (e.g. geography or clients/users). Hence specialization in one direction will ultimately lead to new coordination initiatives. Similarly, designing autonomous organizations raises problems of control. Such basic insights of organization theory are still highly relevant in these modern times and need to be taken into account. However, practice is even more complicated, since specialization and coordination, autonomy and control are all multi-dimensional concepts. A public sector organization's degree of autonomy is actually a product of balancing managerial autonomy with policy autonomy and financial autonomy with structural aspects of autonomy. One needs to be aware that the autonomy granted on one dimension to one agency may in the daily organizational life of this agency become less relevant if autonomy on other dimensions is lacking (see also Verhoest *et al.* 2004a). We question if simple ideas of autonomy is a necessary condition for increased performance and this raises the issue of how much policy-makers should bother about establishing new agency and giving them enhanced autonomy. At least it is necessary to address more systematically the multi-dimensional concept of autonomy and the complicated relationship between autonomy and control.

When political and administrative executives design control arrangements for agencies, there is always a choice to be made in how to combine *ex ante* control with *ex post* result-oriented control, structural forms of control, and control by contacts. When it comes to their formal design, most organizations show very hybrid combinations of specific kinds of autonomy with specific, multiple kinds of control. This is the case even in countries which embraced NPM ideas whole-heartedly, like New Zealand or the UK. Thus, designers of public sector organizations need to make complex choices and trade-offs when creating agencies, and when doing this, they need to use a multi-dimensional conceptual mapping of the core concepts.

Moreover, when designing forms of affiliation with formal degrees of autonomy and control arrangements, politicians and senior administrators need to bear in mind that formal design and its actual functioning are two different realities. Although agencification does attenuate political steering signals, compared to departments, political control does not always respect the formal logic of organizational form. Where agencies perform tasks with high political salience, or that are of high political significance or value for the agency regarding the possibilities for political appointees, de facto political control may be stronger than originally envisaged by the designers. Similarly, senior managers within agencies use strategic behaviour and build reputations to strengthen their autonomy (Carpenter 2001), or, under other conditions, prefer to be very close to politicians. Formal rules and regulations, which seemed functional when the agencies were created, become obsolete after a while or are not enforced as they were intended to be. Designing an optimal formal–legal agency status by combining degrees of autonomy and control is not the whole story. Reality is much more dynamic, and so are de facto autonomy and control practices.

Lastly, changing organizational form of affiliation, as in agencification, is clearly not a panacea for all diseases, not even for underperformance. Autonomy on its own is not a sufficient condition to improve management and performance. Enhancing organizational performance seems to imply high mutual trust relations, creating a stimulating organizational culture with qualified, motivated, and committed employees and managers, appropriate governance structures, and the right capacity, and all this is contingent on the organization's tasks, technical environment, and the broader political–administrative regime. So organizational restructuring is only one part of a very complex story. The bottom line is that there is no best organizational form that can be used everywhere, at all times, and for all tasks. Rather than searching for a final solution and the best organizational form, one must learn to live with inbuilt tension and partly competing organizational principles.

Bibliography

6, P. (2004) 'Joined-up government in the Western world in comparative perspective: a preliminary literature review and exploration', *Journal of Public Administration Research and Theory*, 14 (1), 103–36.

6, P (2005) 'Joined-Up government in the West beyond Britain: A Provisional Assessment' in V. Bogdanor (ed.) *Joined-Up Government*. British Academy Occasional Paper 5 (Oxford: Oxford University Press).

Aberbach, J. D. and T. Christensen (2001) 'Radical reform in New Zealand: crisis, windows of opportunities, and rational actors', *Public Administration*, 79 (2), 404–22.

Altheide, D. L. and R. P. Snow (1988) 'Toward a Theory of Mediation', *Communication Yearbook*, 11 (S 194), 223.

Andrews R., G. Boyne, J. Law and R. M. Walker (2007) 'Centralization, Organizational Strategy, and Public Service Performance', *Journal of Public Administration Research and Theory*, 19 (1), 57–80.

Armingeon, K. (2002) 'The Effects of Negotiation Democracy: A Comparative Analysis', *European Journal of Political Research*, 41 (1), 81–105.

Askim, J., T. Christensen, A. L. Fimreite and P. Lægreid (2010) 'How To Assess Administrative Reform? Investigating the Adoption and Preliminary Impacts of the Norwegian Welfare Administration Reform', *Public Administration*, 88(1), 232–46.

Aubert, B. A., S. Boudreau, F. Gagné and N. Perreault (2005) 'Analyse évaluative des unités conventionnées et des unités autonomes de services' (Montréal, Q: Centre interuniversitaire de recherche en analyse des organisations), http://www.tresor.gouv.qc.ca/fr/publications/modernisation/unites_conventionnees_UAS.pdf.

Aucoin, P. (1990) 'Administrative Reform in Public Management: Paradigms, Principles, Paradoxes and Pendulums', *Governance*, 3 (2), 115–37.

Aucoin, P. (2007) 'Public Governance and Accountability of Canadian Crown Corporations: Reformation or Transformation', paper presented to Canadian Political Science Association 2007 Annual Conference, University of Saskatchewan, 31 May.

Aucoin, P. and H. Bakvis (1988) *The Centralization–Decentralization Conundrum: Organization and Management in the Canadian Government*, Institute for Research on Public Policy, Halifax, NS.

Australian Public Service Commission (2006) *State of the Service Report 2005–06*, APSC, Canberra.

Australian Public Service Commission (2007a) *Tackling Wicked Problems: A Public Policy Perspective*, APSC, Canberra.

Australian Public Service Commission (2007b) *State of the Service Report 2006–07*, APSC, Canberra.

Bach, T. and W. Jann (2009) 'Structure and Governance of Agencies in Germany: A Lot of Continuity and Little Change', in P. G. Roness and H. Sætren (eds), *Change and Continuity in Public Sector Organizations* (Bergen: Fagbokforlaget).

Bache, I. and M. Flinders (eds) (2004) *Multi-level Governance* (Oxford: Oxford University Press).

Bakvis, K. and L. Juillet (2004) *The Horizontal Challenge: Line Departments, Central Agencies and Leadership* (Ottawa, Canadian School of Public Services).

Balázs, I. (2004) 'A központi közigazgatás különös hatáskörű szerveinek szabályozási koncepciója', *Magyar Közigazgatás*, 54 (9), 513–528.

Balboni., B. (2008) 'Perceived Corporate Credibility as the Emergent Property of Corporate Reputation's Transmission Process', 1–9 in *MPRA Paper*.

Barbieri, D. and E. Ongaro. (2008) 'EU Agencies: What Is Common and What Is Distinctive Compared with National-level Public Agencies', *International Review of Administrative Sciences*, 74 (3), 395–420.

Barro, R. and Gordon, D. (1983) 'Rules, Discretion and Reputation in a Model of Monetary Policy', *Journal of Monetary Economics*, 12, 101–21.

Barzelay, M. (2001) *The New Public Management: Improving Research and Policy Dialogue* (Berkeley University of California Press).

Bégin-Lafontaine, M. (2008) 'Exercice de conformité ou état d'une réelle responsabilisation: l'évaluation de la performance dans quatre agences québécoises' (Master's thesis, HEC Montreal).

Behn, R. D. (2003) 'Why Measure Performance? Different Purposes Require Different Measures', *Public Administration Review*, 63 (5), 586–606.

Bendor, J., A. Glazer and T. Hammond, (2001) 'Theories of Delegation', *Annual Review of Political Science*, 4 (1), 235–69.

Benz, A. and K. H. Goetz (1996) 'The German Public Sector: National Priorities and the International Reform Agenda', in A. Benz and K. H. Goetz (eds), *A New German Public Sector? Reform, Adaption and Stability* (Aldershot: Dartmouth).

Better Regulation Group (2007) Bodies in Ireland with regulatory powers, www.taoiseach.gov.ie/attached_files/pdf%20files/Bodies%20in%20Ireland%20with%20Regulatory%20Powers.pdf.

Bilodeau, N., C. Laurin and A. R. Vining (2007) 'Choice of Organizational Form Makes a Real Difference: The Impact of Corporatization on Government Agencies in Canada', *Journal of Public Administration Research and Theory*, 17 (1), 119–47.

Black, J. (2001) 'Decentring Regulation: The Role of Regulation and Self-regulation in a "Post-regulatory"-world', *Current Legal Problems*, 54, 103–46.

Black, J. (2002). *Critical Reflections on Regulation*, CARR Discussion Paper No. 4 (London: CARR, LSE).

Blinder, A. S. (1999) 'Central Bank Credibility: Why Do We Care? How Do We Build It?', *The American Economic Review*, 90 (5), 1421–31.

Blühdorn, I. (2006) 'Democracy, Efficiency, Futurity: Contested Objectives of Societal Modernization' in I. Bluehdorn and U. Jun (eds), *Economic Efficiency – Democratic Renewal. Contested Modernization in Britain and Germany*, (Lanham: Lexington Press).

Bogdanor, V. (ed.) (2005) *Joined-up Government* (Oxford: Oxford University Press).

Borins, S. (2002) 'Transformation of Public Sector: Canada in Comparative Perspective' in C. Dunn (ed.) *The Handbook of Canadian Public Administration* (Don Mills: Oxford University Press).

Börzel, T. A. and T. Risse (2000) 'Who Is Afraid of a European Federation? How to Constitutionalise a Multi-Level Governance System.' in J. Y. Meny and J. H. H. Weiler (eds), *What Kind of Polity? Responses to Joschka Fischer* (Florence: Robert Schuman Centre).

Boston, J. and C. Eichbaum (2007) 'State Sector Reform and Renewal in New Zealand: Lessons for Governance', in G. E. Caiden and Tsai-Tsu Su (eds), *The Repositioning of Public Governance: Global Experience and Challenges*, (Tapei: Best-Wise Publishing).

Boston, J., J. Martin, J. Pallot and P. Walsh (1996) *Public Management: The New Zealand Model* (Auckland: Oxford University Press).

Bouckaert, G. and J. Halligan (2008) *Managing Performance: International Comparisons* (Routledge: London).

Bouckaert, G. and W. van Dooren, (2003) 'Performance Measurement and Management in Public Sector Organizations', in T. Bovaird and E. Loffler (eds) *Public Management and Governance* (London: Routledge).

Bouckaert, G. and B. G. Peters (2004) 'What Is Available and What Is Missing in the Study of Quangos?' in C. Pollitt and C. Talbot (eds), *Unbundled Government. A Critical Analysis of the Global Trend to Agencies, Quangos and Contractualisation* (London: Routledge).

Bouckaert, G., B. G. Peters and K. Verhoest (2006) 'Janus-faced Re-organization: Specialisation and Co-ordination in Four Countries in the Period 1985–2005', paper presented at the Annual Conference, EGPA, Milan, Italy, 6–8 September 2006.

Bouckaert, G., B. Peters, K. Verhoest (2010) *The Coordination of Public Sector Organizations: Shifting Patterns of Public Management* (Basingstoke: Palgrave Macmillan).

Bovens, M., T. Schillemans and P. t'Hart (2008) 'Does Public Accountability Work? An Assessment Tool', *Public Administration*, 86 (1), 225–42.

Boyne, G. (1998) 'Bureaucratic Theory Meets Reality: Public Choice and Service Contracting in U.S. Local Government', *Public Administration Review*, 58 (6), 474–84.

Boyne, G. A. (2003) 'Sources of Public Service Improvement: A Critical Review and Research Agenda', *Journal of Public Administration Research and Theory*, 13 (3), 367–94.

Boyne, G. (2004) 'Explaining Public Service Performance. Does Management Matter?' *Public Policy and Administration*, 19 (4), 110–17.

Boyne, G. and R. M. Walker (2005) 'Introducing the 'Determinants of Performance in Public Organizations' Symposium', *Journal of Public Administration Research and Theory*, 15 (4), 483–88.

Boyne, G., K. J. Meier, L. O'Toole and R. M. Walker (2005) 'Where Next? Research Directions on Performance in Public Organizations', *Journal of Public Administration Research and Theory*, 15 (4), 633–9.

Brabazon, T. (2000) 'Behavioral Finance: A New Sunrise or a False Dawn?'. 1–8 in *CoIL Summer School 2000.* (Limerick, University of Limerick: Department of Accountancy, University College Dublin).

Braithwaite, J. and P. Drahos (2000) *Global Business Regulation* (Cambridge: Cambridge University Press).

Brambilla, R., C. Francalanci and E. Ongaro (1999) *Modelling the Information Processing Capacity of Local Authorities with Different Degrees of Structural Disaggregation,*

Proceedings of the meeting of the European Conference of Information Technology Evaluation, Brunel University, West London, September 1999.

Braun, D. (1993) 'Who Governs Intermediary Agencies? Principal–Agent Relations in Research Policy-Making', *Journal of Public Policy*, 13 (2), 135–62.

Braun, D. (2003) 'Dezentraler und unitarischer Foderalismus. Die Schweiz und Deutschland im Vergleich', *Swiss Political Science Review*, 9 (1), 57–90.

Bréchemier, D. and S. Saussier (2001) 'What Governance Structure for Non-Contractible Services? An Empirical Analysis' in Plunket, A., C. Voisin, and B. Bellon (eds) *The Dynamics of Industrial Collaboration* (Cheltenham: Edward Elgar).

Brewer, G. A. (2005) 'In the Eye of the Storm: Frontline Supervisors and Federal Agency Performance', *Journal of Public Administration Research and Theory*, 15 (4), 505–27.

Brewer, G. A. and S. C. Selden (2000) 'Why Elephants Gallop: Assessing and Predicting Organizational Performance in Federal Agencies', *Journal of Public Administration Research and Theory*, 10 (4), 685–711.

BRH (2005) *Bericht an den Haushaltsausschuss des Deutschen Bundestages nach § 88 Abs. 2 BHO zur Fachaufsicht der Bundesministerien über ihre nachgeordneten Geschäftsbereiche (Entwurf)* (Bonn: Bundesrechnungshof).

Brickley, J., C. W. Smith and J. L. Zimmerman (1995) 'The Economics of Organizational Architecture', *Journal of Applied Corporate Finance*, 8 (2), 19–31.

Brown, A., Stern, B. Tenebaum, B. and D. Gencer (2006) *Handbook for Evaluating Infrastructure Regulatory Systems* (Washington: The World Bank).

Brown, A. D. (1994) 'Politics, Symbolic Action and Myth Making in Pursuit of Legitimacy', *Organization Studies*, 15 (6), 861–78.

Brown, T. and M. Potoski (2003) 'Transaction Costs and Institutional Explanations for Government Service Production Decisions', *Journal of Public Administration Research and Theory*, 13 (4), 441–68.

Brunetti, A., G. Kisunko and B. Weder (1998) 'Credibility of Rules and Economic Growth: Evidence from a Worldwide Survey of the Private Sector', *The World Bank Economic Review*, 12 (3), 353–84.

Brunsson, N. (1989) *The Organization of Hypocrisy. Talk, Decisions and Actions in Organizations* (Chichester: Wiley).

Brunsson, N. and J. P. Olsen (1993) 'Organizational Forms: Can We Choose Them', in N. Brunsson and J. P. Olsen (eds), *The Reforming Organization* (London: Routledge).

Brunsson, N. and J. P. Olsen (1993) *The Reforming Organization* (London: Routledge).

Bryant, J. and D. Zillmann (2002) *Media Effects: Advances in Theory and Research* (Mahwah: Lawrence Erlbaum).

Burnham, J. and R. Pyper (2008) *Britain's Modernised Civil Service* (Basingstoke: Palgrave Macmillan).

Burns, J. P. (1994) 'Administration Reform in a Changing Political Environment: the Case of Hong Kong', *Public Administration and Development*, 14, 241–52.

Burns, J. P. (2004) *Government Capacity and the Hong Kong Civil Service* (Hong Kong: Oxford University Press).

Cantillon, B., V. De Maesschalck, S. Rottiers and G. Verbist (2006) 'Social Redistribution in Federalised Belgium', *West European Politics*, 29, 1034–56.

Carpenter, D. P. (2001) *The Forging of Bureaucratic Autonomy: Reputations, Networks, and Policy Innovation in Executive Agencies, 1862–1928* (Princeton: Princeton University Press).

Carpenter, D. P. (2002) 'Groups, the Media, Agency Waiting Costs, and FDA Drug Approval', *American Journal of Political Science*, 46 (3), 490–505.

Caulfield, J. and A. Liu (2006) 'Shifting Concepts of Autonomy in the Hong Kong Hospital Authority', *Public Organization Review*, 6, 20–19.

Cavalluzo, K. S. and C. D. Ittner (2004) 'Implementing Performance Measurement Innovations: Evidence from Government', *Accounting, Organizations and Society*, 29, 243–67.

Central Agencies Review 2006 (2006) Review of Central Agencies' Role in Promoting and Assuring State Sector Performance, NZ Treasury, http://www.treasury.govt.nz/publications/informationreleases/exgreviews/ca.

Chester, D. N. (1953) 'Public Corporations and the Classification of Administrative Bodies', *Political Studies*, 1, 34–52.

Cheung, A. B. L. (1997) 'Reform in Search of Politics: The Case of Hong Kong's Aborted Attempt To Corporatize Public Broadcasting', *Asian Journal of Public Administration*, 19 (2), 276–302.

Cheung, A. B. L. (1999) 'Administrative Development in Hong Kong: Political Questions, Administrative Answers', in H. K. Wong and H. S. Chan (eds), *Handbook of Comparative Public Administration in the Asian Pacific Basin* (New York: Marcel Dekker).

Cheung, A. B. L. (2001) 'The "Trading Fund" Reform in Hong Kong: Claims and Performance', in A. B. L. Cheung and J. C. Y. Lee (eds), *Public Sector Reform in Hong Kong: Into the 21st Century* (Hong Kong: The Chinese University Press).

Cheung, A. B. L. (2006a) 'Budgetary Reforms in Two City States: Impact on the Central Budget Agency in Hong Kong and Singapore', *International Review of Administrative Sciences*, 72 (3), 341–61.

Cheung, A. B. L. (2006b) 'Reinventing Hong Kong's Public Service: Same NPM Reform, Different Contexts and Politics', *International Journal of Organization Theory and Behavior*, 9 (2), 212–34.

Cheung, A. B. L. (2006c) 'How Autonomous Are Public Corporations in Hong Kong? The Case of the Airport Authority', *Public Organization Review*, 6, 221–36.

Christensen, J. G. (2001) 'Bureaucratic Autonomy as a Political Asset', in B. G. Peters and J. Pierre (eds), *Politicians, Bureaucrats and Administrative Reform* (London: Routledge).

Christensen, J. G. (2005) *Delegation and Administrative Organization: An Overview of Danish Regulatory Administration 1950–2000*, http://www.publicmanagement-cobra.org/pub/paper/DelegationandAdministrativeOrg.pdf.

Christensen, J. G. (forthcoming) 'Public Interest Regulation Reconsidered', in D. Levi-Faur, J. Braithwaite, and S. K. Vogel (eds) *Handbook of Regulation* (Cheltenham: Edward Elgar).

Christensen, J. G. and K. Yesilkagit (2006a) 'Delegation and Specialization in Regulatory Administration: A Comparative Analysis of Denmark, Sweden and the Netherlands', in T. Christensen and P. Lægreid (eds) *Autonomy and Regulation: Coping with Agencies in the Modern State* (Cheltenham: Edward Elgar).

Christensen, J. G. and K. Yesilkagit (2006b) 'Political Responsiveness and Credibility in Regulatory Administration', paper presented at the ECPR conference on Regulatory Governance. Bath 7–8 Sept. 2006.

Christensen, T. and M. Egeberg (1997) 'Sentraladministrasjonen – en oversikt over trekk ved departementer og direktorater', in T. Christensen and M. Egeberg (eds), *Forvaltningskunnskap* (Oslo: Tano Aschehoug).

Christensen, T. and P. Lægreid (1998a) *Den moderne forvaltning* (Oslo: Tano Aschehoug).

Christensen, T. and P. Lægreid (1998b) 'Administrative Reform Policy: The Case of Norway', *International Review of Administrative Sciences*, 64 (4), 457–75.

Christensen, T. and P. G. Roness (1999) 'Den historiske arven – Norge', in P. Lægreid and O. K. Pedersen (eds), *Fra opbygning til ombygning i staten. Organisationsforandringer i tre nordiske lande* (Copenhagen: DJØF Publishing).

Christensen, T. and P. Lægreid (2001a) *New Public Management. The Transformation of Ideas and Practice* (Aldershot: Ashgate).

Christensen, T. and Lægreid, P. (2001b) 'New Public Management: The Effects of Contractualism and Devolution on Political Control', *Public Management Review*, 3 (1), 73–94.

Christensen, T. and P. Lægreid (2001c) 'A Transformative Perspective on Administrative Reforms', in T. Christensen and P. Lægreid (eds), *New Public Management. The Transformation of Ideas and Practice* (Aldershot: Ashgate).

Christensen, T. and P. Lægreid (2001d) 'New Public Management – Undermining Political Control?' in T. Christensen and P. Lægreid (eds), *New Public Management. The Transformation of Ideas and Practice* (Aldershot: Ashgate).

Christensen, T. and P. Lægreid (2003a) 'Coping with Complex Leadership Roles: the Problematic Redefinition of Government-owned Enterprises', *Public Administration*, 81 (4), 803–31.

Christensen, T. and P. Lægreid (2003b) 'Administrative Reform Policy: The Challenges of Turning Symbols into Practice', *Public Organization Review*, 3 (1), 3–27.

Christensen, T. and P. Lægreid (2006a) 'Agencification and Regulatory Reform', in T. Christensen and P. Lægreid (eds), *Autonomy and Regulation. Coping with Agencies in the Modern State* (Cheltenham: Edward Elgar).

Christensen, T. and P. Lægreid (2006b) 'Rebalancing the State: Reregulation and the Reassertion of the Centre', in T. Christensen and P. Lægreid (eds), *Autonomy and Regulation. Coping with Agencies in the Modern State* (Cheltenham: Edward Elgar).

Christensen, T. and P. Lægreid (eds) (2006c) *Autonomy and Regulation. Coping with Agencies in the Modern State* (Cheltenham: Edward Elgar).

Christensen, T., P. Lægreid and A. R. Ramslien (2006a) *Styring og autonomi. Organisasjonsformer i norsk utlendingsforvaltning* (Oslo: Universitetsforlaget).

Christensen, T., P. Lægreid and I. Stigen (2006b) 'Performance Management and Public Sector Reform: The Norwegian Hospital Reform', *International Public Management Journal*, 9 (2), 113–39.

Christensen, T. and P. Lægreid (2007a) 'The Whole-of-Government Approach to Public Sector Reform' *Public Administration Review*, 67 (6), 1057–64.

Christensen, T. and P. Lægreid (eds) (2007b) *Transcending New Public Management.* (Aldershot: Ashgate).

Christensen, T. and P. Lægreid (2007c) 'Regulatory Agencies – the Challenges of Balancing Agency Autonomy and Political Control', *Governance*, 20 (3), 479–519.

Christensen, T. and P. Lægreid (2007d) 'Introduction – Theoretical Approach and Research Questions', in T. Christensen and P. Lægreid (eds), *Transcending New Public Management. The Transformation of Public Sector Reform* (Aldershot: Ashgate).

Christensen, T. and P. Lægreid (2008a) 'The Regulatory Orthodoxy in Practice', in U. Sverdrup and J. Trondal (eds), *The Organizational Dimension of Politics. Essays in Honour of Morten Egeberg* (Bergen: Fagbokforlaget).

Christensen, T. and P. Lægreid (2008b) 'NPM and Beyond – Structure, Culture and Demography', *International Review of Administrative Sciences*, 74 (1), 7–24.

Christensen, T. and P. Lægreid (2008c) 'The Study of Public Management in Norway. Combining Organization Theory and Political Science', in W. Kickert (ed.), *The Study of Public Management in Europe and the US* (London: Routledge).

Christensen, T. and P. Lægreid (2008e) 'Modern Regulatory Policy – Ideas and Practice', *Policy and Society*, 26 (7), 19–38.

Christensen, T. and P. Lægreid (eds) (2008f) 'Transcending New Public Management: A Transformative Approach To Increased Complexity and the Challenge of Balancing Autonomy and Control', paper presented at 'Kindred Spirits – Developing Ideas to Catch and Release', Celebrating Scancor's 20th Anniversary, 21–23 Nov. 2008, Stanford University.

Christensen, T. and P. Lægreid (2009) 'Living in the Past? Tenure, Roles and Attitudes in the Central Civil Service', *Public Administration Review*, 69 (5), 951–61.

Christensen, T. and P. Lægreid (forthcoming) 'NPM-related Regulatory Reforms: The Problem of Putting the New Regulatory Orthodoxy into Practice', in D. Levi-Faur, J. Braithwaite and S. K. Vogel (eds), *Handbook of Regulation* (Cheltenham: Edward Elgar).

Christensen, T., Lægreid, P. Roness, and K. A. Røvik (2007a) *Organization Theory and the Public Sector. Instrument, Culture and Myth* (London and New York City: Routledge).

Christensen, T., P. Lægreid and R. Norman (2007) 'Organizing Immigration – a Comparison of New Zealand and Norway 'in T. Christensen. and P. Lægreid (eds), *Transcending New Public Management* (Aldershot: Ashgate).

Christensen, T., A. L. Fimreite and P. Lægreid (2007) 'Reform of the Employment and Welfare Administrations – the Challenges of Coordinating Diverse Public Organizations', *International Review of Administrative Sciences*, 73 (3), 389–408.

Christensen, T., A. Lie and P. Lægreid (2007) 'Still Fragmented Government or Reassertion of the Centre?' in T. Christensen and P. Lægreid (eds), *Transcending New Public Management. The Transformation of Public Sector Reform* (Aldershot: Ashgate).

Christensen, T., A. Lie and P. Lægreid (2008) 'Beyond New Public Management: Agencification and Regulatory Reform in Norway', *Financial Accountability & Management*, 24 (1), 15–30.

Chun, Y. H. and H. G. Rainey (2005) 'Goal Ambiguity and Organizational Performance in US Federal Agencies', *Journal of Public Administration Research and Theory*, 15 (4), 529–57.

Clark, M. (2005) 'Scandalous! The Electoral Effects of Valence Issues in Western Europe, 1976–1998' in *Annual Meeting of the Midwest Political Science Association*, Chicago.

Coen, D. and M. Thatcher (2005) 'The New Governance of Markets and Non-Majoritarian Regulators', *Governance: An International Journal of Policy, Administration, and Institutions*, 18 (3), 329–46.

Coglianese, C. and M. Howard (1998) 'Getting the Message Out: Regulatory Policy and the Press', *Politics*, 3 (3), 39–55.

Cohen, M. D. and J. G. March (1974) *Leadership and Ambiguity: The American College President* (Harvard: Harvard Business School Press).

Commissie Stevens (2007) *Regels op maat: eindrapport commissie-Stevens. Slotaanbevelingen aan het kabinet voor de aanpak van regeldruk* (Den Haag: Commissie Stevens).

Commons, J. (1924) *Legal Foundations of Capitalism* (New York: Macmillan).

Cooley, Alexander (2000) 'International Aid to the Former Soviet States: Agent of Change or Guardian of the Status Quo?' *Problems of Post-Communism*, 47 (4), 34–44.

Cooper, D. J. and K. Ogata (2005) 'New Public Management Reforms in Canada' in J. Guthrie, C. Humphrey, L. R. Jones and O. Olson (eds) *International Public Financial Management Reform* (Greenwich: Information Age Publishing).

Cooray, M. J. A. (2000) 'Ombudsman in Asia: A Case-study of Hong Kong and Sri Lanka', in R. Gregory and P. Giddings (eds), *Righting Wrongs: the Ombudsman in Six Continents* (Amsterdam: IOS Press).

Côté, L. (2006) 'L'expérience québécoise en matière de réforme administrative: la loi sur l'administration publique', *Canadian Public Administration*, 49 (1), 1–22.

CPAP [Commission permanente de l'administration publique] (2001) 'Audition du directeur général de l'Aide financière aux études conformément à la Loi sur l'administration publique', Les Travaux Parlementaires, 36ᵉ législature, 1re session, 2 novembre 2000.

Cukierman, A., S. Webb and B. Neyapti (1992) 'Measuring the Independence of Central Banks and Its Effects on Policy Outcomes', *World Bank Economic Review*, 6 (3), 353–98.

Cyert, R. M. and J. G. March (1963) *A Behavioral Theory of the Firm* (Englewood Cliffs, NJ: Prentice-Hall).

David, R. and S. Han (2004) 'A Systematic Assessment of the Empirical Support for Transaction Cost Economics', *Strategic Management Journal*, 25, 39–58.

de Jonge, J., H. van Trijp, R. J. Renes and L. Frewer (2007) 'Understanding Consumer Confidence in the Safety of Food: Its Two-Dimensional Structure and Determinants', *An International Journal*, 27 (3), 729–40.

Deephouse, D. L. (2000) 'Media Reputation as a Strategic Resource: An Integration of Mass Communication and Resource-Based Theories', *Journal of Management*, 26 (6), 1091–1112.

Denters, B. and K. Mossberger (2006) 'Building Blocks for a Methodology for Comparative Urban Political Research', *Urban Affairs Review*, 41 (4), 550–71.

Department of the Taoiseach (2004) *Regulating Better. A Government White Paper Setting Out Six Principles of Better Regulation* (Dublin: Department of the Taoiseach).

Deschouwer, K. (2006) 'And the Peace Goes On? Consociational Democracy and Belgian Politics in theTwenty-first Century', *West European Politics*, 29, 895–911.

Dienst Wetsmatiging (2008) *Nulmeting van de administratieve lasten van het beleidsdomein Werk en Sociale Economie. Onderzoek uitgevoerd door Departement Werk en Sociale Economie, Vlaamse subsidieagentschap Werk en Sociale Economie, Syntra Vlaanderen, Vlaamse Dienst voor Arbeidsbemiddeling en Beroepsopleiding, Dienst Wetsmatiging* (Brussel: Vlaamse Overheid).

DiMaggio, P. J. and W. W. Powell (1983) 'The Iron Cage Revisited: Institutional Isomorphism and Collective Rationality in Organizational Fields', *American Sociological Review*, 48 (2), 147–60.

Dixit, A. (1996) *The Making of Economic Policy: A Transaction-Cost Politics Perspective* (Massachusetts: MIT Press).

Doern, B. and R. Johnson (2006) *Rules, Rules, Rules, Rules. Multilevel Regulatory Governance* (Toronto: Toronto University Press).

Doern, B., M. Hill, M. Prince and R. Schultz (1999) *Changing the Rules. Canadian Regulatory Regimes and Institutions* (Toronto: University of Toronto Press).

Döhler, M. (2007) *Die politische Steuerung der Verwaltung* (Baden-Baden: Nomos).

Dollery, B. (2001) 'New Institutional Economics and the Analysis of the Public Sector', *Policy Studies Review*, 18 (1), 185–211.

Domberger, S. and P. Jensen (1997) 'Contracting Out by the Public Sector: Theory, Evidence, Prospects', *Oxford Review of Economic Policy*, 13 (4), 67–78.

Donahue, A. K., S. C. Selden and P. W. Ingraham (2000) 'Measuring Government Management Capacity: A Comparative Analysis of City Human Resources management Systems', *Journal of Public Administration and Research Theory*, 10 (2), 381–412.

Dow, G. (1987) 'The Function of Authority in Transaction Cost Economics', *Journal of Economic Behavior and Organization*, 8 (1), 13–38.

Drazen, A. and P. Masson (1994) 'Credibility of Policies versus Credibility of Policymakers', *Quarterly Journal of Economics*, 109 (3), 735–54.

Dunleavy, P. (1991) *Democracy, Bureaucracy and Public Choice: Economic Explanations in Political Science* (Hemel Hempstead: Harvester Wheatsheaf).

Dunleavy, P. and H. Margetts (2001) 'From Majoritarian to Pluralist Democracy?: Electoral Reform in Britain Since 1997', *Journal of Theoretical Politics*, 13 (3), 295–319.

Dunsire, A., K. Hartley and D. Parker (1991) 'Organizational Status and Performance: Summary of the Findings', *Public Administration*, 69 (1), 21–40.

Ebinger, F. (2007). 'Agencies and Effects – Autonomy and Functional Politicization in the German Core Executive', paper presented at the Permanent Study Group on Governance of Public Sector Organizations, European Group of Public Administration conference.

Efficiency Unit (1995) *Serving the Community – A Management Guide for Civil Servants* (Hong Kong: Government Printer).

Egeberg, M. (1989) 'Om å organisere konkurrerende beslutningsprinsipper inn i myndighetstrukturer', in M. Egeberg (ed.), *Institusjonspolitikk og forvaltningsutvikling – bidrag til en anvendt statsvitenskap* (Oslo: TANO).

Egeberg, M. (1994) 'Bridging the Gap Between Theory and Practice: The Case of Administrative Policy', *Governance*, 7 (1), 83–98.

Egeberg, M. (1999) 'The Impact of Bureaucratic Structure on Policy Making', *Public Administration*, 77 (1), 155–70.

Egeberg, M. (2003) 'How Bureaucratic Structure Matters: An Organizational Perspective', in B. G. Peters and J. Pierre (eds), *Handbook of Public Administration* (London: Sage).

Egeberg M. and J. Trondal (2009a) 'Political Leadership and Bureaucratic Autonomy: Effects of Agencification', *Governance*, 22 (4), 673–88.

Egeberg, M. and J. Trondal (2009b) 'National Agencies in the European Administrative Space: Government-driven, Commission-driven or Networked?' *Public Administration*, 87 (4), 779–90.

Eilders, C. (2000) 'Media as Political Actors? Issue Focusing and Selective Emphasis in the German Quality Press', *German Politics*, 9 (3), 181–206.

Eilders, C. (2002) 'Conflict and Consonance in Media Opinion: Political Positions of Five German Quality Newspapers', *European Journal of Communication*, 17 (1), 25–63.

Elder, N. C. M. and E. C. Page (1998) 'Culture and Agency: Fragmentation and Agency Structures in Germany and Sweden', *Public Policy and Administration*, 13 (4), 28–45.

Elgie, R. and I. McMenamin (2005) 'Credible Commitment, Political Uncertainty or Policy Complexity? Explaining Variations in the Independence of Non-majoritarian Institutions in France', *British Journal of Political Science*, 35, 531–48.

Emery, Y. and D. Giauque (2003) 'Emergence of Contradictory Injunctions in Swiss NPM Projects', *International Journal of Public Sector Management*, 16 (6), 468–81.

Epstein, D. and S. O'Halloran (1999) *Delegating Powers: A Transaction Cost Politics Approach to Policy Making Under Separate Powers* (Cambridge: Cambridge University Press).

Euréval in association with Rambøll-Management (2008) *Meta-study on Decentralised Agencies: Cross-cutting Analysis of Evaluation Findings*. Final Report September 2008. Evaluation for the European Commission Contract ABAC-101930.

Ezzy, D. (2002) *Qualitative Analysis: Practice and innovation* (London: Routledge).

Fedele, P., D. Galli and E. Ongaro (2007) 'Disaggregation, Autonomy and Re-regulation, Contractualism: Public Agencies in Italy (1992–2005)', *Public Management Review*, 9 (4), 557–85.

Fimreite, A. L. and P. Lægreid (2009) 'Reorganization of the Welfare State Administration: Partnerships, Networks and Accountability', *Public Management Review*, 11 (3), 281–97.

Finance Branch (1995) *Management of Public Finances* (Hong Kong: Government Printer).

Flinders, M. (2004) 'Distributed Public Governance in Britain', *Public Administration*, 82, 883–909.

Flynn, N. (2002) *Public sector management*, 4th edn (London: Pearson).

Forbes, M. and L. E. Lynn, (2005) 'How Does Public Management Affect Government Performance? Findings from International Research', *Journal of Public Administration Research and Theory*, 15 (4), 559–84.

Frant, H. (1991) 'The New Institutional Economics: Implications for Policy Analysis' in Weimer, D. (ed.), *Policy Analysis and Economics: Developments, Tensions, Prospects* (Boston: Kluwer Academic Publishers).

Friedland, R. and R. R. Alford (1991) 'Bringing Society Back In. Symbols, Practice and Institutional Contradictions', in W. W. Powell and P. J. DiMaggio (eds), *The New Institutionalism in Organizational Analysis* (Chicago: University of Chicago Press).

Furubotn, E. and S. Pejovich (1974), *The Economics of Property Rights* (Massachusetts: Cambridge University Press).

Gains, F. (2004) 'Adapting the Agency Concept. Variations within 'Next Steps', in C. Pollitt and C. Talbot (eds), *Unbundled Government. A Critical Analysis of the Global Trend to Agencies, Quangos and Contractualisation* (London: Routledge).

GCR (2006) 'The 2006 Handbook of Competition Enforcement Agencies', *Global Competition Review,* Special Report.

Gehring, T. (2004) 'The Consequences of Delegation to Independent Agencies: Separation of Powers, Discursive Governance and the Regulation of Telecommunications in Germany', *European Journal of Political Research,* 43 (4), 677–98.

Gentzkow, M. and J. M. Shapiro (2006) 'Media Bias and Reputation', *Journal of Political Economy,* 114 (2), 280–316.

Geradin, D. and J. A. McCahery (2004) 'Regulatory Co-opetition: Transcending the Regulatory Competition Debate', in J. Jordana and D. Levi-Faur (eds), *The Politics of Regulation. Institutions and Regulatory Reforms for the Age of Governance* (Cheltenham: Edward Elgar).

Gilardi, F. (2002) 'Policy Credibility and Delegation to Independent Regulatory Agencies: A Comparative Empirical Analysis', *Journal of European Public Policy,* 9 (6), 873–93.

Gilardi, F. (2004) 'Institutional Change in Regulatory Policies: Regulation Through Independent Agencies and the Three New Institutionalisms', in J. Jordana and D. Levi-Faur (eds), *The Politics of Regulation. Institutions and Regulatory Reforms for the Age of Governance* (Cheltenham, Edward Elgar), 57–89.

Gilardi, F. (2005a) 'The Institutional Foundations of Regulatory Capitalism: The Diffusion of Independent Regulatory Agencies in Western Europe', *Annals, AAPSS,* 598, 84–101.

Gilardi, F. (2005b) 'The Formal Independence of Regulators: A Comparison of 17 Countries and 7 Sectors', *Swiss Political Science Review,* 11 (4), 139–67.

Gilardi, F. (2006) 'Delegation to Independent Regulatory Agencies in Western Europe. Credibility, Political Uncertainty and Diffusion', in Braun, D. and Gilardi (eds), *Delegation in Contemporary Democracy* (London: Routledge).

Gilardi , F. (2008) *Delegation in the Regulatory State: Independent Regulatory Agencies in Western Europe* (Cheltenham: Edward Elgar).

Gill, D. (2008a) 'Crown Entity Reform in Aotearoa-New Zealand – Pendulum Shift?', paper presented at International Research Symposium for Public Management, Queensland University of Technology, Brisbane, 26–28 March.

Gill, D. (2008b) 'By Accident or Design: Changes in the structure of the State in New Zealand', *Policy Quarterly,* 4 (2), 27–32.

Gouvernement du Québec (1999) 'Pour de meilleurs services aux citoyens: Un nouveau cadre de gestion pour la fonction publique', *Énoncé de politique sur la gestion gouvernementale* (Québec: QC).

Gouvernement du Québec (2005) 'Cinq années de gestion axée sur les résultats au gouvernement du Québec', *Rapport sur la mise en œuvre de la Loi sur l'administration publique* (Québec: QC).

Government Secretariat (1998) *Staff List of the Government of the Hong Kong Special Administrative Region* (Hong Kong: Printing Department).

Gray, W. and W. G. Sanders (2006) *Views from the Top of the 'Quiet Revolution': Secretarial Perspectives on the New Arrangements in Indigenous Affairs*, Discussion Paper 282, Centre for Aboriginal Economic Policy Research, Australian National University.

Greer, P. (1992) 'The Next Steps Initiative: An Examination of the Agency Framework Documents', *Public Administration*, 70 (1), 89–100.

Greer, P. (1994) *Next Steps Origins: Transforming Central Government* (Buckingham: Open University Press).

Gregory, R. (2001) 'Transforming Governmental Culture: A Sceptical View of New Public Management', in T. Christensen and P. Lægreid (eds), *New Public Management. The Transformation of Ideas and Practice* (Aldershot: Ashgate).

Gregory, R. (2003) 'All the King's Horses and all the King's Men: Putting New Zealand's Public Sector Back Together Again', *International Public Management Review*, 4 (2), 41–58.

Gregory, R. (2003) 'Accountability in Modern Government', in B. G. Peters and J. Pierre (eds), *Handbook of Public Administration* (London: Sage).

Gregory, R. (2006) 'Theoretical Faith and Practical Works: De-Autonomization and Joining-Up in the New Zealand State Sector, in T. Christensen and P. Lægreid (eds), *Autonomy and Regulation. Coping with Agencies in the Modern State* (Cheltenham: Edward Elgar).

Greve, C., M. Flinders and S. Van Thiel (1999) 'Quangos – What's in a Name? Defining Quangos from a Comparative Perspective', *Governance*, 12 (2), 129–46.

Gulick, L. (1937) 'Notes on the Theory of Organization. With a Special Reference to Government', in L. Gulick and L. Urwick (eds), *Papers on the Science of Administration* (New York: A. M. Kelly).

Hajnal, G. (2006) 'Public Management Reforms in Hungary' (NISPAcee, NISPAcee 14th Annual Conference, Ljubljana, Slovenia, 11–13 May 2006.)

Hajnal, G. (2008) *Adalékok a magyarországi közpolitika kudarcaihoz* (Budapest: KSZK).

Hajnal, G. and G. Jenei (2007) 'The Study of Public Management in Hungary. Management and the Transition to Democratic Rechtsstaat', in W. J. M. Kickert (ed), *The Study of Public Management in Europe and the United States. A Comparative Analysis of National Distinctiveness* (London: Routledge), 208–32.

Hall, C., C. Scott, C. and C. Hood (2000) *Telecommunications Regulation. Culture, Chaos and Interdependence Inside the Regulatory Process* (London: Routledge).

Hall, P. A. and R. Taylor (1998) 'The Potential of Historical Institutionalism: A Response to Hay and Wincott', *Political Studies*, 48: 958–62.

Halligan, J. (2006) 'The Reassertion of the Centre in a First Generation of NPM System', in T. Christensen and P. Lægreid (eds), *Autonomy and Regulation. Coping with Agencies in the Modern State* (Cheltenham: Edward Elgar).

Halligan, J. (2007a) 'Advocacy and Innovation in Interagency Management: The Case of Centrelink', *Governance*, 20 (3), 445–67.

Halligan, J. (2007b) 'Reintegrating Government in Third Generation Reforms of Australia and New Zealand', *Public Policy and Administration*, 22 (2), 217–38.

Halligan, J. (2007c) 'Reform Design and Performance in Australia and New Zealand', in T. Christensen and P. Lægreid (eds), *Transcending New Public Management* (Aldershot: Ashgate).

Halligan, J. (2008a) 'Australian Public Service: Combining the Search for Balance and Effectiveness with Deviations on Fundamentals', in C. Aulich and R. Wettenhall (eds), *Howard's Fourth Government* (Sydney: University of New South Wales Press).

Halligan, J. (2008b) *The Centrelink Experiment: An Innovation in Service Delivery* (Canberra: Australian National University Press).

Hamburger, P. (2007) 'Coordination and Leadership at the Centre of the Australia Public Service', in R. Koch and J. Dixon (eds), *Public Governance and Leadership*, (Wiesbaden: Deutscher Universitats-Verlag).

Hampton, P. (2005) *Reducing Administrative Burdens: Effective Inspection and Enforcement* (London: HM Treasury).

Hansen, H. F. and L. H. Pedersen, L. H. (2006) 'The Dynamics of Regulatory Reform', in T. Christensen and P. Lægreid (eds), *Autonomy and Regulation. Coping with Agencies in the Modern Sate* (Cheltenham: Edward Elgar).

Hayes, A. F. and K. Krippendorff (2007) 'Answering the Call for a Standard Reliability Measure for Coding Data', *Communication Methods and Measures*, 1 (1), 77–89.

Heckman, J. J., C. Heinrichand and J. Smith (1997) 'Assessing the Performance of Performance Standards in Public Bureaucracies', *American Economic Review*, 87, 389–96.

Heffron, F. (1989), *Organization Theory and Public Organizations* (Prentice Hall: New Jersey).

Helm, D. (1994) 'British Utility Regulation: Theory, Practice and Reform', *Oxford Review of Economic Policy*, 10, 17–39.

Hemerijck, A. and J. Visser (2000) 'Change and Immobility: Three Decades of Policy Adjustment in the Netherlands and Belgium', *West European Politics*, 23, 229–56.

Hendriks, F. and P. Tops (2003) 'Local Public Management Reforms in the Netherlands: Fads, Fashions and Winds of Change', *Public Administration*, 81 (2), 301–23.

Hodge, G. (2000) *Privatization: An International Review of Performance* (Boulder: Westview Press).

Henisz, W. J. (2000), 'The Institutional Environment for Economic Growth', *Economics and Politics*, 12, 1–31.

Hesse, J. J., C. Hood and B. G. Peters (eds) (2003) *Paradoxes in Public Sector Reform: An International Comparison* (Berlin: Duncker & Humblot).

Hetling, A., M. L. McDermott and M. Mapps (2008) 'Symbolism Versus Policy Learning: Public Opinion of the 1996 U.S. Welfare Reform', *American Politics Research*, 36 (3), 335–57.

Hill, G. H. (2005). 'The Effects on Managerial Succession on Organizational Performance', *Journal of Public Administration Research and Theory*, 15 (4), 585–97.

Hill, C. J. and L. E. Lynn (2005). 'Is Hierarchical Governance in Decline? Evidence from Empirical Research', *Journal of Public Administration Research and Theory*, 15 (2), 173–95.

Ho, P. Y. (2004) *The Administrative History of Hong Kong Government Agencies 1841–2002* (Hong Kong: Hong Kong University Press).

Hogwood, B., W. D. Judge and M. McVicar (2000) 'Agencies and Accountability', in R. A. W. Rhodes (ed.), *Transforming British Government, Volume 1* (Basingstoke: Macmillan).

Home Affairs Bureau (2005) Review of Advisory and Statutory Bodies: Interim Report No. 14 – Review of Classification System of Advisory and Statutory Bodies in the Public Sector (Panel on Home Affairs of the Legislative Council of Hong Kong, Legislative Co.)

Hood, C. (1991) 'A Public Management for All Seasons?', *Public Administration*, 69 (1), 3–19.

Hood, C. (1996) 'Exploring Variations in Public Management Reform of the 1980s' in H. A. G. M. Bekke, J. L. Perry and T. A. J. Toonen (eds), *Civil Service Systems* (Bloomington: Indiana University Press).

Hood, C. (1998) *The Art of the State: Culture, Rhetoric, and Public Management* (Oxford: Clarendon Press).

Hood, C. and A. Dunsire (1981) *Bureaumetrics* (Farnborough: Gower).

Hood, C. and G. F. Schuppert (eds) (1988) *Delivering Public Services in Western Europe* (London: Sage).

Hood, C., H. Rothstein and R. Baldwin (2001) *The Government of Risk: Understanding Risk Regulation Regimes* (Oxford: Oxford University Press).

Hooghe, L. and G. Marks (2001) *Multi-level Governance and European Integration* (Lanham, MD: Rowman and Littlefield).

Hopenhayn, H. and S. Lohmann (1996) 'Fire-Alarm Signals and the Political Oversight of Regulatory Agencies', *Journal of Law, Economics, and Organization*, 12 (1), 196–213.

Horn, M. (1995) *The Political Economy of Public Administration: Institutional Choice in the Public Sector* (Cambridge: Cambridge University Press).

Howard, J. (2002) 'Strategic Leadership for Australia: Policy Directions in a Complex World', Address to the Committee for Economic Development of Australia, 20 Nov.

Humphreys, P. C. and J. Mair (2006) 'Ireland's Complex Regulatory Landscape', paper presented at the ECPR Conference on regulatory governance, University of Bath, 7–8 September 2008.

Huque, S. A., M. R. Hayllar, A. B. L. Cheung, N. Flynn and H. K. Wong (1999) *Public Sector Reform in Hong Kong: The Performance of Trading Funds* (Hong Kong: Department of Public and Social Administration, City University of Hong Kong).

Ingraham, P. and D. Moynihan (2001) 'Beyond Measurement: Managing for Results in State Government', in Dall Forsythe (ed.), *Quicker, Better, Cheaper?: Managing Performance in American Government* (Albany: Rockefeller Institute Press).

Ingraham, P., P. Joyce, and Donahue (2003) *Government Performance: why Management Matters?* (Baltimore: Johns Hopkins University Press).

Jacobsson, B. (1995) 'Ideer om forvaltning og politikk', in P. Lægreid and O. K. Pedersen (eds), *Nordiske forvaltningsreformer* (Copenhagen: Danmarks forvaltningshöjskoles forlag).

Janssen, L., C. Kegels and B. Verschueren (2005), *De administratieve lasten in België voor het jaar 2004* (Brussel: Federaal planbureau).

Jensen, M. C. and W. H. Meckling (1976) 'Theory of the Firm: Managerial Behavior, Agency Costs and Ownership Structure', *Journal of Financial Economics*, 3, 305–60.

Jordana, J. and D. Sancho (2004) 'Regulatory Design, Institutional Constellations and the Study of the Regulatory State', in J. Jordana and D. Levi-Faur (eds), *The Politics of Regulation. Institutions and Regulatory Reforms for the Age of Governance* (Cheltenham: Edward Elgar), 296–319.

Jordana, J. and D. Levi-Faur (eds) (2004) *The Politics of Regulation. Institutions and Regulatory Reforms for the Age of Governance* (Cheltenham: Edward Elgar).

Jordana, J., D. Levi-Faur and X. Fernandez, (2007) 'The Global Diffusion of Regulatory Agencies: Institutional Emulation and the Restructuring of Modern Bureaucracy', paper presented at the IV ECPR General Conference, Pisa.

Joskow, P. (1991) 'The Role of Transaction Cost Economics in Antitrust and Public Utility Regulatory Policies', *Journal of Law, Economics and Organization*, 7 (Special Issue), 53–83.

Joyce, P. and S. Sieg (2000) 'Using Performance Information for Budgeting: Clarifying the Framework and Investigating Recent State Experience', paper presented at the 2000 Annual Conference of the American Society of Public Administration, San Diego, CA.

Judge, D., B. W. Hogwood and M. McVicar (1997) 'The 'Pondlife' of Executive Agencies: Parliament and 'Informatory' Accountability', *Public Policy and Administration*, 12 (2), 95–115.

Kähkönen, L. (2005) 'Costs and Efficiency of Quasi-Markets in Practice', *Local Government Studies*, 31 (1), 85–97.

Kamarck, E. C. (2004) 'Applying 21st-Century Government to the Challenge of Homeland Security', in J. F. Kamensky and T. J. Burlin (eds), *Collaboration* (Lanham: Rowan and Littlefield).

Katzenstein, P. J. (2003) 'Small States and Small States Revisited', *New Political Economy*, 8 (1), 9–30.

Kaufman, H. (1956) 'Emerging Conflicts in the Doctrines of Public Administration', *American Political Science Review*, 50 (4), 1057–73.

Kaufman, H. (1976) *Are Government Organizations Immortal?* (Washington, DC: Brookings Institution).

Kaufmann, F. X. (1986) 'The Relationship between Guidance, Control and Evaluation' in F. X. Kaufmann, G. Majone and V. Ostrom (eds), *Guidance, Control, and Evaluation in the Public Sector* (Berlin: De Gruyter).

Kaufmann, F. X., G. Majone, and V. Ostrom (eds.) (1986) *Guidance, Control and Evaluation in the Public Sector* (Berlin: de Gruyter).

Kepplinger, H. M. and J. H. Weißbecker (1991) 'Negativität als Nachrichtenideologie', *Publizistik*, 36 (3), 330–42.

Kepplinger, H. M., W. Donsbach, H. B. Brosius and J. F. Staab (2004) 'Media Tone and Public Opinion: A Longitudinal Study of Media Coverage and Public Opinion on Chancellor Kohl', *International Journal of Public Opinion Research*, 1 (4), 326–42.

Kernaghan, K. and D. Siegel (1987) *Public Administration in Canada* (Toronto: Methuen).

Kettl, D. (2000) *The Global Public Management Revolution* (Washington, DC: Brooking Institute Press).

Kilényi, G. (2006) 'A közigazgatási szervek jogi személyiségének problémái', *Magyar Közigazgatás*, 56 (8), 449–68.

Kim K. (2008) 'Agencification in Korea: Governance and Performance', paper presented at the Permanent Study Group on Governance of Public Sector

Organizations, European Group of Public Administration conference, Rotterdam, 3–6 Sept. 2008.

Kim, J. N., Bach, S. B., and I. J. Clelland (2007) 'Symbolic or Behavioral Management? Corporate Reputation in High-Emission Industries', *Corporate Reputation Review*, 10 (2), 77–98.

King, G., R. Keohane, and S. Verba (1994) *Designing Social Inquiry: Scientific Inference in Qualitative Research* (Princeton: Princeton University Press).

Kingdon, J. W. (1984) *Agendas, Alternatives, and Public Policies* (Boston, MA: Little, Brown).

Klijn, E. H. (2005) 'Networks and Inter-organizational Management: Challenging, Steering, Evaluation, and the Role of Public Actors in Public Management' in E. Ferlie, L. E. Lynn and C. Pollitt (eds), *The Oxford Handbook of Public Management* (Oxford: Oxford University Press).

Knill, C. (1998) 'European Policies: The Impact of National Administrative Traditions', *Journal of Public Policy*, 18 (01), 1–28.

Kovryga, O. V. and P. M. Nickel (2004) 'The Inevitability of Enduring Historical and Cultural Patterns: The Paradox of Decentralization Efforts in Ukraine', *Administrative Theory and Praxis*, 26 (4), 609–34.

Kovziridze, T. (2001) 'Federalisme, multi-level governance en twee types van hiërarchie', *Res Publica, Tijdschrift voor Politologie*, 1, 15–36. ['Federalism, multi-level governance and two types of hierarchy', *Res Publica, Flemish Journal of Political Science*].

Krasner, S. D. (1988) 'Sovereignty. An Institutional Perspective', *Comparative Political Studies*, 21 (1), 66–94.

Krause, G. A. and J. W. Douglas (2005) 'Institutional Design versus Reputational Effects on Bureaucratic Performance: Evidence from US Government Macroeconomic and Fiscal Projections', *Journal of Public Administration Research and Theory*, 15 (2), 281–306.

Kriesi, H. and M. Jegen (2001) 'The Swiss Energy Policy Elite: The Actor Constellation of a Policy Domain in Transition', *European Journal of Political Research*, 39, 251–87.

Krippendorff, K. (2004) *Content Analysis: An Introduction to Its Methodology* (Thousand Oaks: Sage).

Kydland, F. and E. Prescott (1977) 'Rules Rather Than Discretion: The Inconsistency on Optimal Plans', *Journal of Political Economy*, 85 (1), 473–91.

Lægreid, P. and J. P. Olsen (1978) *Byråkrati og beslutninger* (Bergen: Universitetsforlaget).

Lægreid, P. and O. K. Pedersen (eds) (1999) *Fra opbygning til ombygning i staten* (Copenhagen: DJØF Publishing).

Lægreid, P. and P. G. Roness (1998) 'Frå einskap til mangfald. Eit perspektiv på indre fristilling i staten', in T. Grønlie and P. Selle (eds), *Ein stat? Fristillingas fire ansikt* (Oslo: Det Norske Samlaget).

Lægreid, P. and P. G. Roness (1999) 'Administrative Reform as Organized Attention', in M. Egeberg and P. Lægreid (eds), *Organizing Political Institutions. Essays for Johan P. Olsen* (Oslo: Scandinavian University Press).

Lægreid, P. and P. G. Roness (2003) 'Administrative Reform Programmes and Institutional Response in Norwegian Central Government', in J. J. Hesse, C. Hood and B. G. Peters (eds), *Paradoxes in Public Sector Reform* (Berlin: Duncker & Humblot).

Lægreid, P., V. W. Rolland, P. G. Roness and J. E. Agotnes (2003) *The Structural Anatomy of the Norwegian State 1947–2003, Working paper 21* (Bergen: Stein Rokkan Centre for Social Studies).

Lægreid, P., S. Opedal and I. M. Stigen (2005) 'The Norwegian Hospital Reform. Balancing Political Control and Enterprise Autonomy', *Journal of Health Politics, Policy and Law*, 30 (6), 1035–72.

Lægreid, P., P. G. Roness and K. Rubecksen (2006a) 'Autonomy and Control in the Norwegian Civil Service: Does Agency Form Matter?' in T. Christensen and P. Lægreid (eds), *Autonomy and Regulation: Coping with Agencies in the Modern State* (Cheltenham: Edward Elgar).

Lægreid, P., P. G. Roness and K. Rubecksen (2006b) 'Performance Management in Practice: The Norwegian Way', *Financial Accountability and Management*, 22 (6), 251–70.

Lægreid, P., P. G. Roness and K. Rubecksen (2007) 'Modern Management Tools in State Agencies: The Case of Norway', *International Public Management Journal*, 10 (4), 387–413.

Lægreid, P., P. G. Roness and K. Rubecksen (2008a) 'Performance Information and Performance Steering: Integrated System or Loose Coupling?', in W. Van Dooren and S. Van de Walle (eds), *Performance Information in the Public Sector: How It Is Used* (London: Palgrave Macmillan).

Lægreid, P., P. G. Roness and K. Rubecksen (2008b) 'Controlling Regulatory Agencies', *Scandinavian Political Studies*, 31 (1), 1–26.

Laffont, J.-J. and D. Martimort (1999) 'Separation of Regulators Against Collusive Behavior', *RAND Journal of Economics*, 30, 232–62.

Lam, W. (2005) 'Coordinating the Government Bureaucracy in Hong Kong: An Institutional Analysis', *Governance*, 18 (4), 633–54.

Lane, J. (1995) *The Public Sector: Concepts, Models and Approaches* (London: Sage).

Lang, G. E. and K. Lang (1984) *Politics and Television Re-viewed* (Beverly Hills: Sage).

Lee, M. (1999) 'Reporters and Bureaucrats: Public Relations Counter-strategies by Public Administrators in an Era of Media Disinterest in Government', *Public Relations Review*, 25 (4), 451–63.

Legislative Council Secretariat (2005) Background brief on broadcasting services of Radio Television Hong Kong (Legislative Council of Hong Kong, Legislative Council Paper NO. CB(1)237/05-06, 8 Nov. 2005).

Levi-Faur, D. (2005) 'The Global Diffusion of Regulatory Capitalism', *Annals, AAPSS*, 598, 12–32.

Levy, B. and P. T. Spiller (1996) *Regulations, Institutions and Commitment: Comparative Studies of Telecommunications* (Cambridge: Cambridge University Press).

Light, P. C. (1997) *The Tides of Reform: Making Government Work 1945–1995* (New Haven: Yale University Press).

Loeser, R. (1994) *System des Verwaltungsrechts, Bd. 2, Verwaltungsorganisationsrecht* (Baden-Baden: Nomos).

Lonti, Z. (2005) 'How Much Decentralization? Managerial Autonomy in the Canadian Public Service', *American Review of Public Administration*, 35 (2), 122–36.

Lowi, T. (1999) 'Distribution, Regulation, Redistribution: The Functions of Government', in P. Nivola and D. Rosenbloom (eds), *Classic Readings in American Politics: Third Edition* (Worth: St Martin's).

Lowi, T. J. (1964) 'American Business, Public Policy, Case Studies and Political Theory', *World Politics*, 16, 677–715.

Lübbe-Wolff, G. (2000) *Symbolische Umweltpolitik* (Frankfurt a. M.: Suhrkamp).

MAC/Management Advisory Committee (2004) *Connecting Government: Whole of Government Responses to Australia's Priority Challenges*, Canberra.

Maeda, Y. and M. Miyahara (2003) 'Determinants of Trust in Industry, Government, and Citizen's Groups in Japan', *Corporate Reputation Review*, 10 (2), 303–10.

MAG/Ministerial Advisory Group (2001) *Report of the Advisory Group of the Review of the Centre* (Wellington: State Services Commission).

Maggetti M. (2007) 'De Facto Independence After Delegation: A Fuzzy-Set Analysis', *Regulation & Governance*, 1 (4), 271–94.

Mahon, J. F. and S. L. Wartick (2003) 'Dealing with Stakeholders: How Reputation, Credibility and Framing Influence the Game', *Corporate Reputation Review*, 6 (1), 19–35.

Majone, G. (1994) 'The Rise of the Regulatory State in Europe', *West European Politics*, 17 (3), 77–101.

Majone, G. (1996) *Regulating Europe* (London, New York: Routledge).

Majone, G. (1997a) 'From the Positive to the Regulatory State: Causes and Consequences of Changes in the Mode of Governance', *Journal of Public Policy*, 17 (2), 139–67.

Majone, G. (1997b) 'Independent Agencies and the Delegation Problem; Theoretical and Normative Dimensions', in B. Steuenberg and F. Van Vught (eds), *Political Institutions and Public Policy: Perspectives on European Decision Making* (Dordrecht: Kluwer).

Majone, G. (1999) 'The Regulatory State and Its Legitimacy Problems', *West European Politics*, 22 (1), 1–24.

Majone, G. (2001a) 'Nonmajoritarian Institutions and the Limits of Democratic Governance: A Political Transaction-Cost Approach', *Journal of Institutional and Theoretical Economics* 157, 57–78.

Majone, G. (2001b) 'Regulatory Legitimacy in the United States and the European Union' in K. Nicolaidis and R. Howse (eds), *The Federal Vision. Legitimacy and Levels of Governance in the United States and the European Union* (Oxford: Oxford University Press).

Majone, G. (2001c) 'Two Logics of Delegation: Agency and Fiduciary Relations in EU Governance', *European Union Politics*, 2 (103), 103–22.

March, J. G. (1984) 'How We Talk and How We Act: Administrative Theory and Administrative Life' in T. J. Sergiovanni and J. E. Corbally (eds), *Leadership and Organizational Culture: New Perspectives on Administrative Theory and Practice*: (Illinois: University of Illinois Press).

March, J. G. (1994) *A Primer on Decision Making* (New York: Free Press).

March, J. G. (2008) *Explorations in Organizations* (Stanford: Stanford University Press).

March, J. G. and J. P. Olsen (1976) *Ambiguity and Choice in Organizations* (Bergen: Universitetsforlaget).

March, J. G. and J. P. Olsen (1983) 'Organizing Political Life: What Administrative Reorganization Tells Us About Government', *The American Political Science Review*, 77 (2), 281–96.

March, J. G. and J. P. Olsen (1989a) *Rediscovering Institutions: The Organizational Basis of Politics* (New York: The Free Press).

March, J. G. and J. P. Olsen (1994) *Democratic Governance* (New York: the Free Press).

March, J. G. and J. P. Olsen (1996) 'Institutional Perspectives on Political Institutions', *Governance*, 9 (3), 247–64.

March, J. G. and R. I. Sutton (1997) 'Organizational Performance as a Dependent Variable', *Organization Science*, 8, 697–706.

Massey, A. and R. Pyper (2005) *Public Management and Modernisation in Britain* (Basingstoke: Palgrave Macmillan).

Masten, S. (1993) 'Transaction Costs, Mistakes, and Performances: Assessing the Importance of Governance', *Managerial and Decision Economics*, 14 (2), 119–29.

Masten, S., J. Meehan and E. Snyder (1991) 'The Costs of Organization', *Journal of Law, Economics and Organization*, 7 (1), 1–25.

Mayntz, R. and F. W. Scharpf (1975) *Policy-making in the German Federal Bureaucracy* (Amsterdam: Elsevier).

Mazzoleni, G. (1987) 'Media Logic and Party Logic in Campaign Coverage: The Italian General Election of 1983', *European Journal of Communication*, 2 (1), 81–103.

McCubbins, M. D., R. G. Noll and B. R. Weingast (1987) 'Administrative Procedures as Instruments of Political Control', *Journal of Law, Economics, and Organization*, 3 (2), 243–77.

McGauran, A.-M., K. Verhoest and P. C. Humphreys (2005) *The Corporate Governance of Agencies in Ireland. Non-commercial National Agencies*, CPMR Research Report 6 (Dublin: Institute of Public Administration).

McGowan, F. and H. Wallace (1996) 'Towards a European Regulatory State', *Journal of European Public Policy*, 3 (4), 560–76.

Mckinsey & Co. (1973) *The Machinery of Government: A New Framework for Expanding Services* (Hong Kong: Government Printer).

McNamara, K. R. (2002) 'Rational Fictions: Central Bank Independence and the Social Logic of Delegation', *West European Politics*, 25 (1), 47–76.

Meier, K. J. and G. C. Hill (2005) 'Bureaucracy in the Twenty-First Century' in Ewan Ferlie, Laurence E. Lynn and Christopher Pollitt (eds), *The Oxford Handbook of Public Management* (New York: Oxford University Press).

Meier, K. J. and J. L. O'Toole (2002) 'Public Management and Organizational Performance: The Effect of Managerial Quality', *Journal of Policy Analysis and Management*, 21 (4), 659–43.

Ménard, C. and S. Saussier (2002) 'Contractual Choice and Performance: The Case of Water Supply in France' in Brousseau E. and J. Glachant (eds), *The Economics of Contracts: Theories and Applications* (Cambridge: Cambridge University Press).

Metcalfe, L. and S. Richards (1987) *Improving Public Management* (London: Sage).

Meyer, J. and B. Rowan (1977) 'Institutionalized Organizations: Formal Structure as Myth and Ceremony', *American Journal of Sociology*, 83 (2), 340–63.

Meyer, J. W. and B. Rowan (1977) 'Institutionalized Organizations: Formal Structure as Myth and Ceremony', *American Journal of Sociology*, 83 (2), 340–63.

Miners, N. (1998) *The Government and Politics of Hong Kong*, 5th edn (Hong Kong: Oxford University Press).

Mintzberg, H. (1979) *The Structuring of Organizations* (Englewood Cliffs, NJ: Prentice-Hall).

Mintzberg, H. (1983) *Designing Effective Organizations: Structures in Five* (Englewood Cliffs, NJ: PrenticeHall).

Mitnick, Barry M. (1980) *The Political Economy of Regulation* (New York: Columbia University Press).

Moe, T. M. (1984) 'The New Economics of Organization', *American Journal of Political Science*, 28 (4), 739–77.

Moe, T. M. (1989) 'The Politics of Structural Choice: Toward a Theory of Public Bureaucracy', in O. E. Williamson (ed.), *Organization Theory: From Chester Barnard to the Present and Beyond* (New York: Oxford University Press).

Mónus, L. (1994) 'Az országos hatáskörű szervek helyzete az újraszabályozás után', *Magyar Közigazgatás*, 44 (1), 30–4.

Moran, M. (2003) *The British Regulatory State: High Modernism and Hyper-innovation* (Oxford: Oxford University Press).

Moran, T. (2008) 'Splicing the Perspectives of the Commonwealth and States into a Workable Federation', ANZSOG Annual Conference on Federalism, 11–12 Sep., Melbourne.

Moynihan, D. P. (2006a) 'Managing for Results in State Government: Evaluating a Decade of Reform', *Public Administration Review*, 66 (1), 77–89.

Moynihan, D. P. (2006b) 'Ambiguity in Policy Lessons: The Agencification Experience', *Public Administration*, 84 (4), 1029–50.

Moynihan, D. P. and S. K. Pandey (2005) 'Testing How Management Matters in an Era of Government by Performance Management', *Journal of Public Administration Research and Theory*, 15 (3), 421–39.

Mulgan, R. (2000) 'Accountability: An Ever-expanding Concept', *Public Administration*, 78 (3), 555–73.

Nakrošis V. and Ž. Martinaitis (2009) 'The Setting Up, Autonomy, Control and Performance of the Lithuanian Public Sector Organisations: Tentative Findings and Suggestions for Further Research', paper presented at the Permanent Study Group on Governance of Public Sector Organizations, Malta, 2–5 Sept. 2009.

Narad, R. A. (2006) 'The Multicratic Organization: A Model for Management of Functional Interdependence' in T. D. Lynch (ed.), *Handbook of Organization Theory and Management. The Philosophical Approach* (New York: Taylor & Francis).

Naschold, F. (1989), *New Frontiers in Public Sector Management* (Berlin: De Gruyter).

Nicholson-Crotty, S. and L. J. O'Toole (2004) 'Testing a Model of Public Management and Organizational Performance: The Case of Law Enforcement agencies', *Journal of Public Administration Research and Theory*, 14 (1), 1–18.

Newig, J. (2003) *Symbolische Umweltgesetzgebung: rechtssoziologische Untersuchungen am Beispiel des Ozongesetzes, des Kreislaufwirtschafts- und Abfallgesetzes sowie der Grossfeuerungsanlagenverordnung* (Berlin Duncker & Humboldt).

Norman, R. (2008) 'At the Centre or in Control: Central Agencies in Search of a New Identity', *Policy Quarterly*, 4 (2), 33–8.

Nørreklit, H. (2003) 'The Balanced Scorecard: What Is the Core? A Rhetorical Analysis of the Balanced Scorecard', *Accounting, Organizations and Society*, 28 (6), 591–619.

Norris, P. (2001) 'The Twilight of Westminster? Electoral Reform and Its Consequences', *Political Studies*, 49 (5), 877–900.

North, D. C. and B. R. Weingast (1989) 'Constitutions and Commitment: the Evolution of Institutions Governing Public Choice in Seventeenth Century England', *Journal of Economic History*, 69, 803–32.

NOU (1989) 5 *En bedre organisert stat* (Hermansen Commission).

Nyitrai, P. (1996) 'Adalékok az országos hatáskörű szervek rendszerében 1990–94 között bekövetkezett változások elemzéséhez', in Fogarasi, József (1996) (ed.), *A magyar közigazgatás korszerűsítésének elvi és gyakorlati kérdései: Oktatási anyag* (Budapest).

O'Toole, L. J. Jr. and K. J. Meier (2003) 'Plus ça change: public management, personnel stability and organizational performance' *Journal of Public Administration Research and Theory*, 13 (1), 43–64.

OECD (1997) *Report on Regulatory Reform* (Paris: OECD).

OECD (2002a) *Distributed Public Governance. Agencies, Authorities and Other Government Bodies* (Paris: OECD).

OECD (2002b) *Regulatory Policies in OECD Countries. From Interventionism to Regulatory Governance* (Paris: OECD).

OECD (2005a) 'Switzerland – The Role of Competition Policy in Regulatory Reform', *OECD Reviews of Regulatory Reform*.

OECD (2005b) Multilevel Regulatory Governance. *OECD papers*, 5, 80–163.

Olsen, J. P. (1989) *Petroleum og politikk* (Oslo: TANO).

Olsen, J. P. (1992) 'Analyzing Institutional Dynamics' (*Staatswissenschaften und Staatspraxis*, (2), 247–71.)

Olsen, J. P. (1996) 'Norway: Slow Learner – or Another Triumph of the Tortoise?' in J. P. Olsen and B. G. Peters (eds), *Lessons from Experience. Experimental Learning in Administrative Reforms in Eight Democracies* (Oslo: Scandinavian University Press).

Olsen, J. P. (1997) 'Institutional Design in Democratic Context', *Journal of Political Philosophy*, 5 (3), 203–29.

Olsen, J. P. (2006) 'May Be It Is Time To Rediscover Bureaucracy', *Journal of Public Administration Research and Theory*, 16, 1–24.

Olsen, J. P. (2007) *Europe in Search of Political Order* (Oxford: Oxford University Press).

Olsen, J. P. (2009) 'Change and Continuity: An Institutional Approach to Institutions of Democratic Government', *European Political Science Journal*, 1 (1), 3–32.

Olsen, J. P., P. G. Roness and H. Sætren (1982) 'Norway: Still Peaceful Coexistence and Revolution in Slow Motion?', in J. J. Richardson (ed.), *Policy Styles in Western Europe* (London: Allen & Unwin).

Olsen, J. P. and B. G. Peters (1996) 'Learning from Experience?', in J. P. Olsen and B. G. Peters (eds), *Lessons from Experience. Experimental Learning in Administrative Reforms in Eight Democracies* (Oslo: Scandinavian University Press).

Ombudsman (2007) *Annual Report of the Ombudsman 2007*, http://www.ombudsman.gov.hk/annual_reports.html, date accessed 15 June 2009.

Ongaro, E. (ed.) (2006) *Le Agenzie Pubbliche: Modelli Istituzionali ed Organizzativi* (Rome: Rubbettino).

Ongaro, E. (ed.) (2008) *L'Organizzazione dello Stato tra Autonomia e Policy Capacity* (Rome: Rubbettino).

Ongaro, E. (2009) *Public Management Reform and Modernization: Trajectories of Administrative Change in Italy and France, Greece, Portugal, Spain* (Cheltenham: Edward Elgar).

Ongaro, E. (forthcoming) 'The role of politics and institutions in the Italian administrative reform trajectory', *Public Administration*.

Ongaro, E. and G. Valotti (2008) 'Public Management Reform in Italy: Explaining the Implementation Gap', *The International Journal of Public Sector Management*, 21 (2), 174–204.

Osborne, S. (1998) *Voluntary Organisations and Innovation in Public Services* (London: Routledge).

Osborne, D. and Gaebler, T. (1992) *Reinventing Government: How the Entrepreneurial Spirit Is Transforming the Public Sector* (Reading:Addison-Wesley).

Ouchi, W. (1980) 'Markets, Bureaucracies and Clans', *Administrative Science Quarterly*, 25, 129–42.

Painter, M. (1987) *Steering the Modern State* (Sydney: Sydney University Press).

Painter, M. (2005) 'Transforming an Administrative State: Administrative Reform in Hong Kong and the Future of the Developmental State', *Public Administration Review*, 65 (3), 335–46.

Painter, M. and B. Carey (1979) *Politics Between Departments* (St Lucia: University of Queensland Press).

Painter, M. and Pierre, J. (2005) *Challenges to State Policy Capacity: Global Trends and Comparative Perspectives* (Basingstoke: Palgrave Macmillan).

Painter, M. and S. F. Wong (2007) 'The Telecommunications Regulatory Regimes in Hong Kong and Singapore: When Direct State Intervention Meets Indirect Policy Instruments', *Pacific Review*, 20, 173–95.

Papadopoulos, Y. (2003) 'Cooperative Forms of Governance: Problems of Democratic Accountability in Complex Environments', *European Journal of Political Research*, 43, 473–501.

Papadopoulos, Y. (2008) 'Europeanization? Two Logics of Change of Policy-Making Patterns in Switzerland', *Journal of Comparative Policy Analysis*, 10 (3), 255–78.

Pearce, J. L. and J. L. Perry (1983) 'Federal Merit Pay: A Longitudinal Analysis', *Public Administration Review*, 43 (4), 325–25.

Pehle, H. (1998) *Das Bundesministerium für Umwelt, Naturschutz und Reaktorsicherheit: Ausgegrenzt statt integriert?* (Wiesbaden: DUV).

Peres, L. (1968) 'The Resurrection of Autonomy: Organization Theory and the Statutory Corporation', *Public Administration* (Sydney), 27 (4), 360–9.

Peters, B. G. (2004) 'Back to the Centre? Rebuilding the State', in A. Gamble and T. Wright (eds), *Restating The State?* (Oxford: Blackwell).

Peters, B. G. (1988) *Comparing Public Bureaucracies. Problems of Theory and Methods* (Tuscaloosa: University of Alabama Press).

Peters, G. B. (1998) 'Managing Horizontal Government: The Politics of Co-ordination', *Public Administration*, 76, 295–311.

Peters, B. G. (2001) *The Politics of Bureaucracy* (London: Routledge).

Peters, B. G. (2004) 'Administrative Traditions and the Anglo-American Democracies' in J. Halligan (ed.), *Civil Service Systems in Anglo-American Countries* (Cheltenham: Edward Elgar).

Peters, B. G. (2006) 'Concepts and Theories of Horizontal Policy Management', B. G. Peters, and J. Pierre (eds) *Handbook of Public Policy* (London: Sage).

Peters, B. G. and J. Pierre (2005) 'Swings or roundabouts? Multilevel governance as a source of and contraint on policy capacity', in M. Painter and J. Pierre (eds), *Challenges to State Policy Capacity* (Basingstoke: Palgrave Macmillan).

Peters, B. G. and D. J. Savoie (1996) 'Managing Incoherence: The Coordination and Empowerment Conundrum', *Public Administration Review*, 56 (3), 281–90.

Peters, R. G., V. T. Covello and D. B. McCallum (1997) 'The Determinants of Trust and Credibility in Environmental Risk Communication: An Empirical Study', *Risk Analysis*, 17 (1), 43–54.

Pierson, P. (2004) *Politics in Time: History, Institutions, and Social Analysis* (Princeton: Oxford University Press).

Pollack, M. A. (1996) 'The New Institutionalism and EC Governance: The Promise and Limits of Institutional Analysis', *Governance*, 9 (4), 429–58.

Pollitt, C. (1995a) 'Justification by Works or by Faith?: Evaluating the New Public Management', *Evaluation*, 1 (2), 133–54.

Pollitt, C. (1995b). *Management Techniques for the Public Sector. Pulpit and Practice/ Techniques De Gestion Pour Le Secteur Public. De La Doctrine à La Practice* (Ottawa: Centre Canadien de Gestion/Canadian Centre for Management Development).

Pollitt, C. (2001) 'Convergence: The Useful Myth?' *Public Administration*, 79 (4), 933–48.

Pollitt, C. (2003a) *The Essential Public Manager* (Buckingham: Open University Press).

Pollitt, C. (2003b) 'Joined'Up Government: a Survey', *Political Studies Review*, 1, 34–49).

Pollitt, C. (2004a) 'Theoretical Overview' in C. Pollitt and C. Talbot (eds), *Unbundled Governement: A Critical Analysis of the Global Trend to Agencies, Quangos and Contractualisation* (London: Routledge).

Pollitt, C. (2004b) From There to Here, from Now to Then: Buying and Borrowing Public Management Reforms (Clad Ninth International Conference, Madrid, 3 Nov. 2004).

Pollitt, C. (2005) 'Decentralization. A Central Concept in Contemporary Public Management', in E. Ferlie, L. E. Lynn, Jr. and C. Pollitt (eds), *The Oxford Handbook of Public Management* (Oxford: Oxford University Press), 371–97.

Pollitt, C. (2006) 'Performance Management in Practice: A Comparative Study of Executive Agencies', *Journal of Public Administration Research and Theory*, 16 (1), 25–44.

Pollitt, C. (2007) 'Convergence or Divergence: What Has Been Happening in Europe?', in C. Pollitt, S. Van Thiel and V. Holmburg (eds), *New Public Management in Europe* (Basingstoke: Palgrave Macmillan).

Pollitt, C. (2009) 'Structural Change and Public Service Performance: International Lessons?' *Public Money & Management*, 29 (5), 285–91.

Pollitt, C., K. Bathgate, J. Caulfield, A. Smullen and C. Talbot (2001) 'Agency Fever? Analysis of an International Policy Fashion', *Journal of Comparative Policy Analysis*, 3 (3), 271–90.

Pollitt, C. and G. Bouckaert (2004) *Public Management Reform. A Comparative Analysis*, 2nd edn (Oxford: Oxford University Press).

Pollitt, C. and C. Talbot (2004) *Unbundled Government: A Critical Analysis of the Global Trend to Agencies, Quangos and Contractualisation* (London: Routledge).

Pollitt, C. and G. Bouckaert (2009) *Change and Continuity in Public Policy and Management* (Cheltenham: Edward Elgar).

Pollitt, C, C. Talbot, J. Caufield, and A. Smullen (2004) *Agencies: How Governments Do Things Through Ssemi-autonomous Organizations* (New York: Palgrave Macmillan).

Pollock, T. G. and V. P. Rindova (2003) 'Media Legitimation Effects in the Market for Initial Public Offerings, *Academy of Management Journal*, 46 (5), 631–42.

Pound, R. (1910) 'Law in Books and Law in Action', *American Law Review*, 44, 12–36.

Powell, W. and P. DiMaggio (eds) (1991) *The New Institutionalism in Organizational Analysis* (Chicago: University of Chicago Press).

Powell, W. W. and P. J. DiMaggio (1991) 'The Iron Cage Revisited: Institutional Isomorphism and Collective Rationality in Organizational Fields', in W. W. Powell and P. J. DiMaggio (eds), *The New Institutionalism in Organizational Analysis* (Chicago: University of Chicago Press).

Power, M. (2005) 'The Theory of Audit Explosion' in E. Ferlie, L. E. Lynn and C. Pollitt (eds), *The Oxford Handbook of Public Management* (New York: Oxford University Press).

Pratt J. W. and R. J. Zeckhauser (1991), 'Principals and Agents: An Overview', in J. W. Pratt and R. J. Zeckhauser (eds), *Principals and Agents: The Structure of Business* (Boston: Harvard Business School Press).

Prebble, M. (2005) 'Annual Report of the State Services Commissioner' in *Annual Report of the State Services Commission for year ended 30 June 2005*.

Radaelli, C. M. (2000) 'Policy Transfer in the European Union: Institutional Isomorphism as a Source of Legitimacy', *An International Journal of Policy and Administration*, 13 (1), 25–43.

Radaelli, C. M. and F. De Francesco (2007) *Regulatory Quality in Europe: Concepts, Measures and Policy Processes* (Mancheste:, Manchester University Press).

Rennie, I. (2008) 'Annual Report of the State Services Commissioner' in *Annual Report of the State Services Commission for year ended 30 June 2008*.

Rhodes, R. A. W. (1996) 'The New Governance: Governing without Government', *Political Studies*, 44, 652–67.

Richards, D. (2008) *New Labour and the Civil Service: Reconstituting the Westminster Model* (Basingstoke: Palgrave Macmillan).

Richards, D. and M. Smith (2006) 'The Tension of Political Control and Administrative Autonomy: from NPM to a Reconstituted Westminster Model' in T. Christensen and P. Lægreid (eds), *Autonomy and Regulation. Coping with Agencies in the Modern State* (Cheltenham: Edward Elgar).

Richman, B. and C. Boerner (2006) 'A Transaction Cost Economizing Approach to Regulation: Understanding Government Responses to the NIMBY Problem', *Yale Journal on Regulation*, 23 (1), 29–76.

Rindfleisch, A. and J. Heide (1997) 'Transaction Cost Analysis: Past, Present, and Future Applications', *Journal of Marketing*, 61 (4), 30–54.

Rolland, V. W. and P. G. Roness (2009) 'Mapping Organizational Units in the State: Challenges and Classifications', paper presented at 'COST-CRIPO meeting', Brussels 20–21 Apr. 2009.

Rolland, V. W. and J. E. Ågotnes (2003) 'A database on the organization of the Norwegian state administration (NSA) 1947–2003', COBRA network, Seminar on organizational forms, autonomy and control in the public sector, Norway, Bergen, 1–2 Dec.

Romzek, B. (2000) 'Dynamics of Public Sector Accountability in an Era of Reform', *International Review of Administrative Sciences*, 66 (1), 21–44.

Roness, P. G. (2001) 'Transforming State Employees' Unions', in T. Christensen and P. Lægreid (eds), *New Public Management. The Transformation of Ideas and Practice* (Aldershot: Ashgate).

Roness, P. G. (2007) 'Types of State Organizations: Arguments, Doctrines and Changes Beyond New Public Management', in T. Christensen and P. Lægreid (eds), *Transcending New Public Management. The Transformation of Public Sector Reform* (Aldershot: Ashgate Publishers).

Roness, P. G. (2009) 'Handling Theoretical Diversity on Agency Autonomy', in P. G. Roness and H. Sætren (eds), *Change and Continuity in Public Sector Organizations* (Bergen: Fagbokforlaget).

Roness, P. G., K. Rubecksen, K. Verhoest, B. Verschuere and M. MacCarthaigh (2007) 'Explaining Autonomy of Public Sector Agencies in Norway, Ireland and Flanders', paper presented at the EGPA Annual Conference, Study Group 'Governance of Public Sector Organizations, Madrid, 19–21 Sept. 2007.

Roness, P. G., K. Verhoest, K. Rubecksen and M. MacCarthaigh (2008) 'Autonomy and Regulation of State Agencies: Reinforcement, Indifference or Compensation?' *Public Organization Review*, 8 (2), 155–74.

Roness, P. G. and H. Sætren (eds) (2009) *Change and Continuity in Public Sector Organizations. Essays in Honor of Per Lægreid* (Bergen: Fagbokforlaget).

Røvik, K. A. (1996) 'Deinstitutionalization and the Logic of Fashion' in B. Czarniawska and G. Sevon (eds), *Translating Organizational Change* (New York: De Gruyter).

Røvik, K. A. (2002) 'The Secrets of the Winners: Management Ideas That Flow' in K. Sahlin-Andersson and L. Engwall (eds), *The Expansion of Management Knowledge – Carriers, Flows and Sources* (Stanford: Stanford University Press).

Rubecksen, K. (2009), 'Autonomy, Control and Tasks in State Agencies', PhD dissertation (Bergen: University of Bergen).

Ryan, Gery W. and H. Russell Bernard (2003) 'Techniques to Identify Themes', *Field Methods*, 15 (1), 8 –109.

Sahlin-Andersson, K. (1996) 'Imitating by Editing Success: The Construction of Organizational Fields', in B. Czarniawska and G. Sevon (eds), *Translating Organizational Change* (Berlin: de Gruyter).

Sahlin-Andersson, K. and L. Engwall (eds) (2002) *The Expansion of Management Knowledge* (Stanford, CA: Stanford University Press).

Saint-Martin, D. (2000) *Building the New Managerial State: Consultants and the Politics of Public Sector Reform in Comparative Perspective* (Oxford: Oxford University Press).

Sankey, C. (1993) 'Public Sector Reform in Hong Kong: Recent Trends', *Hong Kong Public Administration*, 2 (1), 78–85.

Sankey, C. (1995) 'Public Sector Reform: Past Development and Recent Trends', in J. C. Y. Lee and A. B. L. Cheung (eds), *Public Sector Reform in Hong Kong: Key Concepts, Progress to Date, and Future Directions* (Hong Kong: The Chinese University Press).

Sankey, C. (2001) 'An Overview of Public Sector Reform Initiatives in the Hong Kong Government since 1989', in A. B. L. Cheung and J. C. Y. Lee (eds), *Public Sector Reform in Hong Kong: Into the 21st Century* (Hong Kong: The Chinese University Press).

Sárközy, T. (2006) *Államszervezetünk potenciazavarai–Javaslat egy hatékony és modern kormányzati szervezet kialakítására* (Budapest: HVG–Orac).

Savas, E. (2000) *Privatization and Public–Private Partnerships* (New York: Chatham House).

Savoie, D. J. (1999), *Governing from the Centre: The Concentration of Power in Canadian Politics* (Toronto: University of Toronto Press).

Schattschneider, E. E. (1965) *The Semisovereign People* (New York: Holt, Rinehart and Winston).

Schein, E. H. (1985) *Organizational Culture and Leadership* (San Francisco: Jossey-Bass).

Schick, A. (1996) *The Spirit of Reform: Managing the New Zealand State Sector in a Time of Change*, A report prepared for the State Services Commission and the Treasury, Wellington.

Schick, A. (2003) 'The Performing State: Reflection on an Idea Whose Time Has Come but Whose Implementation Has Not', *OECD Journal of Budgeting*, 3 (2), 71–103.

Schröter, E. (2007) 'Reforming the Machinery of Government: The Case of the German Federal Bureaucracy', in R. Koch and J. Dixon (eds), *Public Governance and Leadership* (Wiesbaden: Deutscher Universitäts-Verlag).

Sclar, E. (2000) *You Don't Always Get What You Pay For: The Economics of Privatization* (Ithaca: Cornell University Press).

Scott, C. (2004) 'Regulation in the Age of Governance: The Rise of the Post-regulatory State' in J. Jordana and D. Levi-Faur (eds), *The Politics of Regulation. Institutions and Regulatory Reforms for the Age of Governance* (Cheltenham: Edward Elgar).

Scott, G. (2008) 'After the Reforms: Some Questions about the State of the State in New Zealand', *Policy Quarterly*, 4 (2), 3–14.

Scott, I. (1989) *Political Change and the Crisis of Legitimacy in Hong Kong* (Hong Kong: Oxford University Press).

Scott, I. (2003) 'Organizations in the Public Sector in Hong Kong: Core Government, Quasi-Government and Private Bodies with Public Functions', *Public Organization Review*, 3 (3), 247–67.

Scott, I. (2005) *Public Administration in Hong Kong: Regime Change and Its Impact on the Public Sector* (Singapore: Marshall Cavendish International).

Scott, I. and I. Thynne (2006) 'Guest Editors' Preface', *Public Organization Review*, 6, 167–9.

Scott, W. R. and G. Davies (2006) *Organizations and Organizing: Rational, Natural and Open Systems Perspectives*, 6th rev. edn (Upper Saddle River, NJ: Prentice-Hall).

Selden, S. C. and D. P. Moynihan (2000) 'A Model of Voluntary Turnover in State Government' , *Review of Public Personal Administration*, 20 (2), 63–75.

Selden, S. C. and Sowa J. E. (2004) 'Testing a Multi-dimensional Model of Organizational Performance: Prospects and Problems', *Journal of Public Administration Research and Theory*, 14 (3), 395–416.

Selznick, P. (1957) *Leadership in Administration* (New York City: Harper & Row).

Sepe, S., L. Mazzone, I. Portelli and G. Vetritto (2003) *Lineamenti di Storia dell'Amministrazione Italiana* (Rome: Carocci).

Shapiro, S. P. (2005) 'Agency Theory', *Annual Review of Sociology*, 31, 263–384.

Shepsle, K. A. (1991) 'Discretion, Institutions, and the Problem of Government Commitment' in P. Bourdieu and J. Coleman (eds), *Social Theory for a Changing Society*, (Boulder, New York: Westview Press).

Shergold, P. (2003) 'A Foundation of Ruined Hopes?', Address to Public Service Commission, Canberra, 15 Oct.

Shergold, P. (2004a) 'Connecting Government: Whole-of-government Responses to Australia's Priority Challenges', Canberra, 20 Apr.

324   *Bibliography*

Shergold, P (2004b) 'Plan and Deliver: Avoiding Bureaucratic Hold-up', Australian Graduate School of Management/Harvard Club of Australia, Canberra, 17 Nov.

Shergold, P (2005) 'Foundations of Governance in the Australian Public Service', Speech delivered at launch of *Foundations of Governance in the Australian Public Service*, 1 June, Canberra.

Simon, H. A. (1946) 'The Proverbs of Administration', *Public Administration Review*, 6 (1), 53–67.

Simon, H. A. (1957) *Administrative Behaviour* (New York: Macmillan).

Smullen, A (2004) 'Lost in translation? Shifting Interpretations of the Concept of Agency: The Dutch Case', in C. Pollitt and C. Talbot (eds), *Unbundled Government. A Critical Analysis of the Global Trend to Agencies, Quangos and Contractualisation* (London: Routledge).

Sotiropoulos, D. A. (2002) 'From an Omnipresent and Strong to a Big and Weak State: Democratization and State Reform in Southeastern Europe', *Journal of Southeast European and Black Sea Studies*, 2 (1), 63–74.

Spicer, B., D. Emanuel and M. Powell (1996) *Transforming Government Enterprises* (St. Leonards, Australia: Centre for Independent Studies).

State Services Commission (1998) *Assessment of the New Zealand Public Service*, Occasional Paper No. 1, Wellington.

State Services Commission (2007) *Transforming the State Services: State of the Development Report 2007*, SSC, Wellington.

Steigenberger, K. and G. Hammerschmid (2009) 'Public Corporate Governance in a Country with a Pronounced Administrative Law Tradition – Current empirical findings from Austria', paper presented at the Permanent Study Group on Governance of Public Sector Organizations, European Group of Public Administration conference, Malta, 2–5 Sept. 2009.

Stimson, J. A., M. B. MacKuen, and R. S. Erikson (1994) 'Opinion and Policy: A Global View', *PS: Political Science and Politics*, 27 (1), 29–34.

Strauss, A. L. and J. Corbin (1990) *Basics of Qualitative Research: Grounded Theory Procedures and Techniques* (Thousand Oaks: Sage).

Streeck, W. and K. Thelen (2005) *Beyond Continuity. Institutional Change in Advanced Economies* (Oxford: Oxford University Press).

Swanson, D. L. (1981) 'A Constructivist Approach', in D. D. Nimmo and K. R. Sanders (eds), *Handbook of Political Communication* (London: Sage.).

Swenden, W. and M. T. Jans (2006) 'Will It Stay Or Will It Go?' Federalism and the sustainability of Belgium', *West European Politics*, 29, 877–94.

Talbot, C. (2004) 'Executive Agencies: Have They Improved Management in Government?', *Public Money & Management*, 24 (2), 104–12.

Talbot, C. (2004) 'The Agency idea', in C. Pollitt and C. Talbot (eds), *Unbundled Government. A Critical Analysis of the Global Trend to Agencies, Quangos and Contractualisation* (London: Routledge).

Talbot, C. (2005) 'Performance Management', in E. Ferlie, L. E. Lynn Jr. and C. Pollitt (eds), *The Oxford Handbook of Public Management* (Oxford: Oxford University Press).

Tavits, M. and T. Annus (2006) 'Agencification in Estonia', *Public Administration and Development*, 26, 3–14.

Taylor, F. W. (1998 [1911]) *The Principles of Scientific Management* (Mineola: Dover).

Tepeci, M. (2001). 'The Effect of Personal Values, Organizational Cultures, and Person – Organization Fit on Individual Outcomes in the Restaurant Industry', doctoral dissertation, Pennsylvania State University.

Ter Bogt, H. (2003) 'A Transaction Cost Approach to the Autonomization of Government Organizations: A Political Transaction Cost Framework Confronted with Six Cases of Autonomization in the Netherlands', *European Journal of Law and Economics*, 16 (2), 149–1.

Thatcher, Mark (2002a) 'Delegation to Independent Regulatory Agencies: Pressures, Functions and Contextual Mediation', *West European Politics*, 25 (1), 125–47.

Thatcher, M. (2002b) 'Regulation After Delegation: Independent Regulatory Agencies in Europe', *Journal of European Public Policy*, 9 (6), 954–72.

Thatcher, M. (2005) 'The Third Force? Independent Regulatory Agencies and Elected Politicians in Europe', *Governance*, 18 (3), 347–73.

Thatcher, M. and Stone, A. Sweet (2002) 'Theory and Practice of Delegation to Non-majoritarian Institutions', *West European Politics*, 25 (1), 1–22.

Thelen, K. (1999) 'Historical Institutionalism in Comparative Politics', *Annual Review of Political Science*, 2, 369–404.

Thibodeau, N., J. H. Evans III, N. J. Nagarajan and J. Whittle (2007) 'Value Creation in Public Enterprises: An Empirical Analysis of Coordinated Organizational Changes in the Veterans Health Administration', *The Accounting Review*, 82 (2), 483–520.

Thompson, F. (1993) 'Matching Responsibilities with Tactics. Administrative Controls and Modern Government', *Public Administration Review*, 24 (2), 303–18.

Thompson, G., J. Frances, R. Levacic, and J. Mitchell (1991) *Markets, Hierarchies and Networks. The Coordination of Social Life* (London: Sage).

Thompson, J. D. (1967) *Organization in Action: Social Science Bases of Administrative Theory* (New York: McGraw-Hill).

Thynne, I. (2004) 'State Organizations as Agencies: An Identifiable and Meaningful Focus of Research?', *Public Administration and Development*, 24, 91–9.

Uhrig, J. (2003) *Review of the Corporate Governance of Statutory Authorities and Office Holders Report*, Commonwealth of Australia, Canberra.

Unizo (2007) *Ondernemersprioriteiten voor de federale verkiezingen 2007* (Brussels: Unizo) [*Priorities of entrepreneurs for the federal elections 2007* (Brussels: Union of entrepreneurs)].

Vadál, I. (2006) *A közigazgatási jog kodifikációja–Stabil kormányzás, változó közigazgatás* (Budapest–Péc: Dialóg Campus).

Van Dooren, W. and S. Van de Walle (eds) (2008) *Performance Information in the Public Sector: How it is Used* (London: Palgrave Macmillan).

Van Genugten, M. (2008) 'The Art of Alignment: Transaction Cost Economics and the Provision of Public Services at the Local Level', PhD thesis (Enschede; University of Twente).

Van Humbeeck, P. (2006) *Wetgevingsbeleid in Vlaanderen: een update van de uitdagingen voor betere regelgeving.* (Brussel: SERV).

Van Thiel, S. (2001) *Quangos: Trends, Causes and Consequences* (Aldershot: Ashgate).

Van Thiel, S. (2004a) 'Quangos in Dutch Government' in Pollitt, C. and C. Talbot (eds) *Unbundled Government: A Critical Analysis of the Global Trend to Agencies, Quasi-Autonomous Bodies and Contractualization* (London: Routledge).

van Thiel, S. (2004b) 'Trends in the Public Sector: Why Politicians Prefer Quasi-Autonomous Organizations', *Journal of Theoretical Politics*, 16 (2), 175–201.

Van Thiel, S. (2006) 'Styles of Reform. Differences in Quango Creation Between Policy Sectors in the Netherlands', *Journal of Public Policy*, 26 (2), 115–39.

Varone, F. (2007) 'The Federal Administration' in U. Klöti, P. Knoepfel, H. Kriesi, W. Linder, Y. Papadopoulos, and P. Sciarini (eds), *Handbook of Swiss Politics* (Zürich: Neue Zürcher Zeitung Publishing).

Verhoest, K. (2005) 'Effects of Autonomy, Performance Contracting and Competition on the Performance of a Public Agency: A Case Study', *The Policy Studies Journal*, 33 (2), 235–58.

Verhoest, K., B. G. Peters, G. Bouckaert and B. Verschuere (2004a) 'The Study of Organisational Autonomy: A Conceptual Review', *Public Administration and Development*, 24 (2), 101–18.

Verhoest, K., Verschuere, B., Peters, G. and Bouckaert, G. (2004b) 'Steering and Controlling Autonomous Public Agencies as an Indicator of New Public Management', *Management International*, 9 (1), 25–35.

Verhoest, K. and Bouckaert, G. (2005) 'Machinery of Government and Policy Capacity', in Painter, M. and Pierre, J, (eds) *Challenges to State Policy Capacity* (Basingstoke: Palgrave).

Verhoest, K., K. Rubecksen and P. Humphreys (2006) 'Structure and Autonomy of Public Sector Agencies in Norway, Ireland and Flanders (Belgium): Does Politico-Administrative Culture Help Us To Understand Similarities and Differences?', EGOS, Bergen.

Verhoest, K., B. Verschuere, G. Bouckaert (2007a) 'Pressure, Legitimacy and Innovative Behaviour by Public Organizations', *Governance*, 20 (3), 469–98.

Verhoest, K., Bouckaert, G. and Peters, G. (2007b) 'Janus-faced Re-organization: Specialization and Coordination in Four Countries in the Period 1980–2005', *International Review of Administrative Sciences*, 73 (3), 325–48.

Verhoest, K., P. Roness, B. Verschuere, K. Rubecksen, M. MacCarthaigh (2010) *Autonomy and Control of State Agencies: Comparing States and Agencies* (Basingstoke: Palgrave Macmillan).

Verschuere, B. (2006) *Autonomy & Control in Arm's Length Public Agencies: Exploring the Determinants of Policy Autonomy*, PhD dissertation, KULeuven.

Verschuere, B. (2007) 'The Autonomy – Control Balance in Flemish Arm's Length Public Agencies, *Public Management Review*, 9 (1), 107–33.

Verschuere, B. (2009) 'The Role of Public Agencies in the Policy Making Process: Rhetoric versus Reality', *Public Policy and Administration*, 24 (1), 23–46.

Verschuere, B. and D. Barbieri (2009) 'Investigating the "NPM-ness" of Agencies in Italy and Flanders: The Effect of Place, Age and Task', *Public Management Review*, 11 (3), 345–73.

VGQ [Vérificateur Général du Québec] (1998) *Rapport à l'assemblée nationale pour l'année 1997–1998 Tome II, chapitre 2: Gestion par résultats, vérification menée auprès de deux organismes centraux et de cinq unités autonomes de service.*

VGQ [Vérificateur Général du Québec] (2004) *Rapport à l'assemblée nationale pour l'année 2003–2004, Québec, Tome I, chapitre 5.*

Vining, A. and D. Weimer (2005) 'Economic Perspectives on Public Organizations' in E. Ferlie, L. E. Lynn and C. Pollitt (eds), *The Oxford Handbook of Public Management* (New York: Oxford University Press).

VOKA (2006) *Administratieve vereenvoudiging. Prioriteiten uit de bedrijfspraktijk* (Brussel: Voka).

Voltmer, K. (1998) *Medienqualität und Demokratie: eine empirische Analyse publizistischer Informations-und Orientierungsleistungen in der Wahlkampfkommunikation* (Baden-Baden: Nomos).

Voltmer, K. and C. Eilder (2003) 'The Media Agenda: The Marginalization and Domestication of Europe', in K. Dyson and K. H. Goetz (eds), *Germany, Europe and the Politics of Constraint* (Oxford: Oxford University Press).

Waller, S. and J. de Haan (2004) 'Credibility and Transparency of Central Banks: New Results Based on Ifo's World Economic Survey', *Ifo Survey Data in Business Cycle and Monetary Policy Analysis.*

Walls, M. (2005) 'How Local Governments Structure Contracts with Private Firms: Economic Theory and Evidence on Solid Waste and Recycling Contracts', *Public Works Management and Policy*, 9 (3), 206–22.

Walsh, K. (1995) *Public Services and Market Mechanisms: Competition, Contracting and the New Public Management* (London: Macmillan).

Wanna, J. (2006) 'From Afterthought to Afterburner: Australia's Cabinet Implementation Unit,' *Journal of Comparative Policy Analysis*, 8/4, 347–69.

Warner, M. and R. Hebdon (2001) 'Local Government Restructuring: Privatization and its Alternatives', *Journal of Policy Analysis and Management*, 20 (2), 315–36.

Waterman, R. W. and K. J. Meier (1998) 'Principal–Agent Models: An Expansion?', *Journal of Public Administration Research and Theory*, 8 (2), 173–202.

Waterman, R. W. and A. Rouse (1999) 'The Determinants of the Perceptions of Political Control of the Bureaucracy and the Venues of Influence', *Journal of Public Administration Research and Theory*, 9 (4), 527–69.

Waterman, R. W., A. Rouseand and R. Wright (1998) 'The Venues of Influence: A New Theory of Political Control of the Bureaucracy', *Journal of Public Administration Research and Theory*, 8 (1), 13–38.

Weber, M. (1997 [1922]) *The Theory of Social and Economic Organization* (New York: Simon & Schuster (first published in German)).

Welz, W. (1988) *Ressortverantwortung im Leistungsstaat: Zur Organisation, Koordination und Kontrolle der selbständigen Bundesoberbehörden unter besonderer Berücksichtigung des Bundesamtes für Wirtschaft* (Baden-Baden: Nomos).

Wettenhall, R. L. (1968) 'Government Department or Statutory Authority?', *Public Administration* (Sydney), 27 (4), 350–9.

Wettenhall, R. (2004) 'Statutory Authorities, the Uhrig Report, and the Trouble with Internal Inquiries', *Public Administration Today* 2, 6–76.

Wettenhall, R. (2005) 'Agencies and Non-departmental Public Bodies. The Hard and Soft Lenses of Agencification Theory', *Public Management Review*, 7 (4), 615–35.

Widmer, T. and P. Neuenschwander (2004) 'Embedding Evaluation in the Swiss Federal Administration: Purpose, Institutional Design and Utilization', *Evaluation*, 10 (4), 388–409.

Wildavsky, A. (1984) *The Politics of the Budgetary Process* (Boston: Little, Brown and Company).

Wilks, S. (2007) 'Agencies, Networks, Discourses and the Trajectory of European Competition Enforcement', *European Competition Journal*, 3 (2), 437–64.

Wilks, S. and I. Bartle (2002) 'The Unanticipated Consequences of Creating Independent Competition Agencies', *West European Politics*, 25 (1), 148–72.

Williamson, O. (1979) 'Transaction-Cost Economics: The Governance of Contractual Relations', *Journal of Law and Economics*, 22 (2), 233–61.

Williamson, O. (1985) *The Economic Institutions of Capitalism: Firms, Markets, Relational Contracting* (New York: Free Press).

Williamson, O. (1991) 'Comparative Economic Organization: The Analysis of Discrete Structural Alternatives', *Administrative Science Quarterly*, 36 (2), 269–96.

Williamson, O. (1996) *The Mechanisms of Governance* (Oxford: Oxford University Press).

Williamson, O. (1999) 'Public and Private Bureaucracies: A Transaction Cost Economics Perspective', *Journal of Law, Economics and Organization*, 15 (1), 306–42.

Williamson, O. E. (1985) *The Economic Institutions of Capitalism* (New York: London).

Willner J. and Parker D. (2002) 'The Relative Performance Of Public And Private Enterprise Under Conditions Of Active And Passive Ownership', Centre on Regulation and Competition Research Paper No. 22. Oct. http://www. competition-regulation.org.uk/w

Wilson, J. Q. (1989) *Bureaucracy: What Government Agencies Do and Why They Do It* (New York: Basic Books).

Wintringham, M. (2003) 'Annual Report of the State Services Commissioner' in *Annual Report of the State Services Commission for year ended 30 June 2003*.

Wirth, W. (1986) 'Control in Public Administration: Plurality, Selectivity and Redundancy' in F. X. Kaufmann, G. Majone and V. Ostrom (eds) *Guidance, Control, and Evaluation in The Public Sector* (Berlin: De Gruyter).

Wollmann, H. (2000) 'Comparing institutional development in Britain and Germany: (Persistent) divergence or (progressing) convergence?' in H. Wollmann and E. Schröter (eds), *Comparing Public Sector Reform in Britain and Germany: Key Traditions and Trends of Modernisation* (Aldershot: Ashgate).

World Bank (2000) *Reforming Public Institutions and Strengthening Governance. A World Strategy* (Washington, DC: World Bank).

Wright, V. (1994) 'Reshaping the State. The Implications for Public Administration', *West European Politics*, 17, 102–37.

Yamamoto, K. (2006) 'Performance of Semi-autonomous Public Bodies: Linkage Between Autonomy and Performance in Japanese Agencies', *Public Administration and Development*, 26, 35–44.

Yesilkagit, K. (2004) 'The Design of Public Agencies: Overcoming Agency Costs and Commitment Problems', *Public Administration and Development*, 24 (2), 119–27.

Yesilkagit, K. and J. G. Christensen (2006) *Institutional Design Within National Contexts: Agency independence in Denmark, The Netherlands and Sweden (1945–2000)* (Utrecht: Utrecht School of Governance).

Yesilkagit, K. and J. G. Christensen (2009) 'Institutional Design and Formal Autonomy: Political versus Historical and Cultural Explanations', *Journal of Public Administration Research and Theory Advance Access published online on 1 Apr. 2009*.

Yesilkagit K. and S. van Thiel (2008) 'Political Influence and Bureaucratic Autonomy', *Public Organization Review*, 8 (2), 137–53.

Yvrande-Billon, A. and S. Saussier (2005) 'Do Organizations Matter? Assessing the Importance of Governance through Performance' in Harvey, J. (ed.) *New Ideas in Contracting and Organizational Economics Research* (Hauppauge: Nova Science Publishers).

Zaller, J. (1992) *The Nature and Origins of Mass Opinion* (Cambridge: Cambridge University Press).

Zuna, H. R. (2001) 'The Effects of Corporatization on Political Control', in T. Christensen and P. Lægreid (eds), *New Public Management. The Transformation of Ideas and Practice* (Aldershot: Ashgate).

Index